DATE			

Teaching Movement & Dance

HIGH/SCOPE
EDUCATIONAL RESEARCH FOUNDATION
Ypsilanti, Michigan

Teaching Movement & Dance

Intermediate Folk Dance

by Phyllis S. Weikart

THE
HIGH/SCOPE
PRESS

Published by
THE HIGH/SCOPE PRESS

High/Scope Educational Research Foundation
600 North River Street
Ypsilanti, Michigan 48197
(313) 485-2000

Mary Hohmann and Nancy Altman Brickman, Editors
Gary Easter, Designer/Photographer
Dianne Macut Kreis, Associate Designer
Linda Eckel, Cover Designer
Carolyn Ofiara, Production Assistant

Library of Congress Cataloging in Publication Data

Weikart, Phyllis S., 1931-
  Teaching movement & dance.

  1. Folk dancing—Study and teaching. I. Title. II.
Title: Teaching movement and dance.
GV1753.5.W45   1984   793.3'07   84-15673

ISBN 0-931114-30-6

Printed in the United States of America

To my folk dancing friends

Contents

Preface

I am writing this book for all the folk dancers and folk dance teachers who wish to have a library of folk dance material. After completing *Teaching Movement & Dance: A Sequential Approach to Rhythmic Movement*, my friends and colleagues urged me to convert my intermediate teaching material to a second volume using the same consistent language-to-dance vocabulary and the same format for writing the dances and notating their rhythmic structure.

I am also writing this book because international folk dance is such an exciting educational tool for teachers and recreational leaders. Through folk dance, we are exposing students to the music and movement of different countries and providing them with the opportunity to experience a group activity in which every participant can be successful.

I designed *Teaching Movement & Dance: A Sequential Approach to Rhythmic Movement* and *Teaching Movement & Dance: Intermediate Folk Dance* for folk dancers who would like descriptions of the dances they have learned, and for folk dance teachers and recreation leaders who will be teaching these dances. The dance descriptions in these two volumes provide a quick recall of over 300 dances enabling dancers to become teachers and teachers to expand their repertoire of dances and teaching techniques.

I wish to express my sincere thanks to all the people who have provided the leadership that enabled me to learn the dances. These folk dance teachers include Fred Berk, Sunni Bloland, Dick Crum, Andor Czompo, Eliahu Gamliel, Rickey Holden, Athan Karras, Martin Koenig, Atanas Kolarovsky, Judith and Kalman Magyar, Yves Moreau, Moshe Itzchak-Halevy, Bora Ozkok, Ken Spear, and Ron Waxman.

I also wish to thank my friends and colleagues who have attended my workshops and classes. Through them I gained the opportunity to teach the dances I learned.

In addition, I am most grateful to my workshop assistants, Gloria Abrams and Carolyn Tower, and to the many professionals at the High/Scope Press who have assisted me with this book including Mary Hohmann and Lynn Spencer, editors.

And, with special appreciation, I thank my husband David, my daughters Cindy, Cathy, Jenny, and Gretchen, and my son-in-law Dale for the joy I have experienced dancing with them.

Teaching Movement & Dance

1.
Introduction to Intermediate Folk Dance

Teaching Movement & Dance: Intermediate Folk Dance is a continuation of *Teaching Movement & Dance: A Sequential Approach to Rhythmic Movement.* This new volume helps teachers extend folk dancing for students who have mastered the basic level of this organized dance form by introducing them to a more difficult level of folk dance as well as to an awareness of the cultures the dances represent.

The first volume of *Teaching Movement & Dance* enables teachers to lead large groups of all ages through a sequence of basic movement activities at which they can succeed regardless of their previous movement and dance experience. Such success permits students to progress to organized dance activities, specifically to beginning international folk dance, the easiest form of recreational dance.

This volume of *Teaching Movement & Dance* emphasizes intermediate-level folk dance. It therefore assumes that students have mastered the following skills taught in the first volume:

- Basic rhythmic competency

- Comfort with movement

- Rhythmic movement through time and space

- Beginning folk dance steps

- Combining folk dance steps with locomotor movement sequences and other dance steps

- Using simple combinations of beats, divided beats, and rests

- Using the language-to-dance vocabulary

The same language-to-dance vocabulary and the same dance steps developed in the first volume are used throughout *Teaching Movement & Dance: Intermediate Folk Dance.* This vocabulary simplifies the teaching of dances and helps students of all ages learn and remember each dance. The additional words necessary for the intermediate dances in this volume are included in the glossary, beginning on page 333. New dance steps used in the more difficult intermediate dances are described on pages 7-14.

New to *Teaching Movement & Dance: Intermediate Folk Dance* are dances with uncommon meters such as 5/4, 7/8, and 9/16. The book offers suggestions for introducing students to these meters, beginning on page 5.

Teaching Movement & Dance: A Sequential Approach to Rhythmic Movement and *Teaching Movement & Dance: Intermediate Folk Dance* provide a library of beginning and intermediate folk dances that teachers can use to provide students with an enjoyable and comprehensive folk dance experience. Let us now turn to the focus of this volume—intermediate folk dance.

What Is Intermediate Folk Dance?

Folk dances are recreational dances that people have passed along to their children for at least one generation. Since folk dances are part of a country's cultural heritage, they are also transmitted from one country to another as national dance performing groups travel around the world. People watching these colorful performances are treated to folk dance spectacles replete with authentic costumes and folk music and are often inspired to join folk dance classes and clubs.

Folk dances can be classified by level of difficulty. Beginning folk dance is built around basic coordination, simple locomotor movement sequences, and uncomplicated dance steps. Intermediate folk dance introduces the following complexities:

- Ethnic music played on folk instruments

- Fast music requiring quick footwork

- Unusual musical form and phrasing

- Uncommon meters (5/4, 7/8, 9/16)

- More difficult dance steps

- More difficult combinations of locomotor movements and dance steps

- Sequences of dance steps that are longer or shorter than the accompanying musical phrase

- Long sequences of dance steps organized into multiple parts

- Dances beginning with a movement on the weight-bearing foot

Are There Different Types of Intermediate Folk Dances?

Intermediate folk dances include circle and line dances; single-partner, mixed-partner, and individual dances; group performance dances; leader-led improvisatory dances; and dances in uncommon meters.

The dances in *Teaching Movement & Dance: Intermediate Folk Dance* are primarily from Eastern Europe and Israel. I selected these dances for several reasons. First, these line and circle dances allow people of all ages to dance together regardless of the number of participants. Second, partners can be of the same or of the opposite sex because the dance steps are virtually the same in either case. Third, these are dances I have learned from national folk dance leaders who, in turn, learned and studied these dances in their countries of origin.

Since intermediate folk dance requires a broad spectrum of abilities, I have grouped the dances into three ability levels. Fifth and sixth

graders as well as adults and older children who have mastered the material in the first volume should be able to perform the dances presented in this book.

When Should Intermediate Folk Dance Be Attempted?

When students have mastered the following folk dance skills, they are ready to try intermediate folk dances:

- Maintaining balance while changing direction

- Maintaining group orientation while changing direction

- Stopping movement at the end of a phrase during a resting beat

- Adding a nonweight-transfer motion at the end of 4 or 8 beats

- Moving sideward ("side, cross, side, cross")

- Executing a 2-beat recurring ("in, out") or alternating sequence ("side, lift, side, lift")

- Executing a recurring ("in, kick, out, touch") or alternating ("side, close, side, touch") 4-beat sequence

- Executing simple movement patterns to a quick tempo

- Executing dance steps to a very slow tempo

- Executing beginning dance steps (CHERKESSIYA, GRAPEVINE, STEP HOP, SCHOTTISCHE, THREE, TWO STEP, YEMENITE, and POLKA) starting with either foot

- Combining beginning dance steps with each other and with other locomotor movements

To be successful with intermediate folk dance, students must master these basic skills. Age makes no difference; a beginner is a beginner at any age. If children have had a great deal of movement and beginning folk dance experience in grades one through four, fifth grade is a good time to start intermediate folk dance. Special folk dance clubs and performing groups can be very successful in the upper-elementary and middle-school years.

When I work in a residential setting with teenagers who have little or no beginning folk dance experience, I find that it takes approximately 30 minutes of rhythmic coordination activities (divided into 10 three-minute segments), one or two sessions working on the language-to-dance vocabulary, and approximately five to ten hours of beginning folk dance using the language-to-dance vocabulary to prepare them for the intermediate folk dance. Taken together, rhythmic coordination, competency with the language-to-dance vocabulary, and beginning dance experiences help teens attain a high skill level quite rapidly. In a nonresidential setting where teenagers dance once or twice a week it would take several months to prepare them for intermediate folk dance.

How Do You Introduce Uncommon Meter?

We call music written in 5/4, 7/8, or 9/16 music in uncommon meter. What distinguishes uncommon meter is the subdivision of measures into groups of 2 beats and 3 beats.

Intermediate folk dance students need to "feel" the groups of beats in uncommon meters in the same way beginning folk dancers need to "feel" the underlying beat in common meters. To help students feel beats organized into groups of 2 and 3, refer to *Teaching Movement & Dance: A Sequential Approach to Rhythmic Movement*, page 20, for a discussion of how tactile stimulation can produce beat awareness.

Language* will help students who are aware of beat understand uncommon meter. To illustrate the following stages use the words

*Turn to *Teaching Movement & Dance: A Sequential Approach to Rhythmic Movement*, pages 15-19, for a discussion of language as a bridge to movement and dance.

"apple," a two-syllable word representing 2 beats, and "pineapple," a three-syllable word representing 3 beats, to help students understand a 7/8 meter (3 beats, plus 2 beats, plus 2 beats).

Stage One

First, students say aloud "Pineapple, Apple, Apple" several times. Then they pat their legs on each syllable as they say the words (PINE-AP-PLE, AP-PLE, AP-PLE; PINE-AP-PLE, AP-PLE, AP-PLE) in order to feel the subdivision of 7 beats into a group of 3 beats, a group of 2 beats, and a group of 2 beats. Next, they whisper the syllables as they pat their legs on each syllable. Finally, they think the syllables as they pat their legs.

Stage Two

Students pat their legs on the first syllable of each word with more intensity than the other syllables (*PINE*-ap-ple, *AP*-ple, *Ap*-ple) as they say, whisper, and, finally, think the syllables.

Stage Three

Students pat their legs only on the first syllable of each word as they say and whisper the entire word, emphasizing the first syllables.

Stage Four

Students think the words as they pat their legs only on the first syllables.

Stage Five

Students continue Stage Four with music. Then they switch from patting their legs to patting a partner's shoulders. By "feeling" the beat, students prepare for dancing to the beat.

Stage Six

Students walk to the same musical selection used in Stage Five, stepping on the first syllable of each word. Encourage them to whisper the words as they step, then think the words as they step and listen to the music. It is helpful to use this process with each new uncommon-meter dance before teaching the dance.

How Should Intermediate Folk Dance Be Taught?

Many of the teaching techniques and strategies discussed in *Teaching Movement & Dance: A Sequential Approach to Rhythmic Movement* (pages 76-92) are as important to the teaching of intermediate folk dance as they are to the teaching of beginning folk dance. A knowledgeable teacher, sensitive to students' difficulties with each dance, is the key to folk dance success and enjoyment. If students must struggle because the teacher is disorganized or does not understand how each dance is constructed, they may lose interest in pursuing this enjoyable and challenging group experience.

Teaching from the Known to the Unknown

Intermediate folk dances often present a new organization of familiar locomotor patterns and beginning dance steps. When the teacher introduces an intermediate folk dance by reviewing any patterns and steps in it that students have learned in previous dances, students find the dance much easier to master than when the teacher presents it as a totally new experience. Although the style may change, an accent may be different, or a step may be executed in a new direction, it is important to treat the step as a familiar one.

Teaching Quickly

Beginning folk dances should be taught within five minutes. The longer, more difficult intermediate folk dances should take no more than 15 minutes to teach. This time allotment does not include necessary dance-step preparation and warm-up or the addition of style. It simply allows for teaching the dance pattern.

Teaching Rhythmically

Many intermediate-level dances are rhythmically complex. There are syncopated beats in combination with steady beats, rests, and uneven movement sequences. Whatever the rhythm, students need to learn each part of the dance in the same rhythm they will use when they dance with the music. Simplifying a complex rhythm to make teaching easier *does not* help students feel, hear, and execute rhythmically complex dance sequences. Slowing down a dance sequence slightly during practice may help students as long as the exact rhythm remains intact.

Teaching Close to Tempo, Practicing at Tempo, Then Adding the Music

It is difficult for students to learn a dance sequence very slowly because the stepping pattern becomes disjointed and hard to remember. Slow down dance sequences only when students are having difficulty with them. Then be certain that students are aware of the actual tempo for the dance and that they have practiced the dance at that tempo without the music before they dance with the music.

Adding Style

Style refers to dance movements that are added to the sequence of steps after students are thoroughly comfortable with the basic dance pattern. Style movements may include a special way a step is executed; a specific placement of the free foot or leg; a special arm, body, or head movement that accompanies a step.

Students may be needlessly confused when teachers present dance steps and style simultaneously because the human brain focuses best on one learning task at a time. Generally, in this situation, students focus on the style rather than on the steps because the stylistic movements are more visible and easier to imitate than the dance-step sequence. Therefore, style should be added *after* students are comfortable with the dance-step sequence and can execute it automatically.

When adding style, students should continue to say what their feet are doing while they incorporate the special stylistic movements for each step. If the arm or body pattern is complex, students should stand in one place, say what the feet are doing, and then do the arm or body movements as they say the steps they are doing with their feet. For example, *An Dro* calls for a specific arm-circling motion. After students have learned the footwork, have them stand still and continue saying IN/CLOSE, IN; OUT/CLOSE, OUT. Next have them circle their arms to this language first without holding hands and then holding hands. Last, add the footwork to the arm circles, and the dance pattern with its style is complete.

Assuring Success

Specific techniques for teaching folk dances are presented in *Teaching Movement & Dance: A Sequential Approach to Rhythmic Movement* (pages 83-90). At the intermediate level of dance, teachers should use the following teaching techniques to assure students' success:

• Know the dance thoroughly including the transitions from one part to the next and from the end of the entire sequence back to the beginning.

• Be familiar with the music and understand how the dance fits the music.

• Omit style initially. Add style during a review of the dance or during later repetitions of the dance with the music.

• Omit handholds as students learn the dance unless the handhold enhances balance.

Even intermediate dancers need space to try out sequences without the burden of other people hanging onto them.

• Know both parts of a partner dance well enough to understand any differences that exist.

• Use consistent language. Students learn new dances more easily when teachers use a consistent language-to-dance vocabulary.

What Are the Intermediate Folk Dance Steps?

The intermediate folk dance steps follow in order of difficulty. The easiest steps are the SINGLE and DOUBLE CSÁRDÁS, the OPEN and CLOSED RIDA, the DOUBLE CHERKESSIYA, the HARMONICA step, the CIFRA, and the WALTZ, because these steps are based on beginning folk dance steps and patterns.* The MIXED PICKLE step, the STEP HOP/STEP, and HOP/STEP STEP, the KOLO step, and the DRMEŠ are more difficult.

The SINGLE CSÁRDÁS

The SINGLE and DOUBLE CSÁRDÁS steps are found primarily in Hungarian folk dances. Their exact style depends upon the dance and the region of Hungary where the dance originates.

Important Characteristics

1. The SINGLE CSÁRDÁS consists of one step followed by one nonweight-bearing motion.

---

*For the language-to-dance vocabulary for the beginning folk dance steps (CHERKESSIYA, GRAPEVINE, GRAPEVINE PATTERN, STEP HOP, SCHOTTISCHE, THREE, TWO STEP, YEMENITE, POLKA) turn to page 335 of the glossary. For their complete description and analysis, turn to pages 64-75 in *Teaching Movement & Dance: A Sequential Approach to Rhythmic Movement*.

SINGLE CSÁRDÁS
2/4 Meter

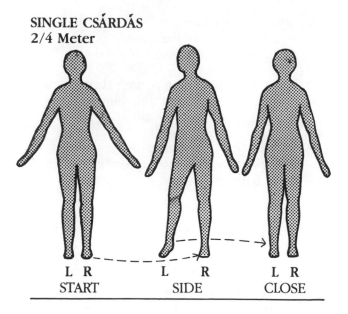

L R — START L R — SIDE L R — CLOSE

2. The step and motion are of equal duration.

3. The SIDE, TOUCH is a lead up to this dance step. The CLICK movement is the style of the touch.

4. The SINGLE CSÁRDÁS may be executed in 2/4 or 4/4 meter:

2/4 Meter R foot

Beat 1	Step R foot sideward right	"SIDE"
&	Click L foot against R foot (no weight transfer)	"CLICK"

4/4 Meter

Beat 1	Step R foot sideward right	"SIDE"
2	Click L foot against R foot	"CLICK"
3	Step L foot sideward left	"SIDE"
4	Click R foot against L foot	"CLICK"

The DOUBLE CSÁRDÁS

Important Characteristics

1. The DOUBLE CSÁRDÁS consists of three sideward steps followed by one nonweight-bearing motion.

2. The steps and motion are of equal duration.

3. The SIDE, CLOSE, SIDE, TOUCH is a lead up to this dance step. The CLICK may occur on the CLOSE and is a part of the final motion. This is the style of the movement.

4. The DOUBLE CSÁRDÁS may be executed in 2/4 or 4/4 meter:

2/4 Meter R foot

Beat 1	Step R foot sideward right	"SIDE"
&	Step L foot next to R foot	"CLOSE"
2	Step R foot sideward right	"SIDE"
&	Click L foot against R foot	"CLICK"

4/4 Meter L foot

Beat 1	Step L foot sideward left	"SIDE"
2	Step R foot next to L foot	"CLOSE"
3	Step L foot sideward left	"SIDE"
4	Click R foot against L foot	"CLICK"

The OPEN RIDA

The OPEN and CLOSED RIDA are generally classified as Hungarian dance steps, but the same steps are used in dances from several East European countries.

Important Characteristics

1. The OPEN RIDA consists of two steps.

DOUBLE CSÁRDÁS
2/4 Meter

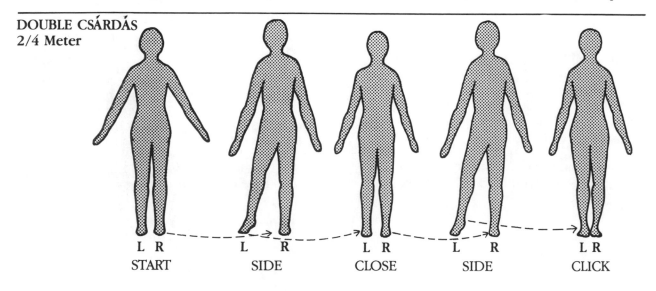

L R — START L R — SIDE L R — CLOSE L R — SIDE L R — CLICK

OPEN RIDA
2/4 Meter

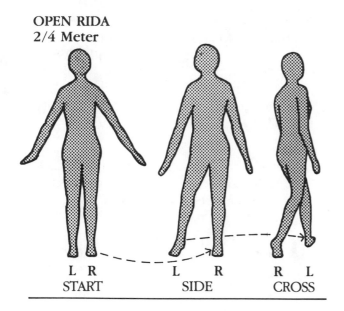

L R
START

L R
SIDE

R L
CROSS

2. The two steps are of equal duration.

3. The OPEN RIDA begins with a sideward step which is generally executed with a slight leap.

4. The OPEN RIDA may be executed in 2/4 or 4/4 meter:

2/4 Meter R foot
Beat 1 Step R foot sideward right   "SIDE"
    & Step L foot crossing in front
       of R foot   "CROSS"
    2 Repeat beat 1&

4/4 Meter L foot
Beat 1 Step L foot sideward left   "SIDE"
    2 Step R foot crossing in front
       of L foot   "CROSS"
   3-4 Repeat beats 1-2

The CLOSED RIDA

The steps and characteristics of the CLOSED RIDA are identical to the OPEN RIDA but occur in the opposite sequence, CROSS, SIDE.

The DOUBLE CHERKESSIYA

The DOUBLE CHERKESSIYA is found primarily in dances from Israel.

Important Characteristics

1. The DOUBLE CHERKESSIYA is the combination of two CROSS, BACK, SIDE patterns.

2. The DOUBLE CHERKESSIYA is a 6-beat pattern often preceded or followed by 2 beats to allow it to conform to an 8-beat phrase.

3. The DOUBLE CHERKESSIYA is a recurring step; each repetition begins on the same foot.

4. The DOUBLE CHERKESSIYA may be executed in 2/4 or 4/4 meter:

4/4 Meter (1 1/2 measures)
Beat 1 Step R foot crossing in front
       of L foot   "CROSS"
    2 Step L foot crossing in back
       of R foot   "BACK"
    3 Step R foot sideward right   "SIDE"
    4 Step L foot crossing in front
       of R foot   "CROSS"
    1 Step R foot crossing in back
       of L foot   "BACK"
    2 Step L foot sideward left   "SIDE"

DOUBLE CHERKESSIYA
2/4 Meter

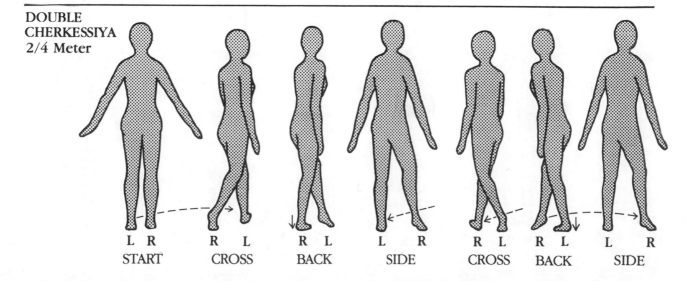

L R
START

R L
CROSS

R L
BACK

L R
SIDE

R L
CROSS

R L
BACK

L R
SIDE

2/4 Meter (1 1/2 measures)

Beat 1	Step L foot crossing in front of R foot	"CROSS"
&	Step R foot crossing in back of L foot	"BACK"
2	Step L foot sideward left	"SIDE"
&	Step R foot crossing in front of L foot	"CROSS"
1	Step L foot crossing in back of R foot	"BACK"
&	Step R foot sideward right	"SIDE"

The HARMONICA Step

The HARMONICA step is found primarily in dances from Israel. The name originated from the dance *Harmonica* in which the step is found.

Important Characteristics

1. The HARMONICA is a SCHOTTISCHE-type step with specific footwork—a CROSS, BACK combined with a SIDE, HOP.

2. Adding a hop to each half of the DOUBLE CHERKESSIYA produces the HARMONICA step.

3. The HARMONICA is an alternating step because the repetition of the HARMONICA step begins on the opposite foot.

4. The HARMONICA may be executed in 4/4 or 2/4 meter:

4/4 Meter

Beat 1	Step R foot crossing in front of L foot	"CROSS"
2	Step L foot crossing in back of R foot	"BACK"
3	Step R foot sideward right	"SIDE"
4	Hop R foot	"HOP"

2/4 Meter

Beat 1	Step L foot crossing in front of R foot	"CROSS"
&	Step R foot crossing in back of L foot	"BACK"
2	Step L foot sideward left	"SIDE"
&	Hop L foot	"HOP"

The CIFRA

The CIFRA is found primarily in Hungarian folk dances. The style depends on the dance and the region of Hungary where the dance originates.

Important Characteristics

1. The CIFRA consists of three steps.

2. The first two steps are of equal duration. The third step takes the same amount of time as the first two steps combined.

3. The CIFRA is an alternating step; each repetition begins with the opposite foot.

4. The CIFRA may be executed in place as a

HARMONICA
2/4 Meter

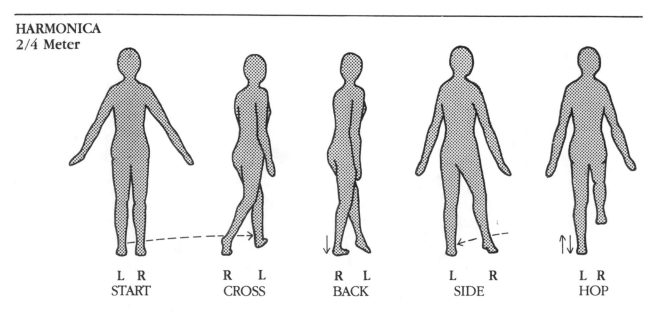

L R	R L	R L	L R	L R
START	CROSS	BACK	SIDE	HOP

CIFRA
2/4 Meter

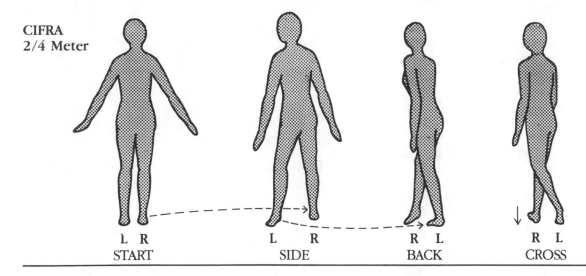

L R	L R	R L	R L
START	SIDE	BACK	CROSS

THREE or moving as a TWO STEP, which serves as a lead up to this dance step.

5. The CIFRA may be executed in 2/4 or 4/4 meter:

2/4 Meter R foot (in place)

Beat 1	Step R foot slightly sideward right	"SIDE"
&	Step L foot crossing in back of R foot	"BACK"
2	Step R foot crossing in front of L foot	"CROSS"

4/4 Meter L foot (moving)

Beat 1	Step L foot forward	"FORWARD"
2	Step R foot behind L foot	"CLOSE"
3	Step L foot forward	"FORWARD"
4	Hold	"REST"

The WALTZ Step

The WALTZ step is most often found in dances from Western Europe, the British Isles, Scandanavia, and North America.

Important Characteristics

1. The running WALTZ uses the same steps as the first three beats of the THREE step.

2. The WALTZ is often executed incorrectly using the TWO-STEP footwork (STEP, CLOSE, STEP).

3. The first step is generally longer and executed with more force than the other two steps creating a "down, up, up" pattern.

4. The WALTZ is an alternating dance step; each repetition begins with the opposite foot.

WALTZ
3/4 Meter

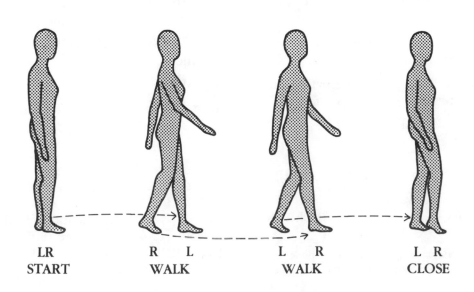

LR	R L	L R	L R
START	WALK	WALK	CLOSE

MIXED PICKLE
4/4 Meter

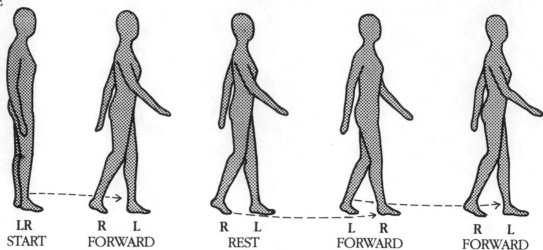

LR	R	L	R	L	L	R	R	L
START	FORWARD		REST		FORWARD		FORWARD	

3/4 Meter (running WALTZ)

Beat 1	Step on the R foot (slight leap)	"LEAP"
2	Step on the L foot	"RUN"
3	Step on the R foot	"RUN"

3/4 Meter (WALTZ)

Beat 1	Step on the L foot	"WALK"
2	Step on the R foot	"WALK"
3	Step L foot next to the R foot	"CLOSE"

The MIXED PICKLE Step*

The MIXED PICKLE step is found in dances throughout Eastern Europe.

Important Characteristics

1. The MIXED PICKLE step consists of three steps.

2. The first step takes the same amount of time as steps two and three combined.

3. The MIXED PICKLE is an alternating step; each repetition begins on the opposite foot.

4. The MIXED PICKLE step may be executed in 2/4 or 4/4 meter:

2/4 Meter R foot

Beat 1	Step R foot forward	"FORWARD"
2	Step L foot forward	"FORWARD"
&	Step R foot forward	"FORWARD"

*MIXED PICKLE is the name given to this rhythmic sequence by Dick Crum, an authority on Balkan dance.

4/4 Meter L foot

Beat 1	Step L foot forward	"FORWARD"
2	Step R foot forward	"REST"
3	Step R foot forward	"FORWARD"
4	Step L foot forward	"FORWARD"

The STEP HOP/STEP

The STEP HOP/STEP is opposite in rhythmic structure to the HOP/STEP STEP. It occurs in dances from Eastern Europe.

Important Characteristics

1. The STEP HOP/STEP is a combination of a step in any direction followed by a hop and a step that together equal the duration of the first step.

2. The STEP HOP/STEP is a recurring step; the next step uses the same footwork.

3. The STEP HOP/STEP usually occurs in 2/4 meter:

2/4 Meter

Beat 1	Step R foot	"STEP"
2	Hop R foot	"HOP"
&	Step L foot	"STEP"

The HOP/STEP STEP

The HOP/STEP STEP is found in dances from Eastern Europe. It is more difficult than the STEP HOP/STEP because the first movement is a hop rather than a weight transfer.

STEP HOP/STEP
2/4 Meter

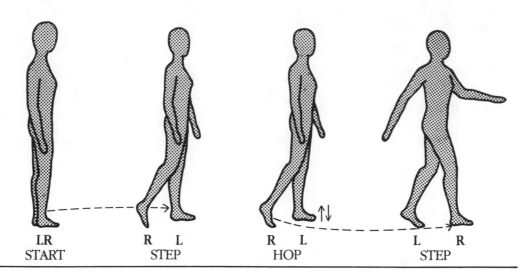

LR	R L	R L	L R
START	STEP	HOP	STEP

Important Characteristics

1. The HOP/STEP STEP consists of a hop followed by two steps.

2. The hop and the first step take the same amount of time as the second step.

3. The HOP/STEP STEP is a recurring step; each repetition has the same footwork and can be executed in any direction.

4. The HOP/STEP STEP is often combined with a STEP HOP or a TWO STEP.

5. The HOP/STEP STEP usually occurs in 2/4 meter:

2/4 Meter

Beat 1	Hop L foot in place	"HOP"
&	Step R foot	"STEP"
2	Step L foot	"STEP"

The KOLO Step

The KOLO step is found primarily in dances from Yugoslavia where kolo means circle. The step is used in kolo or circle dances.

Important Characteristics

1. The KOLO step begins with a hop followed by three sideward steps and a final hop creating two hops in sequence as the step is repeated.

2. The KOLO step takes 2 measures of 2/4 meter to complete.

3. The KOLO step is two dance steps combined—a HOP/STEP STEP and a STEP HOP.

4. The first hop and step combined take the

HOP/STEP STEP
2/4 Meter

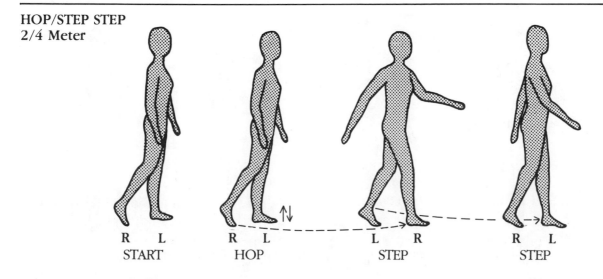

R L	R L	L R	R L
START	HOP	STEP	STEP

KOLO
2/4 Meter

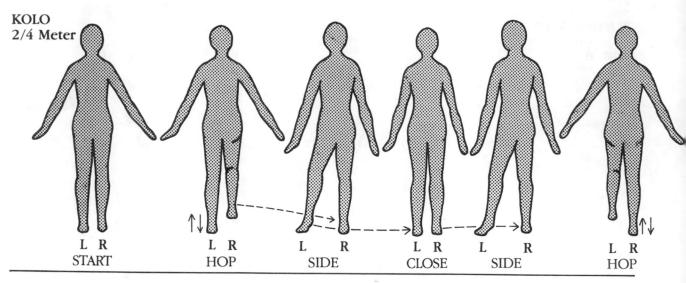

L R	L R	L R	L R	L R	L R
START	HOP	SIDE	CLOSE	SIDE	HOP

same amount of time as each of the other movements.

5. The KOLO step is an alternating step; each repetition begins on the opposite foot.

6. The KOLO step has very little sideward movement.

7. The sideward SCHOTTISCHE is a lead up to the KOLO step or a modification of it.

8. The KOLO step is generally executed in a 2/4 meter:

2/4 Meter

Beat 1	Hop L foot in place	"HOP"
&	Step R foot sideward right	"SIDE"
2	Step L foot next to R foot	"CLOSE"
1	Step R foot sideward right	"SIDE"
2	Hop R foot in place	"HOP"

The DRMEŠ Step

The DRMEŠ step is found primarily in dances from Eastern Europe. It is difficult because it is fast and combines unusual movements.

Important Characteristics

1. The DRMEŠ consists of one movement in which both knees bend slightly followed by two movements in which the heels drop sharply. The knees are straight as the heels drop.

2. There are a number of variations to the DRMEŠ step.

3. The DRMEŠ step usually occurs in 2/4 meter:

2/4 meter

Beat 1	Bend both knees	"BEND"
2 &	Drop both heels sharply	"BOUNCE, BOUNCE"

DRMEŠ
2/4 Meter

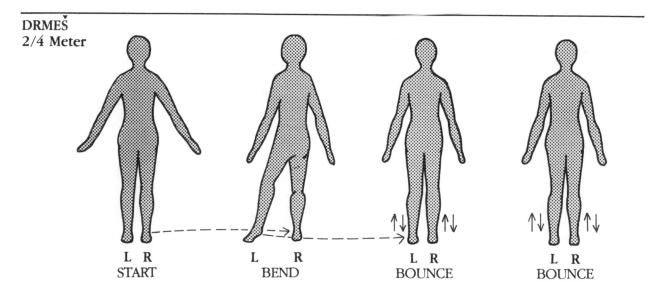

L R	L R	L R	L R
START	BEND	BOUNCE	BOUNCE

2.

Intermediate Folk Dances

Music for Intermediate Folk Dance

Folk dance music is an integral part of folk dancing. If folk dancers do not feel the music as they dance, then the dances are reduced to movement sequences devoid of their ethnicity.

I have been frustrated as over the years many of the standard folk dance recordings have become unavailable. I believe that we as educators are responsible for introducing children and adults to this very exciting recreational dance form. I also believe that we must have good folk dance recordings to keep the folk dance movement alive. Therefore I have planned and directed the recording of nine albums to go with the dances in *Teaching Movement & Dance: A Sequential Approach to Rhythmic Movement*. This music is expertly arranged and sensitively played. The nine-record set is called *Rhythmically Moving*; at this writing, six titles in the series have been released.* Additional records to accompany this volume are also planned.

Levels of Dance Difficulty

The dances in this book cover a wide range of skills and require different levels of ability to dance them successfully. Therefore, they are divided into three groups: easier dances, Level 1; moderately difficult dances, Level 2; and more difficult dances, Level 3. The dances with a fast tempo, dances that begin with a hop, dances with many parts, dances without a predetermined sequence, and dances using a DRMEŠ step are Level 3 dances. Dances in uncommon meters follow dances in common meters in each level of difficulty.

---

*To order records in the Rhythmically Moving series, call or write to the High/Scope Press, 600 N. River St., Ypsilanti, Michigan 48197-2898, (313) 485-2000. Other records can be ordered from the following distributors:

Ed Kremer's Folk Showplace, 155 Turk St., San Francisco, CA 94102, (415) 775-3444
Festival Records, 2773 West Pico Blvd., Los Angeles, CA 90006, (213) 737-0500
Folk Dance Music Center, 4301 Terry Lake Rd., Fort Collins, CO 80524, (303) 493-0207
Folk Dancer Record Service, P.O. Box 201, Flushing, NY 11352, (212) 784-7404
Folkraft, 10 Fenwick St., Newark, NJ 07114, (201) 824-8700
Worldtone Music, Inc., 230 Seventh Ave., New York, NY 10011, (212) 691-1934

Intermediate Level 1 Dances,
Common & Uncommon Meters

Common Meters

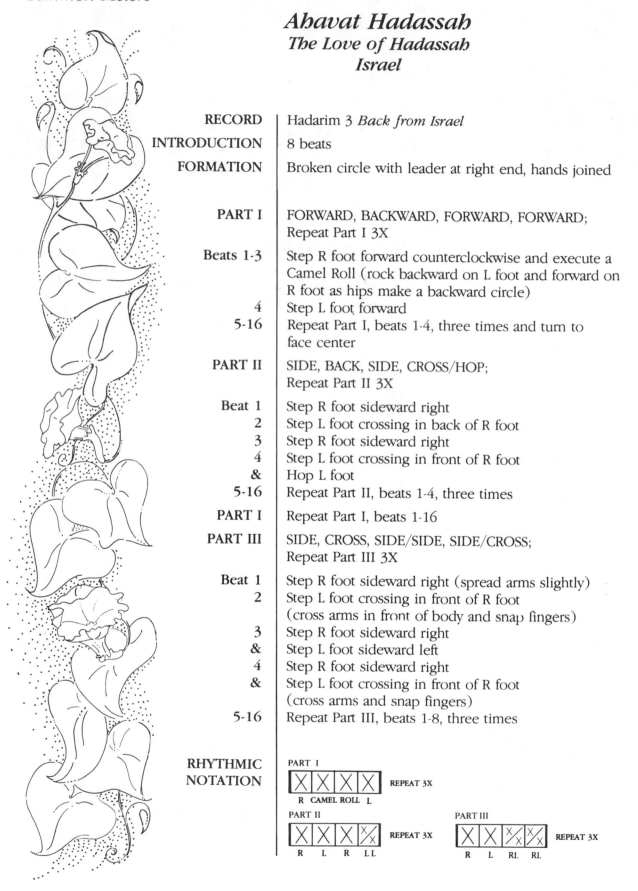

Ahavat Hadassah
The Love of Hadassah
Israel

RECORD	Hadarim 3 *Back from Israel*
INTRODUCTION	8 beats
FORMATION	Broken circle with leader at right end, hands joined
PART I	FORWARD, BACKWARD, FORWARD, FORWARD; Repeat Part I 3X
Beats 1-3	Step R foot forward counterclockwise and execute a Camel Roll (rock backward on L foot and forward on R foot as hips make a backward circle)
4	Step L foot forward
5-16	Repeat Part I, beats 1-4, three times and turn to face center
PART II	SIDE, BACK, SIDE, CROSS/HOP; Repeat Part II 3X
Beat 1	Step R foot sideward right
2	Step L foot crossing in back of R foot
3	Step R foot sideward right
4	Step L foot crossing in front of R foot
&	Hop L foot
5-16	Repeat Part II, beats 1-4, three times
PART I	Repeat Part I, beats 1-16
PART III	SIDE, CROSS, SIDE/SIDE, SIDE/CROSS; Repeat Part III 3X
Beat 1	Step R foot sideward right (spread arms slightly)
2	Step L foot crossing in front of R foot (cross arms in front of body and snap fingers)
3	Step R foot sideward right
&	Step L foot sideward left
4	Step R foot sideward right
&	Step L foot crossing in front of R foot (cross arms and snap fingers)
5-16	Repeat Part III, beats 1-8, three times

RHYTHMIC NOTATION

PART I

| X | X | X | X | REPEAT 3X
R CAMEL ROLL L

PART II

| X | X | X | X | REPEAT 3X
R   R   L LL

PART III

| X | X | X | X | REPEAT 3X
R   L RL RL

An Dro
France (Brittany)

RECORD	*Dances from Brittany*
INTRODUCTION	4 beats of bag pipe
FORMATION	Broken circle, little fingers joined, hands waist level, forearms parallel to floor
PART I	IN/CLOSE, IN; OUT/CLOSE, OUT
Beat 1	Step L foot in (slightly diagonally left) on ball of foot
&	Step R foot next to heel of L foot
2	Step L foot in flat foot, bring R foot up behind
3	Step R foot out (slightly left)
&	Step L foot slightly in front of R foot
4	Step R foot out and bring L foot up behind
ARMS	
Beats 1-2	Arms push in and up, loop back toward the body, and finish up away from body
3-4	Arms reverse by coming down toward body, then looping away from body, and back to starting position

RHYTHMIC NOTATION

PART I

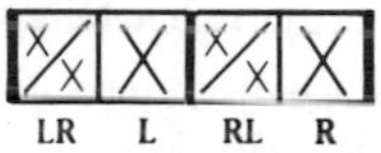

LR   L   RL   R

Baldâzka
Bulgaria

RECORD	Balkanton BHA 734 *Bulgarian Folk Dances*
INTRODUCTION	None
FORMATION	Lines, hands held in "W" position Arms extended to about eye level
PART I	FORWARD, FORWARD; SIDE/BACK, SIDE/TOUCH; Repeat Part I 3X
Beat 1	Step R foot forward moving counterclockwise
2	Step L foot forward and turn to face center
3	Step R foot sideward right
&	Step L foot crossing in back of R foot
4	Step R foot sideward right
&	Touch L foot next to R foot
5-8	Repeat beats 1-4 moving clockwise beginning L foot
9-16	Repeat Part I, beats 1-8
PART II	IN/IN, IN/IN; IN/IN, IN/STAMP; OUT/OUT, OUT/OUT; OUT/OUT, OUT/STAMP; Repeat Part II
Beat 1	Step R foot in with a slight leap
&	Step L foot in bending knee
2-3	Repeat beats 1 & two times
4	Step R foot in with a slight leap
&	Stamp L foot next to R foot
5-8	Repeat beats 1-4 moving out from center beginning L foot
9-16	Repeat Part II, beats 1-8
NOTE	Arms describe a circle in and around on each two beats
	Repeat Parts I and II
PART III	FORWARD, FORWARD; SIDE/BACK, SIDE/STAMP; Repeat Part III 3X
Beats 1-16	Repeat Part I, beats 1-16, substituting a stamp for the touch

Baldâzka *(continued)*

PART IV	IN/IN, IN/IN; IN/STAMP, STAMP; OUT/OUT, OUT/OUT; OUT/STAMP, STAMP; Repeat Part IV
Beats 1-2	Repeat Part II, beats 1-2
3	Step R foot in with a slight leap
&	Stamp L foot next to R foot
4	Stamp L foot next to R foot
5-8	Repeat beats 1-4 moving out from center beginning L foot
9-16	Repeat Part IV, beats 1-8
NOTE	Arms describe one circle in and around as in Part II adding 2 quick circles on the stamps
	Repeat Parts III and IV
PART V	FORWARD, FORWARD; FORWARD/FORWARD, FORWARD; OUT, OUT; ACCENT/ACCENT, ACCENT; Repeat Part V
Beat 1	Step R foot forward moving counterclockwise
2	Step L foot forward
3-4	Step R, L, R foot forward and turn to face center
5	Step L foot out away from the center
6	Step R foot out away from the center
7-8	Step L, R, L foot in place with accents
9-16	Repeat Part V, beats 1-8
	Repeat Parts IV, V, and IV.

RHYTHMIC NOTATION

PART I, III

REPEAT 3X W/OPP. FTWK.

R   L   RL   R(L)

PART II

REPEAT 3X W/OPP. FTWK.

RL   RL   RL   R(L)

PART IV

REPEAT 3X W/OPP. FTWK.

RL   RL   R(L) (L)

PART V

REPEAT 3X W/OPP. FTWK.

R   L   RL   R

Bat Hareem
Israel

RECORD	Electra *Hora*
INTRODUCTION	16 beats
FORMATION	Circle, hands joined in "V" position
PART I	FORWARD, HOP (2X); CROSS, SIDE, BACK, SIDE; FORWARD, HOP (2X); FORWARD, BACKWARD, BACKWARD, FORWARD; Repeat Part I
Beats 1-2	Step hop L foot forward moving counterclockwise
3-4	Step hop R foot forward
5-8	Grapevine counterclockwise beginning L foot crossing in front of R foot
9-12	Repeat beats 1-4
13-16	Cherkessiya facing counterclockwise beginning L foot
17-32	Repeat Part I, beats 1-16
PART II	STAMP, STAMP, BRUSH, HOP; BACKWARD/STEP, STEP; FORWARD/STEP, STEP; FORWARD, HOP (2X); FORWARD, BACKWARD, BACKWARD, FORWARD; Repeat Part II
Beats 1-2	Stamp L foot 2 times
3	Brush L foot forward
4	Hop R foot
5-6	Balance L foot backward clockwise
7-8	Balance R foot forward counterclockwise
9-16	Repeat Part I, beats 9-16
17-32	Repeat Part II, beats 1-16

RHYTHMIC NOTATION

PART I

X	X	X	X	X	X	X	X	REPEAT 3X
L	L	R	R	L	R	L	R	

PART II

X	X	X	X	X/X	X	X/X	X	
(L)	(L)	(L)	R	LR	L	RL	R	

X	X	X	X	X	X	X	X	REPEAT II
L	L	R	R	L	R	L	R	

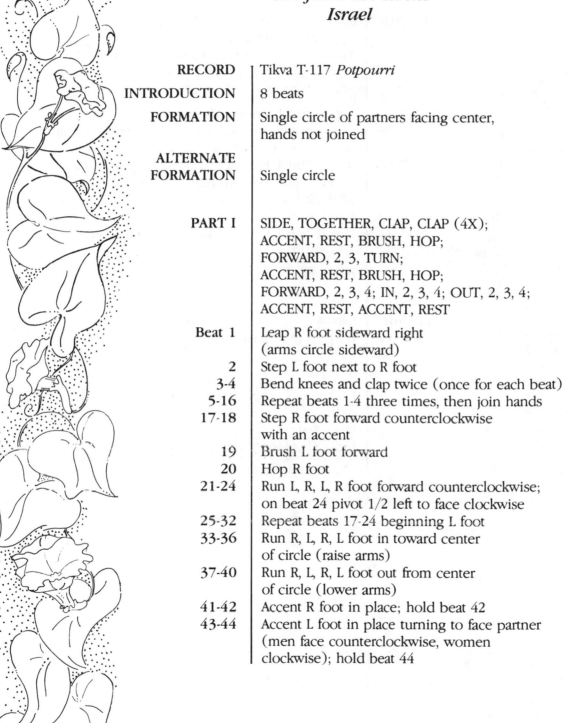

Bat Tsurim
Girl from the Rocks
Israel

RECORD	Tikva T-117 *Potpourri*
INTRODUCTION	8 beats
FORMATION	Single circle of partners facing center, hands not joined
ALTERNATE FORMATION	Single circle

PART I	SIDE, TOGETHER, CLAP, CLAP (4X);
	ACCENT, REST, BRUSH, HOP;
	FORWARD, 2, 3, TURN;
	ACCENT, REST, BRUSH, HOP;
	FORWARD, 2, 3, 4; IN, 2, 3, 4; OUT, 2, 3, 4;
	ACCENT, REST, ACCENT, REST
Beat 1	Leap R foot sideward right (arms circle sideward)
2	Step L foot next to R foot
3-4	Bend knees and clap twice (once for each beat)
5-16	Repeat beats 1-4 three times, then join hands
17-18	Step R foot forward counterclockwise with an accent
19	Brush L foot forward
20	Hop R foot
21-24	Run L, R, L, R foot forward counterclockwise; on beat 24 pivot 1/2 left to face clockwise
25-32	Repeat beats 17-24 beginning L foot
33-36	Run R, L, R, L foot in toward center of circle (raise arms)
37-40	Run R, L, R, L foot out from center of circle (lower arms)
41-42	Accent R foot in place; hold beat 42
43-44	Accent L foot in place turning to face partner (men face counterclockwise, women clockwise); hold beat 44

(continued)

Bat Tsurim (continued)

PART II	QUARTER TURN, CLAP, CLAP (4X); ACCENT, HOLD, BRUSH, HOP; AWAY, 2, 3, 4; ACCENT, HOLD, BRUSH, HOP; TOWARD, 2, 3, 4; ISRAELI TURN; ACCENT, REST, ACCENT, REST
Beats 1-16	Repeat Part I, beats 1-16 with partner; leap 1/4 turn, moving counterclockwise on beat 1 of each four beat sequence; keep facing partner
17-32	Repeat Part I, beats 17-32 but each person move to own right and own left; women toward center of circle, men away from center, then return to partner
33-40	Israeli turn in 8 buzz steps
41-44	Repeat Part I, beats 41-44, end facing center
NOTE	If alternate formation is used, use Part I throughout.

RHYTHMIC NOTATION

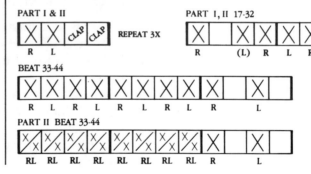

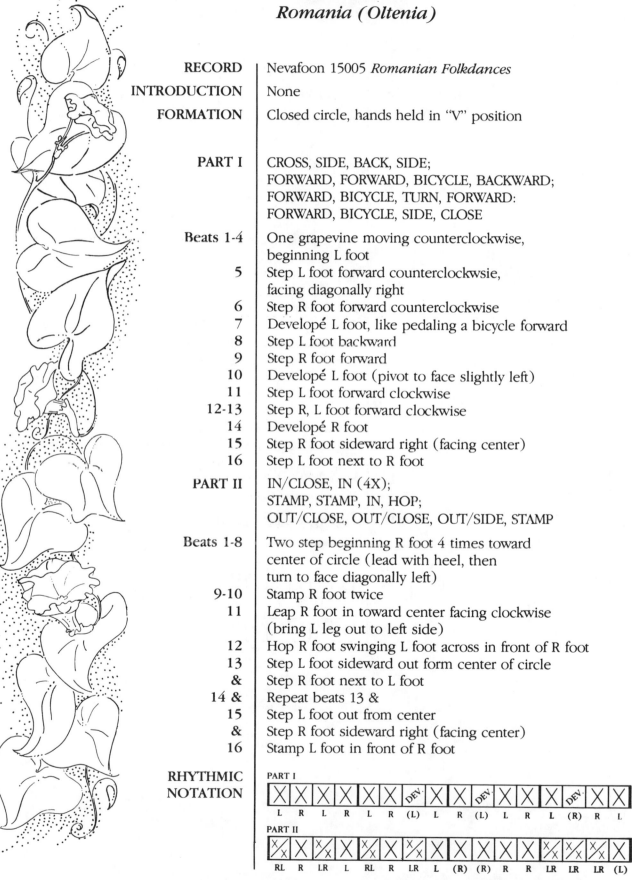

Boeraesca
Romania (Oltenia)

RECORD	Nevafoon 15005 *Romanian Folkdances*
INTRODUCTION	None
FORMATION	Closed circle, hands held in "V" position
PART I	CROSS, SIDE, BACK, SIDE; FORWARD, FORWARD, BICYCLE, BACKWARD; FORWARD, BICYCLE, TURN, FORWARD: FORWARD, BICYCLE, SIDE, CLOSE
Beats 1-4	One grapevine moving counterclockwise, beginning L foot
5	Step L foot forward counterclockwsie, facing diagonally right
6	Step R foot forward counterclockwise
7	Developé L foot, like pedaling a bicycle forward
8	Step L foot backward
9	Step R foot forward
10	Developé L foot (pivot to face slightly left)
11	Step L foot forward clockwise
12-13	Step R, L foot forward clockwise
14	Developé R foot
15	Step R foot sideward right (facing center)
16	Step L foot next to R foot
PART II	IN/CLOSE, IN (4X); STAMP, STAMP, IN, HOP; OUT/CLOSE, OUT/CLOSE, OUT/SIDE, STAMP
Beats 1-8	Two step beginning R foot 4 times toward center of circle (lead with heel, then turn to face diagonally left)
9-10	Stamp R foot twice
11	Leap R foot in toward center facing clockwise (bring L leg out to left side)
12	Hop R foot swinging L foot across in front of R foot
13	Step L foot sideward out form center of circle
&	Step R foot next to L foot
14 &	Repeat beats 13 &
15	Step L foot out from center
&	Step R foot sideward right (facing center)
16	Stamp L foot in front of R foot
RHYTHMIC NOTATION	

PART I

X	X	X	X	X	X	DEV	X	X	DEV	X	X	X	X	DEV	X	X
L	R	L	R	L	R	(L)	L	R	(L)	L	R	L	R	(R)	R	L

PART II

X/X	X	X/X	X	X/X	X	X/X	X	X	X	X	X	X/X	X/X	X/X	X
RL	R	LR	L	RL	R	R	L	(R)	(R)	R	R	LR	LR	LR	(L)

Bosarka
Yugoslavia (East Serbia)

RECORD	Kola K 407
INTRODUCTION	32 beats
FORMATION	Short lines, belt hold with R arm under L arm over
PART I	FORWARD, CROSS; FORWARD, CROSS; FORWARD/CLOSE FORWARD; BACKWARD, HOP; IN, BOUNCE; OUT, CLOSE; STEP/STEP, STEP; IN, BOUNCE; OUT, CLOSE; STEP/STEP, STEP
Beat 1	Step R foot diagonally forward right moving counter-clockwise
2	Step L foot crossing in front of R foot
3	Step R foot diagonally forward
4	Step L foot crossing in front of R foot
5-6	Two step R foot diagonally forward counterclockwise
7	Step L foot diagonally backward clockwise
8	Hop L foot swinging R foot slightly across in front of L leg
9	Step R foot diagonally in toward center bringing right shoulder in (keep L foot in position on floor)
10	Bounce R foot; keep L foot in place
11	Step L foot out and slightly right of "pinned" position
12	Step R foot next to L foot
13-14	Step, L, R, L foot in place
15-20	Repeat beats 9-14
NOTE	Move gradually right during beats 9-20

RHYTHMIC NOTATION

PART I

X	X	X	X	X/X	X	X	X	X	X	X	X	X	X/X	X
R	L	R	L	RL	R	L	L	L	R	R	L	R	LR	L

X	X	X	X	X/X	X
R	R	L	R	LR	L

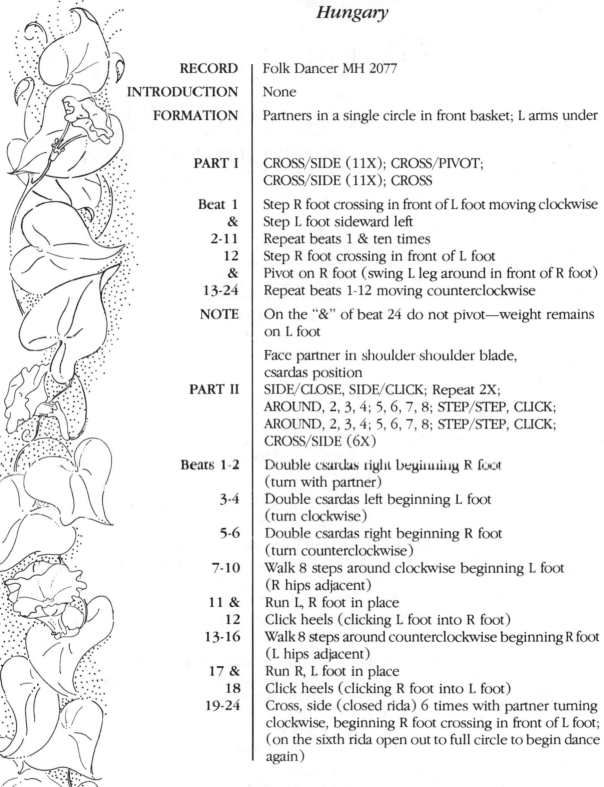

Circle Csárdás
Hungary

RECORD	Folk Dancer MH 2077
INTRODUCTION	None
FORMATION	Partners in a single circle in front basket; L arms under
PART I	CROSS/SIDE (11X); CROSS/PIVOT;
	CROSS/SIDE (11X); CROSS
Beat 1	Step R foot crossing in front of L foot moving clockwise
&	Step L foot sideward left
2-11	Repeat beats 1 & ten times
12	Step R foot crossing in front of L foot
&	Pivot on R foot (swing L leg around in front of R foot)
13-24	Repeat beats 1-12 moving counterclockwise
NOTE	On the "&" of beat 24 do not pivot—weight remains on L foot
	Face partner in shoulder shoulder blade, csardas position
PART II	SIDE/CLOSE, SIDE/CLICK; Repeat 2X;
	AROUND, 2, 3, 4; 5, 6, 7, 8; STEP/STEP, CLICK;
	AROUND, 2, 3, 4; 5, 6, 7, 8; STEP/STEP, CLICK;
	CROSS/SIDE (6X)
Beats 1-2	Double csardas right beginning R foot (turn with partner)
3-4	Double csardas left beginning L foot (turn clockwise)
5-6	Double csardas right beginning R foot (turn counterclockwise)
7-10	Walk 8 steps around clockwise beginning L foot (R hips adjacent)
11 &	Run L, R foot in place
12	Click heels (clicking L foot into R foot)
13-16	Walk 8 steps around counterclockwise beginning R foot (L hips adjacent)
17 &	Run R, L foot in place
18	Click heels (clicking R foot into L foot)
19-24	Cross, side (closed rida) 6 times with partner turning clockwise, beginning R foot crossing in front of L foot; (on the sixth rida open out to full circle to begin dance again)

(continued)

Circle Csárdás (continued)

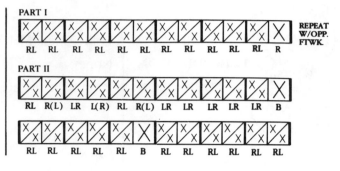

RHYTHMIC NOTATION

Debka Chag
Festive Debka
Israel

RECORD	Tikva T-145 *Party*
INTRODUCTION	16 beats
FORMATION	Line or lines facing counterclockwise, join hands, L arm behind back
PART I	FORWARD, FORWARD; STAMP, STAMP; Repeat Part I 7X
Beat 1-2	Step L, R foot forward counterclockwise; knees bent
3	Stamp L foot and raise L heel (weight is on the R foot)
4	Lower L heel to floor with force
5-32	Repeat Part I, beats 1-4, seven times
PART II	FORWARD/FORWARD, FORWARD; UP, CLOSE; Repeat Part II 3X
Beats 1 &	Run L, R foot forward counterclockwise
2	Run L foot forward reaching R foot sideward out—touch floor with R foot
3	Lift R leg up, knee bent
4	Step R foot next to L foot
5-16	Repeat Part II, beats 1-4, three times
PART III	FORWARD/FORWARD, FORWARD; UP/HOP, FORWARD; FORWARD/HOP, FORWARD; FORWARD/HOP, FORWARD; Repeat Part III

Debka Chag *(continued)*

Beats 1 &	Run L, R foot forward counterclockwise
2	Run L foot forward reaching R foot sideward out—as above
3	Lift R leg up
&	Hop L foot
4	Step R foot forward
5 &	Step hop L foot forward
6	Step R foot forward
7 &	Step hop L foot forward
8	Step R foot forward
9-16	Repeat Part III, beats 1-8

RHYTHMIC NOTATION

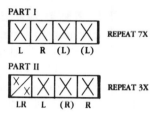

Erev Ba
Evening Falls
Israel

RECORD	Tikva 98 *Dance with Rivka*
INTRODUCTION	16 beats
FORMATION	Open circle, no hands held
PART I	SIDE/CROSS, BACK/SIDE; FORWARD/CLOSE, FORWARD; BACK/SIDE, CROSS/SIDE; BACK/SIDE, TOGETHER; Repeat Part I
Beat 1	Step R foot sideward right
&	Step L foot crossing in front of R foot
2	Step R foot crossing in back of L foot
&	Step L foot sideward left turning to face clockwise
3-4	Two step forward beginning R foot

(continued)

Erev Ba *(continued)*

5-6	Reverse grapevine facing center and moving counterclockwise (beginning L foot crossing in back of R foot)
7	Step L foot crossing in back of R foot
&	Step R foot sideward right
8	Step L foot next to R foot transferring weight to both feet
9-16	Repeat Part I, beats 1-8
PART II	TURN/TURN, SIDE/CROSS; BACK/SIDE, CROSS/BACK; Repeat; IN/CROSS, IN/CROSS; IN/CROSS, IN/OUT; CROSS/OUT, CROSS/OUT; CROSS/OUT, TURN/TURN
Beats 1 &	Step R, L foot turning a full circle counterclockwise (body turns clockwise)
2	Step R foot sideward right
&	Step L foot crossing in front of R foot
3	Step R foot crossing in back of L foot
&	Step L foot sideward left
4	Step R foot crossing in front of L foot
&	Step L foot crossing in back of R foot
5-8	Repeat beats 1-4 (end facing clockwise)
9	Step R foot sideward in (toward center of circle) arms spread low
&	Step L foot crossing in front of R foot, crossing wrists
10-11	Repeat beats 9 & two times
12	Step R foot sideward in
&	Step L foot sideward out
13	Step R foot crossing in front of L foot, crossing wrists
&	Step L foot sideward out, arms spread
14-15	Repeat beats 13 & two times
16	Step R, L foot turning a full circle counterclockwise (body turns clockwise)

RHYTHMIC NOTATION

PART I

X X X X X X X X REPEAT
RL RL RL R LR LR LR B

PART II

X X X X REPEAT 3X
RL RL RL RL

Gaida Avasi
Macedonia

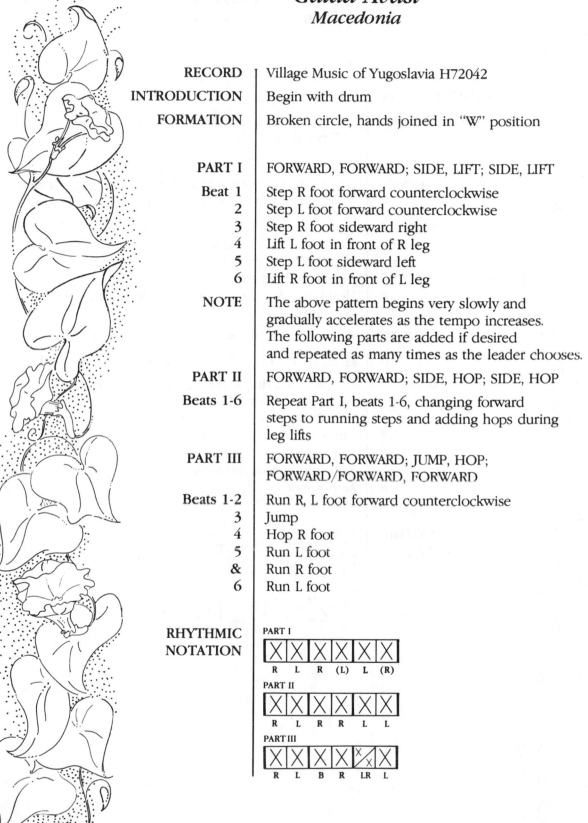

RECORD	Village Music of Yugoslavia H72042
INTRODUCTION	Begin with drum
FORMATION	Broken circle, hands joined in "W" position

PART I	FORWARD, FORWARD; SIDE, LIFT; SIDE, LIFT
Beat 1	Step R foot forward counterclockwise
2	Step L foot forward counterclockwise
3	Step R foot sideward right
4	Lift L foot in front of R leg
5	Step L foot sideward left
6	Lift R foot in front of L leg
NOTE	The above pattern begins very slowly and gradually accelerates as the tempo increases. The following parts are added if desired and repeated as many times as the leader chooses.
PART II	FORWARD, FORWARD; SIDE, HOP; SIDE, HOP
Beats 1-6	Repeat Part I, beats 1-6, changing forward steps to running steps and adding hops during leg lifts
PART III	FORWARD, FORWARD; JUMP, HOP; FORWARD/FORWARD, FORWARD
Beats 1-2	Run R, L foot forward counterclockwise
3	Jump
4	Hop R foot
5	Run L foot
&	Run R foot
6	Run L foot

RHYTHMIC NOTATION

PART I

X	X	X	X	X	X
R	L	R	(L)	L	(R)

PART II

X	X	X	X	X	X
R	L	R	R	L	L

PART III

X	X	X	X	X X	X
R	L	B	R	LR	L

Gavotte D'Honneur
France (Brittany)

RECORD	Dances from Brittany DB2
INTRODUCTION	Begin with vocal
FORMATION	Broken circle or line, hands joined in "W" position

PART I	FORWARD, FORWARD; FORWARD/FORWARD, FORWARD; FORWARD, FORWARD; FORWARD, HOP; Repeat Part I 3X
Beats 1-2	Step L, R foot forward moving clockwise
3-4	Step L, R, L foot forward (3 &, 4)
5-6	Step R, L foot forward
7	Step R foot forward
8	Hop R foot bringing L foot up in front of L leg with bent knee
NOTE	Forward steps are executed with toes apart
PART II	HOP, HOP; SIDE, CROSS; JUMP, HOP; BACK, HOP
Beats 1-2	Hop R foot 2 times moving sideward clockwise
3	Step L foot sideward left
4	Step R foot crossing in front of L foot
5	Jump on both feet facing center
6	Hop L foot
7	Step R foot crossing in back of L foot
8	Hop R foot

RHYTHMIC NOTATION

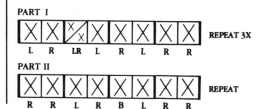

Gruzanka
Yugoslavia (Serbia)

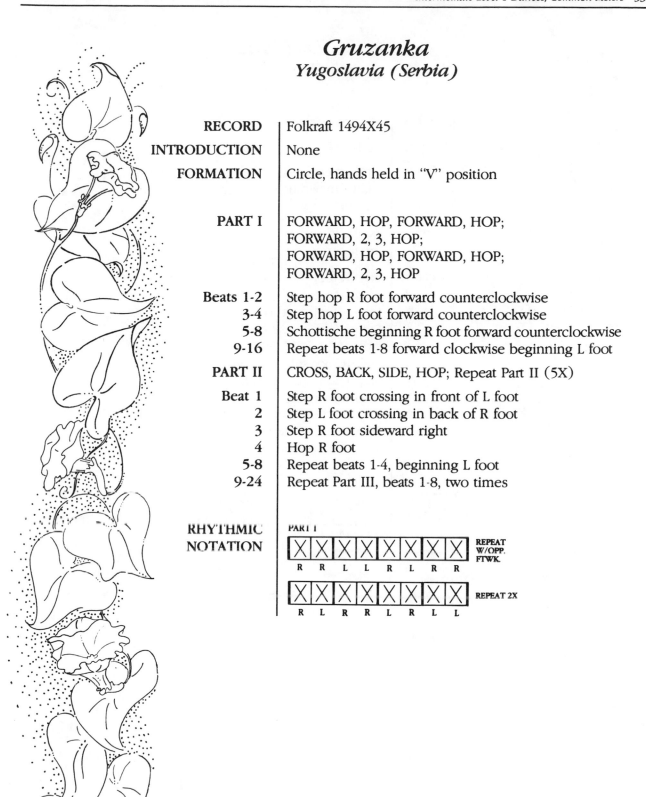

RECORD	Folkraft 1494X45
INTRODUCTION	None
FORMATION	Circle, hands held in "V" position
PART I	FORWARD, HOP, FORWARD, HOP; FORWARD, 2, 3, HOP; FORWARD, HOP, FORWARD, HOP; FORWARD, 2, 3, HOP
Beats 1-2	Step hop R foot forward counterclockwise
3-4	Step hop L foot forward counterclockwise
5-8	Schottische beginning R foot forward counterclockwise
9-16	Repeat beats 1-8 forward clockwise beginning L foot
PART II	CROSS, BACK, SIDE, HOP; Repeat Part II (5X)
Beat 1	Step R foot crossing in front of L foot
2	Step L foot crossing in back of R foot
3	Step R foot sideward right
4	Hop R foot
5-8	Repeat beats 1-4, beginning L foot
9-24	Repeat Part III, beats 1-8, two times

RHYTHMIC NOTATION

PART I

X	X	X	X	X	X	X	X	REPEAT W/OPP. FTWK.
R	R	L	L	R	L	R	R	

X	X	X	X	X	X	X	X	REPEAT 2X
R	L	R	R	L	R	L	L	

Güzelleme
Turkey

RECORD	Boz-Ok-105
INTRODUCTION	16 beats
FORMATION	Broken circle, hands joined with arms straight; right arm behind neighbor's left arm, fingers interlocked
PART I	IN, OUT/CLOSE; CROSS, SIDE/CLOSE; SIDE, HEEL; SIDE, HEEL
Beat 1	Step R foot in (leave L toe in place)
2	Step L foot out
&	Step R foot next to L foot
3	Step L foot crossing in front of R foot (large step and bend knees so body dips)
4	Step R foot sideward right
&	Step L foot next to R foot
5	Step R foot sideward right
6	Touch L heel sideward left
7	Step L foot sideward left
8	Touch R heel sideward right

RHYTHMIC NOTATION

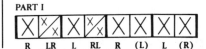

PART I

R   LR   L   RL   R   (L)   L   (R)

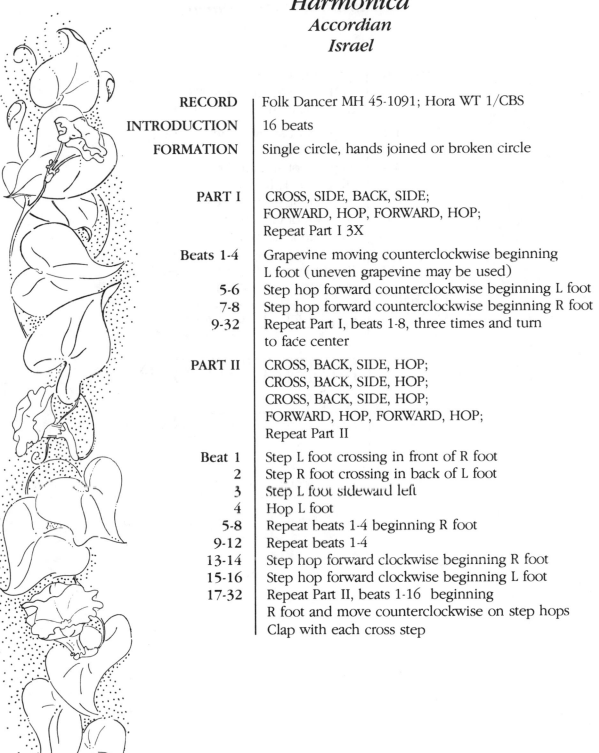

Harmonica
Accordian
Israel

RECORD	Folk Dancer MH 45-1091; Hora WT 1/CBS
INTRODUCTION	16 beats
FORMATION	Single circle, hands joined or broken circle

PART I	CROSS, SIDE, BACK, SIDE; FORWARD, HOP, FORWARD, HOP; Repeat Part I 3X
Beats 1-4	Grapevine moving counterclockwise beginning L foot (uneven grapevine may be used)
5-6	Step hop forward counterclockwise beginning L foot
7-8	Step hop forward counterclockwise beginning R foot
9-32	Repeat Part I, beats 1-8, three times and turn to face center
PART II	CROSS, BACK, SIDE, HOP; CROSS, BACK, SIDE, HOP; CROSS, BACK, SIDE, HOP; FORWARD, HOP, FORWARD, HOP; Repeat Part II
Beat 1	Step L foot crossing in front of R foot
2	Step R foot crossing in back of L foot
3	Step L foot sideward left
4	Hop L foot
5-8	Repeat beats 1-4 beginning R foot
9-12	Repeat beats 1-4
13-14	Step hop forward clockwise beginning R foot
15-16	Step hop forward clockwise beginning L foot
17-32	Repeat Part II, beats 1-16 beginning R foot and move counterclockwise on step hops Clap with each cross step

(continued)

Harmonica *(continued)*

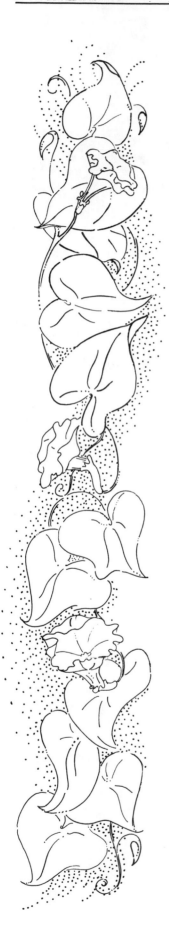

PART III	"T" position of arms SIDE, REST, SIDE, REST; SIDE, CROSS, SIDE, CROSS; Repeat Part III 3X
Beats 1-2	Step L foot sideward left or use a "three" L/R, L foot
3-4	Step R foot sideward right or use a "three," R/L, R foot
5	Step L foot sideward left
6	Step R foot crossing in front of L foot
7	Step L foot sideward left
8	Step R foot crossing in front of L foot
9-32	Repeat Part III, beats 1-8, three times

RHYTHMIC NOTATION

PART I

X	X	X	X	X	X	X	X	**REPEAT 3X**
L	R	L	R	L	L	R	R	

PART II

X	X	X	X	X	X	X	X	X	X	X	X	X	X	X	X	**REPEAT W/OPP. FTWK.**
L	R	L	L	R	L	R	R	L	R	L	L	R	R	L	L	

PART III

X		X		X	X	X	X	**REPEAT 3X**
L		R		L	R	L	R	

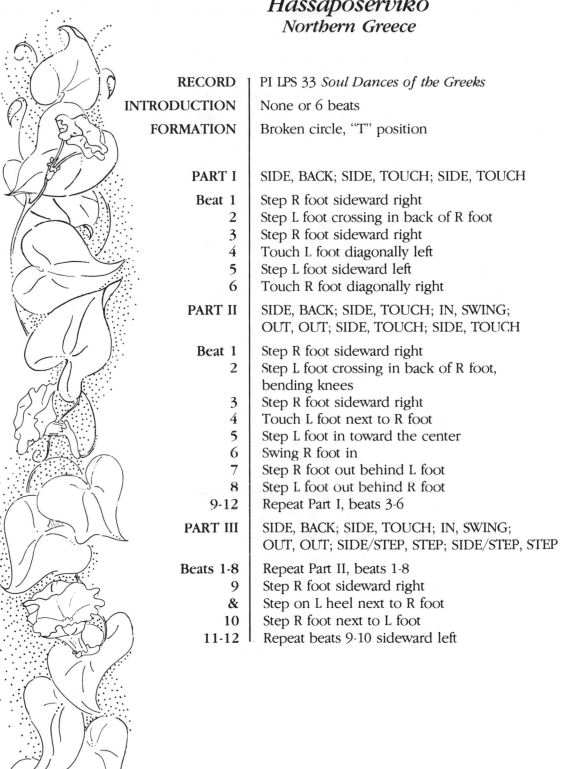

Hassaposerviko
Northern Greece

RECORD	PI LPS 33 *Soul Dances of the Greeks*
INTRODUCTION	None or 6 beats
FORMATION	Broken circle, "T" position

PART I	SIDE, BACK; SIDE, TOUCH; SIDE, TOUCH
Beat 1	Step R foot sideward right
2	Step L foot crossing in back of R foot
3	Step R foot sideward right
4	Touch L foot diagonally left
5	Step L foot sideward left
6	Touch R foot diagonally right

PART II	SIDE, BACK; SIDE, TOUCH; IN, SWING; OUT, OUT; SIDE, TOUCH; SIDE, TOUCH
Beat 1	Step R foot sideward right
2	Step L foot crossing in back of R foot, bending knees
3	Step R foot sideward right
4	Touch L foot next to R foot
5	Step L foot in toward the center
6	Swing R foot in
7	Step R foot out behind L foot
8	Step L foot out behind R foot
9-12	Repeat Part I, beats 3-6

PART III	SIDE, BACK; SIDE, TOUCH; IN, SWING; OUT, OUT; SIDE/STEP, STEP; SIDE/STEP, STEP
Beats 1-8	Repeat Part II, beats 1-8
9	Step R foot sideward right
&	Step on L heel next to R foot
10	Step R foot next to L foot
11-12	Repeat beats 9-10 sideward left

(continued)

Hassaposerviko (continued)

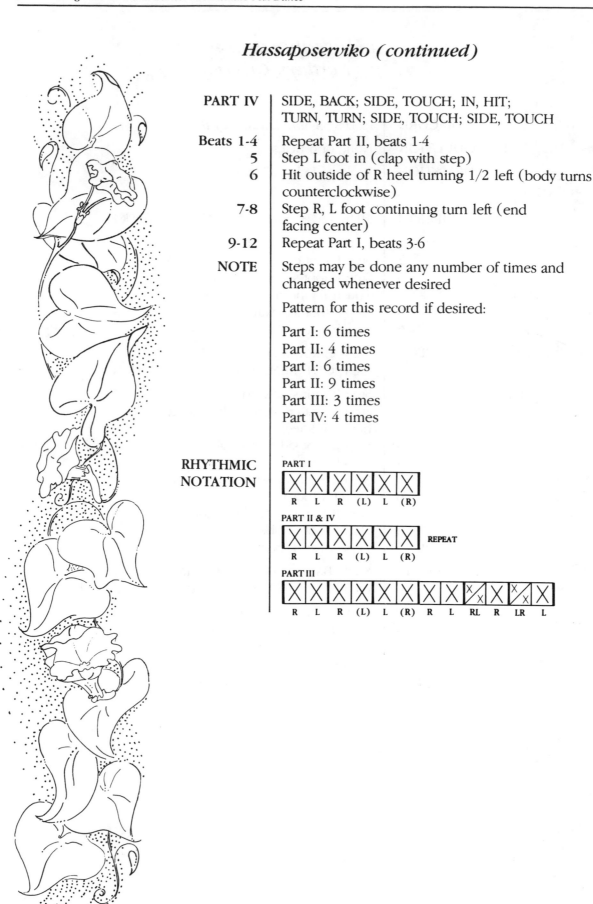

PART IV	SIDE, BACK; SIDE, TOUCH; IN, HIT; TURN, TURN; SIDE, TOUCH; SIDE, TOUCH
Beats 1-4	Repeat Part II, beats 1-4
5	Step L foot in (clap with step)
6	Hit outside of R heel turning 1/2 left (body turns counterclockwise)
7-8	Step R, L foot continuing turn left (end facing center)
9-12	Repeat Part I, beats 3-6
NOTE	Steps may be done any number of times and changed whenever desired

Pattern for this record if desired:

Part I: 6 times
Part II: 4 times
Part I: 6 times
Part II: 9 times
Part III: 3 times
Part IV: 4 times

RHYTHMIC NOTATION

PART I

X	X	X	X	X	X
R	L	R	(L)	L	(R)

PART II & IV

X	X	X	X	X	X	REPEAT
R	L	R	(L)	L	(R)	

PART III

X	X	X	X	X	X	X	X	X/X	X	X/X	X
R	L	R	(L)	L	(R)	R	L	RL	R	LR	L

Hooshig Mooshig
Armenia (Lake Van region Eastern Turkey)

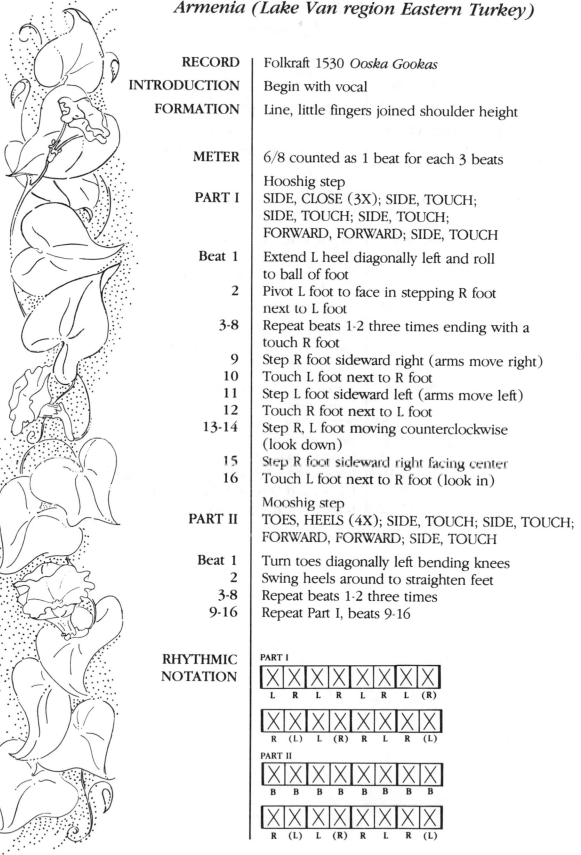

RECORD	Folkraft 1530 *Ooska Gookas*
INTRODUCTION	Begin with vocal
FORMATION	Line, little fingers joined shoulder height
METER	6/8 counted as 1 beat for each 3 beats
PART I	Hooshig step SIDE, CLOSE (3X); SIDE, TOUCH; SIDE, TOUCH; SIDE, TOUCH; FORWARD, FORWARD; SIDE, TOUCH
Beat 1	Extend L heel diagonally left and roll to ball of foot
2	Pivot L foot to face in stepping R foot next to L foot
3-8	Repeat beats 1-2 three times ending with a touch R foot
9	Step R foot sideward right (arms move right)
10	Touch L foot next to R foot
11	Step L foot sideward left (arms move left)
12	Touch R foot next to L foot
13-14	Step R, L foot moving counterclockwise (look down)
15	Step R foot sideward right facing center
16	Touch L foot next to R foot (look in)
PART II	Mooshig step TOES, HEELS (4X); SIDE, TOUCH; SIDE, TOUCH; FORWARD, FORWARD; SIDE, TOUCH
Beat 1	Turn toes diagonally left bending knees
2	Swing heels around to straighten feet
3-8	Repeat beats 1-2 three times
9-16	Repeat Part I, beats 9-16

RHYTHMIC NOTATION

PART I

X	X	X	X	X	X	X	X
L	R	L	R	L	R	L	(R)

X	X	X	X	X	X	X	X
R	(L)	L	(R)	R	L	R	(L)

PART II

X	X	X	X	X	X	X	X
B	B	B	B	B	B	B	B

X	X	X	X	X	X	X	X
R	(L)	L	(R)	R	L	R	(L)

Hora Chadera
Hora from Chader
Israel

RECORD	Worldtone WT 10022
INTRODUCTION	16 slower beats plus 16 faster beats
FORMATION	Circle, L hand at own shoulder with palm up, R hand holding person in front
PART I	FORWARD, 2, 3, 4; HEEL, REST, BACKWARD, CLOSE; Repeat Part I 3X
Beats 1-4	Step R, L, R, L foot forward moving counterclockwise
5-6	Touch R heel forward
7	Step R foot backward clockwise
8	Step L foot next to R foot
9-32	Repeat Part I, beats 1-8, three times
PART II	IN, 2, 3, 4; STAMP, REST, STAMP, REST; OUT, 2, 3, 4; STAMP, REST, STAMP, REST; Repeat Part II
Beats 1-4	Step R, L, R, L foot in toward the center (raise arms)
5	Stamp R foot in front of L foot (raise arms)
6	Rest (lower arms)
7-8	Repeat beats 5-6
9-16	Repeat beats 1-8 moving out from center (lower and raise arms beats 1-4)
17-32	Repeat Part II, beats 1-16

Hora Chadera *(continued)*

PART III	SIDE, BACK, SIDE, STAMP (2X); SIDE, STAMP, SIDE, STAMP; TURN, 2, 3, STAMP; Repeat Part III
Beat 1	Step R foot sideward right
2	Step L foot crossing in back of R foot
3	Step R foot sideward right
4	Stamp L foot next to R foot
5-8	Repeat beats 5-8 sideward left beginning L foot
9	Step R foot sideward right
10	Stamp L foot next to R foot
11-12	Repeat beats 9-10 beginning L foot
13-15	Step R, L, R foot turning right
16	Stamp L foot next to R foot
17-32	Repeat Part II, beats 1-16 beginning L foot

RHYTHMIC NOTATION

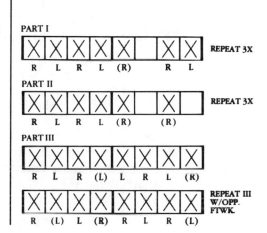

PART I

X X X X   X X   REPEAT 3X

R L R L (R)   R L

PART II

X X X X   X   REPEAT 3X

R L R L (R)   (R)

PART III

X X X X X X X

R L R (L) L R L (R)

X X X X X X X

R (L) L (R) R L R (L)

REPEAT III W/OPP. FTWK.

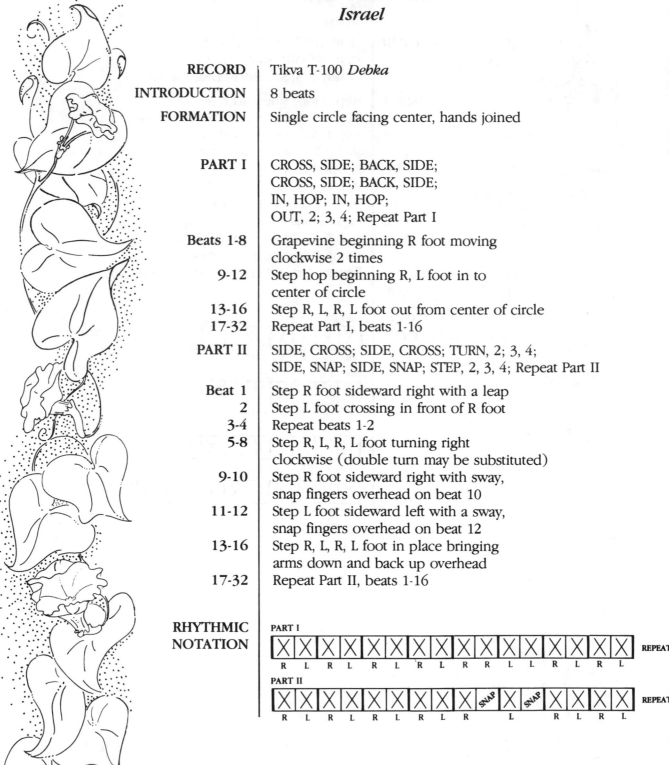

Hora Nirkoda
Israel

RECORD	Tikva T-100 *Debka*
INTRODUCTION	8 beats
FORMATION	Single circle facing center, hands joined
PART I	CROSS, SIDE; BACK, SIDE; CROSS, SIDE; BACK, SIDE; IN, HOP; IN, HOP; OUT, 2; 3, 4; Repeat Part I
Beats 1-8	Grapevine beginning R foot moving clockwise 2 times
9-12	Step hop beginning R, L foot in to center of circle
13-16	Step R, L, R, L foot out from center of circle
17-32	Repeat Part I, beats 1-16
PART II	SIDE, CROSS; SIDE, CROSS; TURN, 2; 3, 4; SIDE, SNAP; SIDE, SNAP; STEP, 2, 3, 4; Repeat Part II
Beat 1	Step R foot sideward right with a leap
2	Step L foot crossing in front of R foot
3-4	Repeat beats 1-2
5-8	Step R, L, R, L foot turning right clockwise (double turn may be substituted)
9-10	Step R foot sideward right with sway, snap fingers overhead on beat 10
11-12	Step L foot sideward left with a sway, snap fingers overhead on beat 12
13-16	Step R, L, R, L foot in place bringing arms down and back up overhead
17-32	Repeat Part II, beats 1-16

RHYTHMIC NOTATION

PART I

X	X	X	X	X	X	X	X	X	X	X	X	X	X	X	X	REPEAT
R	L	R	L	R	L	R	R	L	L	R	L	R	L		

PART II

X	X	X	X	X	X	X	X	SNAP	X	SNAP	X	X	X	X	REPEAT
R	L	R	L	R	L	R	L		L		R	L	R	L	

Hora Nutii
Nuta's Hora (girl's name)
Romania (Muntenia)

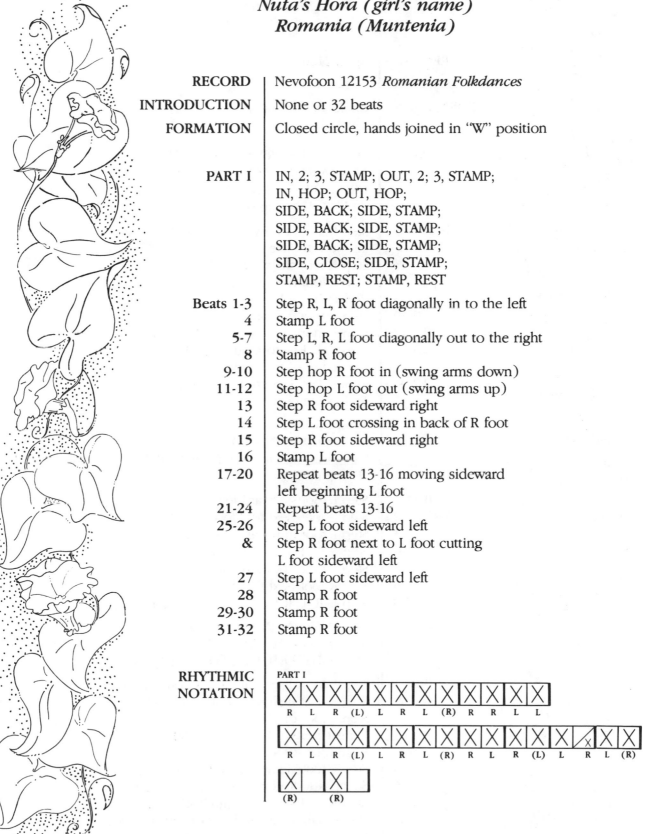

RECORD	Nevofoon 12153 *Romanian Folkdances*
INTRODUCTION	None or 32 beats
FORMATION	Closed circle, hands joined in "W" position

PART I

IN, 2; 3, STAMP; OUT, 2; 3, STAMP;
IN, HOP; OUT, HOP;
SIDE, BACK; SIDE, STAMP;
SIDE, BACK; SIDE, STAMP;
SIDE, BACK; SIDE, STAMP;
SIDE, CLOSE; SIDE, STAMP;
STAMP, REST; STAMP, REST

Beats	
1-3	Step R, L, R foot diagonally in to the left
4	Stamp L foot
5-7	Step L, R, L foot diagonally out to the right
8	Stamp R foot
9-10	Step hop R foot in (swing arms down)
11-12	Step hop L foot out (swing arms up)
13	Step R foot sideward right
14	Step L foot crossing in back of R foot
15	Step R foot sideward right
16	Stamp L foot
17-20	Repeat beats 13-16 moving sideward left beginning L foot
21-24	Repeat beats 13-16
25-26	Step L foot sideward left
&	Step R foot next to L foot cutting L foot sideward left
27	Step L foot sideward left
28	Stamp R foot
29-30	Stamp R foot
31-32	Stamp R foot

RHYTHMIC NOTATION

PART I

X	X	X	X	X	X	X	X	X	X						
R	L	R	(L)	L	R	L	(R)	R	R	L	L				

X	X	X	X	X	X	X	X	X	X	X	X	X	X/x	X	X
R	L	R	(L)	L	R	L	(R)	R	L	R	(L)	L	R	L	(R)

X		X	
(R)		(R)	

Horehronsky Czárdás
Slovakia

RECORD	Apon 2126
INTRODUCTION	16 beats
FORMATION	Circle, hands joined
PART I	FORWARD, FORWARD, SIDE, CLOSE;
	FORWARD, FORWARD, SIDE, CLOSE;
	CROSS, REST, CROSS, REST;
	OUT, 2, 3, 4; Repeat Part I 5X
Beats 1-2	Step R, L foot forward counterclockwise
	and turn to face center
3	Step R foot sideward right
4	Step L foot next to R foot
5-8	Repeat beats 1-4
9-10	Step R foot crossing in front of L foot
11-12	Step L foot crossing in front of R foot
13-16	Step R, L, R, L foot out away from
	the center of the circle
17-96	Repeat Part I, beats 1-16, five times;
	end facing center
	Tempo increases
PART II	SIDE, CLOSE, IN, CLOSE;
	SIDE, CLOSE, OUT/OUT, OUT/OUT
	(Box pattern)
Beat 1	Step L foot sideward left
2	Step R foot next to L foot
3	Step L foot in toward the center
4	Step R foot next to L foot
5	Step L foot sideward left
6	Step R foot next to L foot
7-8	Step L, R, L, R foot out away from the center
CHORUS	IN/CLOSE, IN, IN/CLOSE, IN;
	SIDE/STAMP, SIDE/STAMP;
	OUT/OUT, OUT/OUT (Diagonal pattern)
Beat 1	Step L foot diagonally left in toward center
&	Step R foot next to L foot
2	Step L foot diagonally in again
3-4	Repeat beats 1-2 diagonally right in
	beginning R foot
5	Step L foot sideward left (facing center)
&	Stamp R foot next to L foot (light stamp)
6	Step R foot sideward right (slight leap)
&	Stamp L foot next to R foot (light stamp)
7-8	Step L, R, L, R foot out away from the center

Horehronsky Czárdás (continued)

PART III	SIDE, CLOSE (Side steps)
Beat 1	Step L foot sideward left, raising R hip slightly
2	Step R foot next to L foot
3-8	Repeat beats 1-2 three times
PART IV	SIDE/CROSS (6X); FORWARD/FORWARD, FORWARD/FORWARD (Open Rida, 4 runs)
Beat 1	Step L foot sideward left (slight leap)
&	Step R foot crossing in front of L foot (bend knees)
2-6	Repeat beats 1 & five times
7-8	Run L, R, L, R foot forward clockwise
ENDING	
Beats 1-2	Run L, R foot in place
3-4	Click L foot into R foot

DANCE SEQUENCE

PART I	6 times
PART II	Box pattern 2 times
CHORUS	Diagonal 1 time
	Box pattern 1 time
	Diagonal 1 time
	Box pattern 1 time
	(Repeat Part II and Chorus)
PART III	Side step 8 times
CHORUS	Diagonal 1 time
	Side step 4 times
	Diagonal 1 time
	Side step 4 times
PART IV	Open Rida, 4 runs 2 times
CHORUS	Diagonal 1 time
	Open Rida, 4 runs 1 time
	Diagonal 1 time
	Open Rida, Ending 1 time

RHYTHMIC NOTATION

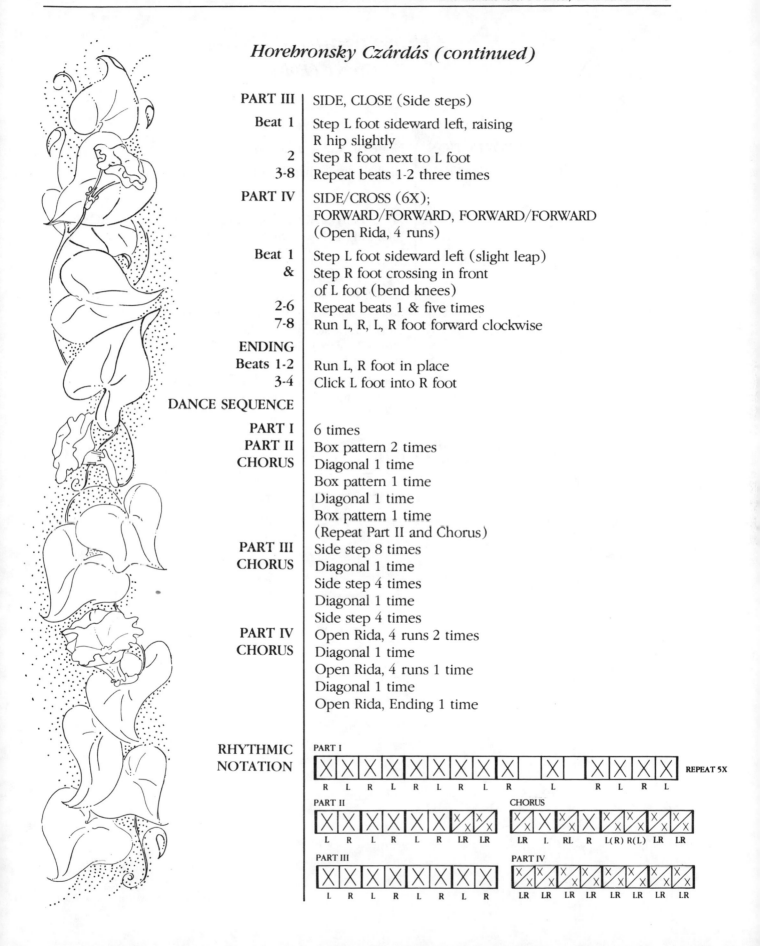

Iatros
Greece (Epirus)

RECORD	KT1001 *Arvanitiko Kofto*
INTRODUCTION	None or wait 4 measures
FORMATION	Broken circle, hands held in "W" position

PART I	SIDE, REST, BACK, SIDE; CROSS, REST, SIDE, CROSS; SIDE, REST, BACK, SIDE; CROSS, REST, TOUCH, REST
Beats 1-2	Step R foot sideward right
3	Step L foot crossing in back of R foot
4	Step R foot sideward right
5-6	Step L foot crossing in front of R foot
7	Step R foot sideward right
8	Step L foot crossing in front of R foot
9-12	Repeat beats 1-4
13-14	Step L foot crossing in front of R foot
15-16	Close R foot to L foot (no weight transfer)

RHYTHMIC NOTATION

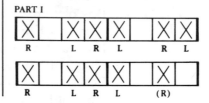

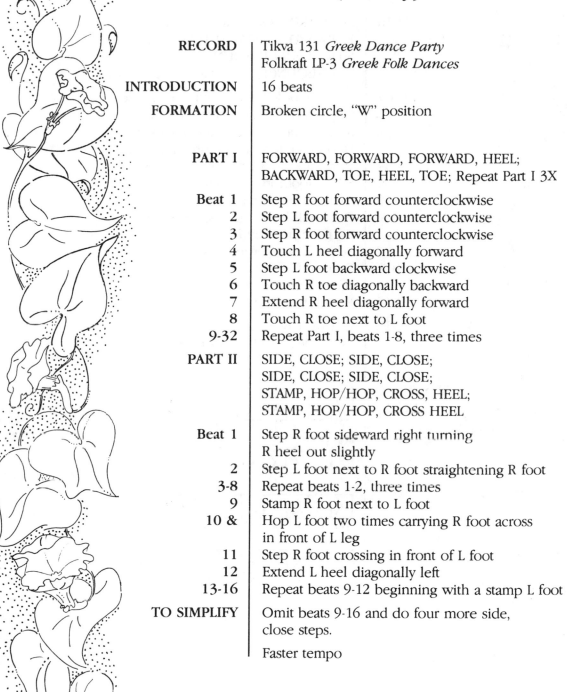

Karagouna
Greece (Thessaly)

RECORD	Tikva 131 *Greek Dance Party* Folkraft LP-3 *Greek Folk Dances*
INTRODUCTION	16 beats
FORMATION	Broken circle, "W" position
PART I	FORWARD, FORWARD, FORWARD, HEEL; BACKWARD, TOE, HEEL, TOE; Repeat Part I 3X
Beat 1	Step R foot forward counterclockwise
2	Step L foot forward counterclockwise
3	Step R foot forward counterclockwise
4	Touch L heel diagonally forward
5	Step L foot backward clockwise
6	Touch R toe diagonally backward
7	Extend R heel diagonally forward
8	Touch R toe next to L foot
9-32	Repeat Part I, beats 1-8, three times
PART II	SIDE, CLOSE; SIDE, CLOSE; SIDE, CLOSE; SIDE, CLOSE; STAMP, HOP/HOP, CROSS, HEEL; STAMP, HOP/HOP, CROSS HEEL
Beat 1	Step R foot sideward right turning R heel out slightly
2	Step L foot next to R foot straightening R foot
3-8	Repeat beats 1-2, three times
9	Stamp R foot next to L foot
10 &	Hop L foot two times carrying R foot across in front of L leg
11	Step R foot crossing in front of L foot
12	Extend L heel diagonally left
13-16	Repeat beats 9-12 beginning with a stamp L foot
TO SIMPLIFY	Omit beats 9-16 and do four more side, close steps. Faster tempo

(continued)

Karagouna (continued)

PART III	FORWARD, FORWARD/FORWARD; FORWARD, FORWARD/FORWARD; SIDE, BOUNCE/BOUNCE; SIDE, BOUNCE/BOUNCE; Repeat Part III
Beat 1	Step R foot forward counterclockwise
2	Step L foot forward counterclockwise
&	Step R foot forward counterclockwise
3	Step L foot forward counterclockwise
4	Step R foot forward counterclockwise
&	Step L foot forward counterclockwise
5	Step R foot sideward right
6 &	Bounce R heel twice (slight bounce), lift L foot in front of R leg
7	Step L foot sideward left
8 &	Bounce L heel twice (slight bounce), lift R foot in front of L leg
9-16	Repeat Part III, beats 1-8
NOTE	Part III may be done in the same way as the Syrtos described in this book.

RHYTHMIC NOTATION

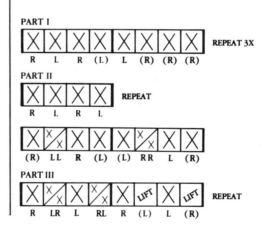

Koftós
Greece (Epirus)

RECORD	FG2735
INTRODUCTION	A pick up
FORMATION	Line, hands held in

PART I	SIDE, BACK/SIDE; CROSS, SIDE/CROSS; Repeat 2X; SIDE, BACK/SIDE; JUMP, REST
Beat 1	Step R foot sideward right
2	Step L foot crossing in back of R foot
&	Step R foot sideward right
3	Step L foot crossing in front of R foot
4	Step R foot sideward right
&	Step L foot crossing in front of R foot
5-12	Repeat beats 1-4 two times
13-14	Repeat beats 1-2
15	Jump
16	Rest
NOTE	An up-beat hop may precede each two beat measure.

RHYTHMIC NOTATION

PART I

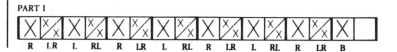

R LR L RL R LR L RL R LR L RL R LR B

Kol Dodi
The Voice of My Beloved
Israel

RECORD	Tikva T-80 *Israeli Folk Dance Festival*
INTRODUCTION	16 beats
FORMATION	Line, facing one behind the other, hands held
PART I	FORWARD, FORWARD; TOUCH, TOUCH; Repeat Part I 3X
Beat 1	Step L foot forward counterclockwise
2	Step R foot forward counterclockwise
3	Touch L foot forward counterclockwise
4	Touch L foot backward counterclockwise
5-16	Repeat Part I, beats 1-4, three times
PART II	FORWARD/HOP, FORWARD/HOP; BRUSH/HOP, BRUSH/HOP; Repeat Part II 3X
Beat 1 &	Step hop L foot forward counterclockwise
2 &	Step hop R foot forward counterclockwise
3	Brush L foot forward bending knee (backward pedaling action)
&	Hop R foot
4 &	Repeat beats 3 &
5-16	Repeat Part II, beats 1-4, three times
PART III	FORWARD, FORWARD; FORWARD/FORWARD, JUMP/HOP; Repeat Part III 3X
Beats 1-2	Step L, R foot forward counterclockwise
3 &	Run, L, R foot forward counterclockwise
4	Jump angling knees left
&	Hop R foot facing forward again
5-16	Repeat Part III, beats 1-4, three times

Kol Dodi (continued)

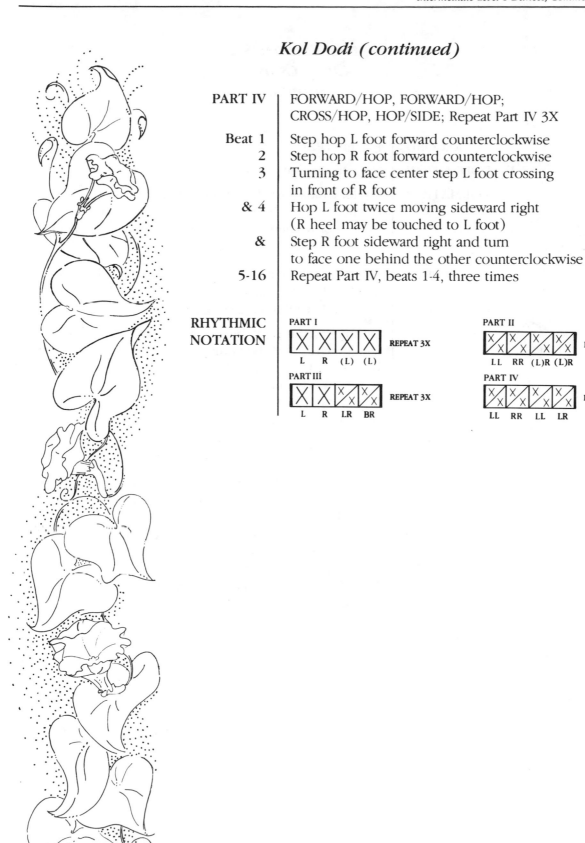

PART IV	FORWARD/HOP, FORWARD/HOP; CROSS/HOP, HOP/SIDE; Repeat Part IV 3X
Beat 1	Step hop L foot forward counterclockwise
2	Step hop R foot forward counterclockwise
3	Turning to face center step L foot crossing in front of R foot
& 4	Hop L foot twice moving sideward right (R heel may be touched to L foot)
&	Step R foot sideward right and turn to face one behind the other counterclockwise
5-16	Repeat Part IV, beats 1-4, three times

RHYTHMIC NOTATION

PART I

☐ X X X X ☐ **REPEAT 3X**
L R (L) (L)

PART II

REPEAT 3X
LL RR (L)R (L)R

PART III

REPEAT 3X
L R LR BR

PART IV

REPEAT 3X
LL RR LL LR

Körcsárdás I
Circle Csardas
Hungary

RECORD	Folkraft LP28
INTRODUCTION	No introduction
FORMATION	Circle, hands joined in reverse basket, or circle of couples with men's hands joined in back of women, women's hands on men's shoulders

PART I	SIDE, CLOSE; SIDE, CLICK; SIDE, CLICK; Repeat 3X; FORWARD (20X); Repeat Part I
Beats 1-4	Double csardas right, beginning R foot
5-6	Single csardas left, beginning L foot
7-24	Repeat beats 1-6, three times
25-44	Step forward counterclockwise 20 steps beginning R foot
45-88	Repeat Part I, beats 1-44
PART II	SIDE/BACK, CROSS; CLICK, REST; SIDE/BACK, CROSS; SIDE/BACK, CROSS; CLICK, REST; Repeat Part II 7X
Beats 1-2	Cifra beginning R foot (left foot crossing in back of R foot)
3-4	Click heels, L foot clicking against R foot
5-6	Cifra beginning R foot
7-8	Cifra beginning L foot
9-10	Click heels, R foot clicking against L foot
11-80	Repeat Part II, beats 1-10, seven times

Körcsárdás I (continued)

PART III	CROSS, SIDE (11X); CROSS, REST; Repeat 3X; CROSS, SIDE (5X); CROSS, REST; Repeat 3X
Beats 1-22	Closed rida steps 11 times moving clockwise beginning R foot crossing in front of L foot
23-24	Step R foot crossing in front of L foot
25-48	Repeat beats 1-24 moving counterclockwise beginning L foot crossing in front of R foot
49-96	Repeat Part III, beats 1-48
97-106	Closed rida steps 5 times moving clockwise
107-108	Step R foot crossing in front of L foot
109-120	Repeat beats 97-108 moving counterclockwise
121-144	Repeat Part III, beats 97-120
NOTE	Hungarian ending: beats 141-144 leap L foot in place, leap R foot in place, and click L foot to R foot.

RHYTHMIC NOTATION

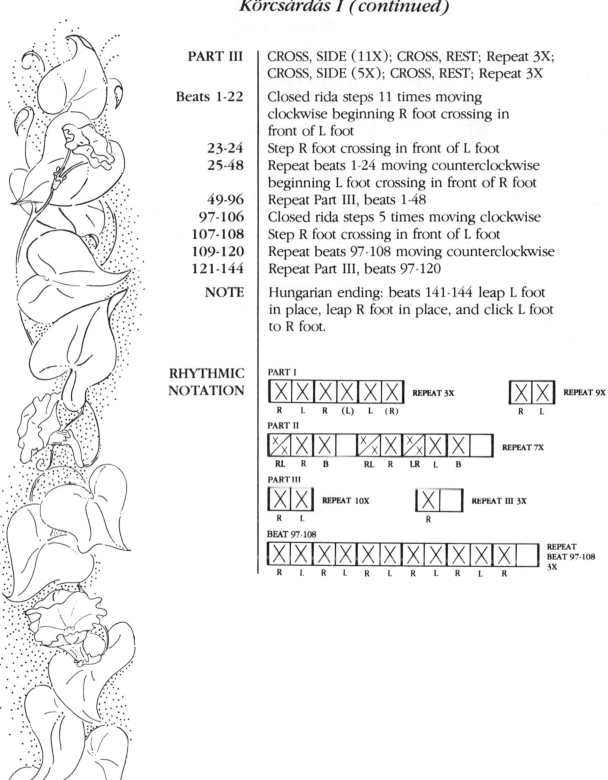

Kritikos
Greece (Crete)

RECORD	Tikva 131 *Greek Dance Party*
INTRODUCTION	8 beats
FORMATION	Broken circle, hands joined in "W" position

PART I	TOUCH, REST, BACK, SIDE; CROSS, REST, FORWARD, FORWARD; FORWARD, REST, FORWARD, FORWARD; FORWARD, PIVOT, SWIVEL, SWIVEL
Beats 1-2	Touch L foot slightly in
3	Step L foot crossing in back of R foot
4	Step R foot sidward right
5-6	Step L foot crossing in front of R foot and turn to face counterclockwise
7	Step R foot forward counterclockwise
8	Step L foot forward
9-10	Step R foot forward
11	Step L foot forward
12	Step R foot forward
13-14	Step L foot forward and pivot to face center
15	Bring feet together swivelling heels right
16	Swivel heels to straight position
VARIATION I	TOUCH, REST, BACK, SIDE; CROSS, REST, IN, IN; IN, REST, OUT, OUT; OUT, REST, SWIVEL, SWIVEL
Beats 1-4	Repeat Part I, beats 1-4
5-6	Step L foot crossing in front of R foot
7-8	Step R, L foot in toward center
9-10	Step R foot in toward the center
11-12	Step L, R foot out away from center
13-14	Step L foot out away from the center
15	Bring feet together swivelling heels right
16	Swivel heels to straight position

Kritikos (continued)

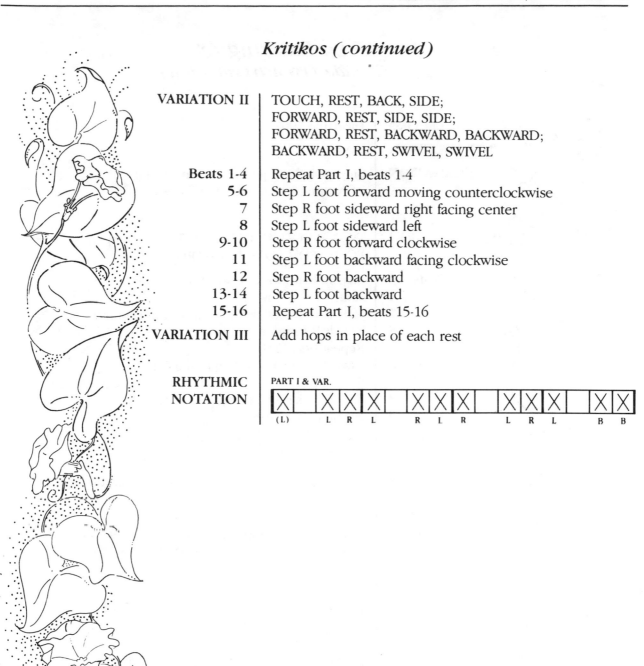

VARIATION II	TOUCH, REST, BACK, SIDE; FORWARD, REST, SIDE, SIDE; FORWARD, REST, BACKWARD, BACKWARD; BACKWARD, REST, SWIVEL, SWIVEL
Beats 1-4	Repeat Part I, beats 1-4
5-6	Step L foot forward moving counterclockwise
7	Step R foot sideward right facing center
8	Step L foot sideward left
9-10	Step R foot forward clockwise
11	Step L foot backward facing clockwise
12	Step R foot backward
13-14	Step L foot backward
15-16	Repeat Part I, beats 15-16
VARIATION III	Add hops in place of each rest

RHYTHMIC NOTATION

PART I & VAR.

X		X	X	X		X	X	X		X	X	X		X	X
(L)		L	R	L		R	L	R		L	R	L		B	B

La Bastringue
Cànada (French-Canadian)

RECORD	Laridaine 7902
INTRODUCTION	None
FORMATION	Single circle of partners, men on right of partner, hand held in "V" position
PART I	IN, 2, 3, TOUCH; OUT, 2, 3, TOUCH; Repeat; FORWARD/CLOSE, FORWARD (8X)
Beats 1-3	Step R, L, R foot in toward the center
4	Touch L foot in
5-7	Step L, R, L foot out away from the center
8	Touch R foot out
9-16	Repeat beats 1-8
17-18	Two step clockwise beginning R foot
19-24	Repeat beats 17-18, three times beginning L foot
25-32	Repeat beats 17-24, four times moving counterclockwise
PART II	UNDER, 2; 3, 4; BUZZ TURN (12X); FORWARD/CLOSE, FORWARD (8X)
Beats 1-4	Right-hand person turn to person on left under L arm with 4 walking steps
5-16	Buzz turn clockwise in social dance position
17-32	Eight two steps moving counterclockwise, partners side-by-side (R hand person on the inside)

RHYTHMIC NOTATION

PART I

X	X	X	X
R	L	R	(L)

REPEAT 3X W/OPP. FTWK.

X /	X	X /	X
R L	R	L R	L

REPEAT 3X

PART II

X	X	X	X
R	L	R	L

X /	X /
R L	R L

REPEAT 5X

X /	X	X /	X
R L	R	L R	L

REPEAT 3X

Lamnatseach
To the Victor
Israel

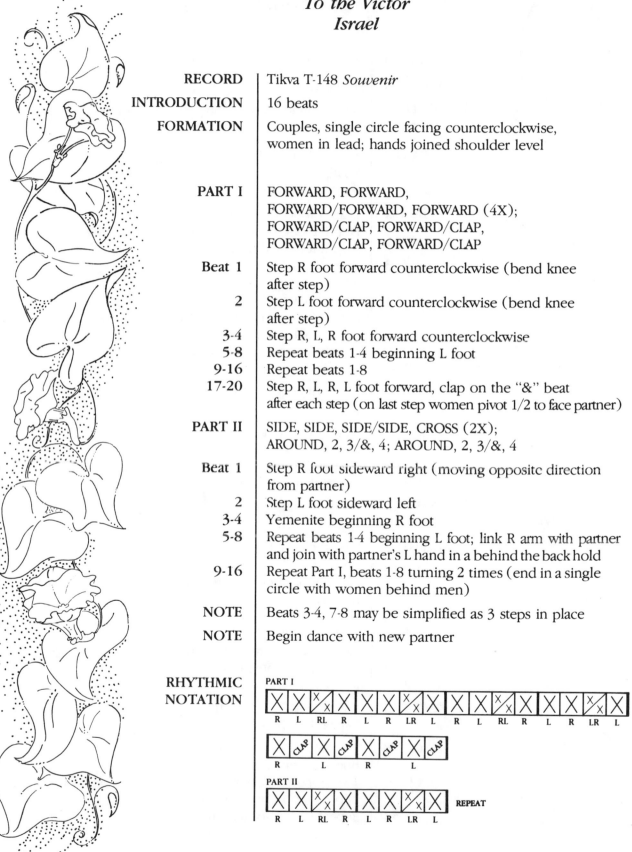

RECORD	Tikva T-148 *Souvenir*
INTRODUCTION	16 beats
FORMATION	Couples, single circle facing counterclockwise, women in lead; hands joined shoulder level
PART I	FORWARD, FORWARD, FORWARD/FORWARD, FORWARD (4X); FORWARD/CLAP, FORWARD/CLAP, FORWARD/CLAP, FORWARD/CLAP
Beat 1	Step R foot forward counterclockwise (bend knee after step)
2	Step L foot forward counterclockwise (bend knee after step)
3-4	Step R, L, R foot forward counterclockwise
5-8	Repeat beats 1-4 beginning L foot
9-16	Repeat beats 1-8
17-20	Step R, L, R, L foot forward, clap on the "&" beat after each step (on last step women pivot 1/2 to face partner)
PART II	SIDE, SIDE, SIDE/SIDE, CROSS (2X); AROUND, 2, 3/&, 4; AROUND, 2, 3/&, 4
Beat 1	Step R foot sideward right (moving opposite direction from partner)
2	Step L foot sideward left
3-4	Yemenite beginning R foot
5-8	Repeat beats 1-4 beginning L foot; link R arm with partner and join with partner's L hand in a behind the back hold
9-16	Repeat Part I, beats 1-8 turning 2 times (end in a single circle with women behind men)
NOTE	Beats 3-4, 7-8 may be simplified as 3 steps in place
NOTE	Begin dance with new partner

RHYTHMIC NOTATION

PART I

X	X	X/X	X	X	X	X/X	X	X	X	X/X	X	X	X	X/X	X
R	L	RL	R	L	R	LR	L	R	L	RL	R	L	R	LR	L

X	CLAP	X	CLAP	X	CLAP	X	CLAP
R		L		R		L	

PART II

X	X	X/X	X	X	X/X	X	
R	L	RL	R	L	R	LR	L	**REPEAT**

Lech Lamidbar
Israel

RECORD	Israeli Music Foundation LP 5/6
INTRODUCTION	16 beats
FORMATION	Single circle, facing center, do not join hands
PART I	SIDE; CROSS, CLOSE, REST, REST; SIDE, CLOSE, SIDE, TOUCH; Repeat Part I 3X
Beat &	Leap R foot sideward right
1	Step L foot crossing in front of R foot
2	Step R foot next to L foot
3	Rest
4	Rest
5	Step L foot sideward left
6	Step R foot next to L foot (clap hands over head)
7	Step L foot sideward left
8	Touch R foot next to L foot (clap hands over head)
9-32	Repeat Part I, beats 1-8, three times, then join hands
PART II	STEP, HOP, STEP, HOP; CROSS, SIDE, BACK, SIDE; Repeat Part II 3X
Beats 1-2	Step hop R foot in place
3-4	Step hop L foot in place
5-8	Grapevine clockwise beginning R foot
9-32	Repeat Part II, beats 1-8, three times
PART III	SIDE, TOUCH, SIDE, TOUCH; IN, TOUCH, OUT, TOUCH; Repeat Part III
Beats 1-2	Step R foot sideward right (touch L foot next to R foot on beat 2)
3-4	Step L foot sideward left (touch R foot next to L foot on beat 4)
5	Step R foot in toward center, bring arms up
6	Touch L foot behind R foot
7	Step L foot out away from the center, bring arms down
8	Touch R foot next to L foot
9-16	Repeat Part III, beats 1-8
PART IV	CROSS, SIDE, BACK, SIDE; CROSS, SIDE, BACK, HOP; Repeat Part IV 3X
Beats 1-8	Two grapevines clockwise beginning R foot, end with hop R foot beat 8
9-16	Two grapevines counterclockwise beginning L foot, end with hop L foot on beat 16
17-32	Repeat Part IV, beats 1-16

Lech Lamidbar (continued)

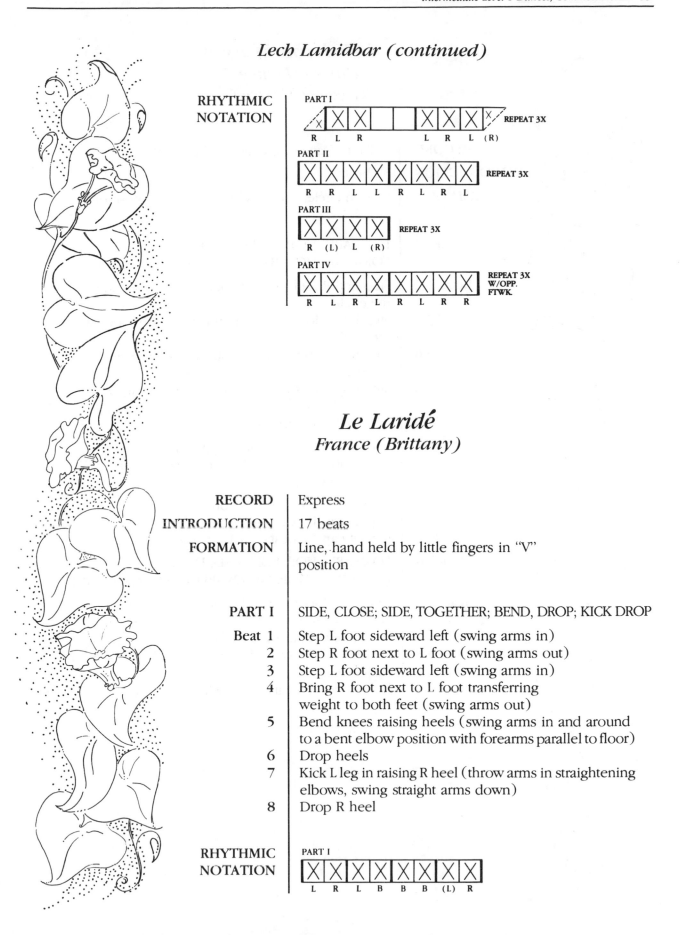

RHYTHMIC NOTATION

PART I

REPEAT 3X

R L R   L R L (R)

PART II

REPEAT 3X

R R L L R L R L

PART III

REPEAT 3X

R (L) L (R)

PART IV

REPEAT 3X
W/OPP.
FTWK.

R L R L R L R R

Le Laridé
France (Brittany)

RECORD	Express
INTRODUCTION	17 beats
FORMATION	Line, hand held by little fingers in "V" position

PART I	SIDE, CLOSE; SIDE, TOGETHER; BEND, DROP; KICK DROP
Beat 1	Step L foot sideward left (swing arms in)
2	Step R foot next to L foot (swing arms out)
3	Step L foot sideward left (swing arms in)
4	Bring R foot next to L foot transferring weight to both feet (swing arms out)
5	Bend knees raising heels (swing arms in and around to a bent elbow position with forearms parallel to floor)
6	Drop heels
7	Kick L leg in raising R heel (throw arms in straightening elbows, swing straight arms down)
8	Drop R heel

RHYTHMIC NOTATION

PART I

L R L B B B (L) R

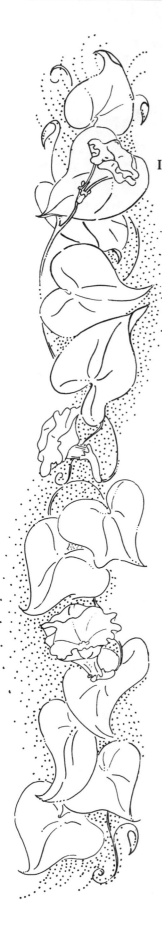

Len Irthe Mais
Harvest Dance
Greece (Thrace)

RECORD	Folklore Dances of Greece M7C23590A
INTRODUCTION	32 beats
FORMATION	Broken circle, hands held down in "V" position
PART I	FORWARD, HOP, FORWARD, HOP; FORWARD, HOP, BACKWARD, HOP; Repeat Part I
Beats 1-2	Step hop R foot forward counterclockwise around the circle
3-4	Step hop L foot forward counterclockwise around the circle
5-6	Step hop R foot forward counterclockwise around the circle
7-8	Step hop L foot backward clockwise facing counterclockwise
9-16	Repeat Part I, beats 1-8
PART IA	FORWARD/CLOSE, FORWARD (2X); FORWARD, HOP, BACKWARD, HOP; Repeat Part IA 3X
Beats 1-2	Two step R foot forward counterclockwise
3-4	Two step R foot forward counterclockwise
5-8	Repeat Part I, beats 5-8
9-32	Repeat Part IA, beats 1-8, three times
PART II	FORWARD, HOP, FORWARD, HOP; BACKWARD, HOP, BACKWARD, HOP; Repeat Part II
Beats 1-2	Step hop R foot forward counterclockwise
3-4	Step hop L foot forward counterclockwise around the circle and turn 1/2 to face clockwise
5-8	Step hop R, L foot backward counterclockwise around the circle
9-16	Repeat Part II, beats 1-8 moving clockwise

Len Irthe Mais *(continued)*

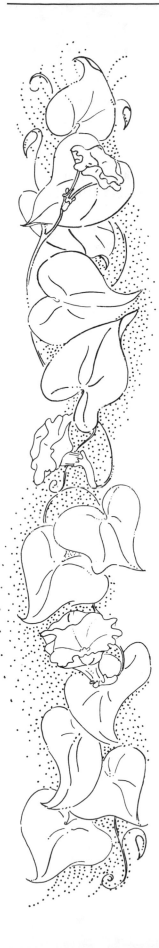

PART IIA	FORWARD/CLOSE, FORWARD (2X); BACKWARD, HOP, BACKWARD, HOP; Repeat Part IIA 3X
Beats 1-2	Two step R foot forward counterclockwise around the circle
3-4	Two step L foot forward counterclockwise around the circle and turn 1/2 to face clockwise
5-8	Step hop R, L foot backward counterclockwise facing clockwise
9-16	Repeat beats 1-8 clockwise
17-32	Repeat Part IIA, beats 1-16
PART III	FORWARD, HOP, FORWARD, HOP; SIDE, BACK, SIDE, HOP; Repeat Part III
Beats 1-4	Step hop R, L foot forward counterclockwise around the circle
5	Step R foot sideward right
6	Step L foot crossing in back of R foot
7	Step R foot sideward right
8	Hop R
9-16	Repeat Part III, beats 1-8 in opposite direction beginning L foot
PART IIIA	FORWARD/CLOSE, FORWARD (2X); SIDE, BACK, SIDE, HOP; Repeat Part IIIA 3X
Beats 1-4	Two step R, L foot forward counterclockwise around the circle and turn to face center
5-8	Repeat Part III, beats 5-8
9-16	Repeat Part IIIA, beats 1-8, in opposite direction beginning L foot
17-32	Repeat Part IIIA, beats 1-16
PART IV	IN HOP, IN HOP, IN HOP, OUT/CLOSE, OUT; Repeat Part IV
Beats 1-6	Step hop R, L, R foot in toward the center of the circle
7-8	Two step L foot out away from the center of the circle
9-16	Repeat Part IV

(continued)

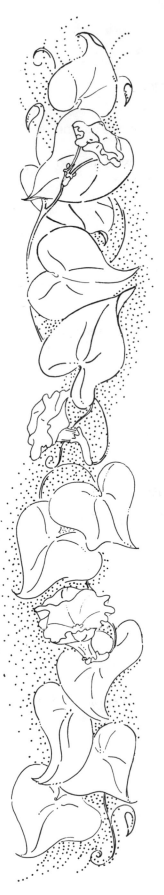

Len Irthe Mais (continued)

PART IVA	IN/CLOSE, IN (2X); IN, HOP, OUT/CLOSE, OUT; Repeat Part IVA 3X
Beats 1-4	Two step R, L foot in toward the center of the circle
5-6	Step hop R foot in toward the center of the circle
7-8	Two step L foot out away from the center of the circle
9-24	Repeat beats 1-8, two times
25-32	Repeat beats 1-8 pausing after the IN HOP then do a slow two step L foot out after the pause

RHYTHMIC NOTATION

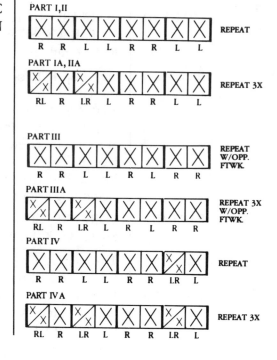

PART I,II

R R L L R R L L   REPEAT

PART IA, IIA

RL R LR L R R L L   REPEAT 3X

PART III

R R L L R L R R   REPEAT W/OPP. FTWK.

PART IIIA

RL R LR L R L R R   REPEAT 3X W/OPP. FTWK.

PART IV

R R L L R R LR L   REPEAT

PART IVA

RL R LR L R R LR L   REPEAT 3X

Likrat Shabat
Welcome of the Sabbath
Israel

RECORD	Tikva T-69 *Dance Along With Sabras*
INTRODUCTION	16 beats
FORMATION	Single circle facing center, hands joined
PART I	SIDE, SIDE, CROSS, SIDE; CROSS, SIDE, CROSS, SIDE; SIDE, SIDE, CROSS, REST; SIDE, SIDE, CROSS, REST; Repeat Part I
Beats 1-3	Yemenite beginning R foot
4	Step L foot sideward left
5	Step R foot crossing in front of L foot
6	Step L foot sideward left
7-8	Repeat beats 5-6
9-12	Yemenite beginning R foot
13-16	Yemenite beginning L foot
17-32	Repeat Part I, beats 1-16
PART II	CROSS, BACK, SIDE, CROSS; BACK, SIDE, OUT, IN; SIDE, BACK, SIDE, REST; SIDE, BACK, SIDE, REST; Repeat Part II
Beat 1	Step R foot crossing in front of L foot (lift arms)
2	Step L foot crossing in back of R foot (lower arms)
3	Step R foot sideward right
4	Step L foot crossing in front of R foot (lift arms)
5	Step R foot crossing in back of L foot (lower arms)
6	Step L foot sideward left
7	Step R foot out from the center (lift arms)
8	Step L foot in toward the center (lower arms)
9	Step R foot sideward right
10	Step L foot crossing in back of R foot
11-12	Step R foot sideward right
13-16	Repeat beats 9-12 beginning L foot to the left side
17-32	Repeat Part II, beats 1-16
PART III	SIDE, SIDE, CROSS, TURN; CROSS, TURN, CROSS, TURN; SIDE, SIDE, CROSS, REST; SIDE, SIDE, CROSS, REST; Repeat Part III
Beats 1-16	Same as Part I but release hands on beats 4-8 and do a full turn left; R arm is raised over head
17-32	Repeat Part III, beats 1-16

(continued)

Likrat Shabat (continued)

PART IV	CROSS, BACK; SIDE, CROSS; BACK, SIDE, OUT, IN; TURN, REST, TOGETHER, REST; TURN, REST, TOGETHER, REST; Repeat Part IV
Beats 1-8	Repeat Part II, beats 1-8 then release hands
9-10	Step R foot turning 1/4 right to face counterclockwise
11-12	Step L foot next to R foot and snap fingers on beat 11 (wrists crossed)
13-14	Step L foot 1/2 turn left to face clockwise
15-16	Step L foot next to R foot and snap fingers
17-32	Repeat Part IV, beats 1-16

RHYTHMIC NOTATION

PART I,II,III

X	X	X	X	X	X	X	X	X	X	X		X	X	X		REPEAT
R	L	R	L	R	L	R	L	R	L	R		L	R	L		

PART IV

X	X	X	X	X	X	X	X		X		X		X		REPEAT
R	L	R	L	R	L	R	L	R		B		L		B	

Makrinitsa
Macedonia (Naoussa)

RECORD	Folklore Dances of Greece M7C23590
INTRODUCTION	14 beats (first three drum beats set the tempo of the beat)
FORMATION	Circle, hands joined in "V" position
PART I	FORWARD, REST, BACKWARD, FORWARD; Repeat Part I 7X
Beats 1-2	Step R foot forward counterclockwise
3	Step L foot backward clockwise
4	Step R foot forward counterclockwise
5-32	Repeat Part I, beats 1-4, seven times (alternate beginning foot)
PART II	IN, REST, OUT, IN (4X); OUT, REST, IN, OUT (4X)
Beats 1-2	Step R foot in toward the center (begin to raise arms parallel to the floor)
3	Step L foot out
4	Step R foot in
5-16	Repeat Part II, beats 1-4, three times (alternate beginning foot)
17-18	Step R foot out with bent knee (begin to lower arms)
19	Step L foot in
20	Step R foot out
21-32	Repeat Part II, beats 17-20, three times
NOTE	On the second repetition of Part II swing the leg in an arc on the first in step of measures two, three, four toward the center. On the succeeding repetitions of Part II a hop may precede the first in step of measures two, three, and four. A full turn may be executed on the fourth in sequence and the fourth out sequence.

RHYTHMIC NOTATION

PART I

X		X	X	REPEAT 7X W/OPP. FTWK.
R		L	R	

PART II

X		X	X	REPEAT 7X W/OPP. FTWK.
R		L	R	

Masquerade
Denmark

RECORD	Folk Dancer MH 1019
INTRODUCTION	4 chords plus a pick-up
FORMATION	Couples in double circle facing counterclockwise
ALTERNATE FORMATION	Single circle, no hands joined
PART I	FORWARD (15X), TURN; FORWARD (15X), TURN (Partners link inside arms with woman's L hand resting on man's R forearm)
Beats 1-16	Walk 16 steps forward counterclockwise beginning with outside foot and turn toward each other to end facing clockwise (link arms again)
17-32	Walk 16 steps forward clockwise and turn to face counterclockwise joining inside hands
PART II	WALTZ (16X)
Beats 1-12	Waltz 4 times counterclockwise beginning with outside foot moving away from partner, toward partner, away, toward. Man then moves in front of woman to assume social dance position
13-24	Waltz 4 times turning clockwise and moving counterclockwise around circle. Man begin L foot backward, woman R foot forward
25-48	Repeat Part II, beats 1-48
NOTE	Where the social dance waltz is inappropriate, substitute 8 waltzes counterclockwise, then 8 waltzes clockwise.
PART III	STEP HOP (16X)
Beats 1-8	Step hop 4 times moving away from partner, toward partner, away, toward (inside hands are joined). Begin on outside foot and swing free leg across body; move into shoulder waist position
9-16	Step hop 4 times turning clockwise moving counterclockwise around circle
17-32	Repeat Part III, beats 1-16
NOTE	If the alternate formation is used, the turning waltz and turning step hop may be executed or continue with the step counterclockwise or clockwise.

Masquerade (continued)

RHYTHMIC
NOTATION

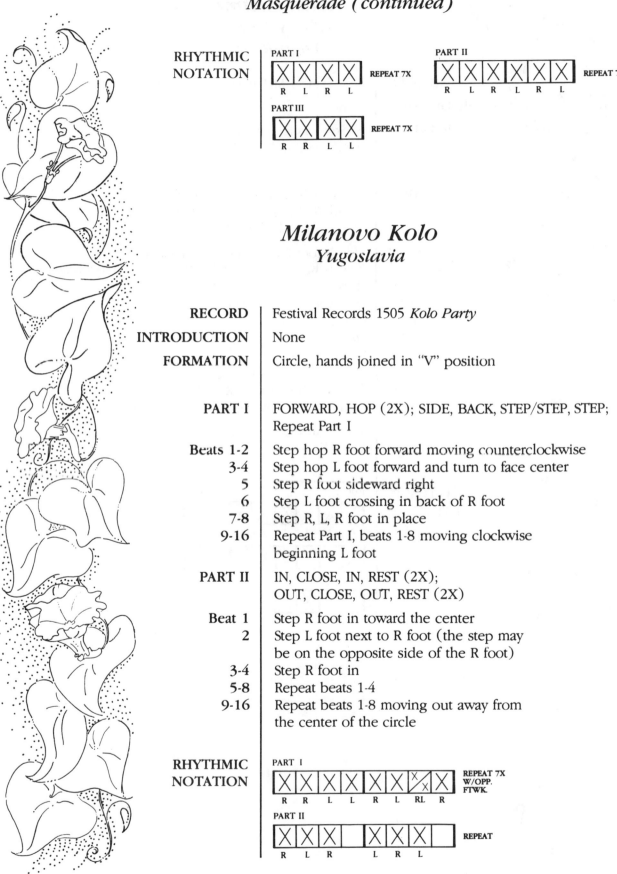

PART I

| X | X | X | X | REPEAT 7X
| R | L | R | L |

PART II

| X | X | X | X | X | X | REPEAT 7X
| R | L | R | L | R | L |

PART III

| X | X | X | X | REPEAT 7X
| R | R | L | L |

Milanovo Kolo
Yugoslavia

RECORD	Festival Records 1505 *Kolo Party*
INTRODUCTION	None
FORMATION	Circle, hands joined in "V" position
PART I	FORWARD, HOP (2X); SIDE, BACK, STEP/STEP, STEP; Repeat Part I
Beats 1-2	Step hop R foot forward moving counterclockwise
3-4	Step hop L foot forward and turn to face center
5	Step R foot sideward right
6	Step L foot crossing in back of R foot
7-8	Step R, L, R foot in place
9-16	Repeat Part I, beats 1-8 moving clockwise beginning L foot
PART II	IN, CLOSE, IN, REST (2X); OUT, CLOSE, OUT, REST (2X)
Beat 1	Step R foot in toward the center
2	Step L foot next to R foot (the step may be on the opposite side of the R foot)
3-4	Step R foot in
5-8	Repeat beats 1-4
9-16	Repeat beats 1-8 moving out away from the center of the circle

RHYTHMIC
NOTATION

PART I

| X | X | X | X | X | X | X/X | X | REPEAT 7X W/OPP. FTWK.
| R | R | L | L | R | L | RL | R |

PART II

| X | X | X | | X | X | X | | REPEAT
| R | L | R | | L | R | L | |

Neda Grivne
Pretty Neda
Yugoslavia

RECORD	Folk Dancer MH 1015
INTRODUCTION	None
FORMATION	Broken circle, leader at the right, hands held in "V" position
PART I	FORWARD, 2, 3, 4; 5, 6, 7, REST; IN, REST, IN, REST; OUT, OUT, OUT, REST; SIDE, TOUCH, SIDE, TOUCH
Beat 1	Step R foot forward counterclockwise
2-7	Step L, R, L, R, L, R foot forward counterclockwise
8	Rest
9-10	Step L foot in toward center
11-12	Step R foot in
13-15	Step L, R, L foot out from center
16	Rest
17	Step R foot sideward right
18	Touch L foot next to R foot
19-20	Step L foot sideward left, touch R foot
NOTE	Two "threes" in place may be substituted beats 17-20.

RHYTHMIC NOTATION

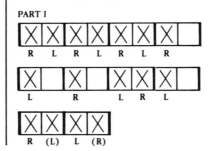

Palamakia/Kofto
Greece (Epirus)

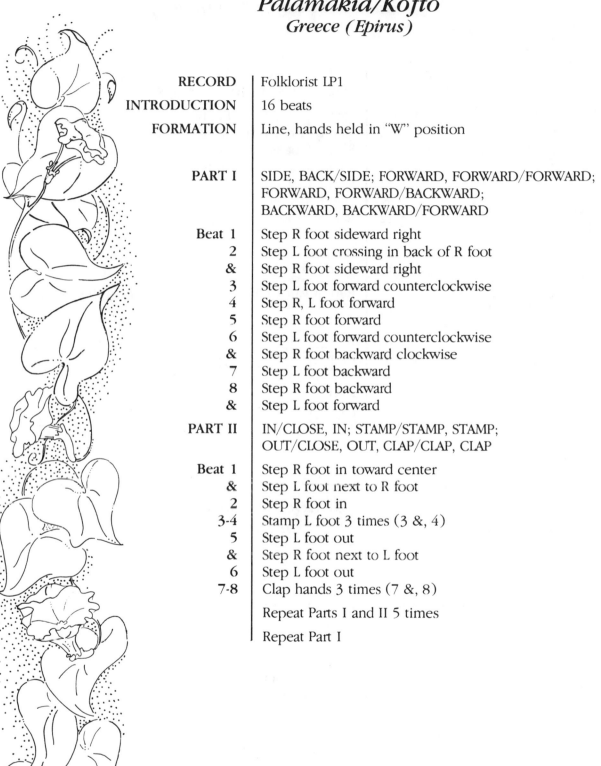

RECORD	Folklorist LP1
INTRODUCTION	16 beats
FORMATION	Line, hands held in "W" position

PART I   SIDE, BACK/SIDE; FORWARD, FORWARD/FORWARD; FORWARD, FORWARD/BACKWARD; BACKWARD, BACKWARD/FORWARD

Beat 1	Step R foot sideward right
2	Step L foot crossing in back of R foot
&	Step R foot sideward right
3	Step L foot forward counterclockwise
4	Step R, L foot forward
5	Step R foot forward
6	Step L foot forward counterclockwise
&	Step R foot backward clockwise
7	Step L foot backward
8	Step R foot backward
&	Step L foot forward

PART II   IN/CLOSE, IN; STAMP/STAMP, STAMP; OUT/CLOSE, OUT, CLAP/CLAP, CLAP

Beat 1	Step R foot in toward center
&	Step L foot next to R foot
2	Step R foot in
3-4	Stamp L foot 3 times (3 &, 4)
5	Step L foot out
&	Step R foot next to L foot
6	Step L foot out
7-8	Clap hands 3 times (7 &, 8)

Repeat Parts I and II 5 times

Repeat Part I

(continued)

Palamakia/Kofto (continued)

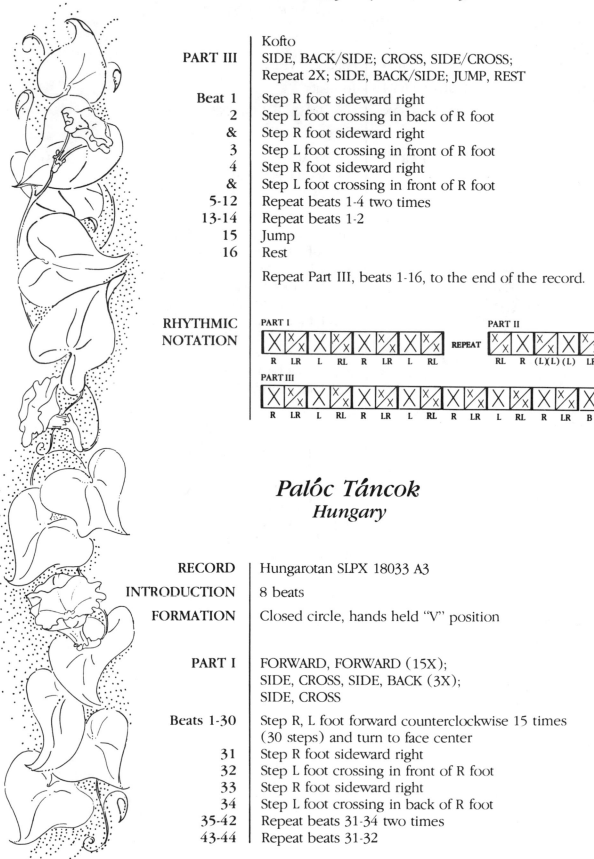

	Kofto
PART III	SIDE, BACK/SIDE; CROSS, SIDE/CROSS; Repeat 2X; SIDE, BACK/SIDE; JUMP, REST
Beat 1	Step R foot sideward right
2	Step L foot crossing in back of R foot
&	Step R foot sideward right
3	Step L foot crossing in front of R foot
4	Step R foot sideward right
&	Step L foot crossing in front of R foot
5-12	Repeat beats 1-4 two times
13-14	Repeat beats 1-2
15	Jump
16	Rest

Repeat Part III, beats 1-16, to the end of the record.

RHYTHMIC NOTATION

PART I

X	X/X	X	X/X	X	X/X	X	X/X
R	LR	L	RL	R	LR	L	RL

REPEAT

PART II

X/X	X	X/X	X/X	X/X	X	CLAP CLAP CLAP
RL	R	(L)(L)	(L)	LR	L	

PART III

X	X/X	X	X/X	X/X	X/X	X	X/X	X/X	X/X	X	X/X	X	X/X	X	
R	LR	L	RL	R	LR	L	RL	R	LR	L	RL	R	LR	B	

Palóc Táncok
Hungary

RECORD	Hungarotan SLPX 18033 A3
INTRODUCTION	8 beats
FORMATION	Closed circle, hands held "V" position
PART I	FORWARD, FORWARD (15X); SIDE, CROSS, SIDE, BACK (3X); SIDE, CROSS
Beats 1-30	Step R, L foot forward counterclockwise 15 times (30 steps) and turn to face center
31	Step R foot sideward right
32	Step L foot crossing in front of R foot
33	Step R foot sideward right
34	Step L foot crossing in back of R foot
35-42	Repeat beats 31-34 two times
43-44	Repeat beats 31-32

Palóc Táncok *(continued)*

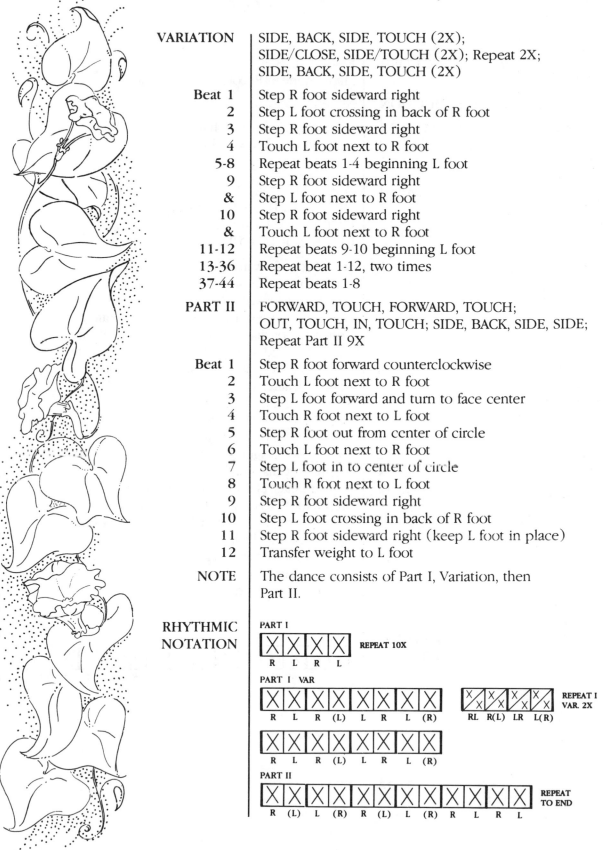

VARIATION	SIDE, BACK, SIDE, TOUCH (2X); SIDE/CLOSE, SIDE/TOUCH (2X); Repeat 2X; SIDE, BACK, SIDE, TOUCH (2X)
Beat 1	Step R foot sideward right
2	Step L foot crossing in back of R foot
3	Step R foot sideward right
4	Touch L foot next to R foot
5-8	Repeat beats 1-4 beginning L foot
9	Step R foot sideward right
&	Step L foot next to R foot
10	Step R foot sideward right
&	Touch L foot next to R foot
11-12	Repeat beats 9-10 beginning L foot
13-36	Repeat beat 1-12, two times
37-44	Repeat beats 1-8
PART II	FORWARD, TOUCH, FORWARD, TOUCH; OUT, TOUCH, IN, TOUCH; SIDE, BACK, SIDE, SIDE; Repeat Part II 9X
Beat 1	Step R foot forward counterclockwise
2	Touch L foot next to R foot
3	Step L foot forward and turn to face center
4	Touch R foot next to L foot
5	Step R foot out from center of circle
6	Touch L foot next to R foot
7	Step L foot in to center of circle
8	Touch R foot next to L foot
9	Step R foot sideward right
10	Step L foot crossing in back of R foot
11	Step R foot sideward right (keep L foot in place)
12	Transfer weight to L foot
NOTE	The dance consists of Part I, Variation, then Part II.

RHYTHMIC NOTATION

PART I

X X X REPEAT 10X

R L R L

PART I VAR

X X X X X X X

R L R (L) L R L (R)

X X X X REPEAT I VAR. 2X

RL R(L) LR L(R)

X X X X X X

R L R (L) L R L (R)

PART II

X X X X X X X X X X X X REPEAT TO END

R (L) L (R) R (L) L (R) R L R L

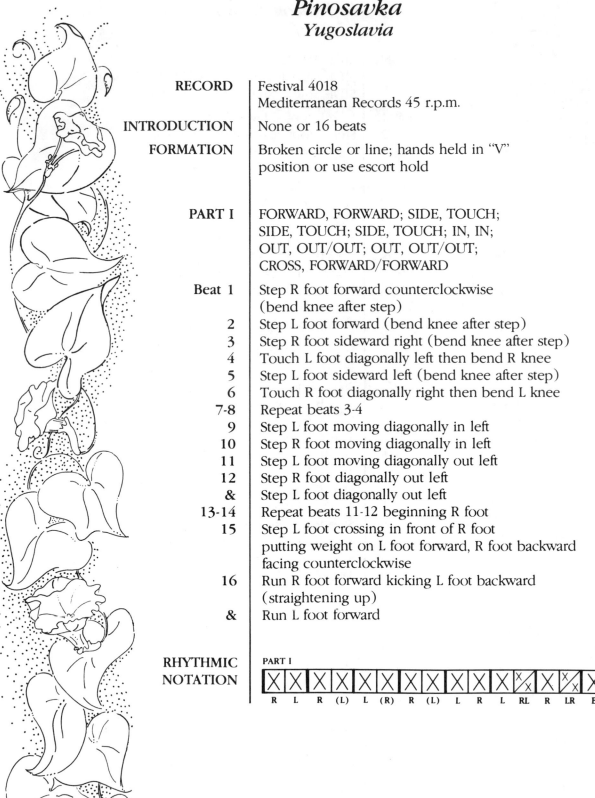

Pinosavka
Yugoslavia

RECORD	Festival 4018 Mediterranean Records 45 r.p.m.
INTRODUCTION	None or 16 beats
FORMATION	Broken circle or line; hands held in "V" position or use escort hold
PART I	FORWARD, FORWARD; SIDE, TOUCH; SIDE, TOUCH; SIDE, TOUCH; IN, IN; OUT, OUT/OUT; OUT, OUT/OUT; CROSS, FORWARD/FORWARD
Beat 1	Step R foot forward counterclockwise (bend knee after step)
2	Step L foot forward (bend knee after step)
3	Step R foot sideward right (bend knee after step)
4	Touch L foot diagonally left then bend R knee
5	Step L foot sideward left (bend knee after step)
6	Touch R foot diagonally right then bend L knee
7-8	Repeat beats 3-4
9	Step L foot moving diagonally in left
10	Step R foot moving diagonally in left
11	Step L foot moving diagonally out left
12	Step R foot diagonally out left
&	Step L foot diagonally out left
13-14	Repeat beats 11-12 beginning R foot
15	Step L foot crossing in front of R foot putting weight on L foot forward, R foot backward facing counterclockwise
16	Run R foot forward kicking L foot backward (straightening up)
&	Run L foot forward

RHYTHMIC NOTATION

PART I

X	X	X	X	X	X	X	X	X	X	X	X	X͞X	X	X͞X	X͞X
R	L	R	(L)	L	(R)	R	(L)	L	R	L	RL	R	LR	B	RL

Polka Alegre
Northern Mexico

RECORD	Express
INTRODUCTION	1 beat
FORMATION	Four couples in a contra set

	Basic Step
PART I	IN/STEP, STEP (4X); OUT/STEP, STEP (4X);
	Repeat
Beats 1 &	Leap R foot toward partner
a	Step L heel in front of R foot } Basic Step
2 & a	Step R foot in place
3-8	Repeat beats 1-2 alternating L, R, L foot
9-16	Repeat beats 1-8 away from partner
17-32	Repeat beats 1-16
PART II	ELBOW TURN (SKIP 16X)
Beats 1-8	Head man, foot lady R elbow turn (8 skips)
9-16	Head lady, foot man R elbow turn (8 skips)
	Head couple join both hands
PART III	HEEL TOE, HEEL TOE, SLIDE, 2, 3, 4; Repeat;
	FORWARD/STEP, STEP (8X)
	IN/STEP, STEP (4X); OUT/STEP, STEP (4X)
Beats 1-2	Man: extend L heel diagonally sideward then touch L toe crossing in front of R foot
	Lady: opposite footwork
3-4	Repeat beats 1-2 with opposite footwork
5-8	Slide 4 times to foot of set
9-16	Repeat beats 1-8 beginning R heel and return
17-24	Head couple: 8 basic steps (as in Part I)— cast off and proceed to bottom of set
25-32	Basic step 4 times in toward partner; 4 basic steps away from partner
NOTE	As head couple casts off, other couples do basic step Part I. Repeat dance until all 4 couples are in head couple position.
ENDING	Part I as in each repeat of dance then in 4 basic steps, do-sa-do around partner 4 basic steps, and honor partner.

RHYTHMIC NOTATION

PART I

X X X X | REPEAT 7X W/ALTERNATING FTWK.

R L R   L R L

PART II

X X X X | REPEAT 3X

R R L L R R L L

PART III

X X X X X X X X | REPEAT W/OPP. FTWK.

R R L L R L R L R L R

Rav B'rachot
Many Blessings
Israel

RECORD	Tikva 145 *Party* Folk Dancer MH 1151
INTRODUCTION	16 beats
FORMATION	Circle, hands joined

PART I	FORWARD, 2, 3, 4; SIDE, BACK, SIDE, BACK; Repeat Part I 3X
Beats 1-4	Run R, L, R, L foot forward counterclockwise
5	Step R foot sideward right (facing center)
6	Step L foot crossing in back to R foot (motion is like a scythe)
7-8	Repeat beats 5-6
9-22	Repeat Part I, beats 1-8, three times
PART II	CROSS, SIDE, BACK, SIDE; CROSS, SIDE, BACK, SIDE; CROSS, SIDE, BACK, SIDE; IN, OUT, CLOSE, REST; Repeat Part II
Beats 1-4	Grapevine beginning R foot moving clockwise
5-12	Repeat beats 1-4, two times
13	Step R foot in toward center of circle
14	Step L foot out
15-16	Step R foot next to L foot
17-32	Repeat Part II, beats 1-16 counterclockwise beginning L foot
PART III	SIDE, CLOSE, SIDE, HOP; BRUSH, HOP, BRUSH, HOP; Repeat Part III 3X
Beat 1	Step R foot sideward right
2	Step L foot next to R foot
3	Step R foot sideward right
4	Hop R foot in place
5	Brush L foot (circular motion)
6	Hop R foot
7	Brush L foot
8	Hop R foot
9-16	Repeat beats 1-8 sideward left beginning L foot
17-32	Repeat Part III, beats 1-16

Rav B'rachot (continued)

PART IV	IN, 2, 3, HOP; BRUSH, HOP, BRUSH, HOP; OUT, 2, 3, HOP; BRUSH, HOP, BRUSH, HOP; Repeat Part IV
Beats 1-4	Schottische R foot in toward center of circle
5	Brush L foot
6	Hop R foot
7	Brush L foot
8	Hop R foot
9-16	Repeat beats 1-8 moving out away from center beginning L foot
17-32	Repeat Part IV, beats 1-16

RHYTHMIC NOTATION

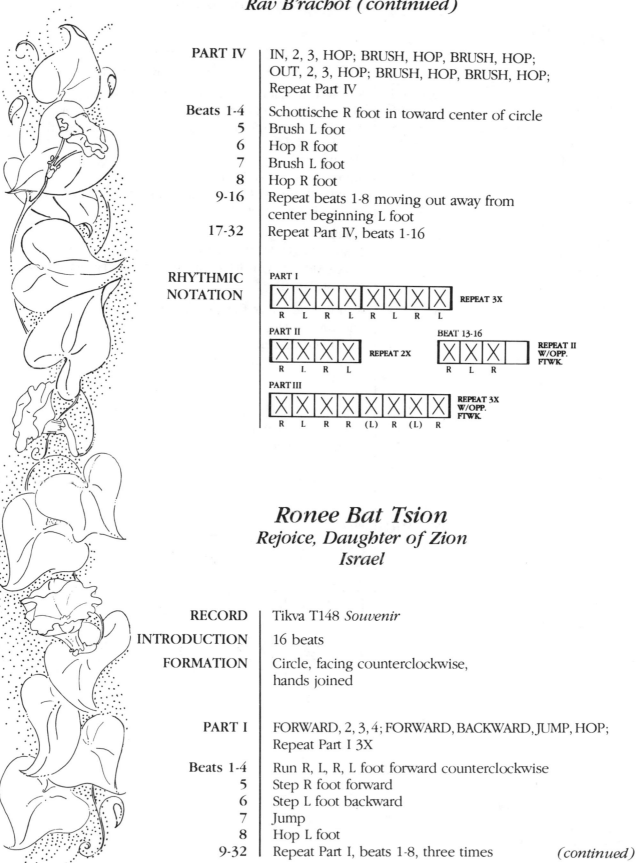

PART I

| X | X | X | X | X | X | X | X | REPEAT 3X |
| R | L | R | L | R | L | R | L | |

PART II

| X | X | X | X | REPEAT 2X |
| R | L | R | L | |

BEAT 13-16

| X | X | X | | REPEAT II W/OPP. FTWK. |
| R | L | R | | |

PART III

| X | X | X | X | X | X | X | REPEAT 3X W/OPP. FTWK. |
| R | L | R | R | (L) | R | (L) | R |

Ronee Bat Tsion
Rejoice, Daughter of Zion
Israel

RECORD	Tikva T148 *Souvenir*
INTRODUCTION	16 beats
FORMATION	Circle, facing counterclockwise, hands joined
PART I	FORWARD, 2, 3, 4; FORWARD, BACKWARD, JUMP, HOP; Repeat Part I 3X
Beats 1-4	Run R, L, R, L foot forward counterclockwise
5	Step R foot forward
6	Step L foot backward
7	Jump
8	Hop L foot
9-32	Repeat Part I, beats 1-8, three times

(continued)

Ronee Bat Tsion (continued)

PART II	IN, 2, 3, 4; HEEL, REST, HEEL, REST; OUT, 2, 3, 4; OUT, IN, OUT, IN; Repeat Part II
Beats 1-4	Run R, L, R, L foot in toward center (raise arms)
5-6	Touch R heel to floor ⎫ lower arms slightly before
7-8	Touch R heel to floor ⎬ touch and raise on touch
9-12	Run R, L, R, L foot out away from center of circle (facing out)
13-16	Step R, L, R, L foot in place turning 1/2 counterclockwise (left) to face center (1/2 buzz turn)
17-32	Repeat Part II, beats 1-16
PART III	FORWARD, 2, 3, 4; JUMP, CROSS, JUMP, CROSS; FORWARD, 2, 3, 4; JUMP, JUMP, BEND, STRAIGHTEN; Repeat Part III
Beats 1-4	Run R, L, R, L foot forward counterclockwise and turn to face center
5	Jump (facing center)
6	Leap L foot crossing in front of R foot (raise R leg in back)
7-8	Repeat beats 5-6
9-12	Run R, L, R, L foot forward counterclockwise
13-14	Debka jump (jump angling knees in then forward)
15	Bend both knees and squat
16	Return to stand
17-32	Repeat Part III, beats 1-16

RHYTHMIC NOTATION

PART I

X	X	X	X	X	X	X	X	REPEAT 3X

R L R L R L B L

PART II

X	X	X	X		X	X	X	X	X	X	X	X	REPEAT

R L R L (R) (R) R L R L R L R L

X	X	X	X	X	X	X	X	X	X	X	X	X	DOWN	UP	REPEAT

R L R L B L B L R L R L B B B B

Rumunjsko Kolo
Yugoslavia

RECORD	Folk Dancer MH 1010 Festival 4811
INTRODUCTION	None
FORMATION	Circle, hands held in "V" position
PART I	BACKWARD, BACKWARD, BACKWARD, HOP; FORWARD, FORWARD, FORWARD, HOP; Repeat Part I
Beats 1-4	Schottische backward beginning R foot moving counterclockwise
5-8	Schottische forward beginning L foot moving counterclockwise
9-16	Repeat Part I, beats 1-8 and turn to face center
PART II	CUT, CUT, CUT, HOP (3X); STAMP, STAMP, STAMP, REST; Repeat Part II
Beat 1	Step R foot cutting L foot out
2	Step L foot cutting R foot in
3	Step R foot cutting L foot out
4	Hop R foot swinging L foot in
5-12	Repeat beats 1-4, two times
13-15	Stamp L foot 3 times
16	Rest
17-32	Repeat Part II, beats 1-16

RHYTHMIC NOTATION

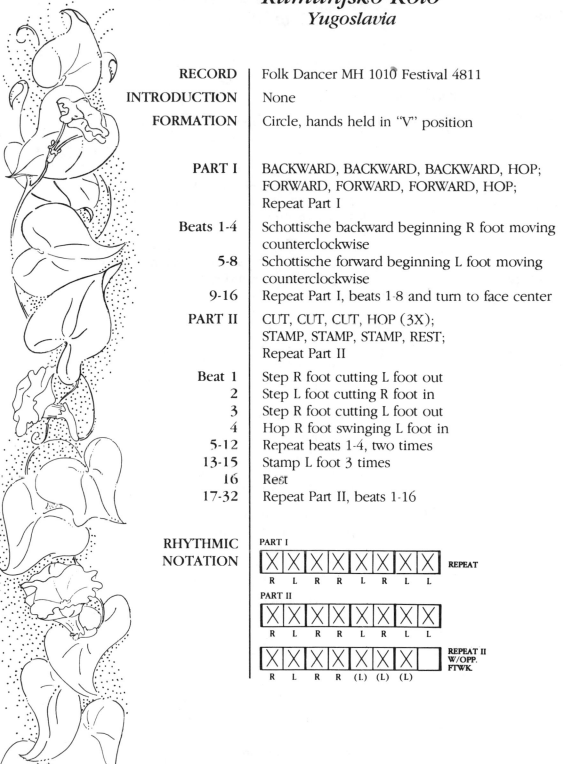

PART I

| X | X | X | X | X | X | X | X | REPEAT |

R L R R L R L L

PART II

| X | X | X | X | X | X | X | X |

R L R R L R L L

| X | X | X | X | X | X | | REPEAT II W/OPP. FTWK. |

R L R R (L) (L) (L)

Sarajevka Kolo
Yugoslavia

RECORD	Folkraft 1496X45
INTRODUCTION	None
FORMATION	Circle, hands joined in "V" position

PART I	FORWARD, HOP; FORWARD, HOP; SIDE, BACK; STEP/STEP, STEP; STEP/STEP, STEP; STEP/STEP, STEP; FORWARD, FORWARD, FORWARD, HOP
Beats 1-2	Step hop R foot forward counterclockwise
3-4	Step hop L foot forward counterclockwise
5	Step R foot sideward right
6	Step L foot crossing in back of R foot
7-8	One "three" in place beginning R foot
9-10	One "three" in place beginning L foot
11-12	One "three" in place beginning R foot
13	Step L foot forward clockwise
14	Step R foot forward clockwise
15-16	Step hop L foot forward clockwise and turn to face counterclockwise
	Slower music
PART II	FORWARD, BEND; FORWARD, BEND; SIDE, CLOSE; SIDE, TOUCH; SIDE, TOUCH; SIDE, TOUCH; FORWARD, FORWARD, FORWARD, PIVOT
Beats 1-2	Step R foot forward counterclockwise then bend R knee
3-4	Step L foot forward counterclockwise then bend L knee
5	Step R foot sideward right
6	Step L foot next to R foot
7	Step R foot sideward right
8	Touch L foot diagonally left
9	Step L foot sideward right
10	Touch R foot diagonally right
11	Step R foot sideward right
12	Touch L foot diagonally left
13	Step L foot forward clockwise
14	Step R foot forward clockwise
15-16	Step L foot forward clockwise and pivot to face counterclockwise

Sarajevka Kolo (continued)

Plan for the dance using above record:
Part I 2 times, Part II 2 times;
from that point on Part I 4 times,
Part II 2 times until end of record.

RHYTHMIC
NOTATION

PART I

| X | X | X | X | X | X | X X X | X X X | X | X X X | X | X | X | X | REPEAT |

R R L L R L RL R LR L RL R L R L L

PART II

| X | | X | | X | X | X | X | X | X | X | X | X | X | | REPEAT 3X |

R L R L R (L) L (R) R (L) L R L

Saüerlaender Quadrille #5
Germany

RECORD	Folk Dancer MH 1129
INTRODUCTION	1 note plus 16 beats
FORMATION	Square sets numbered consecutively clockwise

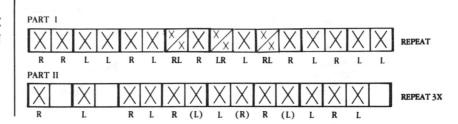

Nieheimer Step
HOP, HOP, HOP, HOP;
SIDE, BACK, TOGETHER, BOUNCE

NOTE	Nieheimer Step to right uses footwork described. Nieheimer Step to left uses opposite footwork.
Beat 1	Hop L foot touching R toe next to L foot with heel turned out
2	Hop L foot touching R toe next to L foot with heel turned in
3	Hop L foot touching R heel next to L foot with toes raised
4	Hop L foot touching R toe next to L foot with heel raised
5	Step R foot sideward right
6	Step L foot crossing in back of R foot
7	Step R foot next to L foot transferring weight to both feet
8	Raise and lower both heels (bounce)

(continued)

Saüerlaender Quadrille #5 (continued)

PART I	PEEK-A-BOO
	Couple #1 lady and couple #3 man do 1 Nieheimer Step (NS) sideward away from partner; look at each other behind couple #4
	Couple #1 lady and couple #3 man do 1 NS sideward to place
	Couple #1 man and couple #3 lady repeat to look behind #2
	Couple #2 lady and couple #4 man repeat to look behind #1
	Couple #2 man and couple #4 lady repeat to look behind #3
PART II	NO HANDS
	Couple #1 face partner and do 1 NS sideward right then 1 NS sideward left (lady toward center of square, man away from center)
	Couple #2, then couple #3, then couple #4 repeat
PART III	CROSSOVER
	Couple #1 and #3 do 1 NS toward each other ending in a line of 4 in middle of square; continue across set with a second NS turning right in a 1/2 turn jump on final beat
	Couple #2 and #4 repeat
	Couple #1 and #3 repeat returning to original place
	Couple #2 and #4 repeat returning to original place
NOTE	In this figure the NS is altered to 3 steps toward center and away from center of square after the 4 hops.
PART IV	RIGHT HAND HOLD
	Couple #1 face partner, join R hands with forearms together; do 1 NS turning 1/2 clockwise then 1 NS turning 1/2 clockwise back to place (begin first NS on R and second NS on L)
	Couple #2, then couple #3, then couple #4, repeat

Saüerlaender Quadrille #5 (continued)

PART V	ALL ACTIVE
	Couples #1 and #3 do a CROSSOVER while couples #2 and #4 separate sideward (PEEK-A-BOO)
	Couples #2 and #4 do CROSSOVER while couples #1 and #3 separate sideward (PEEK-A-BOO)
	Repeat CROSSOVER, PEEK-A-BOO figure to return to place
	All do NO HANDS All do RIGHT HAND HOLD All do NO HANDS All do RIGHT HAND HOLD
RHYTHMIC NOTATION	NIEHEIMER STEP 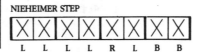 L L L L R L B B

Sharm-el-Sheikh
Israel

RECORD	Hed Arzi MN581
INTRODUCTION	16 beats plus pick-up
FORMATION	Circle, hands joined, moving counterclockwise
PART I	FORWARD, FORWARD, BACKWARD/close, FORWARD; Repeat Part I
Beat 1	Step R foot forward counterclockwise
2	Step L foot forward counterclockwise
3 &	Step R foot backward
a	Step L foot next to R foot
4	Step R foot forward
5-8	Repeat Part I, beats 1-4 beginning L foot
PART II	FORWARD, FORWARD/close, FORWARD, TOUCH; Repeat Part II
Beat 1	Step R foot forward
2 &	Step L foot forward
a	Step R foot next to L foot
3	Step L foot forward and turn to face center
4	Touch R foot next to L foot (facing center)
5-8	Repeat Part II, beats 1-4
PART I	Repeat Part I, beats 1-8
PART II	Repeat Part II, beats 1-8
PART III	TURN/turn, SIDE, SIDE, TOUCH; Repeat Part III
Beats 1 &	Step R foot beginning a full turn right (body turns clockwise)
a	Step L foot completing the full turn (end facing center)
2	Step R foot sideward right
3	Step L foot sideward left
4	Touch R foot next to L foot
5-8	Repeat Part III, beats 1-4
PART IV	FORWARD, FORWARD/side, BACK/side, CROSS; Repeat Part IV
Beat 1	Step R foot forward counterclockwise
2 &	Step L foot forward counterclockwise
a	Step R foot sideward right
3 &	Step L foot crossing in back of R foot
a	Step R foot sideward right
4	Step L foot crossing in front of R foot
5-8	Repeat Part IV, beats 1-4

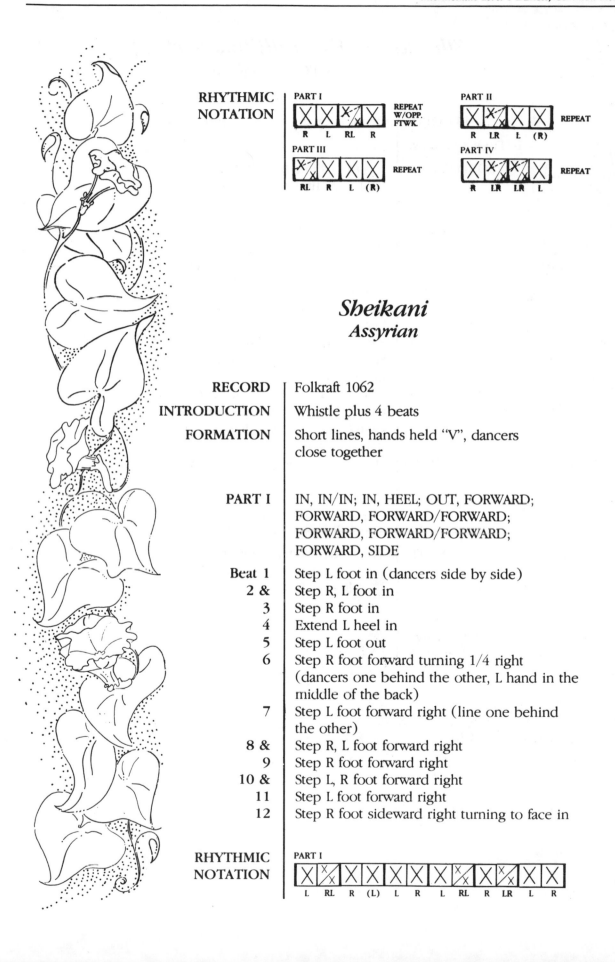

RHYTHMIC NOTATION

PART I — REPEAT W/OPP. FTWK.
R L RL R

PART II — REPEAT
R LR L (R)

PART III — REPEAT
RL R L (R)

PART IV — REPEAT
R LR LR L

Sheikani
Assyrian

RECORD	Folkraft 1062
INTRODUCTION	Whistle plus 4 beats
FORMATION	Short lines, hands held "V", dancers close together
PART I	IN, IN/IN; IN, HEEL; OUT, FORWARD; FORWARD, FORWARD/FORWARD; FORWARD, FORWARD/FORWARD; FORWARD, SIDE

Beat 1	Step L foot in (dancers side by side)
2 &	Step R, L foot in
3	Step R foot in
4	Extend L heel in
5	Step L foot out
6	Step R foot forward turning 1/4 right (dancers one behind the other, L hand in the middle of the back)
7	Step L foot forward right (line one behind the other)
8 &	Step R, L foot forward right
9	Step R foot forward right
10 &	Step L, R foot forward right
11	Step L foot forward right
12	Step R foot sideward right turning to face in

RHYTHMIC NOTATION

PART I
L RL R (L) L R L RL R LR L R

Silivriano (Kykladitikos Syrtos)
Greece (Cycladic Island)

RECORD	Olympic OL-24-13 *Picnic in Greece*
INTRODUCTION	16 beats
FORMATION	Short lines in a front basket with right arms under, left arms over
PART I	SIDE, BACK; SIDE, CROSS; IN/IN, IN; IN/IN, IN; SWING, OUT/OUT; OUT, OUT/OUT; OUT, TOUCH
Beat 1	Step R foot sideward right
2	Step L foot crossing in back of R foot bending knees
3	Step R foot sideward right
4	Step L foot crossing in front of R foot bending knees
5-6	Step R, L, R foot in toward center ("three")
7-8	Step L, R, L foot in toward center ("three")
9	Swing R leg to center (knee straight), rise up on L foot
10 &	Step R, L foot out away from center
11	Step R foot out
12 &	Step L, R foot out
13	Step L foot out
14	Touch R foot next to L foot
NOTE	The leader on the right end of each line may move to the left end of the line ahead by releasing hands and moving on beats 10-14.
RHYTHMIC NOTATION	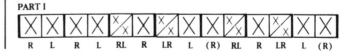

PART I

R L R L RL R LR L (R) RL R LR L (R)

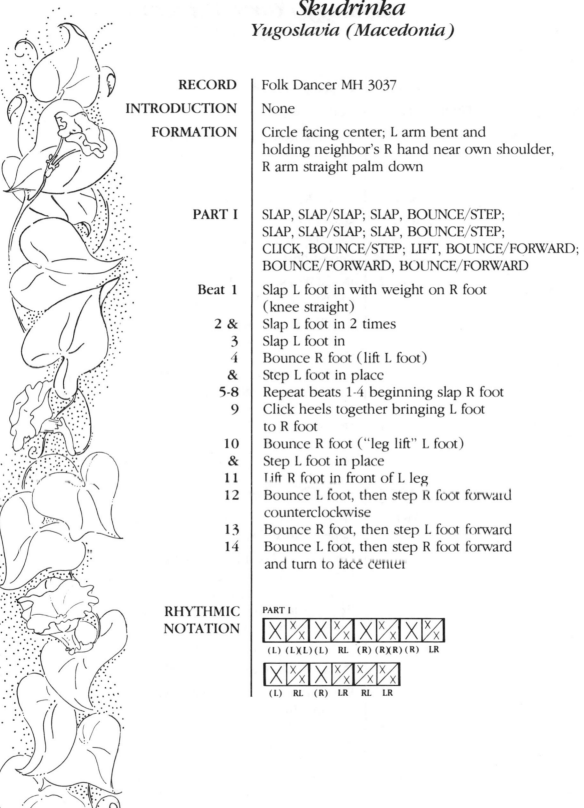

Skudrinka
Yugoslavia (Macedonia)

RECORD	Folk Dancer MH 3037
INTRODUCTION	None
FORMATION	Circle facing center; L arm bent and holding neighbor's R hand near own shoulder, R arm straight palm down
PART I	SLAP, SLAP/SLAP; SLAP, BOUNCE/STEP; SLAP, SLAP/SLAP; SLAP, BOUNCE/STEP; CLICK, BOUNCE/STEP; LIFT, BOUNCE/FORWARD; BOUNCE/FORWARD, BOUNCE/FORWARD
Beat 1	Slap L foot in with weight on R foot (knee straight)
2 &	Slap L foot in 2 times
3	Slap L foot in
4	Bounce R foot (lift L foot)
&	Step L foot in place
5-8	Repeat beats 1-4 beginning slap R foot
9	Click heels together bringing L foot to R foot
10	Bounce R foot ("leg lift" L foot)
&	Step L foot in place
11	Lift R foot in front of L leg
12	Bounce L foot, then step R foot forward counterclockwise
13	Bounce R foot, then step L foot forward
14	Bounce L foot, then step R foot forward and turn to face center

RHYTHMIC NOTATION

PART I

X	X/X	X	X/X	X	X/X	X	X/X

(L) (L)(L) (L)   RL   (R) (R)(R) (R)   LR

X	X/X	X	X/X	X/X	X/X

(L)   RL   (R)   LR   RL   LR

Somogy (Girls' Dance)
Hungary

RECORD	Qualiton LPX 18007
INTRODUCTION	None
FORMATION	Women: front basket with left arms under Men: "T" position behind women's basket
INTRO	SWAY, REST; SWAY, REST (6X)
Beats 1-2	Sway right
3-4	Sway left
5-24	Repeat beats 1-4, five times
PART I	IN, OUT; IN, OUT; IN, OUT; TURN, 2, 3, 4; CROSS/SIDE, CROSS/SIDE; Repeat Part I 5X
Beat 1	Step R foot in toward center
2	Step L foot diagonally out left around the circle
3-6	Repeat beats 1-2, two times
7-10	Step R, L, R, L foot turning right around the perimeter of your own individual circle (body is turning clockwise)
11	Step R foot crossing in front of L foot
&	Step L foot sideward left
12	Step R foot crossing in front of L foot
&	Step L foot sideward left
13-72	Repeat Part I, beats 1-12, five times
PART II	SIDE, CLOSE; SIDE, CLICK; SIDE, CLICK; Repeat Part II 7X
Beats 1-4	Double csardas sideward right
5-6	One single csardas step sideward left
7-24	Repeat Part II, beats 1-6, three times
25-36	Repeat Part II, beats 1-6, four times (executed twice as fast)
PART III	IN/STEP, STEP, OUT/STEP, STEP (6X); IN, REST, OUT/STEP, STEP (6X)
Beat 1	Step R foot in toward center with a Balkan "three"
2	Step L foot diagonally out left with a Balkan "three"
3-12	Repeat beats 1-2, five times
13-24	Repeat Part III, beats 1-12 substituting a single step for each Balkan "three" R foot in toward the center (men accent this single step)

Somogy (Girl's Dance) (continued)

PART IV	CROSS, SIDE (12X)
Beats 1-12	Twelve closed rida steps moving clockwise
PART III	Repeat Part III, beats 1-24
PART IV	Repeat Part IV, beats 1-12 (end with a run R, L foot in place beat 11, and close the feet on beat 12)

RHYTHMIC NOTATION

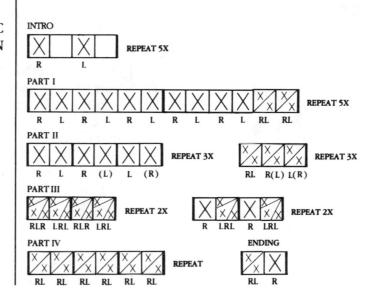

Soude Soude
Armenia

RECORD	Folklore Dances of the Middle East M7C23590
INTRODUCTION	32 beats
FORMATION	Lines, little fingers held in "W" position
PART I	FORWARD/CLOSE, FORWARD (4X); FORWARD/CLOSE, FORWARD (2X); IN/CLOSE, IN; OUT/CLOSE, OUT
Beat 1	Step R foot forward moving counterclockwise (line one behind the other)
&	Step L foot in back of R foot
2	Step R foot forward
3-10	Repeat beats 1-2 four times alternating the starting foot, end facing left
11-12	Repeat beats 1-2 beginning L foot forward moving clockwise, end facing center
13-14	Repeat beats 1-2 in toward the center (line side by side)
15-16	Repeat beats 1-2 moving out away from the center beginning L foot (lower arms)
PART II	SIDE, BACK; SIDE, TOUCH; JUMP, BOUNCE/BOUNCE; JUMP, HOP
Beat 1	Step R foot sideward right (arms raised to "W" position)
2	Step L foot crossing in back of R foot (bend L knee in a dip)
3	Step R foot sideward right
4	Touch L foot (feet spread apart)
5	Jump on both feet (bend knees)
6	Bounce both heels 2 times
7	Jump on both feet accenting the jump (lower arms)
8	Hop L foot, lift R foot in front of L leg (arms raised to "W" position)
RHYTHMIC NOTATION	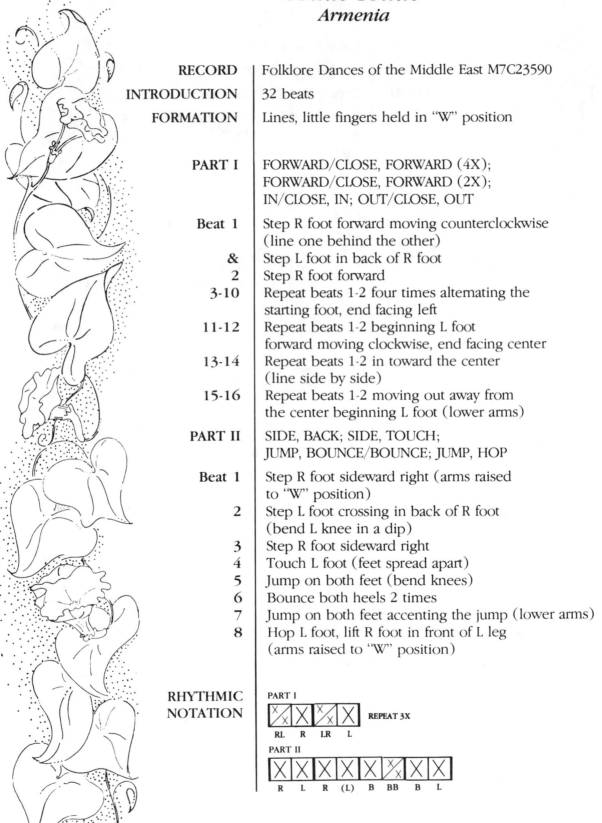

PART I

REPEAT 3X

RL   R   LR   L

PART II

R   L   R   (L)   B   BB   B   L

Soultana
Greece

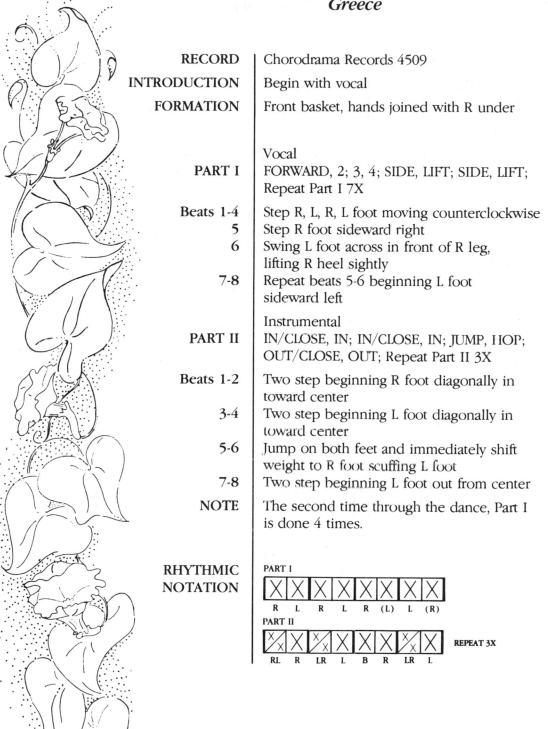

RECORD	Chorodrama Records 4509
INTRODUCTION	Begin with vocal
FORMATION	Front basket, hands joined with R under
	Vocal
PART I	FORWARD, 2; 3, 4; SIDE, LIFT; SIDE, LIFT; Repeat Part I 7X
Beats 1-4	Step R, L, R, L foot moving counterclockwise
5	Step R foot sideward right
6	Swing L foot across in front of R leg, lifting R heel sightly
7-8	Repeat beats 5-6 beginning L foot sideward left
	Instrumental
PART II	IN/CLOSE, IN; IN/CLOSE, IN; JUMP, HOP; OUT/CLOSE, OUT; Repeat Part II 3X
Beats 1-2	Two step beginning R foot diagonally in toward center
3-4	Two step beginning L foot diagonally in toward center
5-6	Jump on both feet and immediately shift weight to R foot scuffing L foot
7-8	Two step beginning L foot out from center
NOTE	The second time through the dance, Part I is done 4 times.

RHYTHMIC NOTATION

PART I

X	X	X	X	X	X	X
R	L	R	L	R	(L)	L (R)

PART II

X/X	X	X/X	X	X	X	X/X	X
RL	R	LR	L	B	R	LR	L

REPEAT 3X

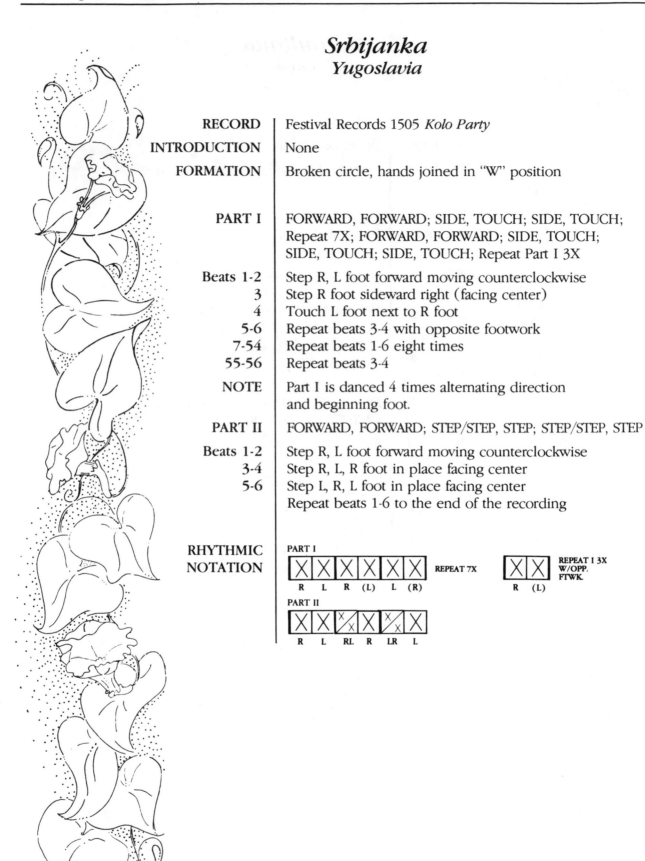

Srbijanka
Yugoslavia

RECORD	Festival Records 1505 *Kolo Party*
INTRODUCTION	None
FORMATION	Broken circle, hands joined in "W" position
PART I	FORWARD, FORWARD; SIDE, TOUCH; SIDE, TOUCH; Repeat 7X; FORWARD, FORWARD; SIDE, TOUCH; SIDE, TOUCH; SIDE, TOUCH; Repeat Part I 3X
Beats 1-2	Step R, L foot forward moving counterclockwise
3	Step R foot sideward right (facing center)
4	Touch L foot next to R foot
5-6	Repeat beats 3-4 with opposite footwork
7-54	Repeat beats 1-6 eight times
55-56	Repeat beats 3-4
NOTE	Part I is danced 4 times alternating direction and beginning foot.
PART II	FORWARD, FORWARD; STEP/STEP, STEP; STEP/STEP, STEP
Beats 1-2	Step R, L foot forward moving counterclockwise
3-4	Step R, L, R foot in place facing center
5-6	Step L, R, L foot in place facing center
	Repeat beats 1-6 to the end of the recording

RHYTHMIC NOTATION

PART I

⊠ ⊠ ⊠ ⊠ ⊠ ⊠   REPEAT 7X   ⊠ ⊠   REPEAT I 3X W/OPP. FTWK.
R L R (L) L (R)   R (L)

PART II

⊠ ⊠ ⊠ ⊠ ⊠
R L RL R LR L

Sulam Yaakov
Jacob's Ladder
Israel

RECORD	Worldtone WT 10016
INTRODUCTION	16 beats
FORMATION	Circle, hands joined in "V" position
PART I	SIDE, CLOSE, SIDE, REST;
	IN, REST, IN, REST;
	SIDE, CLOSE, SIDE, REST;
	OUT, REST, OUT, REST;
	Repeat Part I
Beat 1	Step R foot sideward right
2	Step L foot next to R foot
3-4	Step R foot sideward right
5-6	Step L foot in toward the center
7-8	Step R foot in toward the center
9-12	Repeat beats 1-4 beginning L foot
13-14	Step R foot out away from the center
15-16	Step L foot out
17-32	Repeat Part I, beats 1-16
PART II	SIDE, REST, TOUCH, REST;
	BACK, SIDE, CROSS, PIVOT;
	FORWARD, CLOSE, FORWARD, REST;
	BACKWARD, CLOSE, BACKWARD, REST;
	Repeat Part II
Beats 1-2	Step R foot sideward right
3-4	Touch L foot in toward center
5	Step L foot crossing in back of R foot
6	Step R foot sideward right
7	Step L foot crossing in front of R foot
8	Pivot on L foot to face clockwise
9-12	Two step R foot forward clockwise
13-16	Two step L foot backward counterclockwise
17-32	Repeat Part II, beats 1-16
NOTE	Repeat Parts I and II until the meter of the music changes to 6/8, then repeat Parts I and II changing the timing of the steps to conform to the 6/8 meter.

(continued)

Sulam Yaakov (continued)

PART I	SIDE/close, SIDE; IN, IN, SIDE/close, SIDE, OUT, OUT; Repeat Part I
PART II	SIDE, TOUCH; BACK/side, CROSS; FORWARD/close, FORWARD; BACKWARD/close, BACKWARD; Repeat Part II

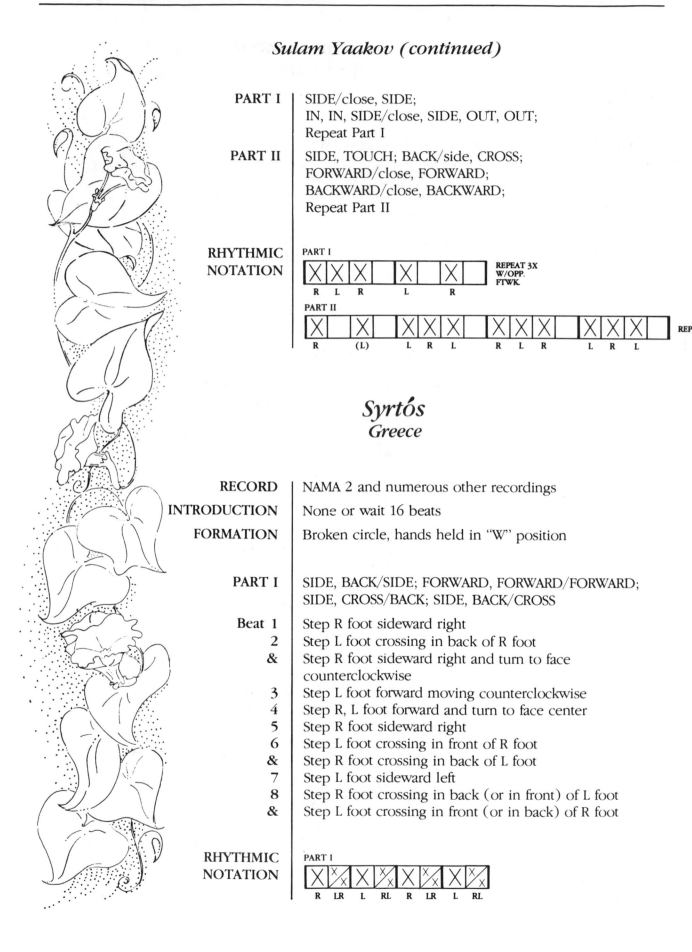

RHYTHMIC NOTATION

PART I

|X|X|X| |X| |X| | REPEAT 3X W/OPP. FTWK.

R L R   L   R

PART II

|X| |X| |X|X|X| |X|X|X| |X|X|X| REPEAT

R   (L)   L R L   R L R   L R L

Syrtós
Greece

RECORD	NAMA 2 and numerous other recordings
INTRODUCTION	None or wait 16 beats
FORMATION	Broken circle, hands held in "W" position
PART I	SIDE, BACK/SIDE; FORWARD, FORWARD/FORWARD; SIDE, CROSS/BACK; SIDE, BACK/CROSS
Beat 1	Step R foot sideward right
2	Step L foot crossing in back of R foot
&	Step R foot sideward right and turn to face counterclockwise
3	Step L foot forward moving counterclockwise
4	Step R, L foot forward and turn to face center
5	Step R foot sideward right
6	Step L foot crossing in front of R foot
&	Step R foot crossing in back of L foot
7	Step L foot sideward left
8	Step R foot crossing in back (or in front) of L foot
&	Step L foot crossing in front (or in back) of R foot

RHYTHMIC NOTATION

PART I

|X|X/X|X|X/X|X|X/X|X|X/X|

R LR L RL R LR L RL

Tai Tai
Greece (Thessaly)

RECORD	Folkraft LP 6
INTRODUCTION	6 beats
FORMATION	Circle or broken circle, hands joined in "V" position Part I, "W" position Part II
PART I	CROSS, SIDE/CROSS; SIDE, SIDE/CLOSE; Repeat 3X; CROSS, SIDE/CROSS; SIDE, SIDE/TOUCH;
Beat 1	Step L foot crossing in front of R foot with slight knee bend
2	Step R foot sideward right
&	Step L foot crossing in front of R foot
3	Step R foot sideward right
4	Step L foot sideward left (slightly out)
&	Step R foot next to L foot
5-20	Repeat beats 1-4, four times (Beat 20 touch R foot next to L foot)
	Raise arms to "W" position
PART II	FORWARD/HOP (3X); IN/HOP, OUT/OUT, TOUCH; Repeat 2X; FORWARD/HOP (3X), IN/HOP; OUT/OUT, CLOSE
Beat 1	Step hop R foot moving counterclockwise
2-3	Step hop L, R foot moving counterclockwise
4	Step hop L foot in toward center
5 &	Step R, L foot out from center
6	Touch R foot on the far side of L foot
7-24	Repeat Part II 3 times (beat 24 step R foot next to L foot)

RHYTHMIC NOTATION

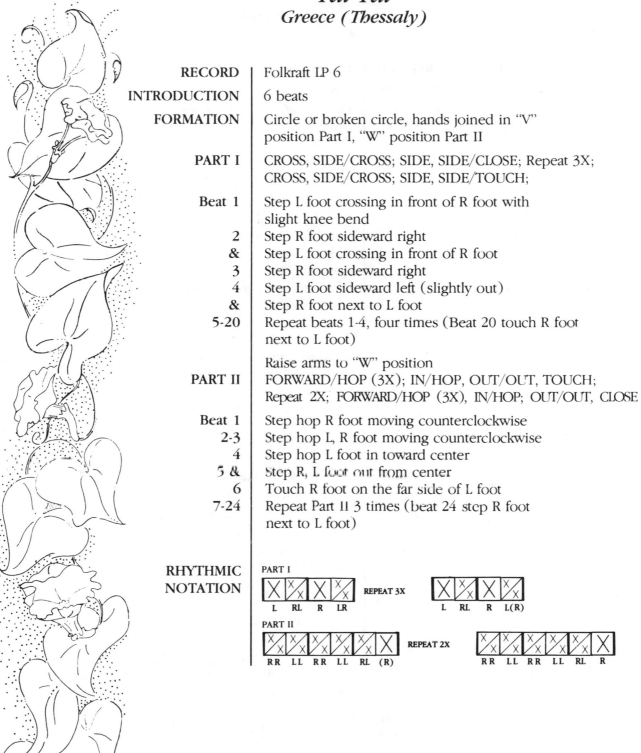

Tarantella
Israel

RECORD	Eretz Zavat
INTRODUCTION	1 beat
FORMATION	Partners in circle facing counterclockwise, man ahead of woman
PART I	FORWARD, 2, 3, 4; JUMP, HOP, JUMP, HOP; FORWARD, 2, 3, 4; JUMP, HOP, SIDE, REST; TURN, TURN, JUMP, CROSS; Repeat Part I
Beats 1-4	Run R, L, R, L foot forward counterclockwise
5	Jump facing center
6	Hop R foot turning body counterclockwise to face diagonally left
7	Jump facing diagonally left
8	Hop L foot turning body clockwise to face counterclockwise again
9-12	Run R, L, R, L foot forward counterclockwise
13	Jump diagonally forward right
14	Hop R foot backward from the diagonal and turn to face center
15-16	Step L foot sideward left
17-18	Step R, L foot turning full turn clockwise
19	Jump facing center
20	Leap L foot crossing in front of R foot
21-40	Repeat Part I, beats 1-20, end facing partner; men facing clockwise, women counterclockwise
PART II	STEP, STEP; AWAY, 2, 3, 4, 5, 6; STEP, STEP, TOWARD, 2, 3, 4, 5, 6; BUZZ TURN
Beats 1-2	Step R, L foot in place clapping hands twice
3-8	Run R, L, R, L, R, L foot away from partner, men toward center, women away from center
9-10	Step R, L foot clapping hands twice
11-20	Run toward partner and do an Israeli turn ending with man ahead of woman
NOTE	The fourth time through the dance, repeat Part I (4 times in all) and end with bump on final beat; do Part II and keep turning until music ends.
RHYTHMIC NOTATION	

PART I

X	X	X	X	X	X	X	X	X	X	X	X	X	X	X	X	
R	L	R	L	B	R	B	L	R	L	R	L	R	L	B	L	

X	X	X	X	REPEAT
R	L	B	L	

PART II

CLAP	CLAP	X	X	X	X	X	X	REPEAT
		R	L	R	L	R	L	

BEATS 17-20

X / X	X / X	X / X	X / X
RL	RL	RL	RL

Trata
Greece (Island of Salamis/Megara)

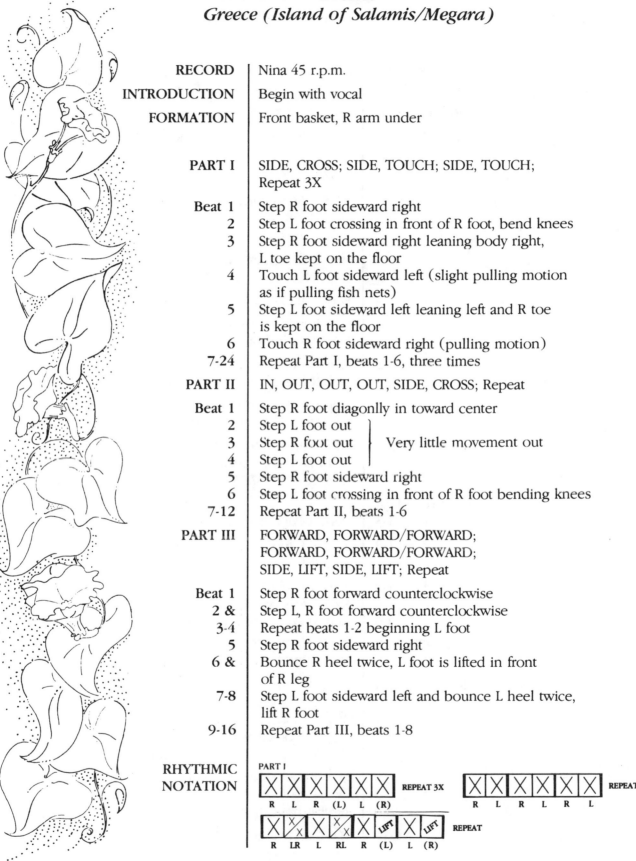

RECORD	Nina 45 r.p.m.
INTRODUCTION	Begin with vocal
FORMATION	Front basket, R arm under
PART I	SIDE, CROSS; SIDE, TOUCH; SIDE, TOUCH; Repeat 3X
Beat 1	Step R foot sideward right
2	Step L foot crossing in front of R foot, bend knees
3	Step R foot sideward right leaning body right, L toe kept on the floor
4	Touch L foot sideward left (slight pulling motion as if pulling fish nets)
5	Step L foot sideward left leaning left and R toe is kept on the floor
6	Touch R foot sideward right (pulling motion)
7-24	Repeat Part I, beats 1-6, three times
PART II	IN, OUT, OUT, OUT, SIDE, CROSS; Repeat
Beat 1	Step R foot diagonlly in toward center
2	Step L foot out ⎫
3	Step R foot out ⎬ Very little movement out
4	Step L foot out ⎭
5	Step R foot sideward right
6	Step L foot crossing in front of R foot bending knees
7-12	Repeat Part II, beats 1-6
PART III	FORWARD, FORWARD/FORWARD; FORWARD, FORWARD/FORWARD; SIDE, LIFT, SIDE, LIFT; Repeat
Beat 1	Step R foot forward counterclockwise
2 &	Step L, R foot forward counterclockwise
3-4	Repeat beats 1-2 beginning L foot
5	Step R foot sideward right
6 &	Bounce R heel twice, L foot is lifted in front of R leg
7-8	Step L foot sideward left and bounce L heel twice, lift R foot
9-16	Repeat Part III, beats 1-8
RHYTHMIC NOTATION	

PART I

☒ ☒ ☒ ☒ ☒ ☒   **REPEAT 3X**   ☒ ☒ ☒ ☒ ☒ ☒   **REPEAT**
R L R (L) L (R)   R L R L R L

☒ ☒ ☒ ☒ ☒ LIFT ☒ LIFT   **REPEAT**
R LR L RL R (L) L (R)

Tsamiko
Greece (Panhellenic)

RECORD		PI LPS 33 *Soul Dances of the Greeks* Tikva 131 *Greek Dance Party*
INTRODUCTION		None
FORMATION		Open circle or line, hands joined head height
METER		3/4 1-2-3
BASIC		*SIDE*, CROSS; *SIDE*, CROSS; *SIDE*, CROSS; *SIDE*, LIFT; *SIDE*, CROSS; *SIDE*, LIFT

Measure	Beat	
1	1-2	Step R foot sideward right
	3	Step L foot crossing in front of R foot
2-3		Repeat measure 1, two times
4	1-2	Step R foot sideward right
	3	Lift L foot in front or in back of R leg
5	1-2	Step L foot sideward left
	3	Step R foot crossing in front of L foot
6	1-2	Step L foot sideward left
	3	Lift R foot in front or in back of L leg

VARIATION I		*SIDE*, CROSS; *TOUCH*, SIDE; *TOUCH*, CROSS; *SIDE*, LIFT; *SIDE*, CROSS; *SIDE*, LIFT

Measure	Beat	
1	1-3	Repeat Basic, measure 1
2	1-2	Touch R foot diagonally forward right
	3	Step R foot sideward right
3	1-2	Touch L foot in
	3	Step L foot crossing in front of R foot
	4-6	Repeat Basic, measures 4-6

VARIATION II		SIDE, BACK, SIDE; CROSS, SIDE, CROSS; *SIDE*, CROSS; *SIDE*, LIFT; *SIDE*, CROSS; *SIDE*, LIFT

Measure	Beat	
1	1	Step R foot sideward right
	2	Step L foot crossing in back of R foot
	3	Step R foot sideward
2	1	Step L foot crossing in front of R foot
	2	Step R foot sideward right
	3	Step L foot crossing in front of R foot
	3-6	Repeat Basic, measures 3-6

NOTE		Basic and Variations may be executed any number of times.

Tsamiko (continued)

VARIATION III

SIDE, CROSS; TOUCH, BACKWARD;
BACKWARD, FORWARD, FORWARD;
BACKWARD, BACKWARD, SIDE;
CROSS, PIVOT, TURN; *SIDE*, LIFT

Measure	Beat	
1		Repeat Basic, measure 1
2	1-2	Touch R foot diagonally forward right
	3	Step R foot backward counterclockwise (facing clockwise)
3	1	Step L foot backward counterclockwise
	2	Step R foot forward counterclockwise
	3	Step L foot forward counterclockwise
4	1	Step R foot backward counterclockwise
	2	Step R foot backward counterclockwise
	3	Leap R foot sideward right
5	1-2	Step L foot crossing in front of R foot and pivot 1/2 clockwise on balls of both feet
	3	Step R foot turning to end facing center
6	1-3	Repeat Basic, measure 6

VARIATION IV

SIDE, CROSS; *SIDE*, CROSS; *SIDE*, CROSS;
SIDE, LIFT/SIDE; CROSS/SIDE; CROSS/SIDE;
CROSS/SIDE; CROSS, SIDE, LIFT

Measure	Beat	
1-3		Repeat Basic, measure 1-3
4	1-2	Step R foot sideward right
	3	Lift L foot in front of R leg
	&	Leap L foot sideward left
5	1	Step R foot crossing in front of L foot
	&	Step L foot sideward left
	2-3	Repeat beats 1 & twice
6	1	Step R foot crossing in front of L foot
	2	Step L foot sideward left
	3	Leg lift R foot in front of L leg

RHYTHMIC NOTATION

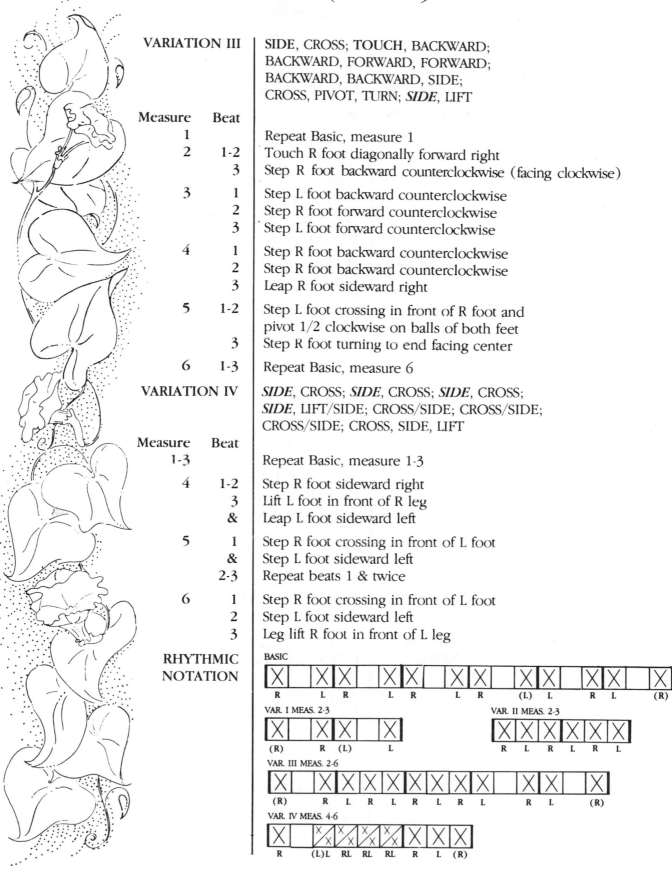

BASIC

R   L R   L R   L R   (L) L   R L   (R)

VAR. I MEAS. 2-3

(R)   R (L)   L

VAR. II MEAS. 2-3

R L R L R L

VAR. III MEAS. 2-6

(R)   R L R L R L R L   R L   (R)

VAR. IV MEAS. 4-6

R   (L)L RL RL RL   R   L   (R)

Tslil Zugim
Shepherd Dance
Israel

RECORD	Tikva 148 *Souvenir*
INTRODUCTION	Begin dance with vocal
FORMATION	Circle facing center, hands joined
PART I	SIDE, SIDE, CROSS, REST (2X); SIDE, SIDE, CROSS, SIDE; CROSS, SIDE, CROSS, REST; Repeat Part I 3X
Beats 1-4	Yemenite beginning R foot
5-8	Yemenite beginning L foot
9-11	Yemenite beginning R foot
12	Step L foot sideward left
13	Step R foot crossing in front of L foot
14	Step L foot sideward left
15-16	Step R foot crossing in front of L foot
17-32	Repeat beats 1-16 beginning L foot and moving right
33-64	Repeat Part I, beats 1-16
	Meter changes to 5/4
PART II	OUT, 2, 3, 4, 5; IN, IN, IN, IN, IN; Repeat Part II 3X
Beats 1-5	Step R, L, R, L, R foot out from center of circle Clap with each step, bend over
6	Leap L foot in toward center
7	Step R foot in
8-9	Repeat beats 6-7
10	Leap L foot in Snap fingers beats 1, 3, 5, arms raised
11-40	Repeat part II, beats 1-10, three times

RHYTHMIC NOTATION

PART I

| X | X | X | | X | X | X | | X | X | X | X | X | X | X | | REPEAT W/OPP. FTWK. |

R L R   L R L   R L R L R L R

PART II

| X | X | X | X | X | | REPEAT 3X |

R L R L R

Tzadik Katamar
Righteousness Shall Flourish
Israel

RECORD	Hadarim LP-3 *Back From Israel*
INTRODUCTION	8 beats
FORMATION	Circle, hands joined in "V" position
PART I	FORWARD, 2, 3, 4; SIDE, SIDE, SIDE, SIDE; Repeat Part I
Beats 1-4	Step R, L, R, L foot forward moving counterclockwise
5	Step R foot sideward right (facing center)
6	Step L foot sideward left
7-8	Repeat beats 5-6
9-16	Repeat Part I, beats 1-8
PART II	FORWARD, FORWARD, BACKWARD, BACKWARD; TURN, TURN, SIDE, CROSS; BACK, SIDE, CROSS, BACK; SIDE, SIDE, SIDE, SIDE; Repeat Part II
Beats 1-2	Step R, L foot forward moving counterclockwise
3-4	Step R, L foot backward moving counterclockwise
5-6	Step R, L foot turning a full turn right
7	Step R foot sideward right
8	Step L foot crossing in front of R foot
9	Step R foot crossing in back of L foot
10	Step L foot sideward left
11	Step R foot crossing in front of L foot
12	Step L foot crossing in back of R foot
13-16	Repeat Part I, beats 5-8
17-32	Repeat Part II, beats 1-16

RHYTHMIC NOTATION

PART I

X	X	X	X	X	X	X	X	REPEAT
R	L	R	L	R	L	R	L	

PART II

X	X	X	X	X	X	X	X	REPEAT 3X
R	L	R	L	R	L	R	L	

Varí Hasápikos
Heavy Butcher's Dance
Greece

RECORD	Folkraft LP-3, Folkraft 1462X45
INTRODUCTION	2 beats
FORMATION	Short lines in "T" position; R arm in back of neighbor's L arm

PART I	IN, SWING, OUT, OUT, SIDE/CROSS, BACK; Repeat; IN, SWING, OUT, OUT
Beat 1	Lunge in on L foot; body in, knee bent
2	Swing R foot in and around in an arc
3	Step R foot out behind L foot
4	Step L foot out behind R foot
5	Step R foot sideward right
&	Step L foot crossing in front of R foot
6	Step R foot crossing in back of L foot
7-12	Repeat beats 1-6
13-16	Repeat beats 1-4
PART II	CROSS/SIDE, CROSS/REST (4X); CROSS, CROSS, CROSS, CROSS; OUT, OUT, SIDE/CROSS, BACK
Beat 1	Step R foot crossing in front of L foot
&	Step L foot sideward left
2	Step R foot crossing in front of L foot
&	Hold and bring L foot in front of R foot
3-4	Repeat beats 1-2 with L foot in front
5-8	Repeat Part II, beats 1-4
9	Step R foot crossing in front of L foot
10	Step L foot crossing in front of R foot
11-12	Repeat beats 9-10
13	Step R foot out behind L foot
14	Step L foot out behind R foot
15-16	Repeat Part I, beats 5-6

RHYTHMIC NOTATION

PART I

X	X	X	X	X/X	X	X	X	X	X	X/X	X	X	X	X/X	X	X
L	(R)	R	L	RL	R	L	(R)	R	L	RL	R	L	(R)	R	L	

PART II

X/X	X	X/X	X	X/X	X	X/X	X	X	X	X	X	X	X	X	X/X	X
RL	R	LR	L	RL	R	LR	L	R	L	R	L	R	L	R	RL	R

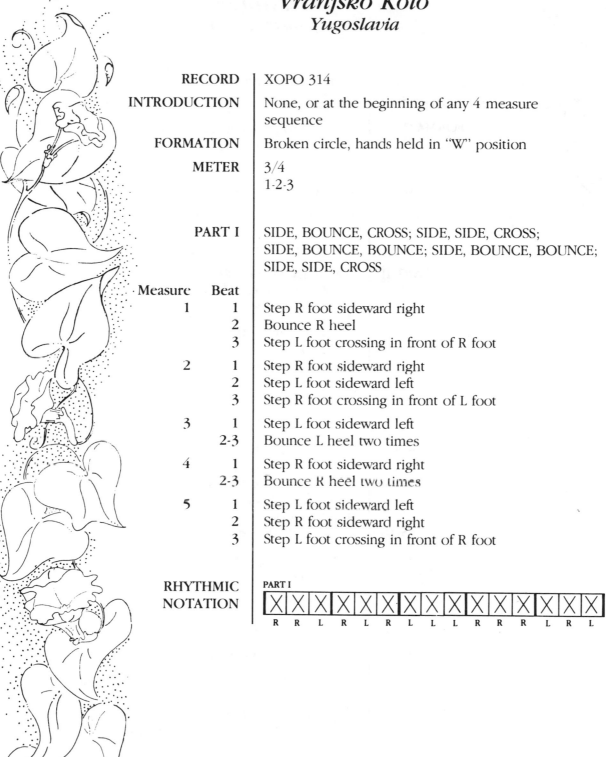

Vranjsko Kolo
Yugoslavia

RECORD	XOPO 314
INTRODUCTION	None, or at the beginning of any 4 measure sequence
FORMATION	Broken circle, hands held in "W" position
METER	3/4 1-2-3

PART I   SIDE, BOUNCE, CROSS; SIDE, SIDE, CROSS; SIDE, BOUNCE, BOUNCE; SIDE, BOUNCE, BOUNCE; SIDE, SIDE, CROSS

Measure	Beat	
1	1	Step R foot sideward right
	2	Bounce R heel
	3	Step L foot crossing in front of R foot
2	1	Step R foot sideward right
	2	Step L foot sideward left
	3	Step R foot crossing in front of L foot
3	1	Step L foot sideward left
	2-3	Bounce L heel two times
4	1	Step R foot sideward right
	2-3	Bounce R heel two times
5	1	Step L foot sideward left
	2	Step R foot sideward right
	3	Step L foot crossing in front of R foot

RHYTHMIC NOTATION

PART I

X	X	X	X	X	X	X	X	X	X	X	X	X	X	X
R	R	L	R	L	R	L	R	L	L	L	R	R	R	L	R	L

Ya Abud
Israel (Arab)

RECORD	MIH3 *Dance with Moshiko*
INTRODUCTION	8 beats
FORMATION	Line, or broken circle, hands held in "V" position; shoulder hold may be used

PART I	SIDE, CLOSE (16X)
Beat 1	Step R foot sideward right (bouncy steps)
2	Step L foot next to R foot
3-32	Repeat beats 1-2, fifteen times
PART II	STAMP, IN, IN, STAMP; STAMP, OUT, OUT, STAMP; Repeat Part II
Beat 1	Stamp R foot next to L foot
2	Step R foot in toward center
3	Step L foot in
4	Stamp R foot next to L foot
5-8	Repeat beats 1-4 moving out of circle
9-16	Repeat Part II, beats 1-8
PART III	HOP, HOP, HOP/IN, OUT (4X)
Beat 1	Hop L foot swinging R foot in (knee straight)
2	Hop L foot swinging R foot out (bend knee)
3	Hop L foot swinging R foot in (knee straight)
&	Step R foot in with flat foot
4	Step L foot out
5-16	Repeat Part III, beats 1-4, three times
	Raise arms to "W" position
PART IV	SIDE, BACK (8X)
Beat 1	Step R foot sideward right (slightly in)
2	Step L foot crossing in back of R foot
3-16	Repeat Part IV, beats 1-2, seven times
PART V	JUMP, JUMP/JUMP (8X)
Beat 1	Jump (R foot slightly in, L foot diagonally out) moving slightly sideward right
2 &	Jump on both feet twice (bend knees)
3-16	Repeat Part V, beats 1-2, seven times

Ya Abud (continued)

	Lower arms to "V" position
PART VI	JUMP, JUMP, LEAP, STAMP (4X)
Beat 1	Jump to forward stride, R foot in and L foot out
2	Jump to forward stride, L foot in nd R foot out
3	Leap L foot in place raising R knee
4	Stamp R foot next to L foot
5-16	Repeat Part VI, beats 1-4, three times
PART VII	FORWARD, 2, 3, STAMP (4X)
Beat 1	Run R foot moving counterclockwise, arms circle
2	Run L foot moving counterclockwise, arms circle
3	Run R foot moving counterclockwise, arms circle
4	Stamp L foot, lower arms forcefully
5-16	Repeat Part VII, beats 1-4, three times beginning I, R, L foot and alternating direction

RHYTHMIC NOTATION

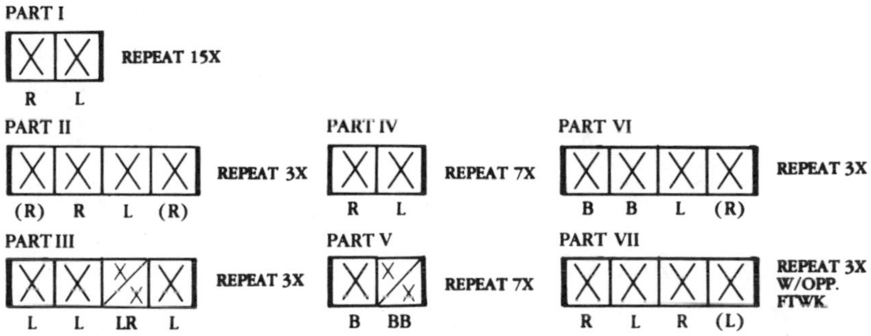

PART I

| X | X | REPEAT 15X
| R | L |

PART II

| X | X | X | X | REPEAT 3X
| (R) | R | L | (R) |

PART IV

| X | X | REPEAT 7X
| R | L |

PART VI

| X | X | X | X | REPEAT 3X
| B | B | L | (R) |

PART III

| X | X | X/X | X | REPEAT 3X
| L | L | LR | L |

PART V

| X | X/X | REPEAT 7X
| B | BB |

PART VII

| X | X | X | X | REPEAT 3X W/OPP. FTWK.
| R | L | R | (L) |

Yibanei Hamigdash
And the Temple Will be Rebuilt
Israel

RECORD	Tikva T-145 *Party*
INTRODUCTION	16 beats
FORMATION	Single circle facing center, hands joined
PART I	SIDE/CLOSE, SIDE; CROSS, PIVOT; FORWARD/CLOSE, FORWARD; BACKWARD/SIDE, CROSS; Repeat Part I
Beat 1	Step R foot sideward right
&	Step L foot next to R foot
2	Step R foot sideward right
3	Step L foot crossing in front of R foot with accent
4	Pivot on L foot turning to face clockwise
5-6	Two step forward clockwise beginning R foot
7	Step L foot backward
&	Step R foot sideward right
8	Step L foot crossing in front of R foot
9-16	Repeat Part I, beats 1-8
PART II	IN/IN, IN; TURN, 2; 3, 4; OUT/OUT, OUT; Repeat Part II
Beats 1-2	Step R, L, R foot in to center of circle; release hands
3-6	Step L, R, L, R foot turning full turn right; arms overhead; (sway in direction of step and snap fingers on steps)
7-8	Step L, R, L foot out
9-16	Repeat Part II, beats 1-8
PART III	FORWARD, FORWARD; FORWARD/FORWARD, TURN; BACKWARD, BACKWARD; BACKWARD/SIDE, CROSS; Repeat Part III
Beats 1-2	Step R, L foot forward counterclockwise
3-4	Step R, L, R foot pivoting on third step to face clockwise
5-6	Step L, R foot backward (facing clockwise)
7	Step L foot backward
&	Step R foot sideward right
8	Step L foot crossing in front of R foot
9-16	Repeat Part III, beats 1-8
RHYTHMIC NOTATION	

PART I

X X	X	X	X X	X	X X	X	REPEAT
RL	R	L	L	L	RL	R	LR L

Yibanei Hamigdash (continued)

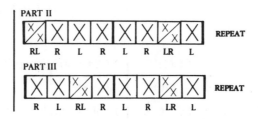

PART II

| X X | X | X | X | X | X X | X | REPEAT |

RL R L R L R LR L

PART III

| X | X | X X | X | X | X | X X | X | REPEAT |

R L RL R L R LR L

Zaplanjski Čačak
Čačak from Zaplanje
Yugoslavia (Serbia)

RECORD	Kola K-407
INTRODUCTION	16 beats
FORMATION	Lines in a belt hold with R arm under

PART I	SIDE, CROSS; SIDE, CROSS; SIDE, CROSS; SIDE, BOUNCE; SIDE, BOUNCE; SIDE, BOUNCE; SIDE, CROSS; SIDE, CROSS; SIDE, BOUNCE; SIDE, BOUNCE; SIDE, CROSS; SIDE, BOUNCE

Beat 1	Step R foot sideward right
2	Step L foot crossing in front of R foot
3-6	Repeat beats 1-2 two times
7-8	Step R foot sideward right then bounce R heel
9-10	Step L foot sideward left then bounce L heel
11-12	Step R foot sideward right then bounce R heel
13	Step L foot sideward left
14	Step R foot crossing in front of L foot
15-16	Repeat beats 13-14
17-18	Step L foot sideward left then bounce L heel
19-20	Step R foot sideward right then bounce R heel
21-22	Repeat beats 13-14
23-24	Step L foot sideward left then bounce L heel (lift R foot in front of L leg)

NOTE	This is an atypical čačak because it does not have a 10 measure sequence.

RHYTHMIC NOTATION	

PART I

| X | X | X | X | X | X | | X | | X | |

R L R L R L R   L   R

| X | X | X | X | X | | X | | X | X | X |

L R L R L   R   L R L

Za Pojas
By the Belt
Bulgaria

RECORD	XOPO 308 *Novo Zagorsko Horo*
INTRODUCTION	None
FORMATION	Broken circle, belt hold
PART I	SIDE, CROSS; SIDE, CROSS; SIDE, CROSS; SIDE, HOP; SIDE, HOP; SIDE, HOP; SIDE, BACK; SIDE, BACK; SIDE, BACK; SIDE, HOP; SIDE, HOP; IN/IN, IN; IN, HOP; OUT, HOP; OUT, HOP; OUT, HOP

Beat 1	Leap R foot sideward right (emphasis on height)
2	Step L foot crossing in front of R foot
3-6	Repeat beats 1-2 two times
7	Step R foot sideward right
8	Hop R foot swinging L foot in front
9	Step L foot sideward left
10	Hop L foot swinging R foot in front
11-12	Repeat beats 7-8
13-18	Repeat beats 1-6 sideward left beginning L foot and cross R foot in back of L foot
19-20	Step hop L foot swinging R foot in front
21-22	Step hop R foot swinging L foot in front
23	Step L foot in toward center
&	Step R foot in toward center
24	Step L foot in toward center
25-26	Step hop R foot in bending L knee raising it high
27-28	Step hop L foot out bending R knee raising it high
29-32	Step hop R, L foot out as in beats 27-28

RHYTHMIC NOTATION

PART I

X	X	X	X	X	X	X	X	X	X
R	L	R	L	R	L	R	R	L	L	R	R

X	X	X	X	X	X	X	X	X	X	X/X	X
L	R	L	R	L	R	L	L	R	R	LR	L

X	X	X	X	X	X
R	R	L	L	R	R	L	L

Zervos Karpathos
Greece (Island of Karpathos)

RECORD	Folkraft 8 *Greek Dances*
INTRODUCTION	Begin with vocal
FORMATION	Broken circle, hands joined in "W" position Slow music
PART I	SIDE, LIFT; SIDE, LIFT; SIDE, CROSS; SIDE, CLOSE; Repeat Part I 3X
Beat 1	Step L foot sideward left
2	Lift R foot in front of L leg
3	Step R foot sideward right
4	Lift L foot in front of R leg
5	Step L foot sideward left
6	Step R foot crossing in front of L foot
7	Step L foot sideward left
8	Step R foot next to L foot
9-	Repeat Part I, beats 1-8, three times
	Faster music
PART II	FORWARD, HOP (3X); FORWARD/CLOSE, FORWARD; Repeat Part II 3X
Beat 1	Step L foot forward moving clockwise
2	Hop L foot
3-6	Repeat beats 1-2 two times
7	Step R foot forward
&	Step L foot next to R foot
8	Step R foot forward
9-32	Repeat Part II, beats 1-8, three times

RHYTHMIC NOTATION

PART I

X	X	X	X	X	X	X	X	REPEAT 3X
L	(R)	R	(L)	L	R	L	R	

PART II

X	X	X	X	X	X	X/X	X	REPEAT 3X
L	L	R	R	L	L	RL	R	

Zibnšrit
Seven Steps
Yugoslavia (Slovenia)

RECORD	33-EP-SD-601 *Slovenian Old Time Dances*
INTRODUCTION	1 note upbeat
FORMATION	Couples facing each other; R hands joined about face level; L hand holding partner at waist
PART I	Directions given for man IN/CLOSE; IN/CLOSE; IN/CLOSE; IN; OUT/CLOSE, OUT/CLOSE; OUT/CLOSE, OUT; IN/CLOSE, IN; OUT/CLOSE, OUT; STEP/HOP; STEP/HOP; STEP/HOP; STEP/HOP; IN/CLOSE, IN; OUT/CLOSE, OUT; STEP/HOP; STEP/HOP; STEP/HOP; STEP/HOP
Beat 1	Step L foot sideward in toward center
&	Step R foot next to L foot
2-3	Repeat beats 1 & two times
4	Step L foot in with accent
5-8	Repeat beats 1-4 out to right
9	Step L foot sideward in
&	Step R foot next to L foot
10	Step L foot sideward in with accent
11-12	Repeat beats 9-10 out
13-16	Four step hops in place for man; woman does 4 step hops with 1 or 2 turns under man's arm, R hands remain held
17-20	Repeat beats 9-12
21-24	Four step hops turning as a couple maintaining hand hold
RHYTHMIC NOTATION	

PART I

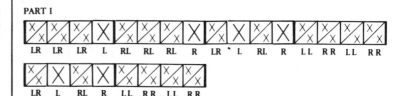

LR LR LR L RL RL RL R LR L RL R LL RR LL RR

LR L RL R LL RR LL RR

Zorba
Greece

RECORD	Tikva 131 *Greek Dance Party*
INTRODUCTION	8 beats
FORMATION	Short lines, shoulder hold

PART I   SIDE, TOUCH; SIDE, TOUCH; TOES, TOES;
IN/TOUCH, SWING; OUT, CLOSE; Repeat Part I 3X

Beat 1	Step R foot sideward right
2	Touch L foot next to R foot
3	Step L foot sideward left
4	Touch R foot next to L foot
5	Turn toes out
6	Turn toes straight
7	Lunge L foot in, touch R foot behind
8	Swing R foot in and around behind L foot
9	Step R foot out behind L foot
10	Step L foot next to R foot
11-40	Repeat Part I, beats 1-10, three times

PART II   CROSS/SIDE, CROSS; CROSS/SIDE, CROSS;
CROSS/SIDE, CROSS; CROSS/SIDE, CROSS;
CROSS, CROSS, CROSS, CROSS;
OUT, OUT, SIDE/CROSS, BACK

Beat 1	Step R foot crossing in front of L foot	Double Travel
&	Step L foot sideward left	
2	Step R foot crossing in front of L foot	
&	Swing L foot around in front of R foot	
3	Step L foot crossing in front of R foot	
&	Step R foot sideward right	
4	Step L foot crossing in front of R foot	
&	Swing R foot around in front of L foot	
5-8	Repeat beats 1-4	
9	Step R foot crossing in front of L foot	Singles
10	Step L foot crossing in front of R foot	
11-12	Repeat beats 9-10	
13	Step R foot out	
14	Step L foot out	
15	Step R foot sideward right	
&	Step L foot crossing in front of R foot	
16	Step R foot crossing in back of L foot	

(continued)

Zorba *(continued)*

PART III	IN/TOUCH, SWING; OUT, OUT; SIDE/CROSS, BACK; IN/TOUCH, SWING; OUT, OUT, SIDE/CROSS, BACK; IN/TOUCH, SWING; OUT, OUT
Beat 1	Lunge L foot in, touch R foot behind
2	Swing R foot in and around behind L foot
3	Step R foot out behind L foot
4	Step L foot out behind R foot
5	Step R foot sideward right
&	Step L foot crossing in front of R foot
6	Step R foot crossing in back of L foot
7-12	Repeat beats 1-6
13-16	Repeat beats 1-4
PART II	Repeat Part II; beat 16 step R foot next to L foot

RHYTHMIC NOTATION

PART I

X	X	X	X	X	X	X/X	X	X	X	**REPEAT 3X**
R	(L)	L	(R)	B	B	L(R)	(R)	R	L	

PART II

X/X	X	X/X	X	X/X	X	X/X	X
RL	R	LR	L	RL	R	LR	L

X	X	X	X	X	X	X/X	X
R	L	R	L	R	L	RL	R

PART III

X/X	X	X	X	X/X	X	X/X	X	X	X	X/X	X
L(R)	(R)	R	L	RL	R	L(R)	(R)	R	L	RL	R

X/X	X	X/X	X
L(R)	(R)	R	L

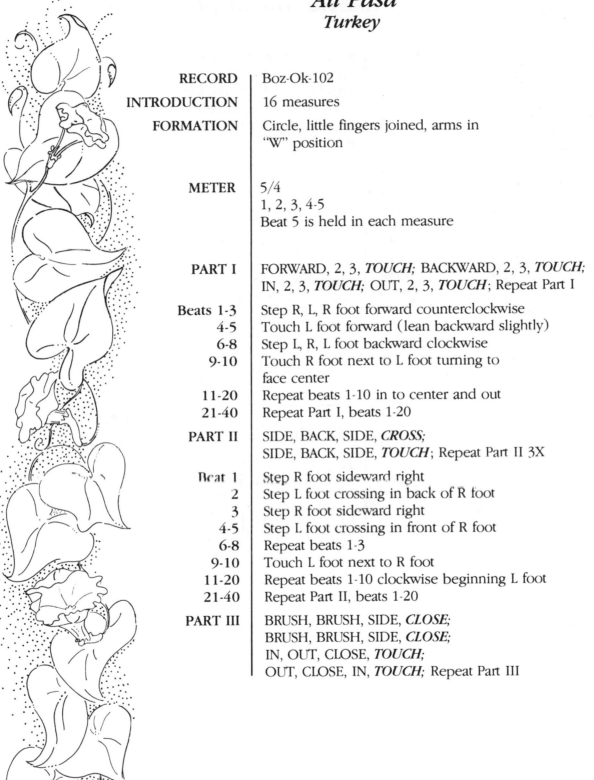

Ali Pasa
Turkey

RECORD	Boz-Ok-102
INTRODUCTION	16 measures
FORMATION	Circle, little fingers joined, arms in "W" position
METER	5/4 1, 2, 3, 4-5 Beat 5 is held in each measure
PART I	FORWARD, 2, 3, *TOUCH*; BACKWARD, 2, 3, *TOUCH*; IN, 2, 3, *TOUCH*; OUT, 2, 3, *TOUCH*; Repeat Part I
Beats 1-3	Step R, L, R foot forward counterclockwise
4-5	Touch L foot forward (lean backward slightly)
6-8	Step L, R, L foot backward clockwise
9-10	Touch R foot next to L foot turning to face center
11-20	Repeat beats 1-10 in to center and out
21-40	Repeat Part I, beats 1-20
PART II	SIDE, BACK, SIDE, *CROSS*; SIDE, BACK, SIDE, *TOUCH*; Repeat Part II 3X
Beat 1	Step R foot sideward right
2	Step L foot crossing in back of R foot
3	Step R foot sideward right
4-5	Step L foot crossing in front of R foot
6-8	Repeat beats 1-3
9-10	Touch L foot next to R foot
11-20	Repeat beats 1-10 clockwise beginning L foot
21-40	Repeat Part II, beats 1-20
PART III	BRUSH, BRUSH, SIDE, *CLOSE*; BRUSH, BRUSH, SIDE, *CLOSE*; IN, OUT, CLOSE, *TOUCH*; OUT, CLOSE, IN, *TOUCH*; Repeat Part III

(continued)

Ali Pasa (continued)

Beat 1	Brush R foot in front of L foot moving it diagonally backward
2	Brush R foot diagonally forward
3	Step R foot sideward right
4-5	Step L foot next to R foot
6-10	Repeat beats 1-5
11	Step R foot in toward center
12	Step L foot out
13	Step R foot next to L foot
14-15	Touch L foot in
16	Step L foot out
17	Step R foot next to L foot
18	Step L foot in
19-20	Touch R foot next to L foot
21-40	Repeat Part III, beats 1-20

RHYTHMIC NOTATION

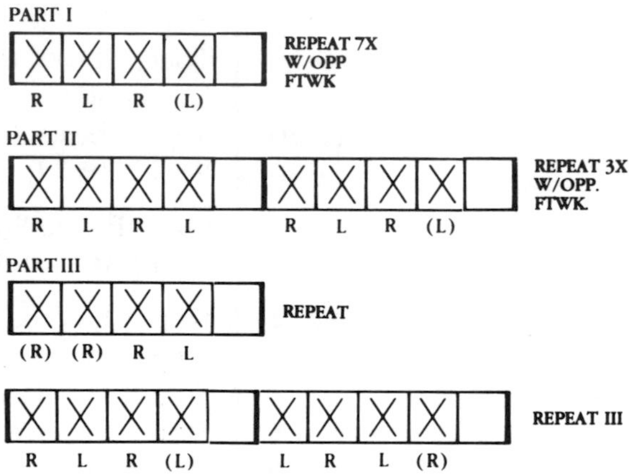

PART I

X	X	X	X		REPEAT 7X W/OPP FTWK

R   L   R   (L)

PART II

X	X	X	X		X	X	X	X		REPEAT 3X W/OPP. FTWK.

R   L   R   L   R   L   R   (L)

PART III

X	X	X	X		REPEAT

(R) (R)   R   L

X	X	X	X		X	X	X	X		REPEAT III

R   L   R   (L)   L   R   L   (R)

Ivanica
Macedonia

RECORD	Worldtone 10009
INTRODUCTION	8 measures (begin with vocal)
FORMATION	Broken circle, arms held in "W" position
METER	7/16
	1-2-3, 4-5, 6-7
	Slow, Quick, Quick (*SQQ*)
PART I	*FORWARD*, FORWARD, FORWARD;
	FORWARD, FORWARD, FORWARD;
	FORWARD, FORWARD, REST;
	SIDE, BOUNCE, BOUNCE;
	SIDE, BOUNCE, BOUNCE;
	SIDE, BOUNCE, BOUNCE;
	SIDE, BACK, REST;
	SIDE, BOUNCE, BOUNCE

Measure	Beat	
1	*S*	Step R foot forward counterclockwise
	Q	Step L foot forward counterclockwise
	Q	Step R foot forward counterclockwise
2		Repeat Measure 1 beginning L foot
3	*S*	Step R foot forward counterclockwise
	QQ	Step L foot forward counterclockwise and turn to face center
4	*S*	Step R foot sideward right
	QQ	Bounce R heel 2 times (lift L foot in front of L leg)
5		Repeat Measure 4 beginning L foot
6		Repeat Measure 4
7	*S*	Step L foot sideward left
	QQ	Step R foot crossing in back of L foot
8	*S*	Step L foot sideward left
	QQ	Bounce L heel 2 times (lift R foot in front of L leg)

Ivanica (continued)

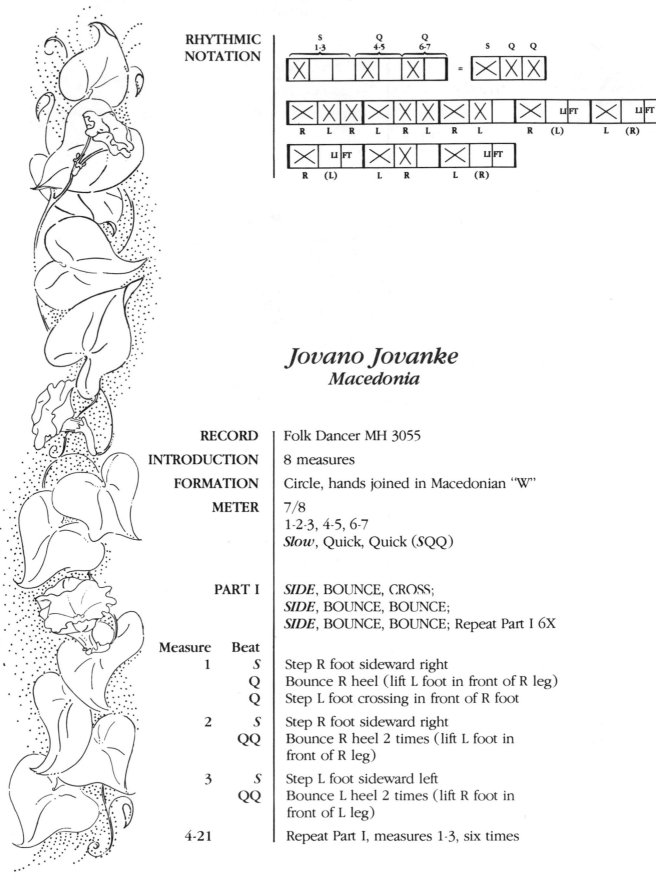

RHYTHMIC NOTATION

Jovano Jovanke
Macedonia

RECORD	Folk Dancer MH 3055
INTRODUCTION	8 measures
FORMATION	Circle, hands joined in Macedonian "W"
METER	7/8
	1-2-3, 4-5, 6-7
	Slow, Quick, Quick (*SQQ*)
PART I	*SIDE*, BOUNCE, CROSS;
	SIDE, BOUNCE, BOUNCE;
	SIDE, BOUNCE, BOUNCE; Repeat Part I 6X

Measure	Beat	
1	S	Step R foot sideward right
	Q	Bounce R heel (lift L foot in front of R leg)
	Q	Step L foot crossing in front of R foot
2	S	Step R foot sideward right
	QQ	Bounce R heel 2 times (lift L foot in front of R leg)
3	S	Step L foot sideward left
	QQ	Bounce L heel 2 times (lift R foot in front of L leg)
4-21		Repeat Part I, measures 1-3, six times

Jovano Jovanke (continued)

PART II | *STEP*, STEP, STEP;
IN, CLOSE, STEP;
OUT, BOUNCE, BACK

Measure	Beat	
1	S	Step R foot next to L foot
	Q	Step L foot next to R foot
	Q	Step R foot next to L foot
2	S	Step L foot in toward center of circle
	Q	Step R foot next to L foot
	Q	Step L foot next to R foot
3	S	Step R foot out from center of circle
	Q	Bounce R foot (lifting L foot in back of R leg)
	Q	Step L foot crossing in back of R foot (close to R foot)
4-9		Repeat Part II, measures 1-3 two times

RHYTHMIC NOTATION

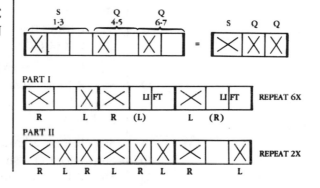

Kalamatianos
From City of Kalamata
Greece

RECORD	Tikva 131 *Greek Dance Party* Numerous other recordings
INTRODUCTION	4 measures
FORMATION	Line or broken circle; leader at right; "W" position
METER	7/8 1-2-3, 4-5, 6-7 *Slow*, Quick, Quick (*SQQ*)
PART I	*SIDE*, BACK, SIDE; *FORWARD*, FORWARD, FORWARD; *SIDE*, CROSS, BACK; *SIDE*, BACK, CROSS

Measure	Beat	
1	S	Step R foot sideward right
	Q	Step L foot crossing in back of R foot
	Q	Step R foot sideward right
2	S	Step L foot forward moving counterclockwise
	Q	Step R foot forward moving counterclockwise
	Q	Step L foot forward moving counterclockwise and turn
3	S	Step R foot sideward right
	Q	Step L foot crossing in front of R foot
	Q	Step R foot crossing in back of L foot
4	S	Step L foot sideward left
	Q	Step R foot crossing in back of L foot
	Q	Step L foot crossing in front of R foot

TO SIMPLIFY	Do measure 1 forward as mcasure 2 Do two side lift steps on measures 3-4
NOTE	This is the national dance of Greece.
RHYTHMIC NOTATION	

Kosovsko Lesno Oro
Yugoslavia (South Serbia)

RECORD	Worldtone WT 10002, "Makedonsko Devojce"
INTRODUCTION	No introduction or begin with vocal
FORMATION	Broken circle, hands joined in "W" position
METER	7/8
	1-2-3, 4-5, 6-7
	Slow, Quick, Quick (SQQ)

PART I | *SIDE*, LIFT, CROSS;
FORWARD, FORWARD, FORWARD;
CLOSE, BOUNCE, BOUNCE

Measure	Beat	
1	S	Step R foot sideward right facing diagonally right
	Q	Lift L leg in with bounce on R heel
	Q	Step L foot crossing in front of R foot
2	S	Step R foot forward counterclockwise
	Q	Step L foot forward counterclockwise
	Q	Step R foot forward counterclockwise
3	S	Step L foot next to R foot (face center)
	Q	Bounce L heel
	Q	Bounce L heel

Men: Lift R foot in front of L leg
Women: Point R toe to center and move hips on QQ

**RHYTHMIC
NOTATION**

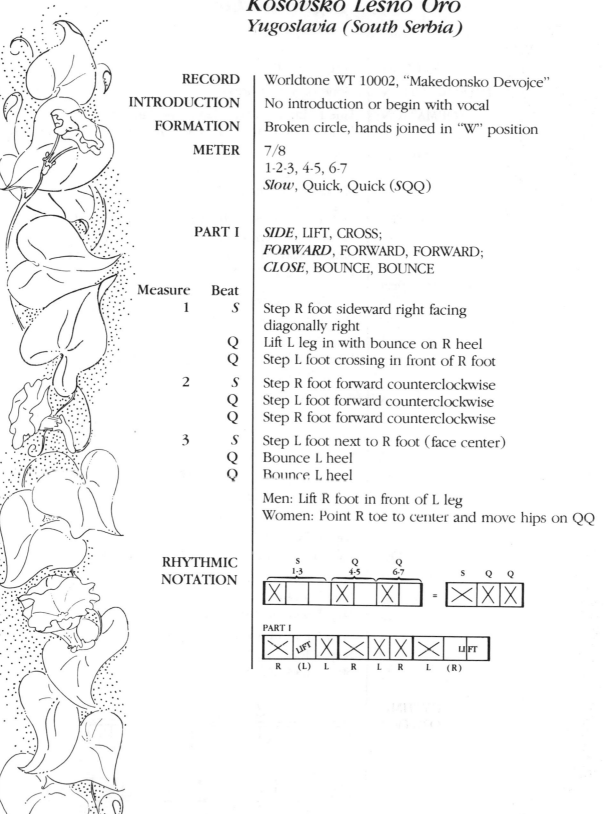

Legnala Dana
Macedonia

RECORD	Festival FS-4011
INTRODUCTION	None or 8 measures
FORMATION	Line facing right with leader at right end; hands joined in "W" position and arms forward from shoulders
METER	7/8 1-2-3, 4-5, 6-7 *Slow*, Quick, Quick (*SQQ*)
PART I	*FORWARD*, FORWARD, REST; *FORWARD*, BOUNCE, BOUNCE; *FORWARD*, FORWARD, FORWARD; *SIDE*, BOUNCE, BOUNCE; *SIDE*, BACK, REST; *SIDE*, BOUNCE, BOUNCE; *IN*, OUT, CLOSE: *IN*, OUT CLOSE

Measure	Beat	
1	S	Step R foot forward
	QQ	Step L foot forward moving counterclockwise
2	S	Step R foot forward
	QQ	Bounce R heel twice (bring L foot to back of R heel, toe pointed)
3	S	Step L foot forward moving counterclockwise
	Q	Step R foot forward — Enlarge steps slightly
	Q	Step L foot forward — in this measure
4	S	Step R foot sideward right
	QQ	Lift L foot in front of R leg bouncing R heel twice
5	S	Step L foot sideward left
	QQ	Step R foot crossing in back of L foot
6	S	Step L foot sideward
	QQ	Lift R foot in front of L leg bouncing L heel twice
7	S	Step R foot in toward the center
	Q	Step L foot out
	Q	Step R foot next to L foot
8	S	Step L foot in toward the center
	Q	Step R foot out
	Q	Step L foot next to R foot

RHYTHMIC NOTATION

PART I

Lemonaki
Little Lemon Tree
Greece (Macedonia)

RECORD	Panhellenion KT 1001
INTRODUCTION	Begin with vocal
FORMATION	Circle, hands held in "V" position
METER	7/8
	1-2-3, 4-5, 6-7
	Slow, Quick, Quick (*SQQ*)

PART I — *SIDE*, BACK, SIDE; *CROSS*, SIDE, BACK; *IN*, IN, IN; *OUT*, OUT, OUT; Repeat Part I

Measure	Beat	
1	S	Step R foot sideward right
	Q	Step L foot crossing in back of R foot
	Q	Step R foot sideward right
2	S	Step L foot crossing in front of R foot
	Q	Step R foot sideward right
	Q	Step L foot crossing in back of R foot
3	S	Step R foot in toward center
	Q	Step L foot in toward center
	Q	Step R foot in with accent
4	S	Step L foot out from center
	Q	Step R foot out from center
	Q	Step L foot out
5-8		Repeat measures 1-4 (instrumental)

PART II

Measure	Beat	
1-4		Repeat measures 1-4, Part I (vocal)
5-6		Repeat measures 3-4, Part I
7-12		Repeat measures 1-6 (instrumental)

NOTE — This dance often is performed by children as a Maypole Dance. The inside circle moves clockwise while the outside moves counterclockwise weaving in and out of each circle. Measures 3-4 move forward/backward rather than in/out.

RHYTHMIC NOTATION

PART I & II

Lesnoto Oro
Macedonia

RECORD	Folk Dancer MH 3037 Nama 2
INTRODUCTION	None or 3 measures
FORMATION	Broken circle, hands held in "W" position, arms brought forward from shoulders.
METER	7/8 1-2-3, 4-5, 6-7 *Slow*, Quick, Quick (*SQQ*)
PART I	*FORWARD*, BOUNCE, CROSS; *SIDE*, BOUNCE, BOUNCE; *SIDE*, BOUNCE, BOUNCE

Measure	Beat	
1	S	Step R foot forward moving counterclockwise
	Q	Bounce R heel and begin L foot crossing in front of R foot
	Q	Step L foot crossing in front of R foot
2	S	Step R foot sideward right
	QQ	Lift L foot in front of R leg bouncing slightly on R foot
3	S	Step L foot sideward left
	QQ	Lift R foot in front of L leg bouncing slightly on L foot

NOTE	When the music quickens to 7/16, do the same step or change measures 2-3 to *SIDE*, CROSS, BACK.
RHYTHMIC NOTATION	

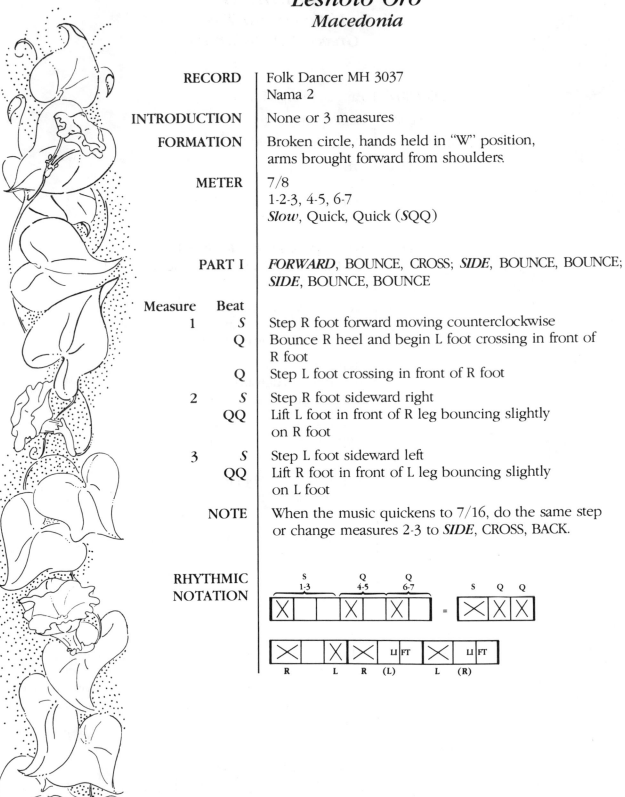

Paiduşca
Romania (Dobrogea)

RECORD	Nevofoon 15005 *Romanian Folkdances*
INTRODUCTION	16 beats
FORMATION	Short lines, hands held in "W" position
METER	5/8 1-2, 3-4-5 Quick, *Slow* (Q*S*)

PART I	HOP, *FORWARD*; HOP, *FORWARD*; HOP, *SIDE*, CROSS, *BACK*; HOP, *SIDE*, CROSS, *BACK*; HOP, *SIDE*, CROSS, *BACK*; HOP, *FORWARD*; HOP, *FORWARD*; HOP, *SIDE*, CROSS, *BACK*; HOP, *SIDE*; CLOSE, *SIDE*; CLOSE, *SIDE*; CLOSE, *SIDE*; HOP, *SIDE*, CROSS, *BACK*; HOP, *SIDE*, CROSS, *BACK*; HOP, *FORWARD*; HOP, *FORWARD*; HOP, *SIDE*, CROSS, *BACK*; HOP, *SIDE*, CROSS, *BACK*; HOP, *SIDE*, CROSS, *BACK*; HOP, *OUT*; HOP, *OUT*; HOP, *OUT*; HOP, *OUT*

Measure	Beat	
1	Q	Hop L foot
	S	Step R foot moving diagonally forward right (arms swing down)
2	Q	Hop R foot
	S	Step L foot moving diagonally forward right (arms swing up)
3	Q	Hop L foot
	S	Step R foot sideward right
4	Q	Step L foot crossing in front of R foot
	S	Step R foot crossing in back of L foot
5-6		Repeat measures 3-4 beginning hop R foot (HOP, SIDE, CROSS, BACK)
7-8		Repeat measures 3-4 (HOP, SIDE, CROSS, BACK)
9	Q	Hop R foot
	S	Step L foot moving diagonally forward left (arms swing down)

(continued)

Paiduşca (continued)

10	Q	Hop L foot
	S	Step R foot moving diagonally forward left (arms swing up)
11	Q	Hop R foot
	S	Step L foot sideward left
12	Q	Step R foot crossing in front of L foot
	S	Step L foot crossing in back of R foot
13	Q	Hop L foot
	S	Step R foot sideward right
14	Q	Step L foot next to R foot
	S	Step R foot sideward right
15-16		Repeat measure 14 two times (CLOSE, SIDE)
17-18		Repeat measures 11-12 (HOP, SIDE, CROSS, BACK)
19-20		Repeat measures 3-4 (HOP, SIDE, CROSS, BACK)
21-22		Repeat measures 9-10 (HOP, FORWARD, HOP, FORWARD)
23-24		Repeat measures 11-12 (HOP, SIDE, CROSS, BACK)
25-26		Repeat measures 3-4 (HOP, SIDE, CROSS, BACK)
27-28		Repeat measures 11-12 (HOP, SIDE, CROSS, BACK)
29	Q	Hop L foot
	S	Step R foot out (arms swing down)
30	Q	Hop R foot
	S	Step L foot out (arms swing up)
31-32		Repeat measures 29-30

RHYTHMIC NOTATION

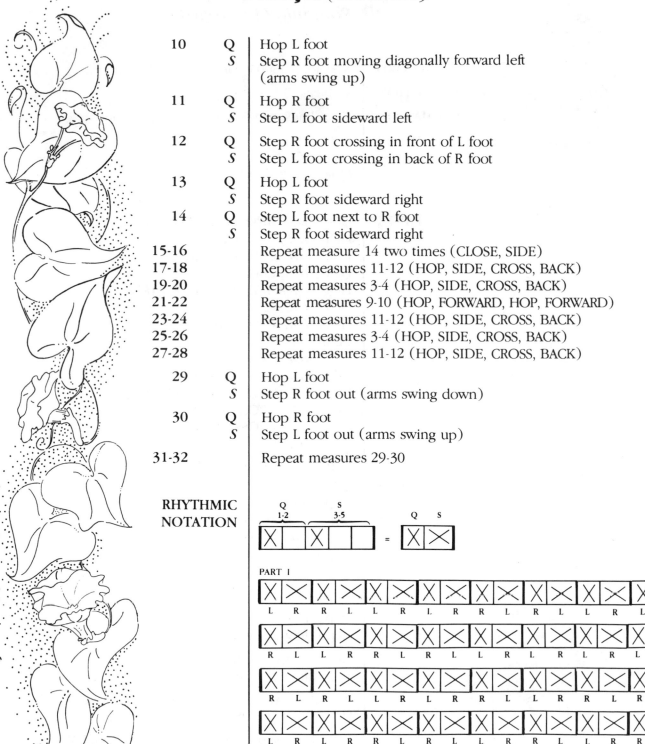

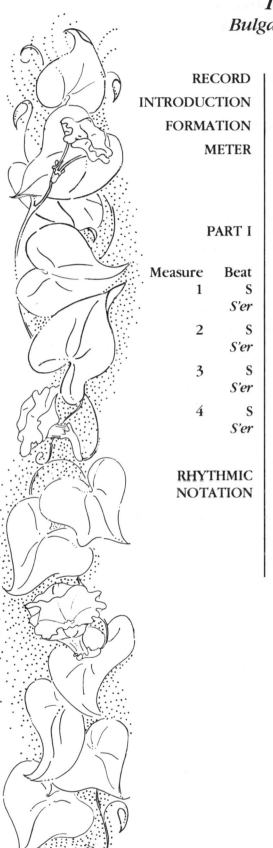

Trŭgnála Rumjana
Bulgaria (Rhodopes & Strandza)

RECORD	XOPO 329
INTRODUCTION	Begin with vocal
FORMATION	Broken circle, "T" position
METER	7/8 1-2-3, 4-5-6-7 Slow, *Slower*, (SS'*er*)

PART I　SIDE, *CROSS*; SIDE, *BACK*; SIDE, *LIFT*; SIDE, *LIFT*

Measure	Beat	
1	S	Step R foot sideward right
	S'*er*	Step L foot crossing in front of R foot
2	S	Step R foot sideward right
	S'*er*	Step L foot crossing in back of R foot
3	S	Step R foot sideward right
	S'*er*	Lift L foot in front of R leg (do not bounce R heel)
4	S	Step L foot sideward left
	S'*er*	Lift R foot in front of L leg (do not bounce L heel)

RHYTHMIC NOTATION

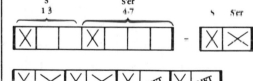

Zagoritikos
Greece (Epirus)

RECORD	Songs of Epirus
INTRODUCTION	None or wait 4 measures
FORMATION	Broken circle, hands joined in "W" position
METER	5/4
	1, 2, 3, 4-5

PART I	TOUCH, TOUCH, CROSS, *HOOK*;
	FORWARD, 2, 3, *4*;
	CROSS, BACK, CLOSE, *STAMP*;
	FORWARD, 2, 3, *CLOSE*

Measure	Beat	
1	1	Touch L foot across in front of R foot
	2	Touch L foot sideward left
	3	Step L foot crossing in front of R foot (long gliding step)
	4-5	Hook R foot behind L knee
STYLE		Women use toe point on touch
		Men use high leg lift without touching
2	1-5	Step R, L, R, L foot moving counterclockwise and turn to face center
3	1	Step R foot crossing in front of L foot
	2	Step L foot crossing in back of R foot
	3	Step R foot next to L foot
	4-5	Stamp L foot next to R foot (R knee bends slightly)
4	1-3	Step L, R, L moving clockwise
	4-5	Step R foot next to L foot

VARIATION I

2		Turn right
4		Turn left

VARIATION II

1	1-2	Touch L foot sideward left and rest beat 2
3	1	Leap R foot
	4-5	Stamp L foot more vigorously

Zagoritikos (continued)

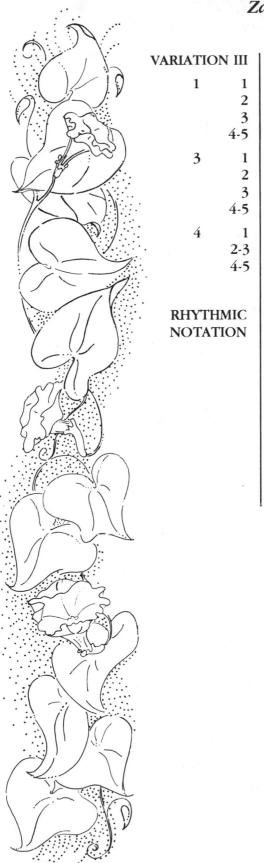

VARIATION III

1	1	Brush L foot in
	2	Brush L foot out
	3	Step L foot in (gliding step)
	4-5	Hook R foot
3	1	Brush R foot across in front of L foot
	2	Brush R foot diagonally right
	3	Brush R foot out
	4-5	Hook 5
4	1	Step R foot out
	2-3	Step L, R out
	4-5	Touch L foot next to R foot

RHYTHMIC NOTATION

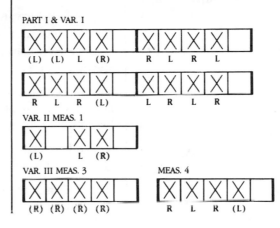

PART I & VAR. I

(L) (L) L (R)   R L R L

R L R (L)   L R L R

VAR. II MEAS. 1

(L)   L (R)

VAR. III MEAS. 3

(R) (R) (R) (R)

MEAS. 4

R L R (L)

Žalna Majka
Yugoslavia (Macedonia)

RECORD	Festival FR 4017
INTRODUCTION	9 measures
FORMATION	Circle, hands joined in "W"
METER	7/8
	1-2-3, 4-5, 6-7
	Slow, Quick, Quick (SQQ)

PART I		*FORWARD*, BOUNCE, CROSS; *SIDE*, BOUNCE, BOUNCE; *OUT*, BOUNCE, BOUNCE; Repeat 6X
Measure	**Beat**	
1	S	Step R foot forward right (face diagonally counterclockwise)
	Q	Bounce R foot and move L foot across in front of R foot
	Q	Step L foot crossing in front of R foot
2	S	Step R foot sideward right
	Q	Lift L foot in front of R leg
	Q	Bring L foot around behind R leg
3	S	Step L foot out
	QQ	Lift R foot (bounce L foot twice)
4-21		Repeat Part I, measures 1-3, six times

PART II		*FORWARD*, BOUNCE, CROSS; *SIDE*, CROSS, BACK; *SIDE*, CROSS, BACK; Repeat 2X
1	S	Step R foot forward counterclockwise (face diagonally counterclockwise)
	Q	Bounce R foot and move L foot across in front of R foot
	Q	Step L foot crossing in front of R foot
2	S	Step R foot sideward right
	Q	Step L foot crossing in front of R foot
	Q	Step R foot crossing in back of L foot
3	S	Step L foot sideward left
	Q	Step R foot crossing in front of L foot
	Q	Step L foot crossing in back of R foot
4-9		Repeat Part II, measure 1-3, two times
		Alternate Part I and II with music

Žalna Majka (continued)

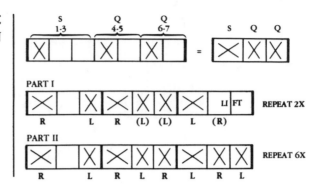

RHYTHMIC NOTATION

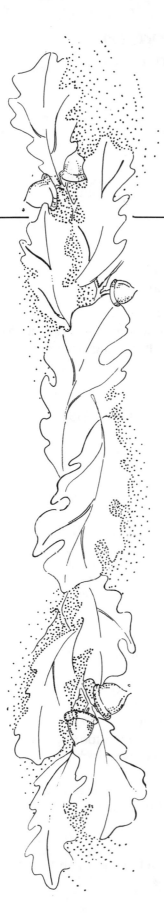

Intermediate Level 2 Dances, Common & Uncommon Meters

Common Meters

Ana Halach Dodech
Where Did Your Beloved Go?
Israel

RECORD	Tikva T-117 *Potpourri*
INTRODUCTION	8 beats
FORMATION	Partners in double circle, facing each other (men on inside); man's R hand joins woman's L hand
PART I	SIDE, BACK, SIDE, HOP; CROSS, BACK, SIDE, HOP; SIDE, BACK, SIDE, HOP; TURN, 2, 3, HOP; Repeat Part I

(Men's step described; women use opposite footwork)

Beats 1-4	Schottische sideward left moving counterclockwise crossing R foot in back of L foot
5	Step R foot crossing in front of L foot; bring joined hands forward
6	Step L foot crossing in back of R foot; bring joined hands down
7	Step R foot sideward right; arms swing out to side
8	Hop R foot
9-12	Repeat beats 1-4
13-16	Schottische turn left, releasing hands; begin by crossing R foot over L foot and complete turn in next two steps
17-32	Repeat Part I, beats 1-16
PART II	AWAY, 2, 3, CLOSE; CLAP, CLAP, TOWARD, 2, 3, 4; ISRAELI TURN; Repeat Part II

(Same footwork for both)

Beats 1-3	Step R, L, R foot away from each other
4	Step L foot next to R foot
5-6	Bend toward partner and clap twice
7	Leap R foot toward partner
8	Run L foot toward partner
9-10	Repeat beats 7-8; end in Israeli turn position
11-16	Six buzz steps turning counterclockwise, starting R foot
17-32	Repeat Part II, beats 1-16; men must hold the "&" of beat 16 to begin dance again
NOTE	Part II may be done as a mixer; on the repeat of Part II, each person "leap-runs" diagonally left to new partner.

Ana Halach Dodech (continued)

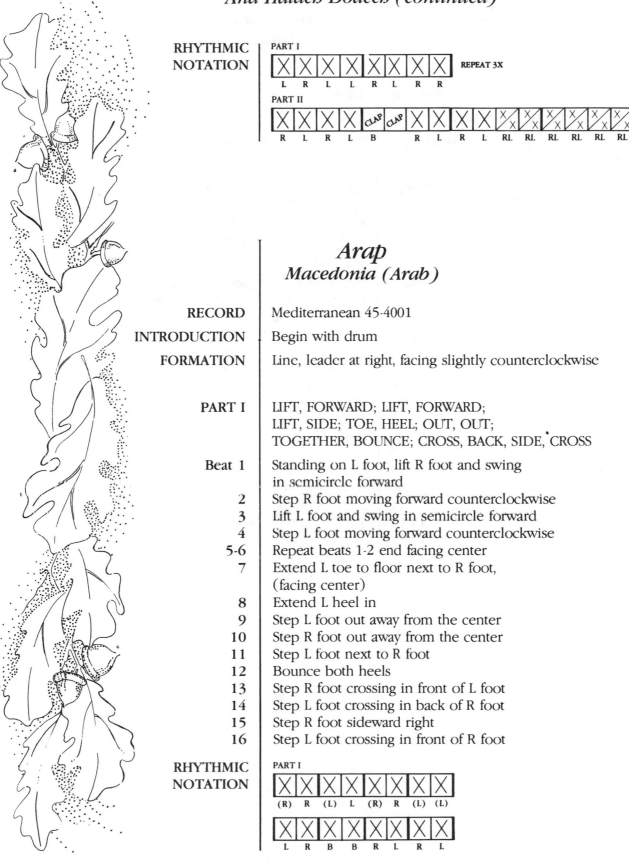

RHYTHMIC NOTATION	PART I

PART I

X	X	X	X	X	X	X	X	REPEAT 3X
L	R	L	L	R	L	R	R	

PART II

X	X	X	X	CLAP	CLAP	X	X	X	X	X X X	X X X	X X X	X X X	X X X	X X X	REPEAT
R	L	R	L	B		R	L	R	L	RL	RL	RL	RL	RL	RL	

Arap
Macedonia (Arab)

RECORD	Mediterranean 45-4001
INTRODUCTION	Begin with drum
FORMATION	Line, leader at right, facing slightly counterclockwise
PART I	LIFT, FORWARD; LIFT, FORWARD; LIFT, SIDE; TOE, HEEL; OUT, OUT; TOGETHER, BOUNCE; CROSS, BACK, SIDE, CROSS
Beat 1	Standing on L foot, lift R foot and swing in semicircle forward
2	Step R foot moving forward counterclockwise
3	Lift L foot and swing in semicircle forward
4	Step L foot moving forward counterclockwise
5-6	Repeat beats 1-2 end facing center
7	Extend L toe to floor next to R foot, (facing center)
8	Extend L heel in
9	Step L foot out away from the center
10	Step R foot out away from the center
11	Step L foot next to R foot
12	Bounce both heels
13	Step R foot crossing in front of L foot
14	Step L foot crossing in back of R foot
15	Step R foot sideward right
16	Step L foot crossing in front of R foot

RHYTHMIC NOTATION

PART I

X	X	X	X	X	X	X
(R)	R	(L)	L	(R)	R	(L)	(L)

X	X	X	X	X	X	X	X
L	R	B	B	R	L	R	L

At Va'ani
You and I
Israel

RECORD	Tikva T-80 *Festival*
INTRODUCTION	8 beats
FORMATION	Single circle facing center, hands joined
PART I	SIDE, BRUSH, BRUSH, BRUSH; SIDE, BRUSH, BRUSH, BRUSH; SIDE/SIDE, CROSS/SIDE; CROSS/SIDE, CROSS; OUT/CLOSE, IN, OUT/CLOSE, IN; Repeat Part I
Beat 1	Step L foot to left side
2	Brush R foot in front of L leg; L knee bends and straightens on beat 2
3-4	Repeat beat 2 two times
5-8	Repeat beats 1-4 beginning R foot
9	Step L foot sideward left
&	Step R foot sideward right
10	Step L foot crossing in front of R foot
&	Step R foot sideward right
11	Repeat beat 10 &
12	Step L foot crossing in front of R foot
13	Step R foot out
&	Step L foot next to R foot
14	Step R foot in
15-16	Repeat beats 13-14 beginning L foot
17-32	Repeat Part I, beats 1-16, beginning R foot

Yemenite Step (beats 9-12)

arms swing out and in with motion of body (beats 13-14)

At Va'ani *(continued)*

PART II	SIDE, CROSS, SIDE, CROSS; TURN, TURN, SIDE/SIDE, CROSS; SIDE, CROSS, SIDE, CROSS; TURN, TURN, SIDE/SIDE, CROSS
Beat 1	Step L foot sideward left
2	Step R foot crossing in front of L foot snapping fingers on beat 3
3-4	Repeat beats 1-2
5-6	Step L, R foot turning a full turn left
7-8	Yemenite beginning L foot
9-16	Repeat Part II, beats 1-8 moving right beginning R foot

**RHYTHMIC
NOTATION**

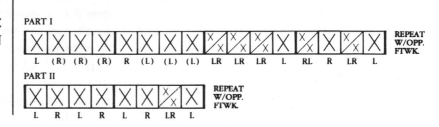

Azul Cielo
Blue Sky
Northern Mexico

RECORD	Express
INTRODUCTION	Dance starts after pause plus 3 notes
FORMATION	Couples in ballroom position; man's back to center; directions given for man
ALTERNATE FORMATION	Single Circle
PART I	SIDE, BACK; SIDE/CROSS, SIDE; BACK, SIDE; CROSS/SIDE, TOUCH; Repeat Part I 3X
Beat 1	Step L foot sideward left moving counterclockwise
2	Step R foot crossing in back of L foot
3	Step L foot sideward left
&	Step R foot crossing in front of L foot
4	Step L foot sideward left
5	Step R foot crossing in back of L foot
6	Step L foot sideward left
7	Step R foot crossing in front of L foot
&	Step L foot sideward left
8	Touch R foot sideward left
9-32	Repeat Part I, beats 1-8, three times, alternating beginning foot and direction
PART II	STEP/HOP (6X); ACCENT/ACCENT, ACCENT; STEP/HOP (6X); ACCENT/ACCENT, ACCENT; Repeat Part II
Beat 1-6	Step/hop 6 times beginning L foot (turn clockwise)
7-8	Accent L, R, L foot
9-16	Repeat beats 1-8 beginning R foot (turn counterclockwise)
17-32	Repeat Part II, beats 1-16
PART III	HEEL, TOE; FORWARD/FORWARD, FORWARD; Repeat Part III 3X
Beat 1	Extend L heel diagonally forward left
2	Point L toe across in front of R foot
3-4	Step L, R, L foot moving counterclockwise (end facing clockwise)
5-8	Repeat beats 1-4 beginning R foot (end facing clockwise)
9-16	Repeat Part III, beats 1-8
PART I	Repeat Part I, beats 1-32

Azul Cielo (continued)

PART IV	HOP/STEP, HOP/STEP; TOWARD/AWAY, TOWARD (2X); SIDE/CLOSE, SIDE/CLOSE; SIDE/STAMP, STAMP (2X); Repeat Part IV 3X
	(Hold both hands)
Beat 1	Hop R foot
&	Step L foot close behind R foot (reeling steps)
2 &	Hop L foot, step R foot close behind L foot
3-4	Rock L foot toward partner, R foot away from partner, L foot toward partner
5	Hop L foot
&	Step R foot close behind L foot
6	Hop R foot
&	Step L foot close behind R foot
7-8	Rock R foot toward, L foot away, R foot toward
9-10	Slide twice beginning L foot moving counterclockwise
11	Step L foot sideward left turning to face clockwise
& 12	Stamp R foot twice
13-16	Repeat beats 9-12 moving clockwise beginning R foot
17-64	Repeat Part IV, beats 1-16, three times
PART I	Repeat Part I, beats 1-32
NOTE	If alternate formation is desired (single circle), dance the woman's part facing center.

RHYTHMIC NOTATION

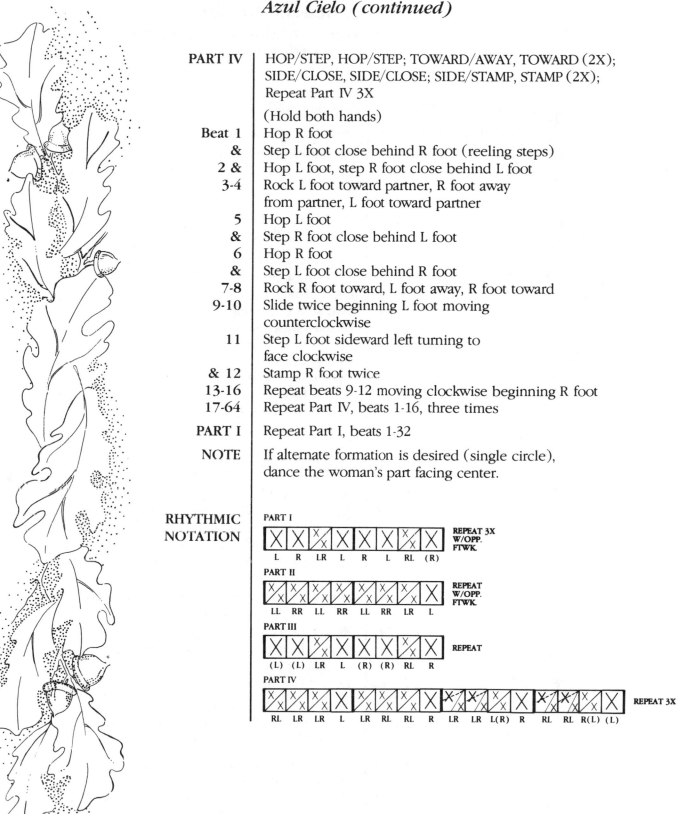

Belasičko Oro
Named for the Mountain Belasica
Macedonia

RECORD	Worldtone WT 10003
INTRODUCTION	None
FORMATION	Broken circle, hands joined in "V" position, leader at right end
PART I	FORWARD, CLOSE; TWO STEP; TWO STEP; SIDE, LIFT; Repeat Part I 3X
Beat 1	Step R foot forward counterclockwise
2	Step L foot close behind R foot; bend L knee and cut R foot forward
3-4	Two step beginning R foot, forward counterclockwise (keep feet flat)
5-6	Repeat beats 3-4 beginning L foot
7	Step R foot sideward right
8	Lift L foot in front of R leg
9-16	Repeat beats 1-8 moving clockwise beginning L foot
17-32	Repeat Part I, beats 1-16
	Arms raised to "W" position
PART II	SIDE, BACK; SIDE/BACK, SIDE; STEP, LIFT; STEP, LIFT; Repeat Part II 3X
Beat 1	Step R foot sideward right
2	Step L foot crossing in back of R foot, knee bent
3	Step R foot sideward right
&	Step L foot crossing in back of R foot
4	Step R foot sideward right, bend R knee and lift L foot in front of R leg
5-6	Step L foot next to R foot, lift R foot in front of L leg while raising and lowering L heel
7-8	Repeat beats 5-6 stepping R and lifting L foot
9-16	Repeat beats 1-8 moving sideward left beginning L foot
17-32	Repeat Part II, beats 1-16
	Arms lowered to "V" position
PART III	SIDE, BEND; TWO STEP; FORWARD, LIFT; TWO STEP; Repeat Part III 3X
Beat 1	Step R foot diagonally sideward right facing counterclockwise
2	Bring L leg behind R calf and bend R knee then turn to face clockwise
3-4	Two step beginning L foot, forward clockwise (flat footed)

Belasičko Oro (continued)

5	Step R foot forward clockwise
6	Lift L foot in front of R leg
7-8	Two step beginning L foot, forward clockwise
9-32	Repeat III, beats 1-8, three times
	Raise arms to "W" position
PART IV	IN, OUT; CLOSE, LIFT; BEND, STRAIGHTEN; STEP/STEP, STEP; Repeat Part IV 3X
Beat 1	Step R foot in front of L foot; raise L leg behind
2	Step L foot out
3	Step R foot next to L foot
4	Lift L foot in front of R leg
5	Bend R knee while turning bent L knee to left
6	Return L knee to position in beat 4
7-8	Step L, R, L in place
9-32	Repeat Part IV, beats 1-8, three times
RHYTHMIC NOTATION	

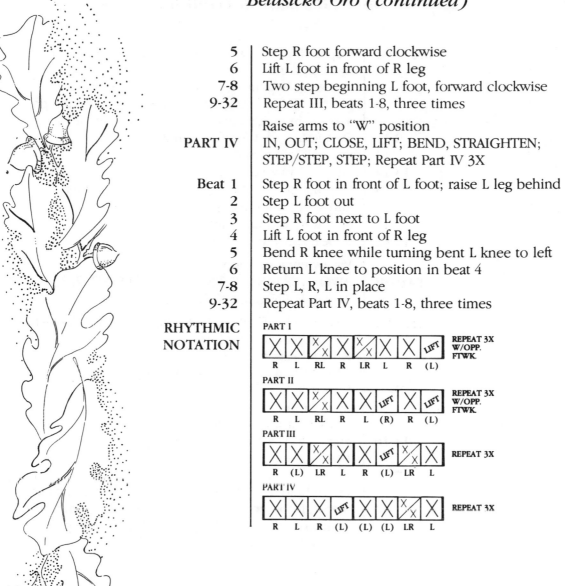

Bisdot Bet-Lechem
The Fields of Bethlehem
Israel

RECORD	Eretz Zavat
INTRODUCTION	Begin with vocal
FORMATION	Couples facing counterclockwise, inside hands held Begin outside foot; directions given for men
PART I	FORWARD, 2, 3, 4; SIDE, SIDE, CROSS, PIVOT; FORWARD, 2, 3, SWING; BACKWARD, BACKWARD, AWAY, TOWARD; Repeat Part I *(continued)*

Bisdot Bet-Lechem *(continued)*

Beats 1-4	Step L, R, L, R forward counterclockwise and turn to face partner
5-7	Yemenite beginning L foot (change hands)
8	Pivot on L foot bringing R foot around and through and rejoin inside hands (both hands now held)
9-11	Step R, L, R foot forward counterclockwise
12	Swing L foot forward
13-14	Step L, R foot backward
15	Step L foot away from partner (look at partner and keep inside hands held)
16	Step R foot toward partner
17-32	Repeat Part I, beats 1-16
	Varsovienne position
PART II	TWO STEP (4X); TURN, 2, 3, 4; AROUND, 2, 3, 4; TURN, TURN, STEP, STEP; Repeat Part II
Beats 1-2	Two step beginning L foot forward counterclockwise
3-4	Two step beginning R foot
5-8	Repeat beats 1-4 with lady making one complete turn away from partner; keep both hands joined on turn
9-12	Step L, R, L, R foot turning one complete turn away from partner and return to face partner (hands have been released)
13-16	Step L, R, L, R foot turning with partner in a behind-the-back hold
17-18	Step L, R foot turning counterclockwise away from partner (keep holding partner's right hand with your left hand)
19-20	Step L, R foot in place turning lady away from you counterclockwise and return to Varsovienne position
21-40	Repeat Part II, beats 1-20

RHYTHMIC NOTATION

PART I

| X | X | X | X | X | X | X | X | | X | X | X | X | X | X | X | X | REPEAT |

L R L R L R L   R L R (L) L R L R

PART II

LR L RL R LR L RL R L R L R L R L R

| X | X | X | X | REPEAT |

L R L R

Bregovsko Horo
Circle Dance from Bregovo
Bulgaria (Vidin District)

RECORD	BG 1001 *Dances from Bulgaria and Macedonia*
INTRODUCTION	None
FORMATION	Short lines in belt hold, L arm under
PART I	SIDE, BACK; SIDE, BACK; SIDE, HOP; CROSS, HOP; CROSS, HOP; SIDE, CROSS; OUT, HOP; IN, HOP; SIDE, CROSS; SIDE, STAMP
Beat 1	Step R foot sideward right
2	Step L foot crossing in back of R foot
3-4	Repeat beats 1-2
5-6	Step hop R foot sideward right (bring L foot in front of R foot)
7-8	Step hop L foot crossed in front of R foot (bring R foot in front of L foot)
9-10	Step hop R foot crossed in front of L foot (move slightly left on the hop)
11	Step L foot sideward left
12	Step R foot crossing in front of L foot
13-14	Step hop L foot out
15-16	Step hop R foot in
17-18	Repeat beats 11-12
19	Step L foot sideward left
20	Stamp R foot
NOTE	This dance falls into the category of ćaćak-type dances because of its 10 measure sequence.

RHYTHMIC NOTATION

PART I

X	X	X	X	X	X	X	X	X	X
R	L	R	L	R	R	L	L	R	R

X	X	X	X	X	X	X	X	X	X
L	R	L	L	R	R	L	R	L	(R)

Čarlama
Yugoslavia (Serbia)

RECORD	Nama 2
INTRODUCTION	None
FORMATION	Broken circle, hands joined in "V" position
PART I	HOP/IN, OUT; CLOSE, HOP; Repeat Part I 7X
Beat 1	Hop L foot
&	Step R foot in toward center
2	Step L foot out
3	Step R foot next to L foot
4	Hop R foot
5-8	Repeat beats 1-4 beginning hop R foot
9-32	Repeat Part I, beats 1-8, three times
PART II	HOP/FORWARD, FORWARD; HOP, HOP; Repeat 2X; HOP/FORWARD, FORWARD; SIDE, HOP; Repeat Part II
Beat 1	Hop L foot
&	Step R foot forward counterclockwise
2	Step L foot forward
3	Hop L foot clicking R heel against L foot (face diagonally in)
4	Repeat beat 3
5-12	Repeat beats 1-4 two times
13-14	Repeat beats 1-2
15	Step R foot forward and turn to face center
16	Hop R foot
27-32	Repeat Part II, beats 1-16 moving clockwise beginning hop R foot

RHYTHMIC NOTATION

PART I

| X̲ X | X | X | X̲ X | X | X | REPEAT 3X |

LR   L   R   R   RL   R   L   L

PART II

| X̲ X | X | X | X | X̲ X | X | X | X |

LR   L   L   L   LR   L   L   L

| X̲ X | X | X | X | X̲ X | X | X | X | REPEAT II W/OPP. FTWK. |

LR   L   L   L   LR   L   R   R

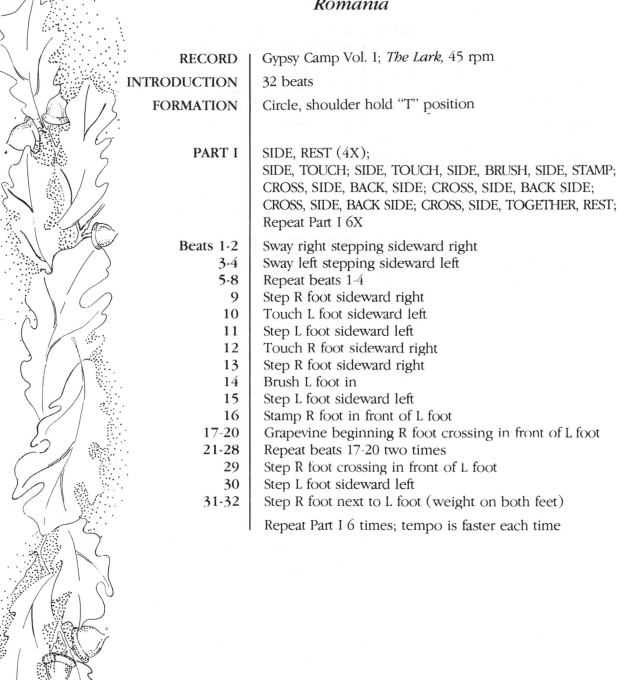

Ciuleandra
Romania

RECORD	Gypsy Camp Vol. I; *The Lark,* 45 rpm
INTRODUCTION	32 beats
FORMATION	Circle, shoulder hold "T" position
PART I	SIDE, REST (4X);
	SIDE, TOUCH; SIDE, TOUCH, SIDE, BRUSH, SIDE, STAMP;
	CROSS, SIDE, BACK, SIDE; CROSS, SIDE, BACK SIDE;
	CROSS, SIDE, BACK SIDE; CROSS, SIDE, TOGETHER, REST;
	Repeat Part I 6X
Beats 1-2	Sway right stepping sideward right
3-4	Sway left stepping sideward left
5-8	Repeat beats 1-4
9	Step R foot sideward right
10	Touch L foot sideward left
11	Step L foot sideward left
12	Touch R foot sideward right
13	Step R foot sideward right
14	Brush L foot in
15	Step L foot sideward left
16	Stamp R foot in front of L foot
17-20	Grapevine beginning R foot crossing in front of L foot
21-28	Repeat beats 17-20 two times
29	Step R foot crossing in front of L foot
30	Step L foot sideward left
31-32	Step R foot next to L foot (weight on both feet)
	Repeat Part I 6 times; tempo is faster each time

(continued)

Ciuleandra (continued)

PART II	SIDE, BACK; SIDE, BACK; SIDE, BACK; SIDE, STAMP; Repeat 3X
Beat 1	Step R foot sideward right
2	Step L foot crossing in back of R foot
3-6	Repeat beats 1-2 two times
7	Step R foot sideward right
8	Stamp L foot
9-16	Repeat beats 1-8 moving left beginning L foot
17-32	Repeat Part II, beats 1-16
	SIDE, STAMP; SIDE, STAMP; SIDE, BACK, SIDE, STAMP; Repeat 3X
Beat 33	Step R foot sideward right
34	Stamp L foot next to R foot
35	Step L foot sideward left
36	Stamp R foot next to L foot
37	Step R foot slightly sideward right
38	Step L foot crossing in back of R foot
39	Step R foot sideward right
40	Stamp L foot next to R foot
41-48	Repeat beats 33-40 beginning L foot
49-64	Repeat Part II, beats 33-48
	Repeat Part II, beats 1-64
	Repeat Part II, beats 1-32

RHYTHMIC NOTATION

PART I

R   L   R   L   R (L) L (R) R (L) L (R)

R L R L R L R L R L R L R L R L R L B   REPEAT I

PART II

R L R L R L R (L)   REPEAT 3X W/OPP. FTWK.

R (L) L (R) R L R (L)   REPEAT 3X W/OPP. FTWK.

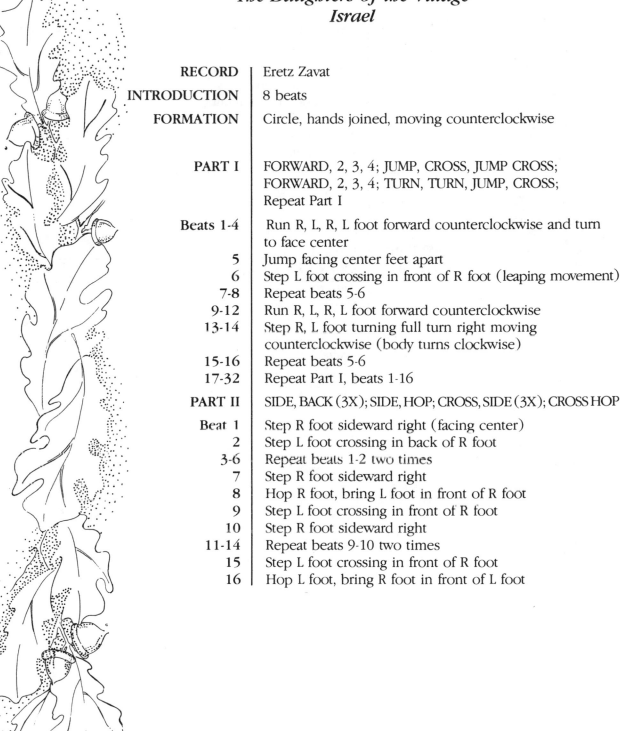

Debka Benot Hakfar
The Daughters of the Village
Israel

RECORD	Eretz Zavat
INTRODUCTION	8 beats
FORMATION	Circle, hands joined, moving counterclockwise
PART I	FORWARD, 2, 3, 4; JUMP, CROSS, JUMP CROSS; FORWARD, 2, 3, 4; TURN, TURN, JUMP, CROSS; Repeat Part I
Beats 1-4	Run R, L, R, L foot forward counterclockwise and turn to face center
5	Jump facing center feet apart
6	Step L foot crossing in front of R foot (leaping movement)
7-8	Repeat beats 5-6
9-12	Run R, L, R, L foot forward counterclockwise
13-14	Step R, L foot turning full turn right moving counterclockwise (body turns clockwise)
15-16	Repeat beats 5-6
17-32	Repeat Part I, beats 1-16
PART II	SIDE, BACK (3X); SIDE, HOP; CROSS, SIDE (3X); CROSS HOP
Beat 1	Step R foot sideward right (facing center)
2	Step L foot crossing in back of R foot
3-6	Repeat beats 1-2 two times
7	Step R foot sideward right
8	Hop R foot, bring L foot in front of R foot
9	Step L foot crossing in front of R foot
10	Step R foot sideward right
11-14	Repeat beats 9-10 two times
15	Step L foot crossing in front of R foot
16	Hop L foot, bring R foot in front of L foot

(continued)

Debka Benot Hakfar (continued)

PART III	IN, 2, 3, 4; IN/PIVOT, REST, STEP HOP; OUT, CLAP (4X)
Beats 1-4	Run R, L, R, L foot in toward center
5	Run R foot in and leap high into the air turning body to face out
6	Rest (body is in the air)
7-8	Step hop L foot facing out
9	Step R foot out of the circle (step on the diagonal)
10	Clap leaning right
11	Step L foot out of the circle (step on the diagonal)
12	Clap leaning left
13-16	Repeat beats 9-12

RHYTHMIC NOTATION

PART I

X	X	X	X	X	X	X	X	X	X	X	X	X	X	X	X	REPEAT
R	L	R	L	B	L	B	L	R	L	R	L	R	L	B	L	

PART II

X	X	X	X	X	X	X	X	X	X	X	X	X	X	X	X
R	L	R	L	R	L	R	R	L	R	L	R	L	R	L	L

PART III

X	X	X	X		X	X	X	CLAP	X	CLAP	X	CLAP	X	CLAP
R	L	R	L		R	L	L	R		L		R		L

Debka Dayagim
Fishermen's Debka
Israel

RECORD	Tikva T-100 *Debka*
INTRODUCTION	16 beats
FORMATION	Circle, or broken circle, facing counterclockwise, hands joined
PART I	FORWARD, FORWARD; FORWARD, HOP; FORWARD, HOP; FORWARD, HOP; Repeat; STEP, HOP; STEP, HOP; STEP, HOP; STEP, HOP; SIDE, HOP; CROSS, HOP; SIDE, HOP; CROSS, HOP
Beats 1-2	Run R, L foot forward counterclockwise (body low)
3-4	Step hop R foot forward (straighten up)
5-8	Step hop L, R foot forward
9-10	Run L, R foot forward body low
11-16	Step hop L, R, L foot forward straighten up (turn to face center on beat 16)
17-18	Step hop R foot in place swinging L leg in
19-20	Step hop L foot in place swinging R leg out
21-24	Repeat beats 17-20
25-32	Repeat beats 17-24 travelling sideward counterclockwise

(continued)

Debka Dayagim (continued)

PART II	FORWARD, FORWARD; FORWARD, HOP; FORWARD, HOP; FORWARD, HOP; Repeat; CROSS, BACK; SIDE, CROSS; BACK, SIDE; CROSS, HOP; IN, HOP; SIDE, HOP; OUT, HOP; CROSS, HOP; TOUCH, HOP; TOUCH, HOP; TOGETHER, REST
Beats 1-16	Repeat Part I, beats 1-16 and turn to face center
17	Step R foot crossing in front of L foot ⎫
18	Step L foot crossing in back of R foot ⎪
19	Step R foot sideward right ⎬ Double
20	Step L foot crossing in front of R foot ⎪ Cherkessiya
21	Step R foot crossing in back of L foot ⎪
22	Step L foot sideward left ⎭
23-32	Step hop R, L, R, L, R foot describing a square with first and last step hops in lower left corner or square
33-34	Touch L toe in while hopping R foot twice
35-36	Touch L toe sideward left while hopping R foot twice
37-38	Step L foot next to R foot (transfer weight to both feet)

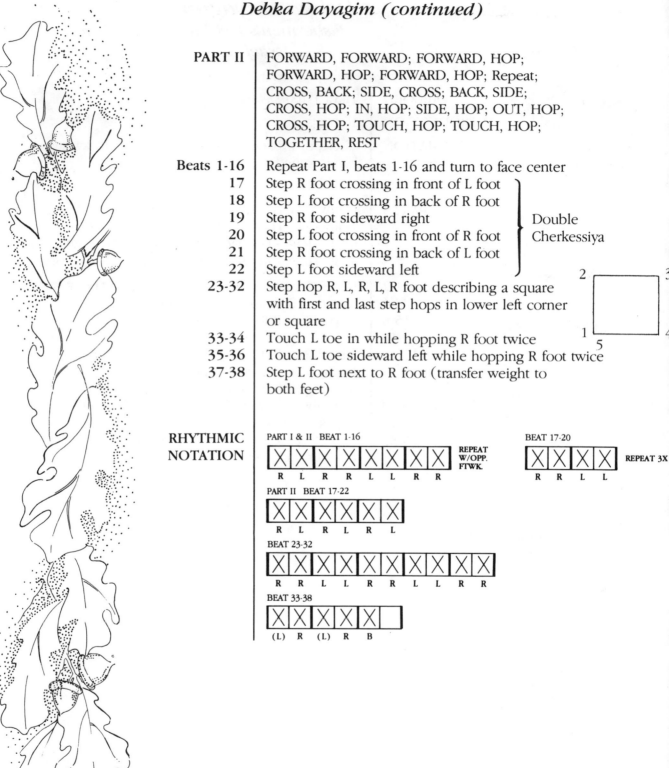

RHYTHMIC NOTATION

PART I & II BEAT 1-16

X X X X X X X X   **REPEAT W/OPP. FTWK.**

R L R R L L R R

BEAT 17-20

X X X X   **REPEAT 3X**

R R L L

PART II BEAT 17-22

X X X X X X

R L R L R L

BEAT 23-32

X X X X X X X X X X

R R L L L R R L L R R

BEAT 33-38

X X X X X

(L) R (L) R B

Dragaicuţa
Romania (Dobrogea)

RECORD	Nevofoon 15005 *Romanian Folkdances*
INTRODUCTION	8 measures
FORMATION	Closed circle of women, hands joined in "V" position
METER	3/4 1-2-3
PART I	OUT; SIDE/*CROSS*; HOP/*FORWARD*; FORWARD; HOP/*FORWARD*; FORWARD; FORWARD; HOP/*FORWARD*; IN; IN; LIFT; REST; OUT; 2; 3; 4; CLOSE; IN; 2; 3; 4; 5; 6; REST; REST/

Measure	Beat	
1	1	Rise up on R foot bringing L foot in back of R foot
	2-3	Step L foot out from center
2	1	Step R foot sideward right
	2-3	Step L foot crossing in front of R foot
3	1	Hop L foot turning to face counterclockwise
	2-3	Step R foot forward counterclockwise
4	2	Step L foot forward counterclockwise
5	1	Hop L foot
	2-3	Step R foot forward counterclockwise
6	2	Step L foot forward counterclockwise
7	2	Step R foot forward counterclockwise
8	1	Hop R foot
	2-3	Step L foot forward counterclockwise and turn to face center
9	2	Step R foot in toward center of circle
10	2	Step L foot and bend knee
11-12	1-6	Raise R leg in front of L foot, straightening L foot

The remainder of the steps will occur on beat 2 of each measure.

(continued)

Dragaicuța (continued)

13	Step R foot out from center of circle
14-16	Step L, R, L foot out
17	Step R foot next to L foot
18-20	Step L, R, L foot in toward center of circle (look across the circle)
21-23	Step R, L, R foot in (bend body in and bend knee on final step)
24	Hold this measure (begin to rise up from bent knee)
NOTE	There is an accented second beat in each measure of music.

RHYTHMIC NOTATION

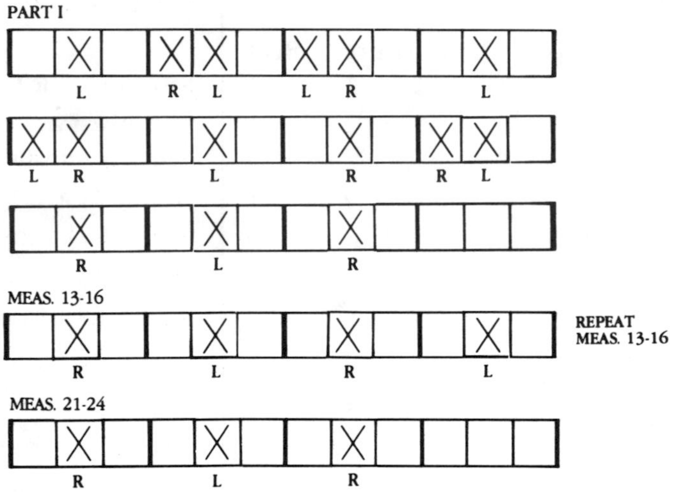
PART I
L R L L R L
L R L R R L
R L R
MEAS. 13-16
R L R L
REPEAT MEAS. 13-16
MEAS. 21-24
R L R

Eretz Zavat
Land of Milk and Honey
Israel

RECORD	*Eretz Zavat*
INTRODUCTION	Begin with vocal
FORMATION	Circle with hands joined

CHORUS	SIDE, REST, TOGETHER, BEND; CLAP, CLAP, SIDE, CLOSE; Repeat Chorus 3X
Beats 1-2	Step R foot sideward right
3	Step L foot next to R foot transferring weight to both feet
4	Bend knees sharply
5-6	Clap hands twice in bent knee position
7	Leap R foot sideward right
8	Step L foot next to R foot
9-32	Repeat Chorus, beats 1-8, three times
PART I	SIDE, REST, SIDE, SIDE; CROSS, REST, SIDE, CLOSE; Repeat Part I 3X
Beats 1-2	Step R foot sideward right with a lunge
3	Step L foot sideward left
4	Step R foot sideward right ⎫ Yemenite
5-6	Step L foot crossing in front of R foot ⎭
7	Step R foot sideward right
8	Step L foot next to R foot
9-32	Repeat Part I, beats 1-8, three times
CHORUS	Repeat Chorus, beats 1-32
PART II	SIDE, REST, SIDE, SIDE; CROSS, HOP, SIDE, CROSS; Repeat Part II 3X
Beats 1-5	Repeat Part I, beats 1-5
6	Hop L foot travelling sideward right
7	Step R foot sideward right
8	Step L foot crossing in front of R foot
9-32	Repeat Part II, beats 1-8, three times
CHORUS	Repeat Chorus, beats 1-32

(continued)

Eretz Zavat (continued)

PART III	SIDE, SIDE, IN, HOP, IN, REST, TOGETHER, CLAP; SIDE, SIDE, OUT, HOP; OUT, REST, TOGETHER, CLAP; Repeat Part III
Beat 1	Step R foot sideward right with a lunge
2	Step L foot sideward left (clap with step)
3	Step R foot in toward the center
4	Hop R foot turning 1/2 clockwise to face out
5-6	Step L foot in toward the center (backing up)
7	Step R foot next to L foot transferring weight to both feet
8	Clap
9-16	Repeat beats 1-8 moving out of the circle
17-32	Repeat Part III, beats 1-16
NOTE	Last time through the dance continue to do Part III until the music ends or return to the Chorus.

RHYTHMIC NOTATION

CHORUS
X		X	X	CLAP	CLAP	X	X	REPEAT 3X
R		B	B			R	L	

PART I
X		X	X	X		X	X	REPEAT 3X
R		L	R	L		R	L	

PART II
X		X	X	X	X	X	X	REPEAT 3X
R		L	R	L	L	R	L	

PART III
X	X	X	X	X		X	CLAP	REPEAT 3X
R	L	R	R	L		B		

Hadarim
Splendor
Israel

RECORD	Hadarim III *Back from Israel*
INTRODUCTION	24 beats
FORMATION	Single circle facing center, hands joined

Hadarim *(continued)*

PART I	CROSS, SIDE, BACK, SIDE; FORWARD, FORWARD, JUMP, HOP; SIDE, REST, SIDE, SIDE; CROSS, HOP, HOP, HOP; Repeat Part I
Beats 1-4	Grapevine moving clockwise beginning R foot
5-6	Run R, L foot forward clockwise
7	Jump facing center
8	Hop L foot in place
9-10	Step R foot sideward right with accent
11-14	Yemenite beginning L foot and add a hop on the L foot
15-16	Hop L foot two times sideward counter- clockwise (keep the R foot out to the side)
17-30	Repeat beats 1-14
31	Jump
32	Hop L foot
PART II	IN, OUT, OUT, IN; IN, OUT, SCISSOR, SCISSOR; SIDE, REST, SIDE, REST; SCISSOR, 2, 3, 4; SIDE, CLOSE; SIDE, CLOSE; SIDE, CLOSE; SIDE, CLOSE; Repeat Part II
Beats 1-4	Cherkessiya beginning R foot facing center
5	Step R foot in
6	Step L foot out
7-8	Step R, L foot kicking L, R foot out
9-10	Step R foot sideward right
11-12	Step L foot sideward left
13-16	Step R, L, R, L foot kicking L, R, L foot out
17	Step R foot sideward right accenting step
18	Step L foot next to R foot
19-24	Repeat beats 17-18, three times
25-48	Repeat Part II, beats 1-24

RHYTHMIC NOTATION

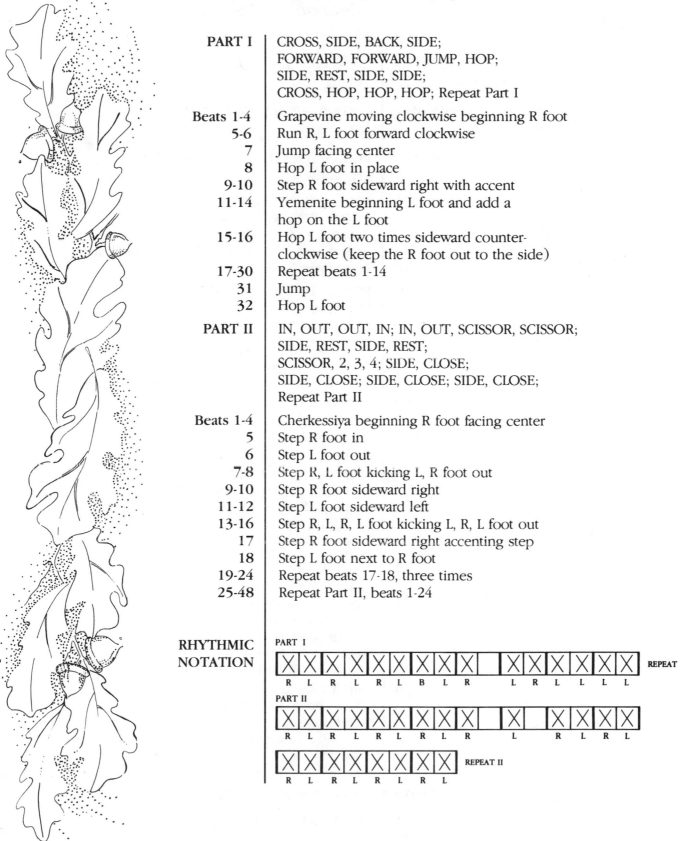

PART I

X X X X X X X [ ] X X X X X X REPEAT
R L R L R L B L R   L R L L L L

PART II

X X X X X X X X X X [ ] X [ ] X X X X
R L R L R L R L R L   L   R L R L

X X X X X X X X REPEAT II
R L R L R L R L

Hora De La Risipiţi
Romania (Oltenia)

RECORD	Noroc Vol. I *Hai La Joc*
INTRODUCTION	32 beats
FORMATION	Circle, hands held "W" position
PART I	IN, 2, 3, TOUCH; OUT, 2, 3, TOUCH; Repeat Part I
Beats 1-3	Step L, R, L foot in toward center (arms jiggle up and down)
4	Touch R foot in with pointed toes
5-8	Repeat beats 1-4 out of circle beginning R foot
9-16	Repeat part I, beats 1-8
PART II	FORWARD, FORWARD, STEP/STEP, STEP; FORWARD, FORWARD, STEP/STEP, STEP; Repeat Part II
Beats 1-2	Step L, R foot forward clockwise (move hands down, up)
3-4	Two step beginning L foot forward clockwise
5-8	Repeat beats 1-4 forward counterclockwise beginning R foot
9-16	Repeat Part II, beats 1-8
PART III	SIDE, TOUCH, SIDE, TOUCH; SIDE, CROSS, SIDE, TOUCH; SIDE, TOUCH, SIDE, TOUCH; SIDE, BACK, SIDE, TOUCH; Repeat Part III
Beat 1	Step L foot sideward left
2	Touch R foot next to L foot (hands move left)
3	Step R foot sideward right
4	Touch L foot next to R foot (hands move right)
5	Step L foot sideward left (hands move left)
6	Step R foot crossing in front of L foot (hands move right)
7	Step L foot sideward left (hands move left)
8	Touch R foot next to L foot
9-16	Repeat beats 1-8 in opposite direction with opposite footwork
NOTE	Beat 14 L foot crosses in back of R foot.
17-32	Repeat Part III, beats 1-16

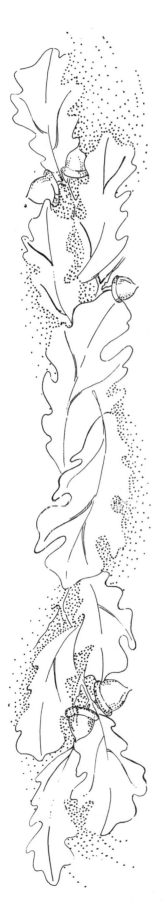

PART IV	FORWARD, FORWARD, STEP/STEP, STEP; CROSS, SIDE, BACK, CROSS; Repeat Part IV 3X
Beats 1-2	Step L, R foot moving clockwise (move hands down, up)
3-4	Two step beginning L foot moving clockwise
5	Step R foot crossing in front of L foot
6	Step L foot sideward left
7	Step R foot crossing in back of L foot
8	Step L foot crossing in front of R foot
9-16	Repeat Part IV, beats 1-8 in opposite direction with opposite footwork
17-32	Repeat Part IV, beats 1-16

**RHYTHMIC
NOTATION**

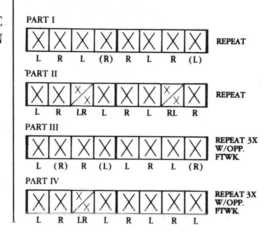

Hora Or
Hora of Light
Israel

RECORD	Hadarim 3 *Back from Israel*
INTRODUCTION	8 beats
FORMATION	Circle, hands joined
PART I	FORWARD, 2, 3, 4; JUMP, CROSS, JUMP, CROSS; Repeat Part I 3X
Beats 1-4	Run R, L, R, L foot forward counterclockwise
5	Jump landing on both feet apart (facing center)
6	Step L foot crossing in front of R foot
7-8	Repeat beats 5-6
9-32	Repeat Part I, beats 1-8, three times
PART II	TURN, 2, 3, JUMP; TURN, 2, 3, JUMP; IN, HOP, IN, HOP; OUT, 2, 3, 4; Repeat Part II
Beats 1-3	Step R, L, R foot moving counterclockwise (body turns clockwise)
4	Jump with feet apart, knees bent (facing center)
5-7	Step L, R, L foot moving clockwise (body turns counterclockwise)
8	Jump with feet apart, knees bent (facing center)
9-10	Step hop R foot in toward center
11-12	Step hop L foot in toward center
13-16	Step R, L, R, L foot out away from the center
17-32	Repeat Part II, beats 1-16
PART III	SIDE, CROSS, BACK, HOP; SIDE, CROSS, BACK, HOP; JUMP, HOP; JUMP, HOP; TURN, 2, 3, 4; Repeat Part III
Beat 1	Step R foot sideward right (accent step)
2	Step L foot crossing in front of R foot
3	Step R foot crossing in back of L foot
4	Hop R foot kicking L foot in front of R foot
5-8	Repeat beats 1-4 beginning with a side step on the L foot
9	Jump with feet apart, knees bent (facing center)
10	Hop on the R foot (lean right)
11	Jump with feet apart, knees bent
12	Hop on the L foot (lean left)
13-16	Turn R, L, R, L foot moving counterclockwise (body turns clockwise)
17-32	Repeat Part III, beats 1-16

Hora Or (continued)

RHYTHMIC NOTATION

PART I

| X | X | X | X | X | X | X | X | REPEAT 3X |

R L R L B L B L

PART II

| X | X | X | X | X | X | X | X | X | X | X | X | X | X | X | X | REPEAT |

R L R B L R L B R R L L R L R L

PART III

| X | X | X | X | X | X | X | X | X | X | X | X | X | X | X | X | REPEAT |

R L R R R L R L L B R B L R L R L

Hora Spoitorilor
Romania

RECORD	Lark MD 3705
INTRODUCTION	None
FORMATION	Lines, hands held at shoulder level. Arms move up and down on walks

PART 1	FORWARD, 2, 3, 4; IN, 2, 3, 4; FORWARD, 2, 3, 4; OUT, 2, 3, CROSS; Repeat Part I
Beats 1-4	Step R, L, R, L foot forward counterclockwise
5-8	Step R, L, R, L foot in toward center
9-12	Step R, L, R, L foot forward clockwise
13-15	Step R, L, R foot out from center
16	Step L foot crossing in front of R foot
17-32	Repeat beats 1-16, step L foot next to R foot beat 32

(continued)

Hora Spoitorilor *(continued)*

PART II	SIDE, CROSS, SIDE/BACK, SIDE;
	CROSS, SIDE, BACK/SIDE, CROSS;
	SIDE, LIFT, SIDE, LIFT;
	SWIVEL, SWIVEL/SWIVEL, REST/SWIVEL, SWIVEL;
	Repeat Part II
Beat 1	Step R foot sideward right
2	Step L foot crossing in front of R foot
3	Step R foot sideward right
&	Step L foot crossing in back of R foot
4	Step R foot sideward right
5	Step L foot crossing in front of R foot
6	Step R foot sideward right
7	Step L foot crossing in back of R foot
&	Step R foot sideward right
8	Step L foot crossing in front of R foot
9	Step R foot sideward right
10	Lift L foot in front of R leg
11	Step L foot sideward left
12	Lift R foot in front of L leg
13	Swivel both heels to the right (bend knees)
14	Swivel both heels to the left (straighten knees)
&	Swivel both heels to the right (bend knees)
15	Rest
&	Swivel both heels to the left (straighten knees)
16	Swivel both heels to the right (bend knees)
17-32	Repeat Part II, beats 1-16 in the opposite direction with opposite footwork
PART III	IN, IN, IN/IN, IN;
	STEP/BRUSH, BOUNCE/BRUSH, BOUNCE/STAMP, ACCENT;
	OUT/BRUSH, HOP/OUT, OUT/BRUSH, HOP/OUT;
	OUT/BRUSH, HOP/OUT, OUT/STAMP, STAMP;
	Repeat Part III
Beats 1-2	Step R, L foot in
3	Step R, L foot in
4	Step R foot in
5	Step L foot next to R foot
&	Brush R toe in
6	Bounce L heel
&	Brush R toe diagonally right
7	Bounce L heel
&	Stamp R foot
8	Accent R foot in place
9	Step L foot out from center
&	Brush R toe in
10	Hop L foot
&	Step R foot out

Hora Spoitorilor *(continued)*

11	Step L foot out
&	Brush R toe in
12	Hop L foot out
&	Step R foot out
13	Step L foot out
&	Brush R foot in
14	Hop L foot
&	Step R foot out
15	Step L foot out
&	Stamp R foot
16	Stamp R foot
17-32	Repeat Part III, beats 1-16
	Repeat Parts I, II, III, I

RHYTHMIC NOTATION

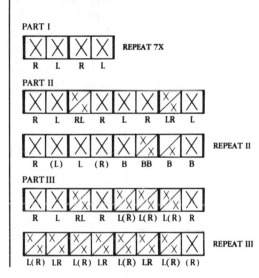

Ikariotikos
Greece (Island of Ikaria)

RECORD	Soul Dances of the Greeks PI-LPS-33 *Dance of Ikaria*
INTRODUCTION	8 beats
FORMATION	Short lines; arms in "T" position or Front Basket
PART I	SIDE, BACK; SIDE, HEEL; SIDE, HEEL; Repeat Part I 3X
Beat 1	Step R foot sideward right
2	Step L foot crossing in back of R foot (dip with the step)
3	Step R foot sideward right
4	Touch L heel diagonally left
5	Step L foot sideward left
6	Touch R heel diagonally right
7-24	Repeat Part I, beats 1-6, three times
PART II	SIDE, HOP/BACK; SIDE, SIDE/CLOSE; IN, OUT/OUT
Beat 1	Step R foot sideward right
2	Hop R foot
&	Step L foot close in back of R foot
3	Step R foot sideward right
4	Step L foot sideward left
&	Step R foot next to L foot
5	Step L foot in toward the center
6	Step R foot out away from the center
&	Step L foot out away from the center

Ikariotikos (continued)

VARIATION I	SIDE, HOP/BACK; SIDE, SIDE/SIDE; SIDE, SIDE/SIDE
Beats 1-2	Repeat Part II, beats 1-2
3	Step R foot sideward right
4 &	Step L foot, R foot sideward left and right
5	Step L foot sideward left
6 &	Step R foot, L foot sideward right and left
VARIATION II	SIDE, HOP/BACK; SIDE, HIT/TURN; HIT, STEP/STEP
Beats 1-2	Repeat Part II, beats 1-2
3	Step R foot sideward right
4	Hit inside of L foot with R hand
&	Step L foot pivoting a full turn
5	Hit outside of R foot with R hand
6 &	Step R foot, L foot in place
NOTE	An additional hit may be added immediately preceding the final step on the L foot. Part II and Variations may be danced in any order and with any number of repeats.

RHYTHMIC NOTATION

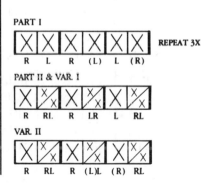

PART I

X X X X X X   **REPEAT 3X**

R   L   R   (L)   L   (R)

PART II & VAR. I

X X X X X X
X X X

R   RL   R   LR   L   RL

VAR. II

X X X X X X
X X X

R   RL   R   (L)L   (R)   RL

Irish Lilt
Ireland

RECORD	Irish Washerwoman *Rhythmically Moving 3*
INTRODUCTION	8 beats
FORMATION	Free formation; hands at sides
	Rock
PART I	STEP, STEP (6X)
Beat 1	Step R foot cutting L leg out
2	Step L foot cutting R leg in
3-12	Repeat Part I, beats 1-2, five times
BREAK (L foot)	APART, TOGETHER, HOP, HOP
13	Jump with feet apart
14	Jump with feet together
15	Hop R foot lifting L foot up behind (knee bent)
16	Hop R foot swinging L foot in (knee straight)
17-32	Repeat Rock beginning L foot; BREAK R foot
NOTE	BREAK (R foot) Use R leg as the swinging leg (hop L foot)
	Swing
PART II	STEP, HOP (6X); BREAK; Repeat Part II
Beat 1	Step R foot lifting L foot up behind (knee bent)
2	Hop R foot swinging L foot in (knee straight)
3	Step L foot lifting R foot up
4	Hop L foot swinging R foot in
5-12	Repeat Part II, beats 1-4, two times
13-16	BREAK L foot
17-32	Repeat Part II, Swing beginning L foot; BREAK R foot

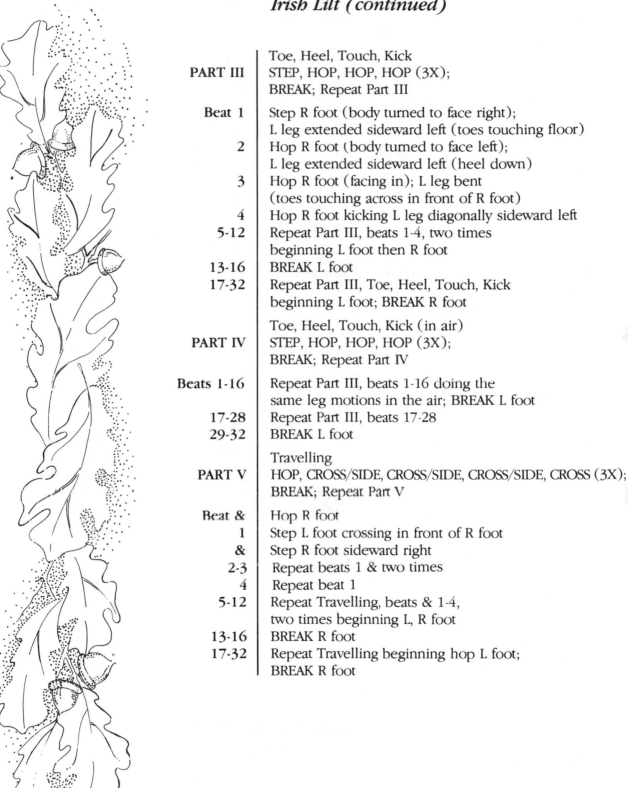

Irish Lilt (continued)

	Toe, Heel, Touch, Kick
PART III	STEP, HOP, HOP, HOP (3X);
	BREAK; Repeat Part III
Beat 1	Step R foot (body turned to face right);
	L leg extended sideward left (toes touching floor)
2	Hop R foot (body turned to face left);
	L leg extended sideward left (heel down)
3	Hop R foot (facing in); L leg bent
	(toes touching across in front of R foot)
4	Hop R foot kicking L leg diagonally sideward left
5-12	Repeat Part III, beats 1-4, two times
	beginning L foot then R foot
13-16	BREAK L foot
17-32	Repeat Part III, Toe, Heel, Touch, Kick
	beginning L foot; BREAK R foot
	Toe, Heel, Touch, Kick (in air)
PART IV	STEP, HOP, HOP, HOP (3X);
	BREAK; Repeat Part IV
Beats 1-16	Repeat Part III, beats 1-16 doing the
	same leg motions in the air; BREAK L foot
17-28	Repeat Part III, beats 17-28
29-32	BREAK L foot
	Travelling
PART V	HOP, CROSS/SIDE, CROSS/SIDE, CROSS/SIDE, CROSS (3X);
	BREAK; Repeat Part V
Beat &	Hop R foot
1	Step L foot crossing in front of R foot
&	Step R foot sideward right
2-3	Repeat beats 1 & two times
4	Repeat beat 1
5-12	Repeat Travelling, beats & 1-4,
	two times beginning L, R foot
13-16	BREAK R foot
17-32	Repeat Travelling beginning hop L foot;
	BREAK R foot

(continued)

Irish Lilt (continued)

	Lift, Touch, Lift, Swing
PART VI	STEP, HOP, HOP, HOP (3X);
	BREAK; Repeat Part VI
Beat 1	Step R foot lift L foot up behind (knee bent)
2	Hop R foot touching L foot behind
3	Hop R foot lifting L foot up behind (knee bent)
4	Hop R foot swinging L foot in
5-12	Repeat beats 1-4 Lift, Touch, Lift, Swing, two times beginning L, R foot
13-16	BREAK L foot
17-32	Repeat Part VI, Lift, Touch, Lift, Swing, beginning L foot; BREAK R foot
NOTE	End with a stamp.

RHYTHMIC NOTATION

PART I
| X | X | X | X | REPEAT 2X |
R   L   R   L

BREAK
| X | X | X | X | REPEAT I & BREAK |
B   B   R   R

PART II
| X | X | X | X | REPEAT 2X |
R   R   L   L

BREAK
| X | X | X | X | REPEAT II & BREAK |
B   B   R   R

PART III & IV
| X | X | X | X | REPEAT 2X W/OPP. FTWK. |
R   R   R   R

BREAK
| X | X | X | X | REPEAT III, IV & BREAK |
B   B   R   R

PART V
| X | X | X | X | REPEAT 2X W/OPP. FTWK. |
R-   LR   LR   LR   L

BREAK
| X | X | X | X | REPEAT V & BREAK |
B   B   L   L

PART VI
| X | X | X | X | REPEAT 2X W/OPP. FTWK. |
R   R   R   R

BREAK
| X | X | X | X | REPEAT VI & BREAK |
B   B   R   R

Kalu Raglayim
Israel

RECORD	Tikva T-100 *Debka*
INTRODUCTION	16 beats
FORMATION	Partners in a single circle, hands held in "V" position

Kalu Raglayim (continued)

PART I	IN, OUT (4X); FORWARD, 2, 3, 4; HOP, HOP, SIDE, CROSS; Repeat Part I
Beat 1	Step R foot in front of L foot cutting L foot out
2	Step L foot in back of R foot cutting R foot in
3-8	Repeat beats 1-2, three times
9-12	Step R, L, R, L foot forward moving counterclockwise
13-14	Hop L foot 2 times moving sideward right (facing center)—heel clicks may be added
15	Step R foot sideward right
16	Step L foot crossing in front of R foot
17-32	Repeat Part I, beats 1-16 and turn to face partner
PART II	AWAY, CLOSE (2X); TURN, TURN; JUMP, HOP; TOWARD, CLOSE; AWAY, CLOSE; TURN, TURN; JUMP, HOP; TOWARD, CLOSE (2X); TURN, TURN; JUMP; HOP; BUZZ TURN (8X)
Beat 1	Step R foot sideward right (partners travel away from one another—one partner toward center, one away from center)
2	Step L foot next to R foot
3-4	Repeat beats 1-2
5-6	Step R, L foot turning a full turn right
7	Jump
8	Hop R foot
9	Step L foot sideward left toward partner
10	Step R foot next to L foot
11-12	Repeat beats 9-10 moving away from partner to the opposite side
13-14	Step L, R foot turning a full turn left
15	Jump
16	Hop L foot
17-24	Repeat beats 9-16 moving toward partner—end facing partner (do not pass partner as in beats 11-12)
25-32	Buzz turn eight times (Israeli turn position)
NOTE	Part II may be used as a mixer. Pass back-to-back with partner to new partner beats 9-24.

**RHYTHMIC
NOTATION**

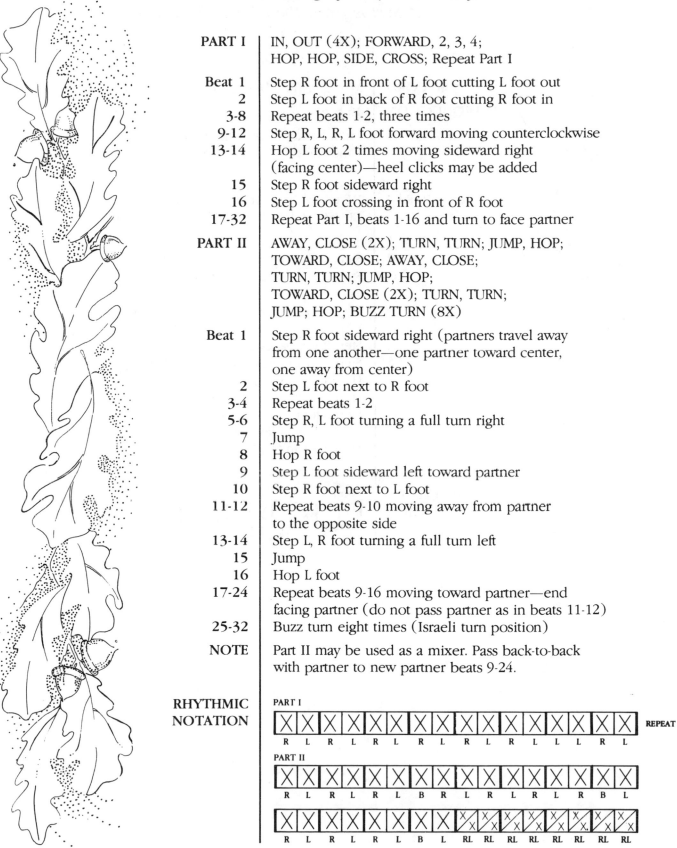

Kamara
A Syrtos from the Island of Skiathos
Greece

RECORD	M7C 23590 *Folklore Dances of Greece*
INTRODUCTION	16 beats
FORMATION	Front basket or broken circle; hands held in "V" position
PART I	IN, OUT/OUT; OUT, BACK/SIDE; CROSS, FORWARD/FORWARD; SIDE, LIFT
Beat 1	Step L foot in toward the center
2	Step R foot out away from the center
&	Step L foot out away from the center (step to outside of R foot)
3	Step R foot out away from the center
4	Step L foot crossing in back of R foot
&	Step R foot sideward right
5	Step L foot crossing in front of R foot (bend the knees)
6	Step R foot forward counterclockwise
&	Step L foot forward counterclockwise
7	Step R foot sideward right
8	Lift L foot in front of R leg

RHYTHMIC NOTATION

PART I

L   RL   R   LR   L   RL   R   (L)

Karagouna (9 Part)
(Danced by Nomads and Farmers called Karagounides)
Greece (Thessaly)

RECORD	Olympic OL-24-13 *Picnic in Greece*
INTRODUCTION	None
FORMATION	Broken circle, "W" position

PART I	FORWARD, FORWARD, SIDE, CLOSE; HEEL, STEP, HEEL, STEP; Repeat Part I 3X
Beat 1	Step R foot forward counterclockwise
2	Step L foot forward counterclockwise
3	Step R foot sideward right (facing center)
4	Step L foot next to R foot
5	Touch R heel in toward center
6	Step R foot next to L foot
7	Touch L heel in toward center
8	Step L foot next to R foot
9-32	Repeat Part I, beats 1-8, three times

PART II	FORWARD, FORWARD, FORWARD, HEEL; BACKWARD, TOE, HEEL, TOE; Repeat Part II 3X
Beat 1	Step R foot forward counterclockwise
2	Step L foot forward counterclockwise
3	Step R foot forward counterclockwise
4	Touch L heel diagonally forward
5	Step L foot backward
6	Touch R toe backward
7	Touch R heel forward
8	Touch R toe next to L foot
9-32	Repeat Part II, beats 1-8, three times

PART III	FORWARD, FORWARD, HOP/HOP, CROSS, HOP/HOP, CROSS; Repeat 4X; FORWARD, FORWARD
Beat 1	Step R foot forward counterclockwise
2	Step L foot forward counterclockwise
3 &	Hop L foot 2 times turning to face clockwise carrying R foot across in front of L leg
4	Step R foot crossing in front of L foot
5 &	Hop R foot 2 times turning to face counterclockwise carrying L foot across in front of R leg
6	Step L foot crossing in front of R foot
7-30	Repeat Part III, beats 1-6, four times
31-32	Step R, L foot forward counterclockwise

(continued)

Karagouna (9 part) (continued)

PART IV	SIDE, CLOSE (8X)
Beat 1	Step R foot sideward right (face center) twisting R heel out slightly
2	Step L foot next to R foot straightening R foot
3-16	Repeat Part IV, beats 1-2, seven times
PART V	FORWARD, FORWARD, BOUNCE/BOUNCE, BOUNCE or FORWARD, FORWARD, DOWN, UP; Repeat Part V 3X
Beat 1	Step R foot forward counterclockwise
2	Step L foot forward counterclockwise
3-4	Step R foot next to L foot transferring weight to both feet (women bounce heels 3 times while men do a deep knee bend and raise up)
5-16	Repeat Part V, beats 1-4, three times
PART VI	SIDE, TOUCH, IN, HEEL; OUT, TOUCH, SIDE, TOUCH; Repeat Part VI 3X
Beat 1	Step R foot sideward right
2	Touch L foot next to R foot
3	Step L foot in toward center (dancers come close together lowering forearms parallel to the floor)
4	Sweep R foot in to center and touch R heel (bend L knee)
5	Step R foot out
6	Touch L foot next to R foot
7	Step L foot sideward left
8	Touch R foot next to L foot
9-32	Repeat Part VI, beats 1-8, three times
PART VII	FORWARD, FORWARD, FORWARD, HEEL; Repeat Part VII 3X
Beats 1-2	Step R, L foot forward counterclockwise
3	Step R foot forward counterclockwise and pivot to face clockwise
4	Touch L heel forward
5-8	Step L, R, L foot forward clockwise and touch R heel counterclockwise
9-16	Repeat Part VII, beats 1-8
PART VIII	SIDE, BACK, SIDE, HEEL; STEP, HOP/HOP, TOGETHER, HEEL; Repeat Part VIII 3X
Beat 1	Step R foot sideward right
2	Step L foot crossing in back of R foot
3	Step R foot sideward right
4	Extend L heel diagonally left

Karagouna (9 part) (continued)

5	Step L foot next to R foot
6 &	Hop L foot two times, extend R leg sideward in air with straight knee
7	Men: Deep knee bend; Women: Partial knee bend or jump twice
8	Extend R heel diagonally in right
9-32	Repeat Part VIII, beats 1-8, three times
PART IX	IN, IN/IN; IN, IN/IN; OUT, OUT/OUT; TURN/TURN, TURN
Beat 1	Step R foot in toward center
2 &	Step L, R foot in toward center
3	Step L foot in toward center
4 &	Step R, L foot in toward center
5-6	Step R, L, R foot (5, 6 &) out away from center
7 &	Step L, R foot turning left moving body counterclockwise (release hands)
8	Step L foot facing center (extend R heel diagonally in)

RHYTHMIC NOTATION

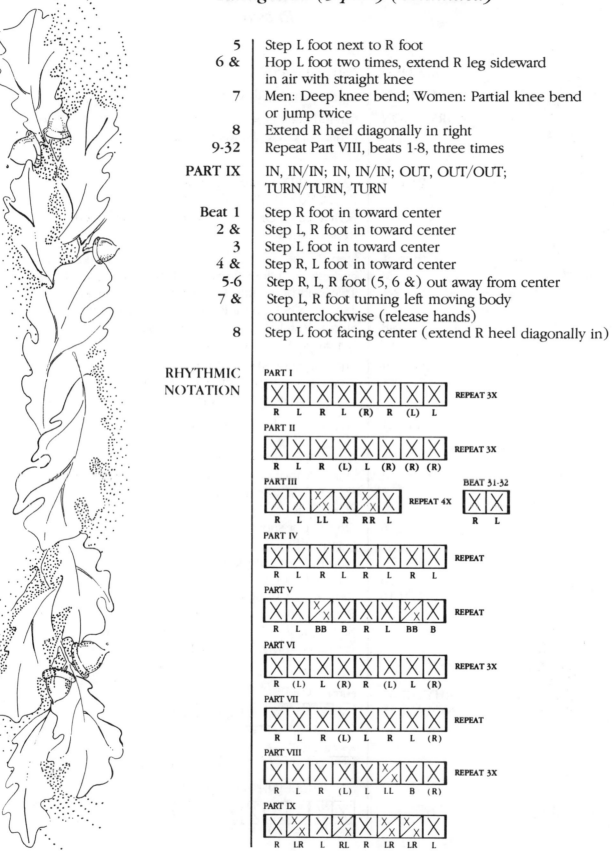

Katia
Russia

RECORD	National N-4520
INTRODUCTION	Begin dance with vocal
FORMATION	Circle facing clockwise, arms straight toward center of circle, hands joined
PART I	BACKWARD, FORWARD/CLOSE; FORWARD, FORWARD/CLOSE; FORWARD, FORWARD; FORWARD, FORWARD; Repeat Part I
Beat 1	Step R foot backward with a leap (bend R knee and extend L foot forward off the floor, knee straight)
2-3	Two step beginning L foot forward clockwise
4-5	Two step beginning R foot forward clockwise
6-8	Step L, R, L foot forward clockwise
9-16	Repeat Part I, beats 1-8
PART II	SIDE, STAMP; SIDE, STAMP; SIDE/STAMP, SIDE/STAMP, STEP/STEP, STAMP; Repeat; SIDE, STAMP, SIDE, STAMP; TURN, 2, 3, 4
Beat 1	Step R foot slightly sideward right
2	Stamp L foot next to R foot
3	Step L foot slightly sideward left
4	Stamp R foot next to L foot
5	Step R foot slightly sideward right
&	Stamp L foot
6	Step L foot slightly sideward left
&	Stamp R foot
7&	Step R, L foot in place
8	Stamp R foot
9-16	Repeat Part II, beats 1-8
17-20	Repeat Part II, beats 1-4
21-24	Step R, L, R, L foot turning a full turn right (airplane turn), L arm high and R arm low
RHYTHMIC NOTATION	

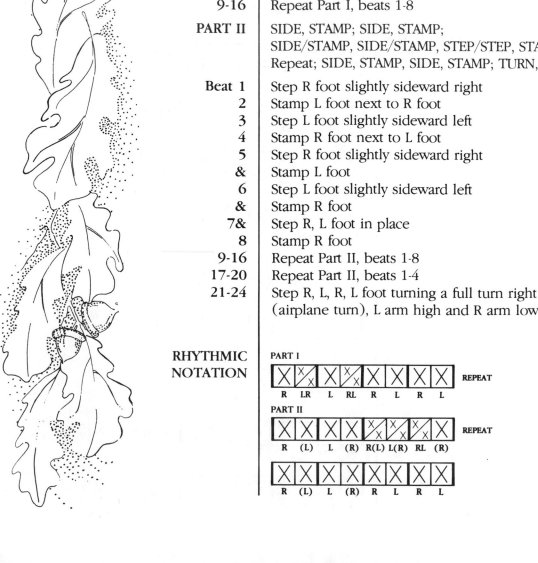

PART I

R   LR   L   RL   R   L   R   L   REPEAT

PART II

R   (L)   L   (R)   R(L)   L(R)   RL   (R)   REPEAT

R   (L)   L   (R)   R   L   R   L

Ki Hivshiloo
For the Vines Have Blossomed
Israel

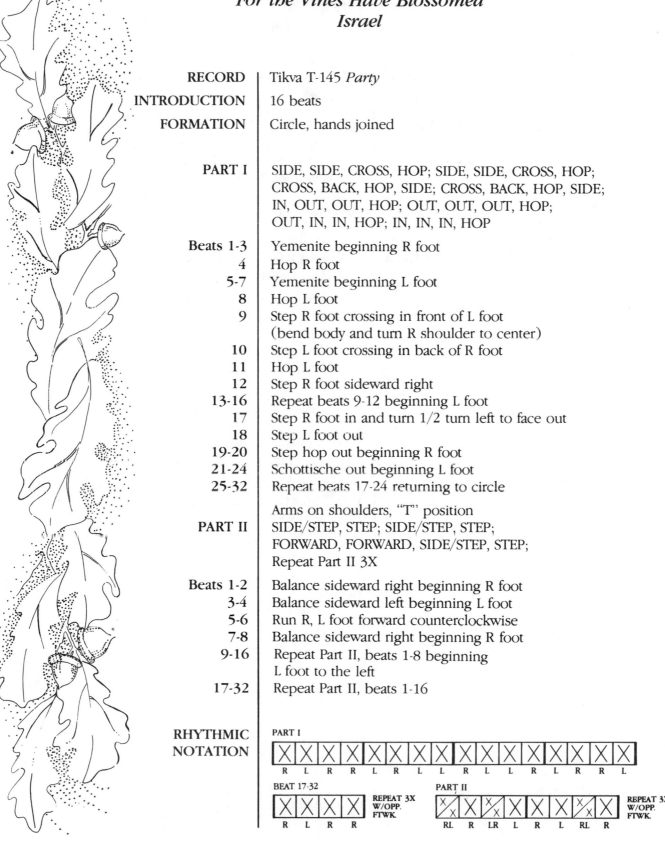

RECORD	Tikva T-145 *Party*
INTRODUCTION	16 beats
FORMATION	Circle, hands joined
PART I	SIDE, SIDE, CROSS, HOP; SIDE, SIDE, CROSS, HOP; CROSS, BACK, HOP, SIDE; CROSS, BACK, HOP, SIDE; IN, OUT, OUT, HOP; OUT, OUT, OUT, HOP; OUT, IN, IN, HOP; IN, IN, IN, HOP
Beats 1-3	Yemenite beginning R foot
4	Hop R foot
5-7	Yemenite beginning L foot
8	Hop L foot
9	Step R foot crossing in front of L foot (bend body and turn R shoulder to center)
10	Step L foot crossing in back of R foot
11	Hop L foot
12	Step R foot sideward right
13-16	Repeat beats 9-12 beginning L foot
17	Step R foot in and turn 1/2 turn left to face out
18	Step L foot out
19-20	Step hop out beginning R foot
21-24	Schottische out beginning L foot
25-32	Repeat beats 17-24 returning to circle
PART II	Arms on shoulders, "T" position SIDE/STEP, STEP; SIDE/STEP, STEP; FORWARD, FORWARD, SIDE/STEP, STEP; Repeat Part II 3X
Beats 1-2	Balance sideward right beginning R foot
3-4	Balance sideward left beginning L foot
5-6	Run R, L foot forward counterclockwise
7-8	Balance sideward right beginning R foot
9-16	Repeat Part II, beats 1-8 beginning L foot to the left
17-32	Repeat Part II, beats 1-16
RHYTHMIC NOTATION	

Kohanochka
Sweetheart or Beloved
Russia

RECORD	Folk Dancer MH 1050
INTRODUCTION	8 beats
FORMATION	Partners side-by-side facing counterclockwise, inside hands joined shoulder level (elbows bent), outside hands in front of chest; directions given for person on left (man); other person opposite footwork
PART I	POLKA; POLKA; POLKA TURN; POLKA TURN; Repeat Part I
Beats 1-4	Two polka steps forward counterclockwise beginning L foot (LEAP/RUN, RUN)
5-8	Two polka steps turning one complete turn away from each other
9-16	Repeat Part I, beats 1-8
NOTE	Arms across chest fling out on first polka and are brought to starting position on second polka; joined hands thrust forward on first and are returned on second.
PART II	Varsovienne position (both begin on L foot) FORWARD/CLOSE, STEP; BACKWARD/CLOSE, STEP; POLKA; POLKA; Repeat Part II
Beats 1-2	Balance L foot forward
3-4	Balance R foot backward
5-8	Two polka steps forward counterclockwise
9-16	Repeat Part II, beats 1-8, and end facing partner

Kohanochka (continued)

PART III	CLAP, CLAP; POLKA; POLKA; POLKA; Repeat 2X; CLAP, CLAP; REST, REST; POLKA; POLKA
Beats 1-2	Clap hands twice (cymbal-like)
3-8	Three polka steps away from partner beginning L foot, women's hands on hips; men's folded on chest
9-10	Clap hands twice
11-16	Three polka steps toward and passing partner (pass R shoulders)
17-18	Clap hands twice
19-24	Three polka steps toward partner backing up (pass L shoulders)
25-26	Clap hands twice
27-28	Rest
29-32	Two polka steps turning away from partner facing counterclockwise
NOTE	Russian Polka: LEAP, RUN, RUN.

RHYTHMIC NOTATION

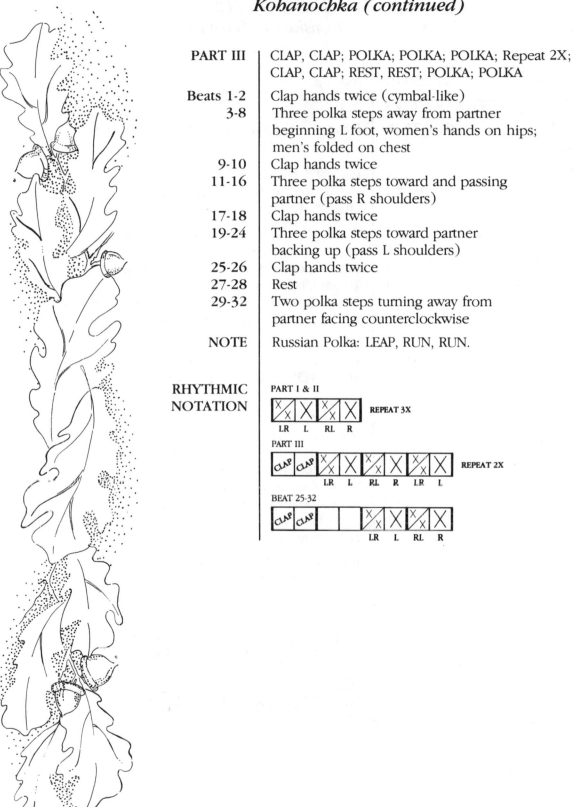

PART I & II

LR L RL R   REPEAT 3X

PART III

CLAP CLAP LR L RL R LR L   REPEAT 2X

BEAT 25-32

CLAP CLAP LR L RL R

Kokonješte
Yugoslavia (Serbia)

RECORD	Nama 2
INTRODUCTION	None
FORMATION	Broken circle, hands joined in "V" position

	Basic
PART I	FORWARD, FORWARD; SIDE, TOUCH; SIDE, TOUCH; SIDE, TOUCH; Repeat Part I 2X
Beat 1	Step R foot forward moving counterclockwise
2	Step L foot forward
3	Step R foot sideward right (facing center)
4	Touch L foot next to R foot
5-8	Repeat beats 3-4 two times alternating beginning foot
9-24	Repeat Part I, beats 1-8, two times

	Fast
PART II	FORWARD, FORWARD; SIDE/STEP, STEP; SIDE/STEP, STEP; SIDE/STEP, STEP; Repeat Part II 7X
Beat 1	Step L foot forward moving clockwise or slightly out from the center
2	Step R foot forward or slightly in
3	Step L foot sideward left (facing center)
&	Step R foot next to L foot
4	Step L foot next to R foot
5-8	Repeat beats 3-4 two times alternating feet
9	Repeat Part II, beats 1-8, seven times alternating beginning foot
NOTE	Part I and II alternate starting foot and direction in which each begins.

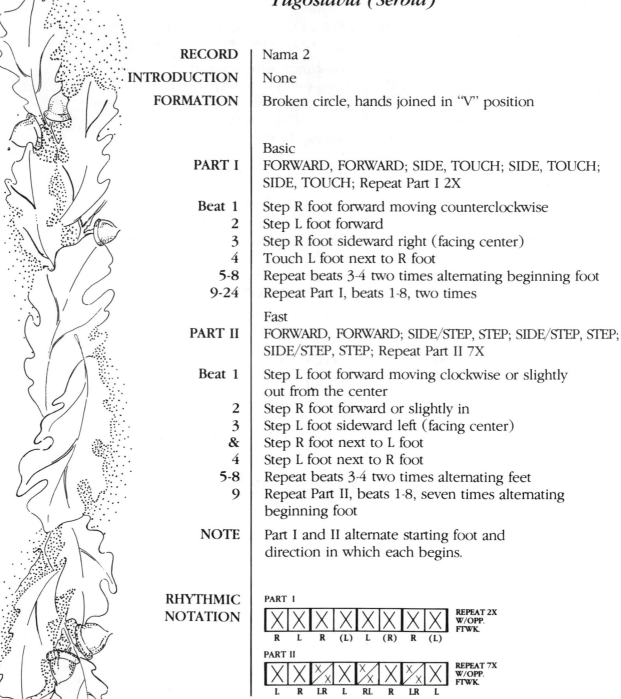

RHYTHMIC NOTATION

PART I

X	X	X	X	X	X	X	X
R	L	R	(L)	L	(R)	R	(L)

REPEAT 2X W/OPP. FTWK.

PART II

X	X	X X	X	X X	X	X X	X
L	R	LR	L	RL	R	LR	L

REPEAT 7X W/OPP. FTWK.

Körcsárdás II
Hungary

RECORD	Hungaroton SLPX 18019 Side 1, Band 8 *Hungarian Zither Music*
INTRODUCTION	None
FORMATION	Closed circle, hands joined in "V" position
PART I	SIDE/CLOSE, SIDE/STAMP; SIDE/CLOSE, SIDE/STAMP; Repeat Part I 5X
Beats 1-2	Double csardas beginning R foot (end with a stamp)
3-4	Double csardas beginning L foot (end with a stamp)
5-24	Repeat Part I, beats 1-4, five times
PART II	APART, TOGETHER; APART, TOGETHER; FORWARD, 2; 3, 4; CLICK, REST; Repeat (3X) APART, TOGETHER; APART, TOGETHER; TURN, 2; 3, 4; CLICK, REST; Repeat
Beat 1	Jump with feet apart (toes in, knees in)
2	Jump with feet together bringing heels in with click
3-4	Repeat beats 1-2
5-8	Step R, L, R, L foot forward counterclockwise
9-10	Click R foot into L foot
11-60	Repeat Part II, beats 1-10, five times
NOTE	On 5th and 6th times turn a full turn right during the 4 steps.
PART III	FORWARD/CLOSE, FORWARD (5X); CLICK, REST; Repeat; STEP HOP (8X); APART, REST; TOGETHER, REST; Repeat Part III 2X
Beats 1-2	Cifra beginning R foot forward counterclockwise (step forward with weight on R heel, step L foot behind R foot, step R foot forward accenting the step)
3-4	Cifra beginning L foot forward counterclockwise
5-10	Repeat cifra beginning R, L, R foot forward counterclockwise
11-12	Click L foot to R foot
13-24	Repeat beats 1-12 beginning L foot forward clockwise and end facing center
25	Step R foot bringing L foot up in back
26	Hop R foot extending L heel in toward the center
27-40	Repeat beats 25-26 seven times alternating feet
41-42	Jump with feet apart (toes in, knees in)
43-44	Jump with feet together bringing heels in with click
45-132	Repeat Part III, beats 1-44, two times

(continued)

Körcsárdás II (continued)

PART IV	SIDE/CROSS; SIDE/CROSS; SIDE/CROSS; SIDE/CROSS; ACCENT/ACCENT, ACCENT; Repeat; SIDE/CROSS (8X); ACCENT/ACCENT; ACCENT; Repeat
Beats 1-4	Open rida steps counterclockwise, beginning R foot sideward right
5-6	Step R, L, R, foot in place accenting steps
7-10	Open rida steps clockwise beginning L foot sideward left
11-12	Step L, R, L foot in place accenting steps
13-22	Repeat with 8 open rida steps counterclockwise and 3 accents
23-32	Repeat with 8 open rida steps clockwise and 3 accents

RHYTHMIC NOTATION

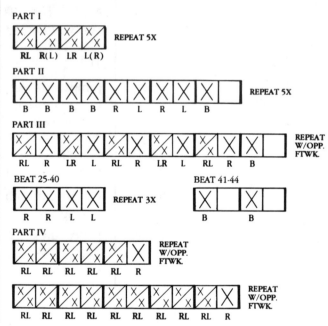

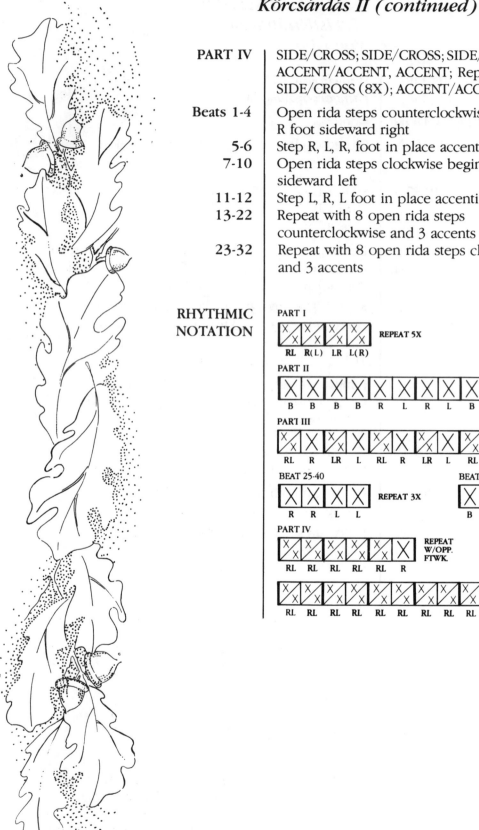

Kriči Kriči Tiček
Whistle Little Birdie
Yugoslavia (Croatia)

RECORD	Festival FM 4002
INTRODUCTION	None
FORMATION	Front basket (L arm under, R arm over)
PART I	SIDE, CLOSE, SIDE, TOUCH (4X)
Beat 1	Step L foot sideward left
2	Step R foot next to L foot
3	Step L foot sideward left
4	Touch R foot next to L foot
5-8	Repeat beats 1-4 to the right beginning R foot
9-16	Repeat Part I, beats 1-8
PART II	SIDE, TOUCH (7X); SIDE, BACK
Beat 1	Step L foot sideward left
2	Touch R foot next to L foot
3-14	Repeat Part II, beats 1-2, six times
15	Step R foot sideward right
16	Step L foot in back of R foot
PART III	CROSS, SIDE (8X)
Beat 1	Step R foot crossing in front of L foot
2	Step L foot sideward left (low leap)
3-16	Repeat Part III, beats 1-2, seven times
PART IV	CROSS, HOP/STEP (7X); CROSS, HOP
Beat 1	Step R foot crossing in front of L foot
2	Hop R foot twisting toward center, bring L knee (bent) in against R leg
&	Step L foot next to R foot
3-14	Repeat Part IV, beats 1-2, six times
15	Step R foot crossing in front of L foot
16	Hop R foot
PART V	FORWARD, FORWARD (8X)
Beats 1-16	Walk 16 steps clockwise beginning L foot (knees quite straight); turn shoulders (R shoulder forward as step L foot)

(continued)

Kriči Kriči Tiček (continued)

PART VI	SIDE, BOUNCE/BOUNCE (8X)
Beat 1	Step L foot sideward left
2	Bounce twice on L heel
3	Step R foot sideward right
4	Bounce twice on R heel
5-16	Repeat Part VI, beats 1-4, three times

RHYTHMIC
NOTATION

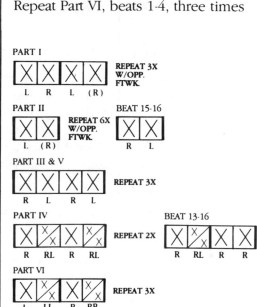

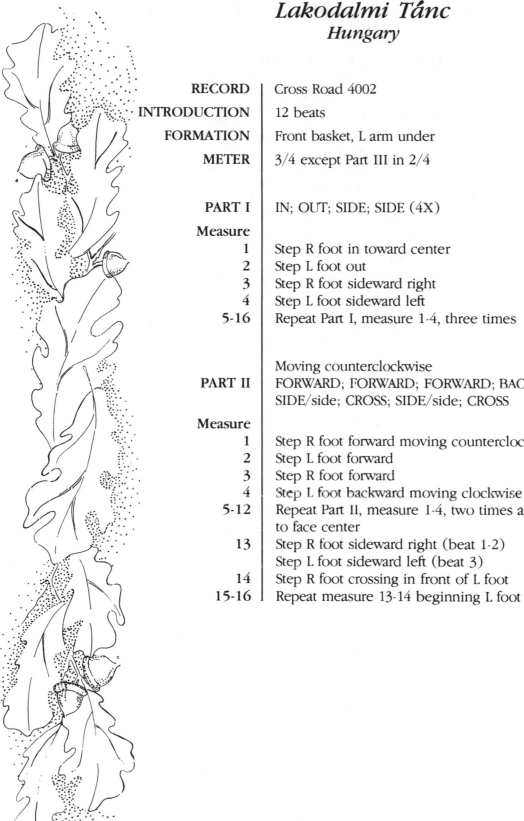

Lakodalmi Tánc
Hungary

RECORD	Cross Road 4002
INTRODUCTION	12 beats
FORMATION	Front basket, L arm under
METER	3/4 except Part III in 2/4

PART I	IN; OUT; SIDE; SIDE (4X)
Measure	
1	Step R foot in toward center
2	Step L foot out
3	Step R foot sideward right
4	Step L foot sideward left
5-16	Repeat Part I, measure 1-4, three times

	Moving counterclockwise
PART II	FORWARD; FORWARD; FORWARD; BACKWARD (3X); SIDE/side; CROSS; SIDE/side; CROSS
Measure	
1	Step R foot forward moving counterclockwise
2	Step L foot forward
3	Step R foot forward
4	Step L foot backward moving clockwise
5-12	Repeat Part II, measure 1-4, two times and pivot to face center
13	Step R foot sideward right (beat 1-2)
	Step L foot sideward left (beat 3)
14	Step R foot crossing in front of L foot
15-16	Repeat measure 13-14 beginning L foot

(continued)

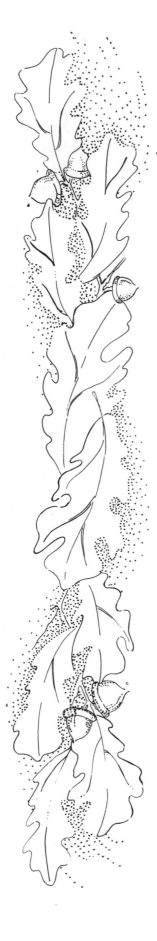

Lakodalmi Tánc (continued)

PART III	CROSS, SIDE, BACK, SIDE (2X); TURN, 2, 3, 4; SIDE/step, STEP; SIDE/step, STEP; Repeat Part III 3X

Measure	
1-8	Two grapevine steps moving clockwise, beginning R foot
9-12	Step R, L, R, L foot turning a full turn right
13	Step R foot sideward right
&	Step L foot next to R foot
14	Step R foot in place
15-16	Repeat beats 13-14 with opposite footwork
17-64	Repeat Part III, measure 1-6, three times
NOTE	The meter changes to 2/4 for Part III.

PART IV	SIDE/side; CROSS/side; CROSS; SIDE; Repeat Part IV 3X

Measure	
1	Step R foot sideward right (beat 1-2)
	Step L foot sideward left (beat 3)
2	Step R foot crossing in front of L foot (beat 1-2)
	Step L foot sideward left (beat 3)
3	Step R foot crossing in front of L foot
4	Step L foot sideward left with sway
5-16	Repeat Part IV, measure 1-4, three times

PART V	FORWARD; FORWARD/side; BACK/side; CROSS Repeat Part V 3X

Measure	
1	Step R foot forward moving counterclockwise
2	Step L foot forward (beat 1-2)
	Step R foot sideward right (beat 3)
3	Step L foot crossing in back of R foot (beat 1-2)
	Step R foot sideward right (beat 3)
4	Step L foot crossing in front of R foot
5-16	Repeat Part V, measure 1-4, three times

Lakodalmi Tánc (continued)

PART VI	CROSS; SIDE; BACK; SIDE (2X); TURN; 2; 3; 4; SIDE; BACK; TOGETHER; BOW

Measure	
1	Step R foot crossing in front of L foot moving clockwise
2	Step L foot sideward left
3	Step R foot crossing behind L foot
4	Step L foot sideward left
5-8	Repeat Part VI, measure 1-4
9-12	Step R, L, R, L foot turning full turn right
13	Step R foot sideward right
14	Step L foot crossing in back of R foot
15-16	Close R foot to L foot and bow

RHYTHMIC NOTATION

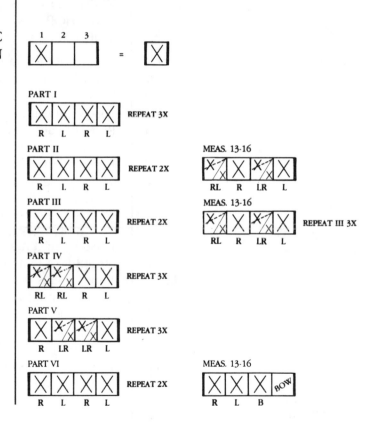

Mátrai Verbunkos
Men's Dance from Matra Mountains
Hungary

RECORD	Qualiton LPX 18007 (Side band 10)
INTRODUCTION	None
FORMATION	Men in an open circle, hands held behind own back (L hand holds R wrist), facing counterclockwise
PART I	FORWARD/CLOSE, FORWARD (4X); HOP, ACCENT (4X); FORWARD/CLOSE, FORWARD (4X); JUMP, HOP, JUMP, HOP; SIDE/BACK, APART, TOGETHER, REST
Beat 1	Step R foot forward moving counterclockwise
&	Step L foot behind R foot
2	Step R foot forward counterclockwise with accent, raise bent L leg behind R leg
3-4	Repeat beats 1-2 beginning L foot (beat 4 extend R leg straight in front slightly off the floor)
5-8	Repeat beats 1-4
NOTE	These are bold leaping steps.
9	Hop L foot sideward right clicking R foot to L foot (R leg begins with a raise of knee high) Raise R hand high, keep L hand behind back
10	Step R foot with accent
11-12	Repeat beats 9-10 hopping R foot sideward left and accent L foot
13-16	Repeat beats 9-12
17-24	Repeat beats 1-8 (end facing center)
25	Jump on both feet clapping hands on jump
26	Hop R foot raising L foot in front and hit inside of L foot with L hand
27	Jump on both feet clapping hands on jump
28	Hop L foot raising R foot in front and hit inside of R foot with R hand
29	Step R hand slightly sideward right
&	Step L foot in back of R foot
30	Jump on both (feet apart, knees in)
31-32	Bring feet together sharply and hold beat 32 Move into a shoulder hold ("T" position)

Beats 1, &, 2 are bracketed with the label: Cifra

Mátrai Verbunkos (continued)

PART II	SIDE, BACK, SIDE, CROSS; BACK, SIDE, TOGETHER, BOUNCE; Repeat 2X; JUMP, HOP, JUMP, HOP; SIDE/BACK, APART, TOGETHER, REST
Beat 1	Step R foot sideward right
2	Step L foot crossing in back of R foot
3	Step R foot sideward right
4	Step L foot crossing in front of R foot with an accent (lift R foot behind L leg)
5	Step R foot crossing in back of L foot
6	Step L foot sideward left
7	Bring R foot to L foot sharply with a click
8	Raise and lower both heels sharply
9-24	Repeat Part II, beats 1-8, two times
25-32	Repeat Part I, beats 25-32

RHYTHMIC NOTATION

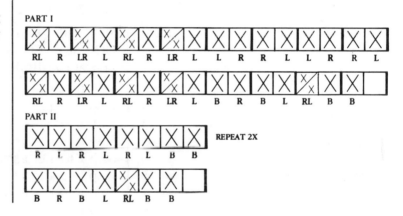

Mishal
A Referendum
Israel

RECORD	Hadarim 3 *Back from Israel*
INTRODUCTION	16 beats
FORMATION	Line, facing counterclockwise, L hand in middle of back, R arm straight, hands joined
PART I	STAMP, STAMP, BACKWARD, STAMP, FORWARD, FORWARD, FORWARD, (4X); STAMP, STAMP
Beats 1-2	Stamp L foot in place next to R foot 2 times
3	Step L foot backward bending body slightly forward
4	Stamp R foot next to L foot
5-7	Step R, L, R foot forward moving counterclockwise
8-28	Repeat beats 1-7 three times
29-30	Repeat beats 1-2
PART II	SIDE, HOP, HOP/SIDE, CROSS; HOP/SIDE, CROSS, SIDE, STAMP; Repeat Part II 3X
Beat 1	Step L foot sideward left
2	Hop L foot
3	Hop L foot
&	Step R foot sideward right
4	Step L foot crossing in front of R foot
5	Hop L foot in place
&	Step R foot sideward right
6	Step L foot crossing in front of R foot
7	Leap R foot sideward; raise arms
8	Stamp L foot next to R foot
9-32	Repeat Part II, beats 1-8, three times; arms lower on beat 1 of each repeat
NOTE	To repeat dance, turn to face one behind the other.
RHYTHMIC NOTATION	

PART I

X	X	X	X	X	X	X		REPEAT 3X
(L)	(L)	L .	(R)	R	L	R		

BEAT 29-30

X	X
(L)	(L)

PART II

X	X	X̲X̲	X	X̲X̲	X	X		REPEAT 3X
L	L	LR	L	LR	L	R	(L)	

Mit Yitneini Ohf
Would That I Were a Bird
Israel

RECORD	Tikva T-117 *Potpourri*
INTRODUCTION	16 beats
FORMATION	Circle, hands joined, facing center
PART I	STEP, BRUSH, UP, REST; SIDE, SIDE, CROSS, REST; FORWARD, UP, BACKWARD, SIDE; CROSS, SIDE, CROSS, REST; Repeat Part I
Beat 1	Step R foot in place
2	Brush L foot in front of R leg (L knee is bent and leg is lifted high)
3	Rise on R toe
4	Hold
5-8	Yemenite beginning L foot and end facing clockwise
9	Step R foot forward clockwise
10	Rise on R toe
11	Step L foot backward and turn to face center
12	Step R foot sideward right
13	Step L foot crossing in front of R foot
14-15	Repeat beats 12-13
16	Hold
17-32	Repeat Part I, beats 1-16
PART II	FORWARD, BRUSH, HOP, HOP; FORWARD, 2, 3, PIVOT; Repeat; IN, REST/IN, IN, REST; OUT, OUT, OUT, REST; Repeat Part II
Beat 1	Step R foot forward clockwise
2	Brush L foot forward
3-4	Hop twice on R foot turning to face counterclockwise
5-7	Step L, R, L, foot forward moving counterclockwise
8	Pivot to face clockwise keeping weight on L foot
9-16	Repeat beats 1-8 and end facing center

(continued)

Mit Yitneini Ohf (continued)

17-18	Step R foot in toward center
&	Leap L foot in
19	Step R foot in lowering L knee to floor (weight on both)
20	Hold and begin to rise
21-23	Step L, R, L foot out
24	Hold and turn to face clockwise
25-48	Repeat Part II, beats 1-24, and end facing center

RHYTHMIC NOTATION

PART I

| X | X | | | X | X | X | | X | | X | X | X | X | X | | REPEAT |

R (L)   L   R   L   R   L   R   L   R   L

PART II

| X | X | X | X | X | X | X | | REPEAT |

R (L)   R   R   L   R   L

BEAT 17-24

| X | X | X | | X | X | X | | REPEAT II |

R   L   B.   L   R   L

Nizamikos
Greece (Macedonia)

RECORD	Panhellenion KT 1001
INTRODUCTION	None
FORMATION	Broken circle, hands joined in "W" position
PART I	SIDE, BACK, FORWARD, HOP; IN, REST, OUT, IN; BRUSH, HOP, OUT, IN; BRUSH, HOP, OUT, IN
Beat 1	Step R foot sideward right
2	Step L foot crossing in back of R foot
3	Step R foot forward counterclockwise
4	Hop R foot
5-6	Step L foot in toward center
7	Step R foot out from center

Nizamikos (continued)

8	Step L foot in toward center
9	Brush R foot in
10	Hop L foot
11-12	Step R, L foot (out, in)
13-16	Repeat beats 9-12
VARIATION	Turn on beats 11-12 and/or beats 15-16

Fast music

PART II	CROSS, BACK/CROSS, BACK, CLOSE; HOP/STEP, STEP, HOP, STEP
Beat 1	Step R foot crossing in front of L foot
2	Step L foot crossing in back fo R foot
&	Step R foot crossing in front of L foot
3	Step L foot crossing in back of R foot
4	Step R foot next to L foot with accent (scuff L foot in simultaneously)
5	Hop R foot
&	Step L heel slightly in
6	Step R foot slightly out
7	Hop R foot
8	Step L foot next to R foot
VARIATION	CROSS/BACK, CROSS/BACK, CLOSE, HOP/CROSS; FORWARD, HOP, FORWARD, HOP
Beat 1	Step R foot crossing in front of L foot
&	Step L foot crossing in back fo R foot
2 &	Repeat beats 1 &
3	Step R foot next to L foot
4	Hop R foot
&	Step L foot crossing in front of R foot
5-6	Step hop R foot moving counterclockwise
7-8	Step hop L foot moving counterclockwise

RHYTHMIC NOTATION

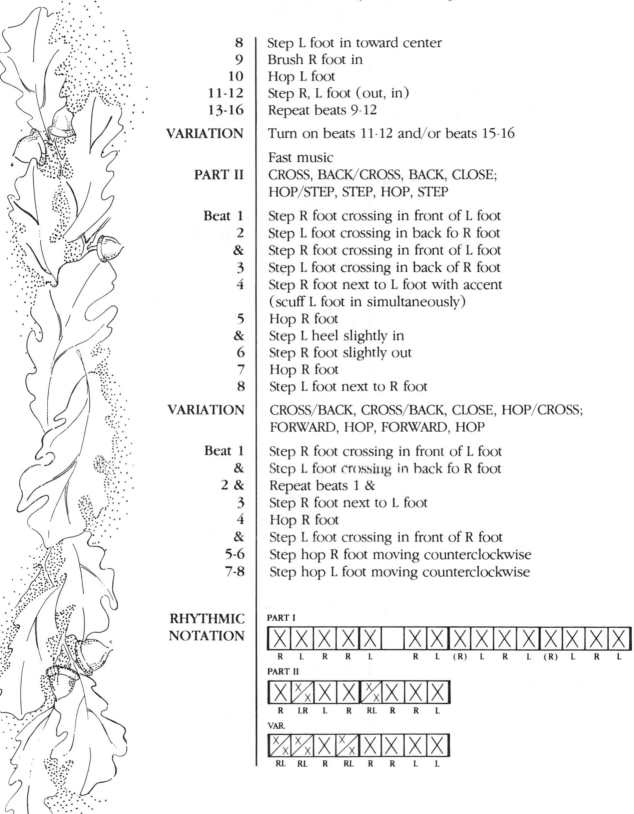

Novo Zagorsko Horo
Bulgaria (Thrace)

RECORD	XOPO 308
INTRODUCTION	None
FORMATION	Short lines, belt hold (men use semi-sitting position, women straight)
PART I	SIDE, BACK; SIDE, BACK; SIDE, HOP; Repeat; IN, REST; TOUCH, REST; APART, TOGETHER; OUT, REST; OUT, REST; APART, TOGETHER; STEP/STEP, STEP; STEP/STEP, STEP; PRANCE, 2; 3, 4; CLICK, REST; CLICK, REST; CLICK, REST; CLICK, REST; STEP, STAMP; HOP, STEP; ACCENT, ACCENT; STAMP, REST

Beat 1	Step L foot sideward left
2	Step R foot crossing in back of L foot
3-4	Repeat beats 1-2
5	Step L foot sideward left
6	Hop L foot (lift R foot in front of L leg)
7	Step R foot sideward right
8	Step L foot crossing in back of R foot
9-10	Repeat beats 7-8
11	Step R foot sideward right
12	Hop R foot (lift L foot in front of R leg)
13-14	Step L foot in
15-16	Touch R foot in front to L foot (bring R foot around sharply)
17	Jump feet apart
18	Jump feet together
19-20	Step R foot out
21-22	Step L foot out
23-24	Repeat beats 17-18
25-26	Step R, L, R foot in place (sharp movements)
27-28	Step L, R, L foot in place (sharp movements)
29-32	Prance, R, L, R, L foot in place
33-34	Click R foot to L foot putting weight on R foot (Lift L foot sideward)
35-36	Click L foot to R foot putting weight on L foot (Lift R foot sideward)
37-38	Repeat beats 33-34
39-40	Click L foot to R foot (keep weight on R foot)

Novo Zagorsko Horo (continued)

STYLE NOTE | Clicks are executed with flat of foot contacting the foot on the floor. Lifts are low and sideward.

41	Step L foot turning to face diagonally left
42	Stamp R foot next to L foot
43	Hop L foot turning to face in
44	Step R foot next to L foot
45-46	Accent L, R foot in place
47	Stamp L foot next to R foot
48	Hold

RHYTHMIC NOTATION

PART I

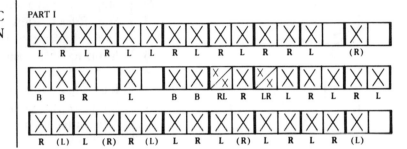

Olahos
Hungary

RECORD	Qualiton LP 18007 Side A, Band 3
INTRODUCTION	None
FORMATION	Individual free formation; women's hands on hips, men's with bent elbows close to sides
PART I	SIDE/BACK, SIDE, JUMP, JUMP; Repeat 2X; SIDE/BACK, SIDE, CLICK, CLICK
Beat 1	Step R foot sideward right
&	Step L foot crossing in back of R foot
2	Step R foot sideward right with bent knee (keep L foot close to R foot)
3	Jump to fifth position, knees straight (L foot in front of R foot, L foot turned to left, R foot turned to right)
4	Jump to fifth position (R foot in front of L foot) knees bent
5-12	Repeat beats 1-4, two times
13-14	Repeat beats 1-2, lift L foot sideward left
15	Hop R foot slightly sideward left clicking L foot to R foot
16	Hop L foot slightly sideward right clicking R foot to L foot
PART II	STEP/IN, OUT; HOP/IN, OUT; HOP/IN, OUT/IN, OUT/IN, OUT; HOP/IN, OUT; HOP/IN, OUT; HOP/IN, OUT/IN; OUT, CLICK
Beat 1	Step R foot in place
&	Step L foot in (weight on the heel)
2	Step R foot out with accent and slightly bent knee
3	Hop R foot in place
& 4	Step L foot in (weight on the heel), step R foot out
5	Hop R foot in place
&	Step L foot in (weight on the heel), clap hands
6	Step R foot out with bent knee
&	Step in (weight on the heel), clap
7	Step R foot out with bent knee
&	Step L foot in (weight on the heel) with clap
8	Step R foot out with bent knee and clap
9-14	Repeat Part II, beats 1-6, no claps (begin with hop R foot)
15	Step R foot out, lift L foot sideward
16	Hop R foot sideward left clicking L foot to R foot

Olahos (continued)

PART III	SIDE/BACK, SIDE; SIDE/BACK, SIDE; SIDE/BACK; SIDE/BACK; SIDE/BACK; SIDE; SIDE/BACK, SIDE; SIDE/BACK; SIDE; SIDE/BACK, SIDE/BACK; SIDE, CLICK
Beat 1	Step R foot sideward right
&	Step L foot crossing in back of R foot
2	Leap R foot sideward right with knee bend
3-4	Repeat beats 1-2 sideward left beginning L foot
5	Step R foot sideward right
&	Step L foot crossing in back of R foot
6-7	Repeat beats 5 & two times
8	Step R foot sideward right with knee bend
9-14	Repeat Part III, beats 1-6 beginning L foot
15	Step L foot sideward left, lift R foot sideward
16	Hop L foot sideward right, clicking R foot to L foot

RHYTHMIC NOTATION

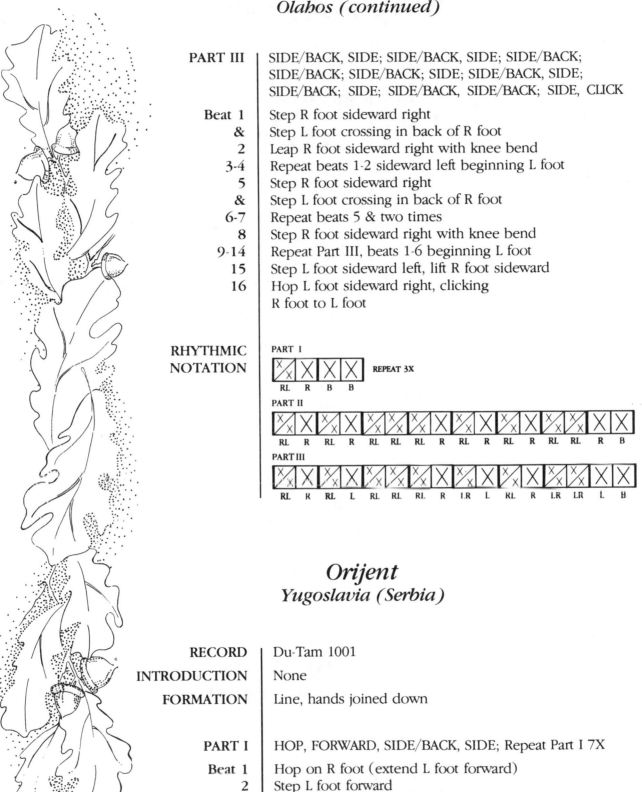

PART I

REPEAT 3X

RL R B B

PART II

RL R RL R RL RL RL R RL R RL R RL RL R B

PART III

RL R RL L RL RL RL R LR L RL R LR LR L B

Orijent
Yugoslavia (Serbia)

RECORD	Du-Tam 1001
INTRODUCTION	None
FORMATION	Line, hands joined down
PART I	HOP, FORWARD, SIDE/BACK, SIDE; Repeat Part I 7X
Beat 1	Hop on R foot (extend L foot forward)
2	Step L foot forward
3	Step R foot sideward right
&	Step L foot crossing in back of R foot
4	Step R foot sideward right and turn to face forward
5-32	Repeat Part I, beats 1-4, seven times *(continued)*

Orijent (continued)

PART II	SIDE, IN, IN, REST; OUT, OUT, OUT, REST; Repeat Part II 3X
Beat 1	Step L foot sideward left (wide step)
2	Step R foot in toward center (in front of L foot)
3-4	Step L foot in toward center
5-7	Step R, L, R foot out
8	Hold
9-32	Repeat Part II, beats 1-8, three times
PART III	IN, IN, IN/IN, IN; IN, IN, IN/IN, IN; OUT, OUT, OUT/OUT, OUT; OUT, OUT, OUT/OUT, OUT; Repeat Part III
Beat 1	Step L foot in turning heels left
2	Step R foot in turning heels right
3 & 4	Step L, R, L foot in turning heels
5-8	Repeat beats 1-4 beginning R foot
9-16	Repeat beats 1-8 moving out turning heels
17-32	Repeat Part III, beats 1-16

Beats 1, 2, 3&4: Keep feet close together

RHYTHMIC NOTATION

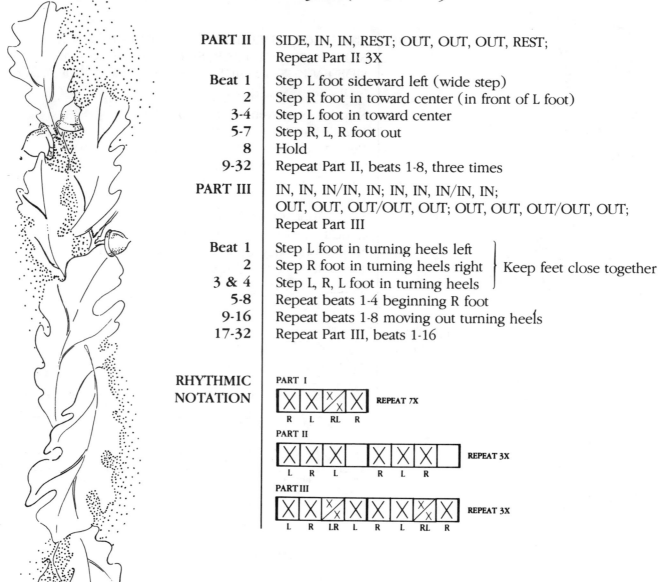

PART I

R L RL R   REPEAT 7X

PART II

L R L   R L R   REPEAT 3X

PART III

L R LR L R L RL R   REPEAT 3X

Pogonissios
Greece (Epirus)

RECORD	Panhellenion
INTRODUCTION	24 beats
FORMATION	Broken circle, hands held "V" position

Pogonissios (continued)

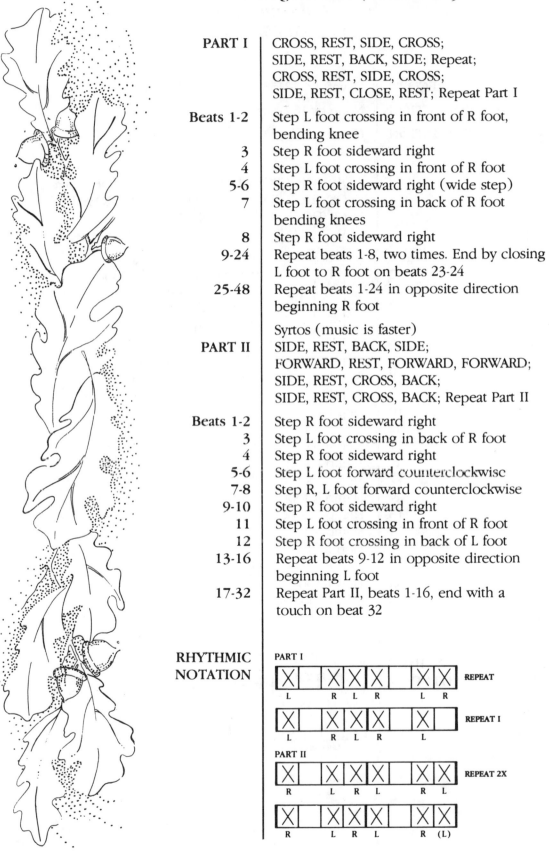

PART I	CROSS, REST, SIDE, CROSS; SIDE, REST, BACK, SIDE; Repeat; CROSS, REST, SIDE, CROSS; SIDE, REST, CLOSE, REST; Repeat Part I
Beats 1-2	Step L foot crossing in front of R foot, bending knee
3	Step R foot sideward right
4	Step L foot crossing in front of R foot
5-6	Step R foot sideward right (wide step)
7	Step L foot crossing in back of R foot bending knees
8	Step R foot sideward right
9-24	Repeat beats 1-8, two times. End by closing L foot to R foot on beats 23-24
25-48	Repeat beats 1-24 in opposite direction beginning R foot
PART II	Syrtos (music is faster) SIDE, REST, BACK, SIDE; FORWARD, REST, FORWARD, FORWARD; SIDE, REST, CROSS, BACK; SIDE, REST, CROSS, BACK; Repeat Part II
Beats 1-2	Step R foot sideward right
3	Step L foot crossing in back of R foot
4	Step R foot sideward right
5-6	Step L foot forward counterclockwise
7-8	Step R, L foot forward counterclockwise
9-10	Step R foot sideward right
11	Step L foot crossing in front of R foot
12	Step R foot crossing in back of L foot
13-16	Repeat beats 9-12 in opposite direction beginning L foot
17-32	Repeat Part II, beats 1-16, end with a touch on beat 32

RHYTHMIC NOTATION

PART I

X		X	X	X		X	X		**REPEAT**
L		R	L	R		L	R		

X		X	X	X		X		**REPEAT I**
L		R	L	R		L		

PART II

X		X	X	X		X	X		**REPEAT 2X**
R		L	R	L		R	L		

X		X	X	X		X	X	
R		L	R	L		R	(L)	

Promuletul
The Little Tree
Romania (Muntenia)

RECORD	Nevofoon 12153 *Romanian Folkdances*
INTRODUCTION	None or 16 beats
FORMATION	Closed circle, hands held in "W" position

PART I SIDE/HOP, CROSS/HOP; BACK/HOP, SIDE/HOP; CROSS/HOP, BACK/HOP; SIDE/HOP, CROSS/HOP; BACK/HOP, IN/STAMP; IN/STAMP, IN/STAMP; STAMP, STAMP/HOP; OUT/HOP, OUT/HOP

Beat	
1	Step hop R foot slightly sideward right
2	Step hop L foot crossing in front of R foot
3	Step hop R foot crossing in back of L foot
4	Step hop L foot slightly sideward left
5	Step hop R foot crossing in front of L foot
6	Step hop L foot crossing in back of R foot
7	Step hop R foot slightly sideward right
8	Step hop L foot crossing in front of R foot
9	Step hop R foot crossing in back of L foot
10	Step L foot slightly in toward the center
&	Stamp R foot
11	Step R foot in
&	Stamp L foot
12	Step L foot in
&	Stamp R foot
13	Stamp R foot
14	Stamp R foot
&	Hop L foot
15	Step R foot out away from the center (reel style)
&	Hop R foot
16	Step L foot out (reel style)
&	Hop L foot

RHYTHMIC NOTATION

PART I

X	X	X	X	REPEAT
X	X	X	X	

RR LL   RR LL

X	X	X	X	X	X	X	X
X	X	X	X		X	X	X

RR L(R) R(L) L(R) (R) (R)L RR LL

Seljančica Kolo
Student Kolo
Yugoslavia (Serbia)

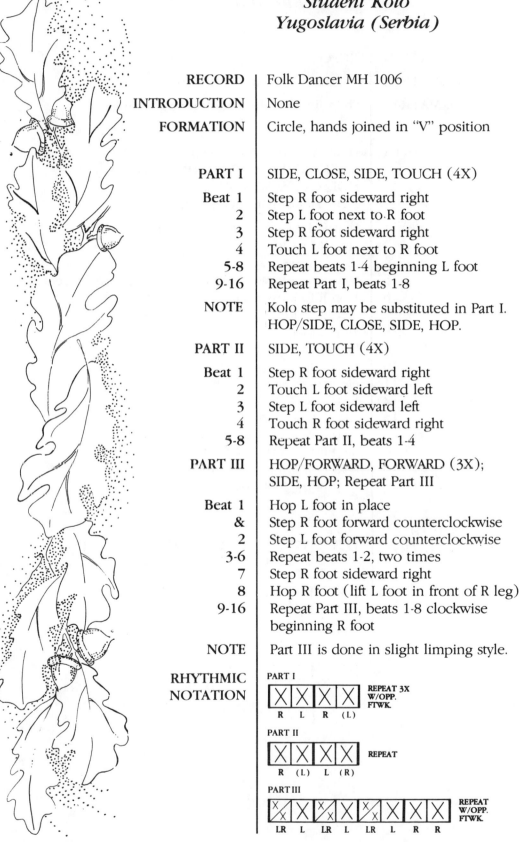

RECORD	Folk Dancer MH 1006
INTRODUCTION	None
FORMATION	Circle, hands joined in "V" position

PART I	SIDE, CLOSE, SIDE, TOUCH (4X)
Beat 1	Step R foot sideward right
2	Step L foot next to R foot
3	Step R foot sideward right
4	Touch L foot next to R foot
5-8	Repeat beats 1-4 beginning L foot
9-16	Repeat Part I, beats 1-8
NOTE	Kolo step may be substituted in Part I. HOP/SIDE, CLOSE, SIDE, HOP.

PART II	SIDE, TOUCH (4X)
Beat 1	Step R foot sideward right
2	Touch L foot sideward left
3	Step L foot sideward left
4	Touch R foot sideward right
5-8	Repeat Part II, beats 1-4

PART III	HOP/FORWARD, FORWARD (3X); SIDE, HOP; Repeat Part III
Beat 1	Hop L foot in place
&	Step R foot forward counterclockwise
2	Step L foot forward counterclockwise
3-6	Repeat beats 1-2, two times
7	Step R foot sideward right
8	Hop R foot (lift L foot in front of R leg)
9-16	Repeat Part III, beats 1-8 clockwise beginning R foot
NOTE	Part III is done in slight limping style.

RHYTHMIC NOTATION	

PART I

X	X	X	X	REPEAT 3X W/OPP. FTWK.
R	L	R	(L)	

PART II

X	X	X	X	REPEAT
R	(L)	L	(R)	

PART III

X X	X	X X	X	X X	X	X	X	REPEAT W/OPP. FTWK.
LR	L	LR	L	LR	L	R	R	

Shopsko Za Pojas
Bulgaria

RECORD	XOPO 331
INTRODUCTION	4 beats or 22 beats
FORMATION	Short line with belt hold; R arm is under
PART I	FORWARD/FORWARD, FORWARD (2X); FORWARD, HOP; CROSS, HOP; SIDE, HOP; SIDE, CROSS; SIDE, BACK; SIDE, HOP; SIDE, HOP; SIDE, HOP
Beat 1	Step R, L foot forward counterclockwise
2	Step R foot forward
3-4	Repeat beats 1-2
5	Step R foot forward turning to face diagonally center
6	Hop R foot extending L leg sideward left
7	Step L foot crossing in front of R foot
8	Hop L foot
9	Step R foot sideward right
10	Hop R foot
11	Step L foot sideward left
12	Step R foot crossing in front of L foot
13	Step L foot sideward left
14	Step R foot crossing in back of L foot
15-16	Step hop L foot sideward left
17-18	Step hop R foot sideward right
19-20	Step hop L foot sideward left

RHYTHMIC NOTATION

PART I

X/X	X	X/X	X	X	X	X	X	X	X	X	X	X	X
RL	R	LR	L	R	R	L	L	R	R	L	R	L	L

X	X	X	X
R	R	L	L

Somogy Csárdás
Couple Dance from Somogy
Hungary (Southwest)

RECORD	Qualiton LP 18007 Side B, band 3
INTRODUCTION	None
FORMATION	Partners (couples); man's step described, woman uses opposite footwork Parts I and II
PART I	SIDE, CROSS, FORWARD, LIFT; SIDE, BACK, SIDE, CLICK
Beat 1	Step L foot sideward left turning slightly left
2	Step R foot crossing in front of L foot
3	Step L foot diagonally forward left
4	Lift R foot
5	Step R foot sideward right turning to face partner
6	Step L foot crossing in back of R foot
7	Step R foot sideward
8	Close L foot to R foot with heel click
PART II	SIDE, CROSS, FORWARD, LIFT; SIDE, BACK, APART, TOGETHER
Beats 1-4	Repeat Part I, beats 1-4
5	Leap R foot sideward right turning to face partner
6	Leap L foot crossing in back of R foot
7	Jump with knees bent, feet slightly apart
8	Jump closing feet with heel click (knees straight) Repeat Parts I and II
PART III	AROUND (8X)
Beats 1-8	Walk clockwise 8 steps, shoulder-waist position, both begin L foot
PART IV	AWAY, TOUCH; AWAY, TOUCH; STEP/STEP, STEP; SIDE, CLICK
Beat 1	Step L foot away from partner, change to two hands held (same footwork)
2	Touch R foot toward partner
3	Step R foot away
4	Touch L foot toward
5-6	Step L, R, L foot in place with accent
7	Step R foot sideward right
8	Bring L foot to R foot with heel click Repeat Parts III and IV

(continued)

Somogy Csárdás (continued)

PART V	Fast music (shoulder, shoulder-blade position) TOWARD, BOUNCE/BOUNCE; AWAY, BOUNCE/BOUNCE; SIDE, BOUNCE/BOUNCE; CLOSE, BOUNCE/BOUNCE; SIDE, BOUNCE/BOUNCE; CLOSE, BOUNCE/BOUNCE; SIDE, BOUNCE/BOUNCE; CLOSE, BOUNCE/BOUNCE
Beat 1	Step L foot toward partner
2&	Bounce L foot twice from ankle
3-4	Step R foot away from partner and bounce twice
5-6	Step L foot sideward left and bounce twice
7-8	Step R foot next to left foot and bounce twice
9-16	Repeat beats 5-8, two times
PART VI	JUMP, REST; SIDE, CROSS; APART, REST; TOGETHER, BOUNCE; Repeat Part VI
Beats 1-2	Jump with knees bent (feet apart)
3	Leap L foot sideward left
4	Leap R foot crossing in front of left foot
5-6	Jump with knees bent (feet apart)
7	Jump closing feet, knees straight
8	Bounce on both feet
9-16	Repeat Part VI, beats 1-8
	Repeat Parts V and VI 2 times

RHYTHMIC NOTATION

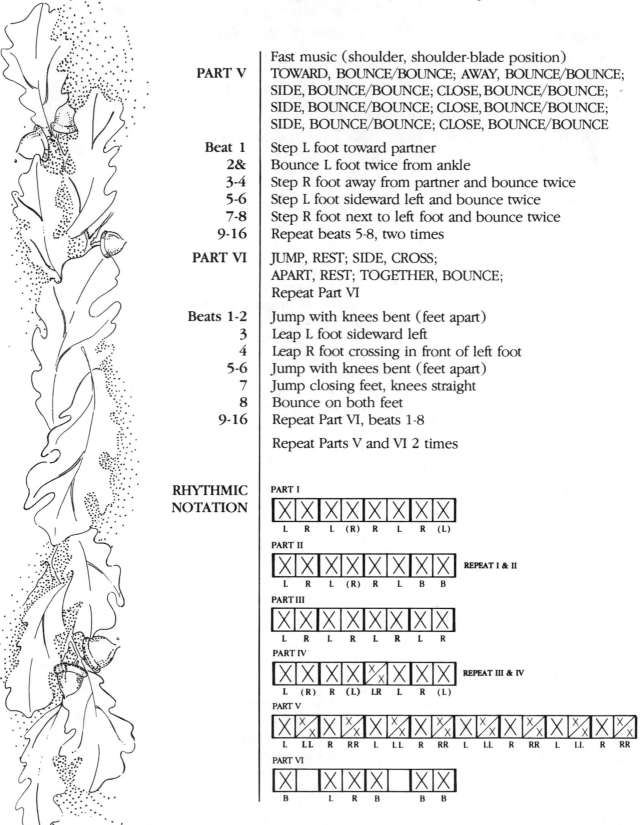

Sukačko Kolo
Yugoslavia (Croatia)

RECORD	Festival FM 4002
INTRODUCTION	16 beats
FORMATION	Front basket (right arm over, left arm under)
PART I	FORWARD (12X)
Beats 1-12	Run 12 steps clockwise, beginning L foot
PART II	HOP/FORWARD, FORWARD (6X)
Beat 1	Hop R foot
&	Step L foot forward clockwise
2	Step R foot forward clockwise
3-12	Repeat Part II, beats 1-2, five times
PART III	SIDE, CLOSE; SIDE, TOUCH;
	SIDE, CLOSE; SIDE, TOUCH;
	SIDE, CLOSE; SIDE, TOUCH;
	SIDE, CLOSE; SIDE, CLOSE
Beat 1	Step L foot sideward left
2	Step R foot next to L foot
3	Step L foot sideward left
4	Touch R foot next to L foot
5-12	Repeat beats 1-4, two times alternating direction
13	Step R foot sideward right
14	Step L foot next to R foot
15-16	Repeat beats 13-14

Repeat dance counterclockwise beginning R foot

Alternate dance clockwise and counterclockwise

RHYTHMIC NOTATION	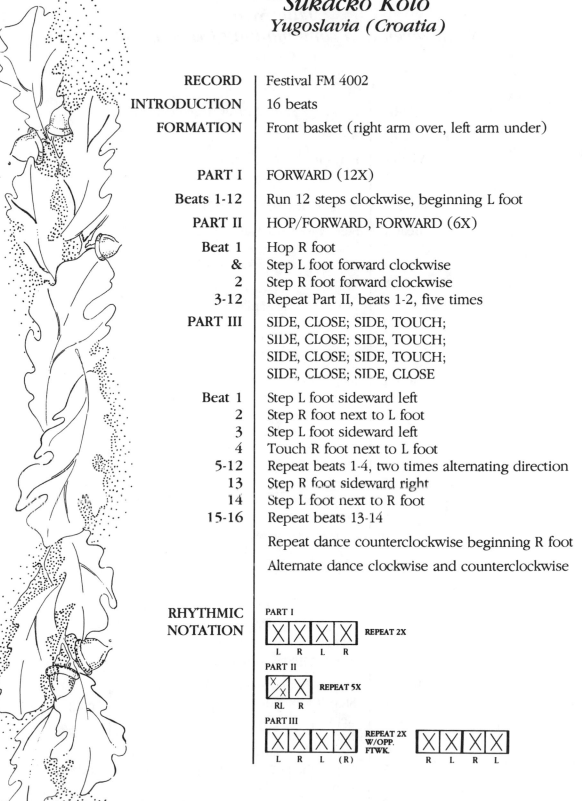

Syrtaki #7
Little Syrto
(Name given to a combination of Hassapiko dances)
Greece

RECORD	PI LPS 33 *Soul Dances of the Greeks*
INTRODUCTION	8 beats
FORMATION	Lines in "T" position

INTRO	SIDE, TOUCH, SIDE, TOUCH; Repeat
Beat 1	Step R foot sideward right
2	Touch L foot next to R foot
3-4	Repeat beats 1-2 sideward left
5-8	Repeat beats 1-4
	Basic Vari Hassapiko
PART I	IN/TOUCH, SWING; OUT, OUT; SIDE/CROSS, BACK; TOUCH; Repeat; IN/TOUCH, SWING; OUT, OUT; SIDE/CROSS, BACK
Beat 1	Step L foot in, lunge and lean body forward
&	Touch R foot in back of L foot
2	Swing R leg in
3	Step R foot directly behind L foot
4	Step L foot directly behind R foot, raising R foot slightly in front
5	Step R foot sideward right (large step)
&	Step L foot crossing in front of R foot (small step)
6	Step R foot crossing in back of L foot
7	Touch L foot on the outside of the R foot
8-20	Repeat beats 1-7 once, then beats 1-6 once
PART II	CROSS/SIDE, CROSS/SIDE, CROSS; CROSS/SIDE, CROSS/SIDE, CROSS; CROSS/SIDE, CROSS; CROSS/SIDE, CROSS; CROSS; CROSS; CROSS: CROSS; TOES, HEELS, TOES, HEELS
Beat 1	Step L foot crossing in front of R foot ⎫
&	Step R foot sideward right ⎬ Triple travel
2 &	Repeat beats 1 &
3	Repeat beat 1 ⎭
&	Bring R foot around in front of L foot
4-6	Repeat beats 1-3 using opposite footwork and direction
7 &	Repeat beats 1 & ⎫
8	Step L foot crossing in front of R foot ⎬ Double travel
&	Bring R foot around to reverse direction ⎭
9-10	Repeat beats 7-8 using opposite footwork and direction

Syrtaki #7 (continued)

11-14	Four single crossovers beginning L foot and ending with feet together Singles
15	Open toes
16	Open heels
17	Close toes
18	Close heels
	Basic Hassaposerviko
PART III	SIDE, BACK; SIDE, TOUCH; SIDE, TOUCH
Beat 1	Step R foot sideward right
2	Step L foot crossing in bck of R foot
3	Step R foot sideward right
4	Touch L foot next to R foot
5	Step L foot sideward left
6	Touch R foot next to L foot
	SIDE, BACK; SIDE, TOUCH; IN, SWING; OUT, OUT; STEP/STEP, STEP; STEP/STEP, STEP; SIDE, BACK; SIDE, TOUCH; SIDE, TOUCH
Beats 7-10	Repeat beats 1-3; beat 4, bring L foot next to R calf
11	Step L foot in toward center
12	Swing R foot in (short, quick swing)
13	Step R foot out from center
14	Step L foot out
15-18	Repeat beats 3-6
	SIDE, BACK,; SIDE, TOUCH; IN, SWING; OUT, OUT; STEP/STEP, STEP; STEP/STEP, STEP
Beats 19-26	Repeat beats 7-14
27-28	Step R, L, R foot in place
29-30	Step L, R, L foot in place
31-36	Repeat beats 1-6
	Basic Hassapiko
PART IV	FORWARD, FORWARD; SIDE, HOP; SIDE, HOP; Repeat 4X TOUCH, REST; TOE, TOE
Beat 1	Step R foot forward counterclockwise (body facing slightly center)
2	Step L foot forward counterclockwise
3	Step R foot sideward right
4	Hop R foot swinging L foot in front of R foot
5	Step L foot sideward left
6	Hop L foot swinging R foot n front of L foot
7-30	Repeat Part IV, beats 1-6, four times; tempo slows down
31-32	Stand still
33	Turn R toe out (weight is on L foot)
34	Turn R toe in (weight is on L foot) *(continued)*

Syrtaki #7 *(continued)*

PART V	
Beats 1-21	Repeat Part I, beats 1-7 of Basic Vari Hassapiko 3 times
PART VI	CROSS/SIDE, BACK/SIDE, CROSS (3X); CROSS, CROSS, CROSS, CROSS; TOES, HEELS, TOES, HEELS
Beat 1	Step L foot crossing in front of R foot
&	Step R foot sideward right
2	Step L foot crossing in back of R foot
&	Step R foot sideward right
3	Step L foot crossing in front of R foot
&	Bring R foot around to reverse direction
4-9	Repeat Part VI, beats 1-3, two times reversing direction to move clockwise, then counterclockwise again
10-17	Repeat Part II, beats 11-18 beginning R foot
PART VII	Basic Hassaposerviko
Beats 1-12	Repeat Part III, beats 1-6, two times
13-36	Repeat Part III, beats 7-18, two times
PART VIII	FORWARD, FORWARD; SIDE, HOP; SIDE, HOP; Repeat 4X; FORWARD, FORWARD; STEP/STEP, STEP; STEP/STEP, STEP; Repeat 4X OUT, BACK; IN/STEP, STEP; SIDE/STEP, STEP; Repeat 7X OUT, OUT; IN, CLOSE; REST, STAMP
Beats 1-30	Repeat Part IV, beats 1-6, five times
31-60	Repeat Part IV, beats 1-6 five times substituting two Balkan threes (R, L foot) in beats 3-6
61-108	Repeat Part IV, beats 1-6, eight times substituting OUT, BACK (R, L foot) in beats 1-2 and Balkan threes (R, L foot) in beats 3-6
109-110	Step R, L foot out
111	Step R foot in
112-113	Step L foot next to R foot
114	Stamp R foot

The bracket grouping Beat 1 through & (beat 3) is labeled: **Zorba**

Syrtaki (continued)

RHYTHMIC NOTATION

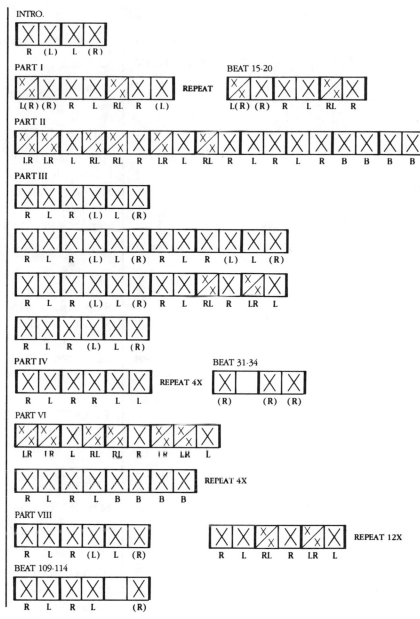

Trei Păzeste Bătrinesc
Romania (Oltenia)

RECORD	Nevofoon 15005 Romanian Folkdances
INTRODUCTION	32 beats
FORMATION	Short lines, "T" position

PART I	STEP, BICYCLE, STEP, STAMP (4X)
Beat 1	Step R foot in place
2	Circle L leg as pedaling a bicycle
3	Step L foot next to R foot
4	Stamp R foot leaning in on stamp
5-16	Repeat Part I, beats 1-4, three times
PART II	SLAP, SLAP, SIDE/BACK, SIDE (4X)
Beats 1-2	Slap R foot in 2 times (leg straight), bend body in
3	Step R foot sideward right
&	Step L foot crossing in back of R foot
4	Step R foot sideward right
5-8	Repeat Part II, beats 1-4, beginning L foot to left
9-16	Repeat Part II, beats 1-8
PART III	CROSS/BACK, SIDE; CROSS/BACK, SIDE; IN/OUT, STEP/STEP; IN/OUT, STEP/STEP; IN/OUT, STEP/STEP; CROSS/SIDE, CROSS/SIDE; CROSS/BACK; SIDE/CROSS; BACK/SIDE, SLAP
Beat 1	Step R foot crossing in front of L foot
&	Step L foot crossing in back of R foot
2	Step R foot slightly sideward right
3-4	Repeat beats 1-2 beginning L foot
NOTE	Beats 1-4 are done with a leaping style
5	Step R foot in toward center with accent (face clockwise)
&	Step L foot out from center
6	Step R foot next to L foot
&	Step L foot next to R foot
7-10	Repeat beats 5-6, two times
11-12	Two closed ridas moving clockwise beginning R foot
13	Step R foot crossing in front of L foot
&	Step L foot crossing in back of R foot
14	Step R foot slightly sideward right
&	Step L foot crossing in front of R foot
15	Step R foot crossing in back of L foot
&	Step L foot slightly sideward left
16	Slap R foot in

Locomotive (bracket grouping beats 5-&-6-&)

Trei Păzeste Bătrinesc (continued)

PART IV	CROSS/SIDE, CROSS/SIDE; CROSS/SIDE, CROSS;
	Repeat 2X
	CROSS, CROSS, CROSS, SLAP

Beat 1	Step R foot crossing in front of L foot	
&	Step L foot sideward left	
2-3	Repeat beats 1 & two times	Body low
4	Step R foot crossing in front of L foot with accent	and forward
&	Swing L foot around in front of R foot	
5-8	Repeat beats 1-4 beginning L foot to the right	
9-12	Repeat beats 1-4	
13	Leap L foot crossing in front of R foot	
14	Leap R foot crossing in front of L foot	
15	Leap L foot crossing in front of R foot	
16	Slap R foot in	

RHYTHMIC
NOTATION

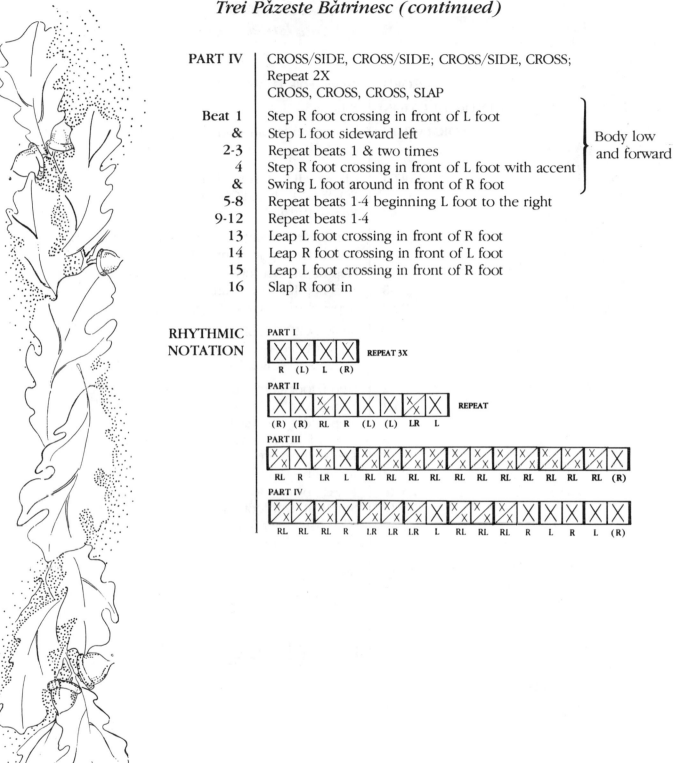

Uri Zion
Israel

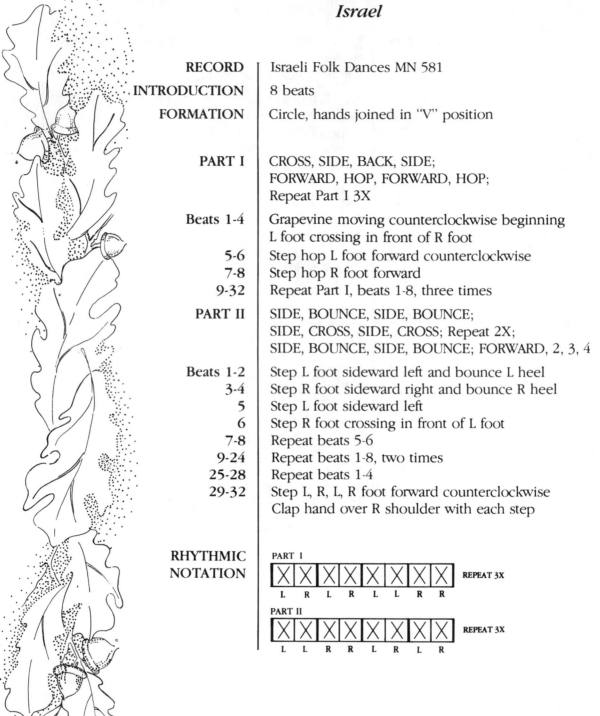

RECORD	Israeli Folk Dances MN 581
INTRODUCTION	8 beats
FORMATION	Circle, hands joined in "V" position
PART I	CROSS, SIDE, BACK, SIDE; FORWARD, HOP, FORWARD, HOP; Repeat Part I 3X
Beats 1-4	Grapevine moving counterclockwise beginning L foot crossing in front of R foot
5-6	Step hop L foot forward counterclockwise
7-8	Step hop R foot forward
9-32	Repeat Part I, beats 1-8, three times
PART II	SIDE, BOUNCE, SIDE, BOUNCE; SIDE, CROSS, SIDE, CROSS; Repeat 2X; SIDE, BOUNCE, SIDE, BOUNCE; FORWARD, 2, 3, 4
Beats 1-2	Step L foot sideward left and bounce L heel
3-4	Step R foot sideward right and bounce R heel
5	Step L foot sideward left
6	Step R foot crossing in front of L foot
7-8	Repeat beats 5-6
9-24	Repeat beats 1-8, two times
25-28	Repeat beats 1-4
29-32	Step L, R, L, R foot forward counterclockwise Clap hand over R shoulder with each step

RHYTHMIC NOTATION

PART I

X	X	X	X	X	X	X	X	**REPEAT 3X**
L	R	L	R	L	L	R	R	

PART II

X	X	X	X	X	X	X	X	**REPEAT 3X**
L	L	R	R	L	R	L	R	

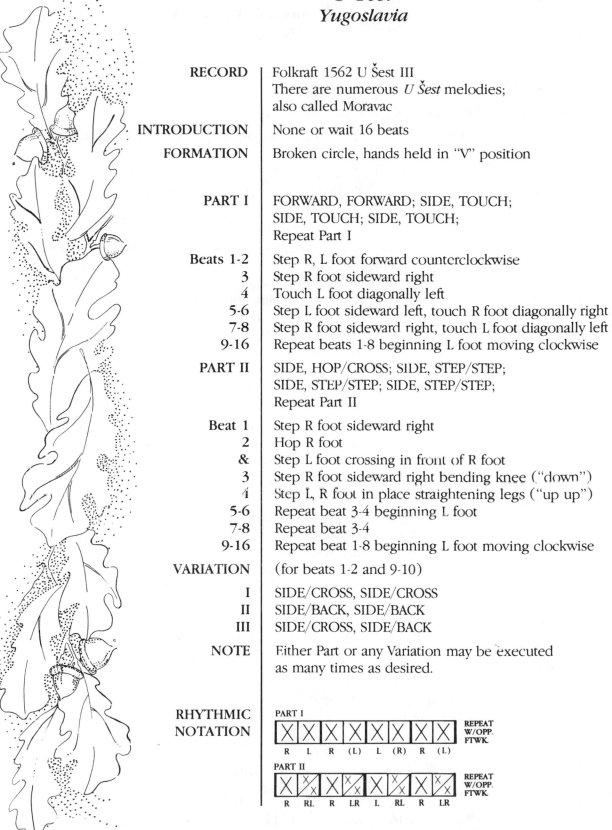

U Šest
Yugoslavia

RECORD	Folkraft 1562 U Šest III There are numerous *U Šest* melodies; also called Moravac
INTRODUCTION	None or wait 16 beats
FORMATION	Broken circle, hands held in "V" position
PART I	FORWARD, FORWARD; SIDE, TOUCH; SIDE, TOUCH; SIDE, TOUCH; Repeat Part I
Beats 1-2	Step R, L foot forward counterclockwise
3	Step R foot sideward right
4	Touch L foot diagonally left
5-6	Step L foot sideward left, touch R foot diagonally right
7-8	Step R foot sideward right, touch L foot diagonally left
9-16	Repeat beats 1-8 beginning L foot moving clockwise
PART II	SIDE, HOP/CROSS; SIDE, STEP/STEP; SIDE, STEP/STEP; SIDE, STEP/STEP; Repeat Part II
Beat 1	Step R foot sideward right
2	Hop R foot
&	Step L foot crossing in front of R foot
3	Step R foot sideward right bending knee ("down")
4	Step L, R foot in place straightening legs ("up up")
5-6	Repeat beat 3-4 beginning L foot
7-8	Repeat beat 3-4
9-16	Repeat beat 1-8 beginning L foot moving clockwise
VARIATION	(for beats 1-2 and 9-10)
I	SIDE/CROSS, SIDE/CROSS
II	SIDE/BACK, SIDE/BACK
III	SIDE/CROSS, SIDE/BACK
NOTE	Either Part or any Variation may be executed as many times as desired.

RHYTHMIC NOTATION

PART I

X	X	X	X	X	X	X	X	REPEAT W/OPP. FTWK.
R	L	R	(L)	L	(R)	R	(L)	

PART II

X	X/X	X	X/X	X	X/X	X	X/X	REPEAT W/OPP. FTWK.
R	RL	R	LR	L	RL	R	LR	

U'Va'u Ha'ovdim
The Lost Ones Will Come Back
Israel

RECORD	Eretz Zavat
INTRODUCTION	Begin with vocal
FORMATION	Lines in grid pattern; everyone facing East, no hands joined
INTRO	SIDE, SNAP, SIDE, SNAP; IN, OUT, OUT, IN; IN/PIVOT, IN, IN, CLOSE; Repeat Intro
Beats 1-2	Step R foot sideward right with snap on beat 2 (arms overhead)
3-4	Step L foot sideward left with snap on beat 4 (arms overhead)
5-8	Repeat beats 1-4
9-12	Cherkessiya beginning R foot
13	Step R foot in and pivot 1/2 clockwise
14	Step L foot in (backing up)
15	Step R foot in (backing up)
16	Step L foot next to R foot
17-32	Repeat beats 1-16 moving in opposite facing direction
PART I	SIDE, CLOSE (4X); IN, IN, OUT, OUT; IN, IN, OUT, OUT; CROSS, SIDE (4X); IN, IN, OUT, OUT; IN, IN, OUT, OUT
Beat 1	Step R foot sideward right (gesture with both hands)
2	Step L foot next to R foot (pull arms toward you)
3-8	Repeat beats 1-2, three times
9-10	Step R, L foot diagonally in right (bring arms up, palms face you)
11-12	Step R, L foot diagonally out (bring arms down)
13-16	Repeat beats 9-12 on left diagonal
17-24	Repeat beats 1-8, beginning R foot crossing in front of L foot (move sideward left)
25-28	Step R, L foot on left diagonal in and out
29-32	Step R, L foot on right diagonal in and out
PART II	IN, 2, 3, 4; IN/PIVOT, IN, IN, CLOSE; Repeat 3X
Beats 1-4	Step R, L, R, L foot (bend and come up with arms in front)
5	Step R foot in (snap fingers) with 1/2 pivot clockwise
6	Step L foot in (backing up)
7	Step R foot in (backing up)
8	Step L foot next to R foot
9-16	Repeat beats 1-8 moving in the opposite direction (end with 1/4 turn right) West

U'va'u Ha'ovdim *(continued)*

17-24	Repeat beats 1-8 (move new direction) North
25-32	Repeat beats 1-8 in fourth direction (end with 1/4 turn right to face beginning direction) South
BRIDGE	SIDE, REST, SIDE, REST
Beats 1-2	Step R foot sideward right facing East
3-4	Step L foot sideward left
PART III	IN, 2, 3, 4; CROSS, REST, CROSS, REST; Repeat 3X; IN, OUT, OUT, IN; IN/PIVOT, IN, IN, CLOSE
Beats 1-4	Step R, L, R, L foot in (raise joined hands) East
5-6	Step R foot crossing in front of L foot
7-8	Step L foot crossing in front of R foot; on beat 4 turn 1/4 left
9-16	Repeat beats 1-8 keeping arms joined and turn 1/4 left (during these 8 beats lines should move close together) North
17-24	Repeat beats 1-8 arms still joined and turn 1/4 left (arms crossed in front of body) West
25-32	Repeat beats 1-8 arms still joined South
33-36	Cherkessiya beginning R foot with hands joined
37	Step R foot in with 1/2 pivot clockwise (let go of hands)
38	Step L foot in (backing up)
39	Step R foot in (backing up)
40	Step L foot next to R foot

Repeat Parts I, II, III 2 times; each time begin facing new direction (North, West)

Fourth time begin with Part III (facing South); then do Part I facing the original direction (East)

ENDING	Raise arms overhead and turn body clockwise; keep turning with everyone moving toward the center of the group

RHYTHMIC NOTATION

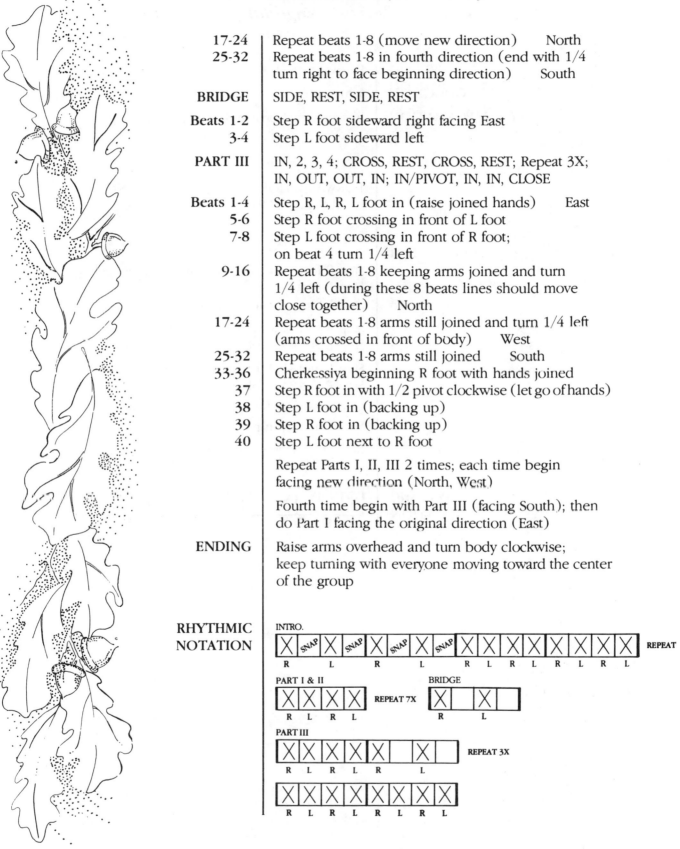

INTRO.

| X | SNAP | X | SNAP | X | SNAP | X | SNAP | X | X | X | X | X | X | X | X | **REPEAT** |

R   L   R   L   R L R L R L

PART I & II   BRIDGE

| X | X | X | X | **REPEAT 7X** | X | | X | |

R L R L   R   L

PART III

| X | X | X | X | | X | | **REPEAT 3X** |

R L R L R   L

| X | X | X | X | X | X | X | X |

R L R L R L R L

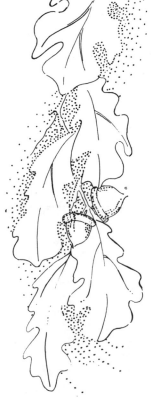

Žikino Kolo
Yugoslavia

RECORD	Festival F-4811
INTRODUCTION	4 measures
FORMATION	Broken circle or line, hands joined "V" position
METER	3/4

FORWARD, HOP, CROSS; SIDE, STEP, STEP;
OUT, STEP, STEP; OUT, STEP, STEP; Repeat

Measure	Beat	
1	1	Step R foot diagonally forward counterclockwise
	2	Hop R foot
	3	Step L foot crossing in front of R foot
2	1	Step R foot sideward right (bend knee)
	2-3	Step L, R foot in place (straighten knees)
3	1	Step L foot slightly diagonally out left
	2-3	Step R, L foot in place
4	1	Step R foot slightly diagonally out right
	2-3	Step L, R foot in place
5-8		Repeat measures 1-4 clockwise beginning L foot

RHYTHMIC NOTATION

R R L R L R L R L R L R   REPEAT W/OPP. FTWK.

Zonarádhikos
Belt Dance
Greece (Thrace)

RECORD	Soul Dances of the Greeks, PI LPS-33
INTRODUCTION	8 beats
FORMATION	Men: Short lines, belt hold Women: lines, front basket
PART I	JUMP/HOP, BACK/SIDE; CROSS/HOP, IN/HOP; IN/HOP, IN/IN; IN/HOP; OUT/HOP; OUT/HOP, OUT/OUT; OUT/HOP; SIDE/BOUNCE; SIDE/BOUNCE

Beat 1	Jump on both feet
&	Hop R foot
2	Step L foot crossing in back of R foot
&	Step R foot sideward right
3	Step L foot crossing in front of R foot
&	Hop L foot
4	Step R foot in toward center
&	Hop R foot
5	Step L foot in
&	Hop L foot
6	Step R, L foot in
&	Step R foot in
&	Hop R foot
8	Step L foot out away from center
&	Hop L foot
9	Step R foot out
&	Hop R foot
10	Step L, R foot out
11	Step L foot out
&	Hop L foot
12	Step R foot sideward right
&	Bounce R heel
13	Step L foot sideward left
&	Bounce L heel

(continued)

Zonarádikos (continued)

PART II	JUMP/HOP, BACK/SIDE; CROSS/HOP, IN/HOP; IN/IN, IN/HOP; IN/HOP, OUT/OUT; OUT/HOP; SIDE/BOUNCE; SIDE/BOUNCE
Beats 1-4	Repeat Part I, beats 1-4
5	Step L, R foot in
6	Step L foot in
&	Hop L foot
7	Step R foot in
&	Hop R foot
8	Step L, R foot out
9	Step L foot out
&	Hop L foot
10-11	Repeat Part I, beats 12-13
PART III	JUMP/HOP, BACK/SIDE; CROSS/HOP, IN/IN; IN/HOP, OUT/OUT; OUT/HOP; SIDE/BOUNCE; SIDE/BOUNCE
Beats 1-3	Repeat Part I, beats 1-3
4	Step R, L foot in
5	Step R foot in
&	Hop R foot
6	Step L, R foot out
7	Step L foot out
&	Hop L foot
8-9	Repeat Part I, beats 12-13
NOTE	Each part may be repeated any number of times and executed in any order.

RHYTHMIC NOTATION

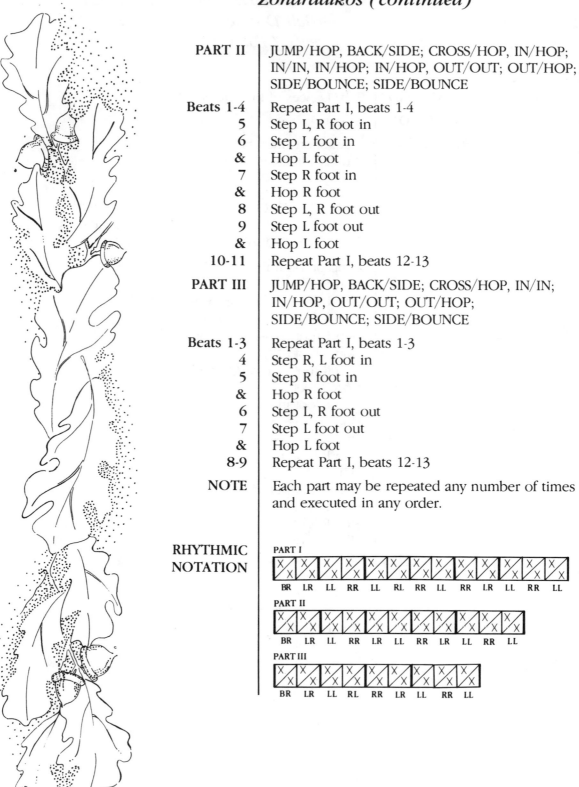

PART I

BR LR LL RR LL RL RR LL RR LR LL RR LL

PART II

BR LR LL RR LR LL RR LR LL RR LL

PART III

BR LR LL RL RR LR LL RR LL

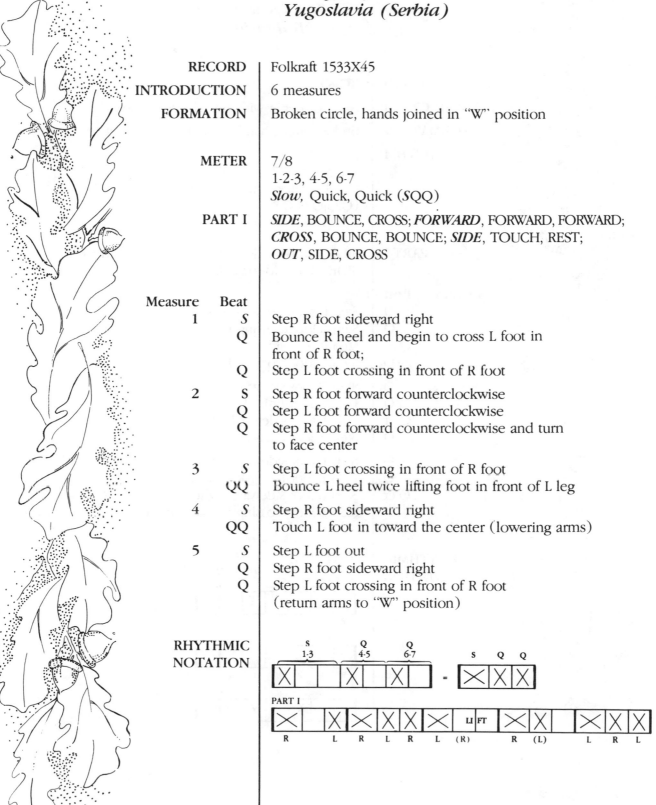

Ajde Jano
Yugoslavia (Serbia)

RECORD	Folkraft 1533X45
INTRODUCTION	6 measures
FORMATION	Broken circle, hands joined in "W" position
METER	7/8
	1-2-3, 4-5, 6-7
	Slow, Quick, Quick (*SQQ*)
PART I	*SIDE*, BOUNCE, CROSS; *FORWARD*, FORWARD, FORWARD; *CROSS*, BOUNCE, BOUNCE; *SIDE*, TOUCH, REST; *OUT*, SIDE, CROSS

Measure	Beat	
1	*S*	Step R foot sideward right
	Q	Bounce R heel and begin to cross L foot in front of R foot;
	Q	Step L foot crossing in front of R foot
2	S	Step R foot forward counterclockwise
	Q	Step L foot forward counterclockwise
	Q	Step R foot forward counterclockwise and turn to face center
3	*S*	Step L foot crossing in front of R foot
	QQ	Bounce L heel twice lifting foot in front of L leg
4	*S*	Step R foot sideward right
	QQ	Touch L foot in toward the center (lowering arms)
5	*S*	Step L foot out
	Q	Step R foot sideward right
	Q	Step L foot crossing in front of R foot (return arms to "W" position)

RHYTHMIC NOTATION

Eleno Mome
Helen, Dear Helen
Bulgaria

RECORD	XOPO 303
INTRODUCTION	None or begin with any phrase of music
FORMATION	Broken circle, hands joined in "W" position
RHYTHM	7/8 1-2, 3-4, 5, 6-7 Quick, Quick, Quicker-Quick (Q,Q,Q'er,Q)

PART I — SIDE, CROSS, side/BACK; SIDE, HOP, side/BACK; SIDE, HOP, side/BACK

Measure	Beat	
1	Q	Step R foot sideward right
	Q	Step L foot crossing in front of R foot
	Q'er	Step R foot sideward right
	Q	Step L foot crossing in back of R foot
2	Q	Step R foot sideward right
	Q	Hop R foot lifting L foot in front of R leg
	Q'er	Step L foot sideward left
	Q	Step R foot crossing in back of L foot
3	Q	Step L foot sideward left
	Q	Hop L foot lifting R foot in front of L leg
	Q'er	Step R foot sideward right
	Q	Step L foot crossing in back of R foot

RHYTHMIC NOTATION

MEAS. 1

Q 1-2	Q 3-4	Q'er 5	Q 6-7
X	X	X	X
R	L	R	L

MEAS. 2

X	X	X	X
R	R	L	R

MEAS. 3

X	X	X	X
L	L	R	L

Fatiše Kolo
Yugoslavia (South Serbia)

RECORD	Worldtone WT 10002
INTRODUCTION	No introduction or begin with vocal
FORMATION	Broken circle, hands joined "W" position
METER	9/16
	1-2, 3-4-5, 6-7, 8-9
	Quick, *Slow*, Quick, Quick (QSQQ)
PART I	BOUNCE, *FORWARD*, BOUNCE, FORWARD;
	BOUNCE, *SIDE*, CROSS, BACK;
	BOUNCE, *SIDE*, CROSS, BACK

Measure	Beat	
1	Q	Bounce L heel (lift R leg)
	S	Step R foot forward counterclockwise
	Q	Bounce R heel (left L leg)
	Q	Step L foot forward counterclockwise
2	Q	Bounce L heel turning to face center
	S	Step R foot sideward right
	Q	Step L foot crossing in back of R foot
	Q	Step R foot crossing in back of L foot
3		Repeat measure 2 beginning bounce R foot and stepping sideward left

RHYTHMIC NOTATION

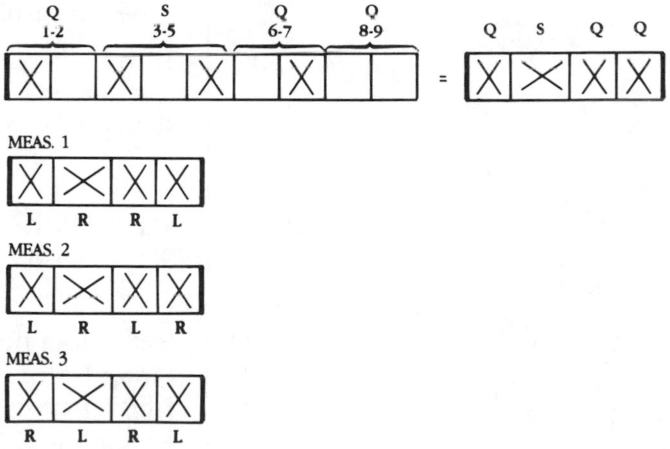

MEAS. 1

L   R   L   L

MEAS. 2

L   R   L   R

MEAS. 3

R   L   R   L

Fissouni
Greece (Epirus)

RECORD	Panhellenion KT1001
INTRODUCTION	None
FORMATION	Circle, hands held in "W" position
METER	9/8
	1-2, 3-4, 5-6, 7-8-9
	Quick, Quick, Quick, *Slow* (QQQS)

PART I		FORWARD, 2, 3, *SWING*;
		BACKWARD, 2, 3, *SWING*

Measure	Beat	
1	Q	Step R foot forward, counterclockwise ⎤
	Q	Step L foot forward counterclockwise ⎬ Bouncy steps
	Q	Step R foot forward counterclockwise ⎦
	S	Swing L foot across in front of R leg raising R heel
2	Q	Step L foot backward clockwise
	Q	Step R foot backward clockwise
	Q	Step L foot backward clockwise
	S	Swing R foot across in front of L leg raising L heel

VARIATION		FORWARD, 2, 3, *SWING*;
		TURN, 2, 3, *SWING*

Measure	Beat	
1		Repeat measure 1, Part I
2	QQQ	Turn body counterclockwise moving clockwise L, R, L foot
	S	Swing R foot across in front of L leg raising L heel

PART II		STEP, SWING, STEP, *SWING*;
		STEP, SWING, STEP *SWING*

Measure	Beat	
1	Q	Step R foot next to L foot
	Q	Swing L foot in front of R leg raising R heel
	Q	Step L foot next to R foot
	S	Swing R foot in front of L leg raising L heel
2		Repeat Part II, measure 1

Fissouni (continued)

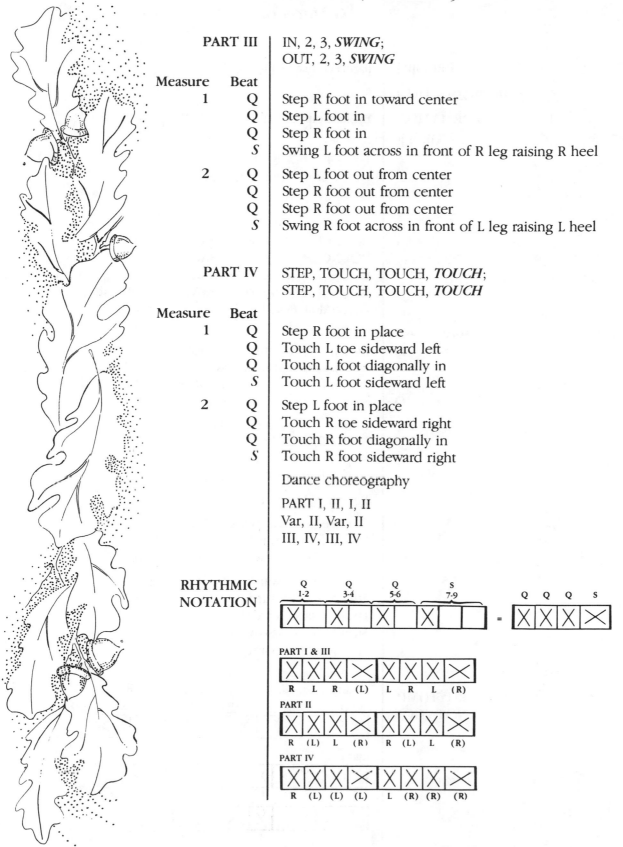

PART III		IN, 2, 3, *SWING*; OUT, 2, 3, *SWING*

Measure	Beat	
1	Q	Step R foot in toward center
	Q	Step L foot in
	Q	Step R foot in
	S	Swing L foot across in front of R leg raising R heel
2	Q	Step L foot out from center
	Q	Step R foot out from center
	Q	Step R foot out from center
	S	Swing R foot across in front of L leg raising L heel

PART IV		STEP, TOUCH, TOUCH, *TOUCH*; STEP, TOUCH, TOUCH, *TOUCH*

Measure	Beat	
1	Q	Step R foot in place
	Q	Touch L toe sideward left
	Q	Touch L foot diagonally in
	S	Touch L foot sideward left
2	Q	Step L foot in place
	Q	Touch R toe sideward right
	Q	Touch R foot diagonally in
	S	Touch R foot sideward right

Dance choreography

PART I, II, I, II
Var, II, Var, II
III, IV, III, IV

**RHYTHMIC
NOTATION**

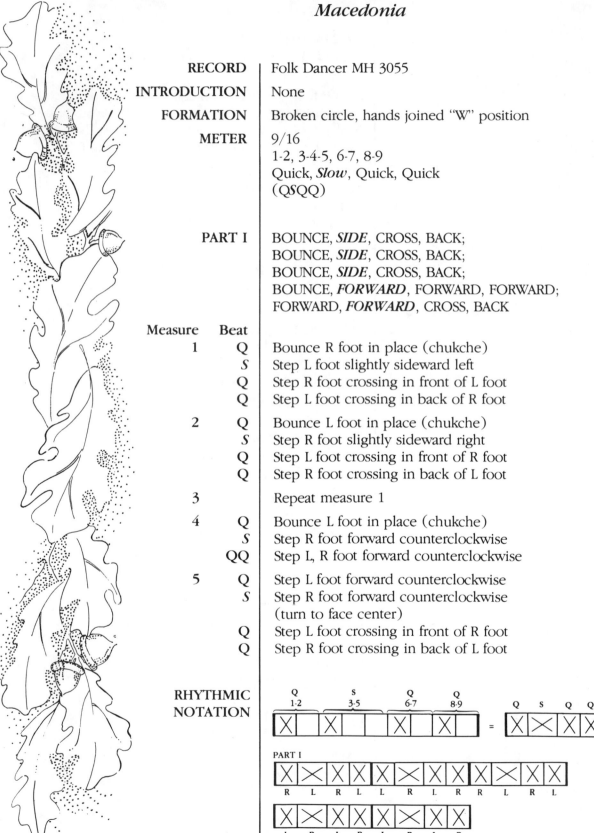

Katushe Mome
Macedonia

RECORD	Folk Dancer MH 3055
INTRODUCTION	None
FORMATION	Broken circle, hands joined "W" position
METER	9/16 1-2, 3-4-5, 6-7, 8-9 Quick, *Slow*, Quick, Quick (QSQQ)
PART I	BOUNCE, *SIDE*, CROSS, BACK; BOUNCE, *SIDE*, CROSS, BACK; BOUNCE, *SIDE*, CROSS, BACK; BOUNCE, *FORWARD*, FORWARD, FORWARD; FORWARD, *FORWARD*, CROSS, BACK

Measure	Beat	
1	Q	Bounce R foot in place (chukche)
	S	Step L foot slightly sideward left
	Q	Step R foot crossing in front of L foot
	Q	Step L foot crossing in back of R foot
2	Q	Bounce L foot in place (chukche)
	S	Step R foot slightly sideward right
	Q	Step L foot crossing in front of R foot
	Q	Step R foot crossing in back of L foot
3		Repeat measure 1
4	Q	Bounce L foot in place (chukche)
	S	Step R foot forward counterclockwise
	QQ	Step L, R foot forward counterclockwise
5	Q	Step L foot forward counterclockwise
	S	Step R foot forward counterclockwise (turn to face center)
	Q	Step L foot crossing in front of R foot
	Q	Step R foot crossing in back of L foot

RHYTHMIC NOTATION

Kostursko Oro
City of Kostur
Greece (Macedonia)

RECORD	XOPO 317
FORMATION	Broken circle, hands held in "W" position Begin with vocal
METER	7/8 1-2-3, 4-5-6-7 Slow, *Slower*, (S, *S'er*)
PART I	FORWARD, *FORWARD*; SIDE, *CLOSE*; OUT, *TOUCH*; SIDE, *BACK*; SIDE, *CIRCLE*; FORWARD, *TOUCH*

Measure	Beat	
1	S	Step R foot moving counterclockwise
	S'er	Step L foot moving counterclockwise
2	S	Step R foot sideward right
	S'er	Step L foot next to R foot
3	S	Step R foot out
	S'er	Touch L foot next to R foot
4	S	Step L foot sideward left
	S'er	Step R foot crossing in back of L foot
5	S	Step L foot sideward left
	S'er	Circle R foot in and to the right and step R foot
6	S	Step L foot forward counterclockwise and pivot to face center
	S'er	Touch R foot next to L foot

RHYTHMIC NOTATION

Lefkaditikos
Ionian Islands (Lefkas)

RECORD	Folkraft LP8
INTRODUCTION	4 beats
FORMATION	Broken circle, hands held in "W" position at shoulder
PART I	BACKWARD, BACKWARD; SIDE, TOUCH; SIDE, TOUCH; Repeat Part I
Beat 1	Step R foot backward moving counterclockwise
2	Step L foot backward and turn to face center
3	Step R foot sideward right
4	Touch L foot across in front of R foot, body facing diagonally right
5	Step L foot sideward left
6	Touch R foot across in front of L foot, body facing diagonally left
7-12	Repeat Part I, beats 1-6
PART II	BACKWARD, BACKWARD; SIDE/CROSS, BACK/SIDE; CROSS, CLOSE; Repeat Part II
Beats 1-2	Repeat Part I, beats 1-2
3	Step R foot sideward right
&	Step L foot crossing in front of R foot
4	Step R foot crossing in back of L foot
4	Step L foot sideward left
5	Step R foot crossing in front of L foot
6	Step L foot next to R foot
7-12	Repeat Part II, beats 1-6
NOTE	Part I may be danced 4 times thus eliminating Part II.

Lefkaditikos (continued)

7/8 meter
1-2-3, 4-5, 6-7
Slow, Quick, Quick (*SQQ*)

PART III *SIDE*, BACK, IN; *IN*, OUT, OUT;
OUT, SIDE, CROSS; *BACK*, SIDE, CROSS;
Repeat Part II 3X

Measure	Beat	
1	S	Step R foot sideward right
	Q	Step L foot crossing in back of R foot
	Q	Step R foot in toward the center
2	S	Step L foot in toward center (low leap) bend L knee and tuck R foot behind L knee
	Q	Step R foot out from center (behind L foot)
	Q	Step L foot out from center (behind R foot)
3	S	Step R foot out from center (behind L foot)
	Q	Step L foot sideward left
	Q	Step R foot crossing in front of L foot
4	S	Step L foot crossing in back of R foot
	Q	Step R foot sideward right
	Q	Step L foot crossing in front of R foot
5-16		Repeat Part III, measures 1-4, three times

RHYTHMIC NOTATION

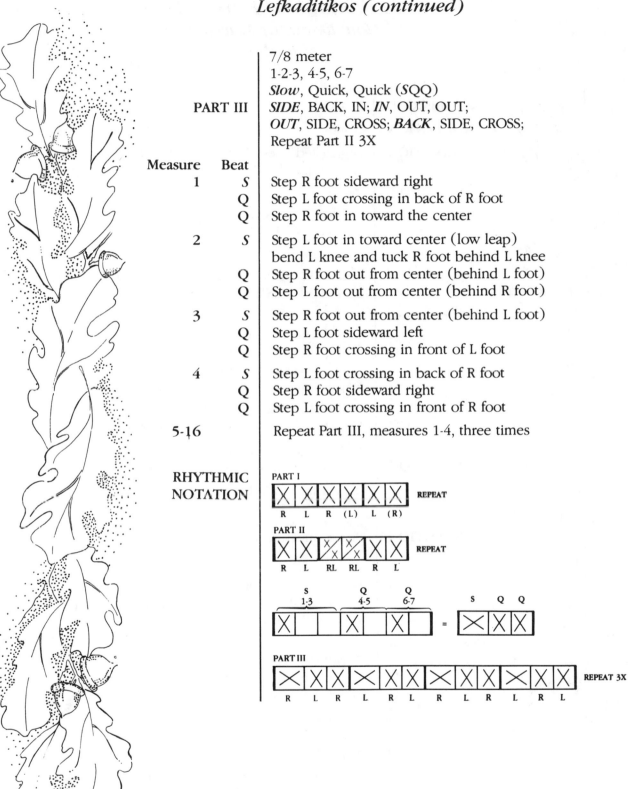

PART I

R L R (L) L (R)   REPEAT

PART II

R L RL RL R L   REPEAT

S (1-3)   Q (4-5)   Q (6-7)   =   S Q Q

PART III

R L R L R L R L R L R L   REPEAT 3X

Makedonsko Bavno Oro
Slow Dance of Macedonia
Macedonia

RECORD	XOPO 301
INTRODUCTION	None
FORMATION	Segregated lines; men in shoulder hold, women join hands in "W" position
METER	7/8
	1-2-3, 4-5, 6-7
	Slow, Quick, Quick (*SQQ*)
PART I	*FORWARD*, TOUCH, CROSS; *SIDE*, LIFT, REST; *SIDE*, LIFT, REST; Repeat Part I 7X

Measure	Beat	
1	S	Step R foot moving counterclockwise, facing diagonally forward
	Q	Touch L foot crossing in front of R foot
	Q	Step L foot crossing in front of R foot
2	S	Step R foot sideward right
	QQ	Lift L foot in front of R leg, no bounce
3	S	Step L foot sideward left
	QQ	Lift R foot in front of L leg, no bounce
4-24		Repeat measures 1-3, seven times

TRANSITION	Repeat measure 1 and turn to face center
PART II	*SIDE*, TOUCH, TOUCH; *CLOSE*, TOUCH, SIDE; *CROSS*, SIDE, BACK; Repeat 4X; *SIDE*, TOUCH, TOUCH; *SIDE*, TOUCH, TOUCH

Measure	Beat	
1	S	Step R foot sideward right
	Q	Touch L heel diagonally sideward left
	Q	Touch L heel in
2	S	Step L foot next to R foot
	Q	Touch R heel in
	Q	Step R foot sideward right
3	S	Step L foot crossing in front of R foot
	Q	Step R foot sideward right
	Q	Step L foot crossing in back of R foot

Makedonsko Bavno Oro (continued)

4-15	Repeat Part II, measures 1-3, four times
16	Repeat Part II, measure 1
17	Repeat Part II, measure 1 beginning L foot
	Repeat Part I without transition
	Repeat measures 1-15 of Part II

TRANSITION Step R foot sideward right and lower arms

PART III

Quick, Quick, *Slow* (QQ*S*)
SIDE, BACK, *SIDE*; SIDE, BACK, side/CROSS;
SIDE, BACK, *SIDE*

Measure	Beat	
1	Q	Step L foot sideward left
	Q	Step R foot crossing in back of L foot
	S	Step L foot sideward left with knee bent, kicking R foot forward
2	Q	Step R foot sideward right
	Q	Step L foot crossing in back of R foot
	Q'er	Step R foot sideward right
	Q	Step L foot crossing in front of R foot
3	Q	Step R foot sideward right
	Q	Step L foot crossing in back of R foot
	S	Step R foot sideward right with knee bent, kicking L foot forward; repeat to end of record ending on measure 2 with a step, lift in place to the Q'er, Q beats

RHYTHMIC NOTATION

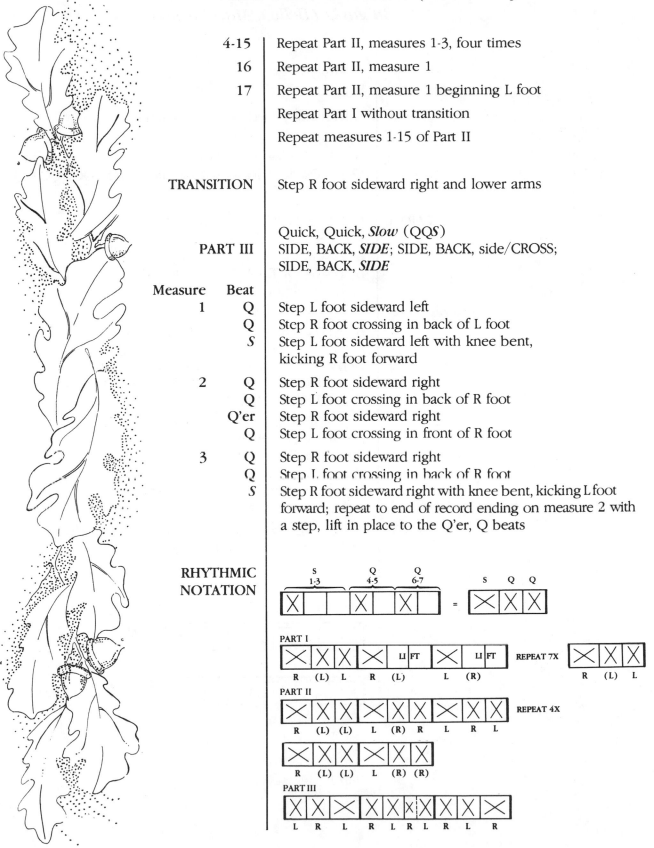

Neda Voda Nalivala
Bulgaria (Belica, Macedonia)

RECORD	Festival 4115
INTRODUCTION	None
FORMATION	Line, hands joined in "W" position
METER	11/8 1-2, 3-4, 5-6, 7-8, 9, 10-11 Quick, Quick, Quick, Quick, Quicker, Quick (QQQQQ'erQ)
PART I	BOUNCE, FORWARD, FORWARD, FORWARD, CROSS/**BACK** (4X) BOUNCE, IN, IN, IN, IN/OUT; BOUNCE, OUT, OUT, OUT, OUT/IN; Repeat In and Out

Measure	Beat	
1	Q	Bounce L heel (R leg raised slightly with knee bent—Chukche)
	QQQ	Step R, L, R foot moving counterclockwise
	Q'er	Step L foot crossing in front of R foot (do not dip)
	Q	Step R foot crossing in back of L foot
2		Repeat measure 1 beginning with chukche R foot and move clockwise
3-4		Repeat measures 1-2
5		Repeat measure 1 moving in toward center
6		Repeat measure 2 moving out away from center
7-8		Repeat measures 5-6
NOTE		Chukche L foot: Raise up on ball of L foot and put heel down on the beat.

RHYTHMIC NOTATION

Osmica
Bulgaria

RECORD	Worldtone WT-YM 002
INTRODUCTION	None
FORMATION	Short lines (about 8 dancers); reverse basket, L hand on top
METER	Pravo 2/4 Račenica 7/16 1-2, 3-4, 5-6-7 Quick, Quick, *Slow* (QQS)
PART I	Pravo OUT, OUT; OUT, LIFT; SIDE, BACK; SIDE, LIFT; SIDE, BACK; SIDE, LIFT; SIDE, BACK; SIDE, LIFT
Beat 1	Step R foot out (line side-by-side)
2	Step L foot out
3	Step R foot out
4	Lift L foot in front of R leg (low lift) use a slight kicking motion on the lift
5	Step L foot sideward left
6	Step R foot crossing in back of L foot
7	Step L foot sideward left
8	Lift R foot in front of L leg (as in beat 4)
9-12	Repeat beats 5-8 with opposite footwork beginning sideward R foot
13-16	Repeat beats 5-8

(continued)

Osmica *(continued)*

		Račenica
PART II		IN, IN *IN* (4X);
		STEP, STEP, *STEP* (3X), STAMP

Measure	Beat	
1	Q	Step R foot in with slight leap, (line side-by-side)
	Q	Step L foot in (running step)
	S	Step R foot in (running step)
2-4		Repeat measure 1 three times alternating footwork
5	Q	Step R foot slightly sideward right (slight leap)
	Q	Step L foot next to R foot
	S	Step R foot next to L foot
6-7		Repeat measure 5 two times alternating footwork
		Stamp L foot next to R foot
NOTE		Dance begins again using opposite footwork.

RHYTHMIC NOTATION

PART I

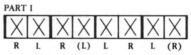

PART II

Pasarelska
Bulgaria

RECORD	XOPO 330 Mediterranian Records 45 r.p.m.
INTRODUCTION	2 measures
FORMATION	Short lines in a "belt hold"
METER	7/8 1-2-3, 4-5, 6-7 *Slow*, Quick, Quick (*SQQ*)

PART I	*FORWARD*, FORWARD, REST; *FORWARD*, FORWARD, REST; *OUT*, OUT, OUT; *OUT*, OUT, OUT; *IN*, IN, HOP; *IN*, IN, HOP; *IN*, STAMP, REST; *OUT*, OUT, OUT; *OUT*, OUT, OUT; *SIDE*, CROSS, BACK

Measure	Beat	
1	*S*	Step R foot forward right body facing slightly counterclockwise
	QQ	Step L foot forward right
2	*S*	Step R foot forward right
	QQ	Step L foot forward right and turn to face center
3	*S*	Step R foot out away from center
	Q	Step L foot out
	Q	Step R foot out
4	*SQQ*	Step L, R, L foot out
5	*S*	Step R foot in toward the center
	Q	Step L foot in
	Q	Hop L foot
6	*SQQ*	Repeat measure 5
7	*S*	Leap R foot in turning body to face diagonally left
	QQ	Stamp L foot
8	*S*	Step L foot out
	Q	Step R foot out
	Q	Step L foot out
9	*SQQ*	Step R, L, R foot out
10	*S*	Step L foot sideward left
	Q	Step R foot crossing in front of L foot
	Q	Step L foot crossing in back of R foot

(continued)

Pasarelska (continued)

| NOTE | Music will increase in tempo; dance ends on the S beat of measure 6. |

RHYTHMIC
NOTATION

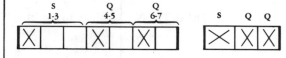

PART I

Tri Godini Kate
Three Years Kate
Yugoslavia (Macedonia)

RECORD	Festival FM 4005
INTRODUCTION	10 measures
FORMATION	Circle, hands joined in "W" position
METER	7/8 1-2-3, 4-5, 6-7 *Slow*, Quick, Quick (*SQQ*)
PART I	*FORWARD*, BOUNCE, FORWARD; *FORWARD*, LIFT, REST; *FORWARD*, PIVOT, REST; *BACKWARD*, BACKWARD, REST; *BACKWARD*, LIFT, REST; Repeat Part I 3X

Tri Godini Kate (continued)

Measure	Beat	
1	S	Step R foot forward counterclockwise
	Q	Bounce R heel bringing L foot forward
	Q	Step L foot forward
2	S	Step R foot forward
	QQ	Lift L foot in front of R leg
3	S	Step L foot forward
	QQ	Pivot 1/2 to face clockwise (body turns counterclockwise)
4	S	Step R foot backward counterclockwise (lower arms)
	QQ	Step L foot backward
5	S	Step R foot backward
	QQ	Lift L foot in front of R leg (raise arms)
6-10		Repeat measures 1-5 clockwise beginning L foot
11-20		Repeat Part I, measures 1-10

PART II   IN, CLOSE, *IN*; IN, CLOSE, *IN*;
SIDE, REST, *LIFT*; SIDE, REST, *LIFT*;
OUT, CLOSE, *OUT*; OUT, CLOSE, *OUT*;
SIDE, REST, *LIFT*; SIDE, REST, *LIFT*

Measure	Beat		
1	Q	Step R foot in toward center	
	Q	Step L foot behind R heel	Two Step
	S	Step R foot in	
2	Q	Step L foot in	
	Q	Step R foot behind L heel	
	S	Step L foot forward in	
3	QQ	Step R foot sideward right	
	S	Lift L foot in front of R leg	
4	QQ	Step L foot sideward left	
	S	Lift R foot in front of L leg	
5-8		Repeat Part II, measures 1-4 out away from the center	

RHYTHMIC NOTATION

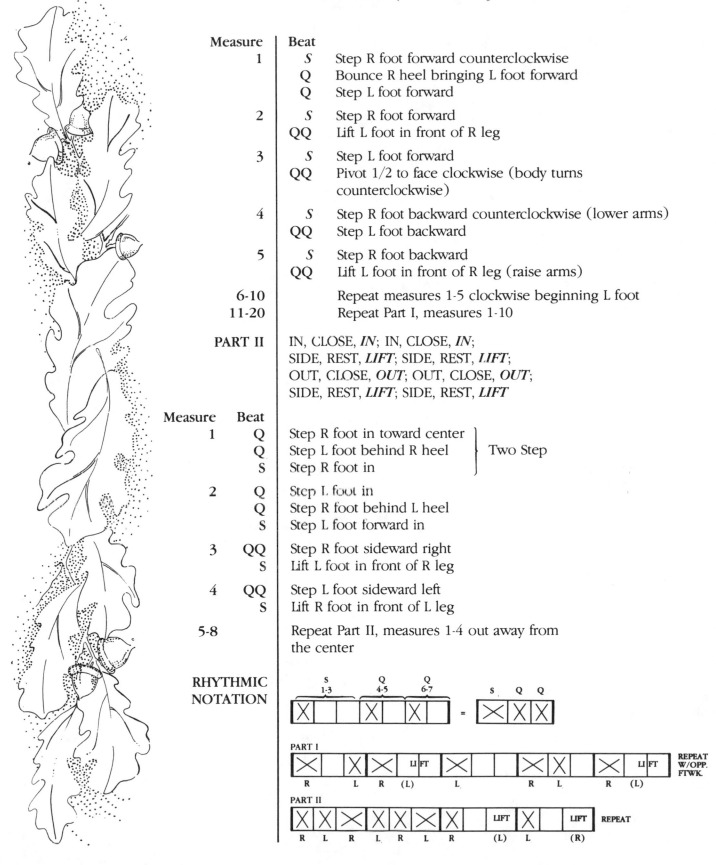

Intermediate Level 3 Dances, Common & Uncommon Meters

Common Meters

Al Gemali
Israel

RECORD	Na'arah IFC1
INTRODUCTION	16 beats
FORMATION	Circle, hands held in "V" position
PART I	SIDE, REST, CROSS, REST; IN, REST, OUT, CLOSE; Repeat
Beats 1-2	Step R foot sideward right
3-4	Step L foot crossing in front of R foot
5-6	Step R foot in toward the center
7	Step L foot out away from the center
8	Step R foot next to L foot
9-16	Repeat beats 1-8 to the left beginning L foot
	SIDE, BACK, SIDE, BACK; TOUCH, TOUCH, CROSS, TOUCH; TURN, TURN, TURN, BRUSH; CROSS, SIDE, CROSS, TOUCH; Repeat
17	Step R foot sideward right
18	Step L foot crossing in back of R foot
19-20	Repeat beats 17-18
21-22	Touch R foot 2 times in front of L foot
23	Step R foot crossing in front of L foot
24	Touch L foot next to R foot
25-27	Step L, R, L foot turning left a full turn
28	Brush R foot in
29	Step R foot crossing in front of L foot
30	Step L foot sideward left
31	Step R foot crossing in front of L foot
32	Touch L foot next to R foot
33-48	Repeat beats 17-32 with opposite footwork beginning L foot

Al Gemali (continued)

PART II	SIDE, REST, CROSS, REST; IN, OUT, TURN, TOUCH; SIDE, CROSS, BACK, TURN; TURN, TURN, TURN, TOUCH; Repeat; SIDE, BACK, SIDE, BACK; TOUCH, TOUCH, CROSS, CLOSE
Beats 1-2	Step R foot sideward right
3-4	Step L foot crossing in front of R foot
5	Step R foot in toward the center of the circle
6	Step L foot out away from the center
7	Step R foot 1/2 right to face out
8	Touch L foot next to R foot
9	Step L foot sideward left
10	Step R foot crossing in front of L foot
11	Step L foot crossing in back of R foot
12-15	Step R, L, R, L foot turning a full turn right
16	Touch R foot next to L foot
17-32	Repeat beats 1-16 and end facing in
NOTE	Step R, L foot out, in on beats 21-22.
33-40	Repeat Part I, beats 17-24 ending with a step L foot next to R foot

RHYTHMIC NOTATION

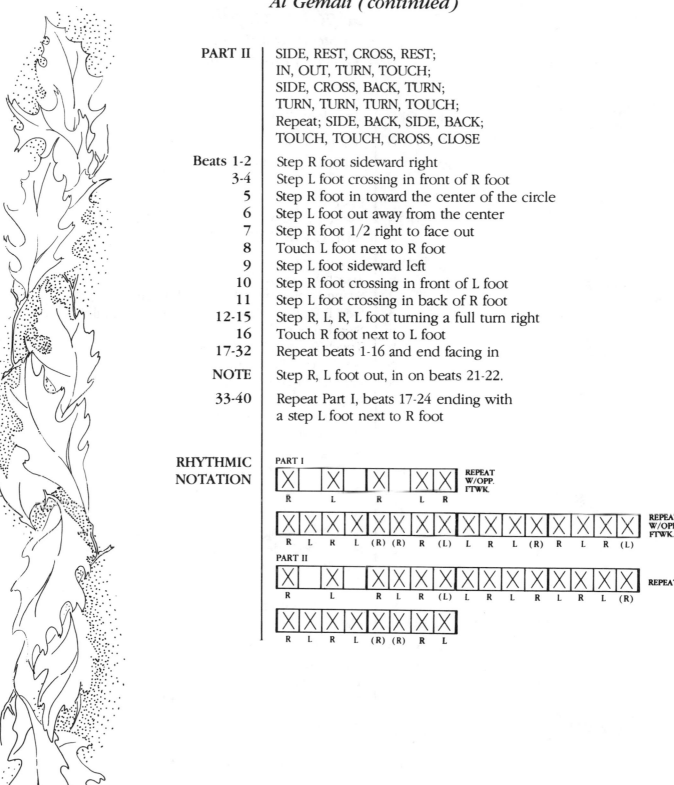

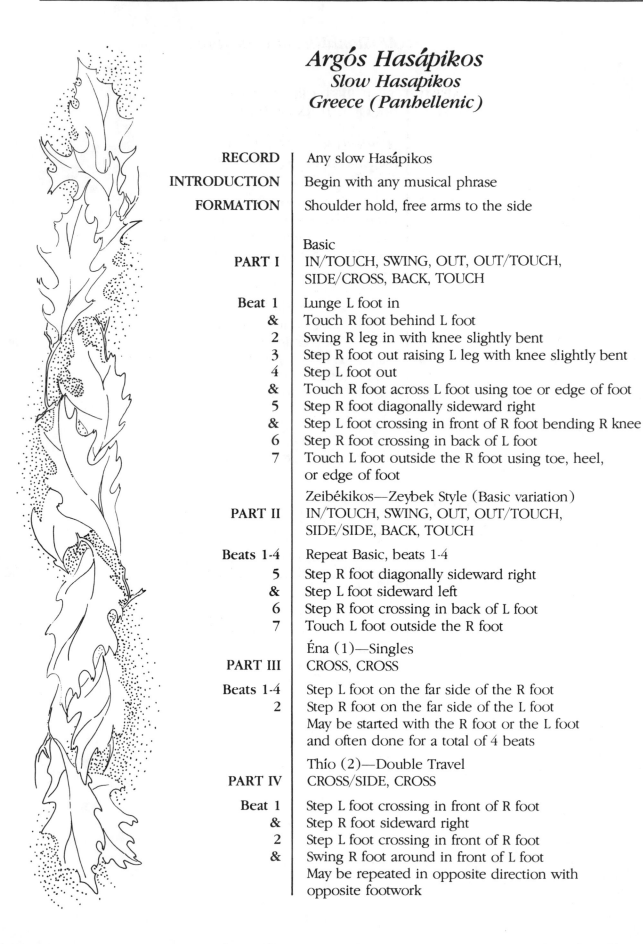

Argós Hasápikos
Slow Hasapikos
Greece (Panhellenic)

RECORD	Any slow Hasápikos
INTRODUCTION	Begin with any musical phrase
FORMATION	Shoulder hold, free arms to the side

Basic

PART I	IN/TOUCH, SWING, OUT, OUT/TOUCH, SIDE/CROSS, BACK, TOUCH
Beat 1	Lunge L foot in
&	Touch R foot behind L foot
2	Swing R leg in with knee slightly bent
3	Step R foot out raising L leg with knee slightly bent
4	Step L foot out
&	Touch R foot across L foot using toe or edge of foot
5	Step R foot diagonally sideward right
&	Step L foot crossing in front of R foot bending R knee
6	Step R foot crossing in back of L foot
7	Touch L foot outside the R foot using toe, heel, or edge of foot

Zeibékikos—Zeybek Style (Basic variation)

PART II	IN/TOUCH, SWING, OUT, OUT/TOUCH, SIDE/SIDE, BACK, TOUCH
Beats 1-4	Repeat Basic, beats 1-4
5	Step R foot diagonally sideward right
&	Step L foot sideward left
6	Step R foot crossing in back of L foot
7	Touch L foot outside the R foot

Éna (1)—Singles

PART III	CROSS, CROSS
Beats 1-4	Step L foot on the far side of the R foot
2	Step R foot on the far side of the L foot
	May be started with the R foot or the L foot and often done for a total of 4 beats

Thío (2)—Double Travel

PART IV	CROSS/SIDE, CROSS
Beat 1	Step L foot crossing in front of R foot
&	Step R foot sideward right
2	Step L foot crossing in front of R foot
&	Swing R foot around in front of L foot
	May be repeated in opposite direction with opposite footwork

Argós Hasápikos *(continued)*

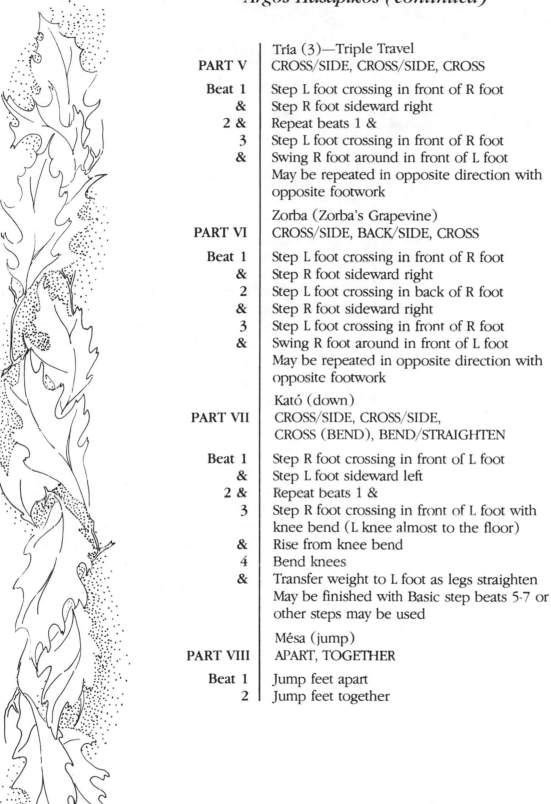

	Tría (3)—Triple Travel
PART V	CROSS/SIDE, CROSS/SIDE, CROSS
Beat 1	Step L foot crossing in front of R foot
&	Step R foot sideward right
2 &	Repeat beats 1 &
3	Step L foot crossing in front of R foot
&	Swing R foot around in front of L foot
	May be repeated in opposite direction with opposite footwork
	Zorba (Zorba's Grapevine)
PART VI	CROSS/SIDE, BACK/SIDE, CROSS
Beat 1	Step L foot crossing in front of R foot
&	Step R foot sideward right
2	Step L foot crossing in back of R foot
&	Step R foot sideward right
3	Step L foot crossing in front of R foot
&	Swing R foot around in front of L foot
	May be repeated in opposite direction with opposite footwork
	Kató (down)
PART VII	CROSS/SIDE, CROSS/SIDE, CROSS (BEND), BEND/STRAIGHTEN
Beat 1	Step R foot crossing in front of L foot
&	Step L foot sideward left
2 &	Repeat beats 1 &
3	Step R foot crossing in front of L foot with knee bend (L knee almost to the floor)
&	Rise from knee bend
4	Bend knees
&	Transfer weight to L foot as legs straighten
	May be finished with Basic step beats 5-7 or other steps may be used
	Mésa (jump)
PART VIII	APART, TOGETHER
Beat 1	Jump feet apart
2	Jump feet together

(continued)

Argós Hasápikos (continued)

PART IX	Aniktós Klistós (open, close) OPEN (TOES), OPEN (HEELS); CLOSE (HEELS), CLOSE (TOES)
Beat 1	Open toes
2	Open heels
3	Close heels
4	Close toes Beats 3, 4 may be reversed
PART X	Pséftikos (lean forward) CROSS/SIDE, CROSS/SIDE, CROSS, BACK
Beat 1	Step R foot crossing in front of L foot
&	Step L foot sideward left
2 &	Repeat beats 1 &
3	Step R foot crossing in front of L foot leaning over and extending L leg backward
4	Step L foot on the far side of the R heel raising body May be finished with Basic step beat 3-7 or beat 5-7 or other steps
NOTE	A 20th century dance form interpreted by the leader. Grew up in the taverns and bars. Done in short lines of 2-6 persons, usually friends.

RHYTHMIC NOTATION

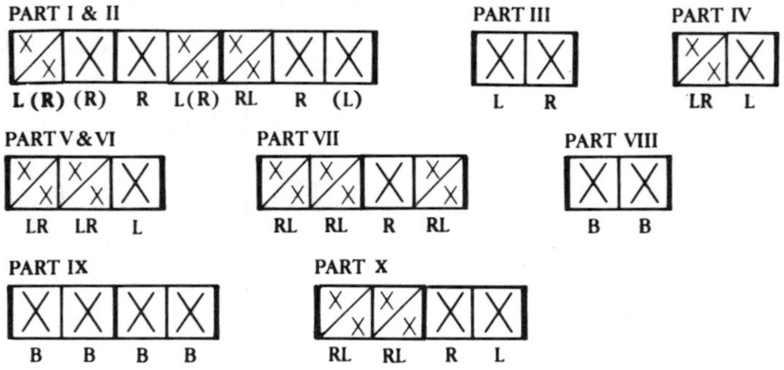

PART I & II
L (R) (R) R L (R) RL R (L)

PART III
L R

PART IV
LR L

PART V & VI
LR LR L

PART VII
RL RL R RL

PART VIII
B B

PART IX
B B B B

PART X
RL RL R L

Bat Arad
Israel

RECORD	Tikva T-80 *Festival*
INTRODUCTION	16 beats
FORMATION	Circle, hands joined in "V" position
PART I	CROSS, SIDE, BACK, SIDE; FORWARD, BACKWARD, BACKWARD, FORWARD; FORWARD, 2, 3, HOP; FORWARD, 2, 3, HOP; Repeat Part I
Beats 1-4	Grapevine moving counterclockwise beginning L foot
5-8	Cherkessiya facing forward counterclockwise
9-12	Schottische moving forward counterclockwise, turn to face clockwise on the hop
13-16	Schottische moving forward clockwise, turn to face counterclockwise on the hop
17-32	Repeat Part I, beats 1-16
PART II	JUMP, REST (2X); JUMP, BOUNCE (2X); IN, HOP, IN, HOP; OUT, 2, 3, HOP; CROSS, SIDE, BACK, SIDE; CROSS, BACK, TURN, TURN; IN, 2, 3, HOP; OUT, 2, 3, 4
Beats 1-2	Jump with feet apart (facing center)
3-4	Jump with feet apart
5	Jump with R foot in, L foot out
6	Bounce R foot in place
7-8	Repeat beats 5-6
9-12	Step hop L, R foot in toward the center
13-16	Schottische out away from the center beginning L foot
17-20	Grapevine moving clockwise beginning R foot
21	Step R foot crossing in front of L foot
22	Step L foot crossing in back of R foot
23-24	Step R, L foot turning a full turn right
25-28	Schottische in toward the center beginning R foot
29-32	Step L, R, L, R foot away from the center
RHYTHMIC NOTATION	

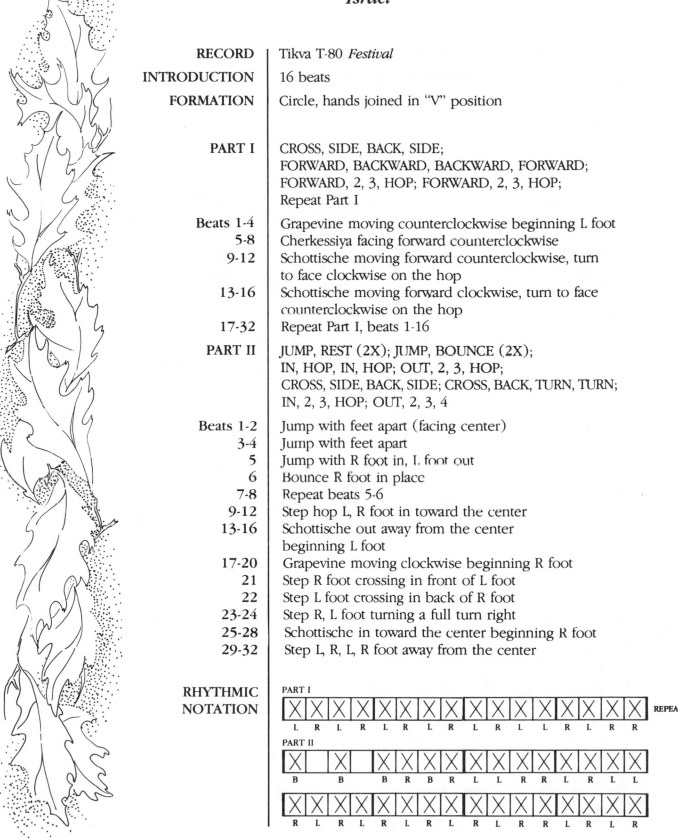

Batuta
Romania

RECORD	Balkan-Arts MK-1H BA 1001
INTRODUCTION	None or begin with any phrase
FORMATION	Lines, hands joined in "V" position

PART I	FORWARD/STAMP, FORWARD/STAMP; FORWARD/FORWARD, FORWARD/STAMP; TURN/TURN, TURN/STAMP; FORWARD/FORWARD, FORWARD/STAMP; SIDE/BACK, SIDE; BOUNCE/STEP, STEP

Beat 1	Step R foot forward counterclockwise
&	Stamp L foot next to R foot
2	Step L foot forward counterclockwise
&	Stamp R foot next to L foot
3	Step R, L foot forward
4	Repeat Beat 1 &
5-6	Repeat beats 3-4 beginning L foot turning to face clockwise on the two beat sequence
7-8	Repeat beats 3-4 forward clockwise end facing center
9	Step L foot sideward left
&	Step R foot crossing in back of L foot
10	Step L foot sideward left
11	Bounce L heel (chukche)
&	Step R foot next to L foot with an accent
12	Step L foot next to R foot with an accent

RHYTHMIC NOTATION	PART I

R(L) L(R) RL R(L) LR L(R) RL R(L) LR L LR L

Betof Utzlil
With Drum and Ring of Bells
Israel

RECORD	MIH 3 *Dance with Moshiko*
INTRODUCTION	16 beats
FORMATION	Circle, hands joined

PART I	FORWARD, FORWARD, JUMP, HOP; FORWARD, FORWARD, JUMP, HOP; IN, OUT, SIDE, SIDE; FORWARD, CLAP, CLAP, REST
Beats 1-2	Run R, L foot forward counterclockwise
3	Jump twisting body diagonally left (feet point diagonally left)
4	Hop L foot raising R knee (body faces forward counterclockwise)
5-6	Run R, L foot forward counterclockwise
7	Jump as in beat 3
8	Hop L foot facing center and raise R knee
9	Step R foot in (raise arms)
10	Step L foot out (lower arms)
11	Step R foot sideward right
12	Step L foot sideward left
13	Leap R foot forward clockwise (L knee raised)
14-15	Clap hands 2 times at head level
16	Hold
	BACKWARD, HOP, BACKWARD, HOP; TURN, HOP, BACKWARD, FORWARD; FORWARD, HOP, FORWARD, HOP; FORWARD, 2, 3, 4; Repeat Part I
Beats 17-18	Step hop L foot backward (counterclockwise)
19-20	Step hop R foot backward (counterclockwise)
21-22	Step hop L foot turning 1/2 to face counterclockwise (body turns away from center of circle)
23	Step R foot backward clockwise
24	Step L foot forward counterclockwise
25-26	Step hop R foot forward counterclockwise
27-28	Step hop L foot forward counterclockwise
29-32	Run R, L, R, L foot forward counterclockwise (do not bend over)
33-64	Repeat Part I, beats 1-32

(continued)

Betof Utzlil (continued)

PART II	BACKWARD, BACKWARD, CLOSE, BACKWARD; BACKWARD, BACKWARD, CROSS, BACKWARD; Repeat 2X; OUT, IN, CROSS, HOP; TURN, 2, 3, HOP; Repeat Part II
Beat 1	Step R foot backward clockwise (facing counterclockwise)
2	Step L foot backward
3	Step R foot next to L foot with accent
4	Step L foot backward
5	Step R foot backward
6	Step L foot backward
7	Step R foot crossing in front of L foot (very close)
8	Step L foot backward
9-24	Repeat beats 1-8, two times
25-27	Yemenite beginning R foot (OUT, IN, CROSS)
28	Hop R foot
29-31	Step L, R, L foot turning out 1/2 clockwise to face clockwise
32	Hop L foot
33-64	Repeat Part II, beats 1-32 (facing clockwise)
NOTE	Yemenite on the repeat is IN, OUT, CROSS.

RHYTHMIC NOTATION

PART I

X	X	X	X	X	X	X	X	X	X	X	X	X	CLAP	CLAP	
R	L	B	L	R	L	B	L	R	L	R	L	R			

X	X	X	X	X	X	X	X	X	X	X	X	X	X	X	X
L	L	R	R	L	L	R	L	R	R	L	L	R	L	R	L

REPEAT

PART II

X	X	X	X	X	X	X	X
R	L	R	L	R	L	R	L

REPEAT 2X

X	X	X	X	X	X	X	X
R	L	R	R	L	R	L	L

REPEAT II

Brîul Pe Opte
Southern Romania

RECORD	Balkan Arts 1001
INTRODUCTION	None
FORMATION	Short lines, belt hold
PART I	HOP/IN, REST/BRUSH, REST/STAMP, STEP; HOP/STEP, STEP; HOP/STEP, STEP; Repeat Part I 3X
Beat 1	Hop L foot lifting R knee
& 2	Step R foot in
& 3	Brush L foot slightly in
&	Stamp L foot next to R foot
4	Step L foot in place
5	Hop L foot lifting R leg diagonally forward right (lift hip-heel turned out)
&	Step R foot next to L foot
6	Step L foot in place
7-8	Repeat beats 5 6
9-32	Repeat Part I, beats 1-8, three times
PART II	HOP/OUT, REST/OUT, REST/IN, IN; HOP/STEP, STEP; HOP/STEP, STEP; REPEAT Part II 3X
Beat 1	Hop L foot in place
& 2	Step R foot out turning body right
& 3	Step L foot out turning body left
&	Step R foot in
4	Step L foot in
5-8	Repeat Part I, beats 5-8
9-32	Repeat Part II, beats 1-8, three times

(continued)

Brîul Pe Opte *(continued)*

PART III	HOP/STEP, STEP/STEP; STEP/STEP; STEP; HOP/STEP, STEP; HOP/STEP, STEP; Repeat; HOP/CROSS, BACK/SIDE; CROSS, BACK, SIDE; HOP/STEP, STEP; HOP/STEP, STEP; Repeat
Beat 1	Hop L foot
&	Step R foot next to L foot
2	Step L foot in place
& 3 & 4	Step R, L, R, L foot in place
5-8	Repeat Part I, beats 5-8
9-16	Repeat Part III, beats 1-8
17	Hop L foot
&	Step R foot crossing in front of L foot
18	Step L foot crossing in back of R foot
&	Step R foot next to L foot
19	Step L foot crossing in front of R foot
&	Step R foot crossing in back of L foot
20	Step L foot sideward left
21-24	Repeat Part I, beats 5-8
25-32	Repeat Part III, beats 17-24

Beats 2, &3&4: Raise knees in front

PART IV	HOP/IN, OUT/IN; OUT/IN, OUT; HOP/OUT, IN/OUT; IN/OUT; IN/OUT; IN; Repeat Part IV 3X
Beat 1	Hop L foot
&	Step R foot diagonally in right (face diagonally left)
2 & 3 & 4	Step L, R, L, R, L, R foot without changing position of feet
5-8	Repeat beats 1-4 with R foot diagonally out (face diagonally right)
9-32	Repeat Part IV, beats 1-8, three times
	Repeat Parts I-IV
	Repeats Parts I and II through beat 30 of Part II
Ending 31	Jump slightly pidgeon-toed
32	Jump landing on heels and balancing

RHYTHMIC NOTATION

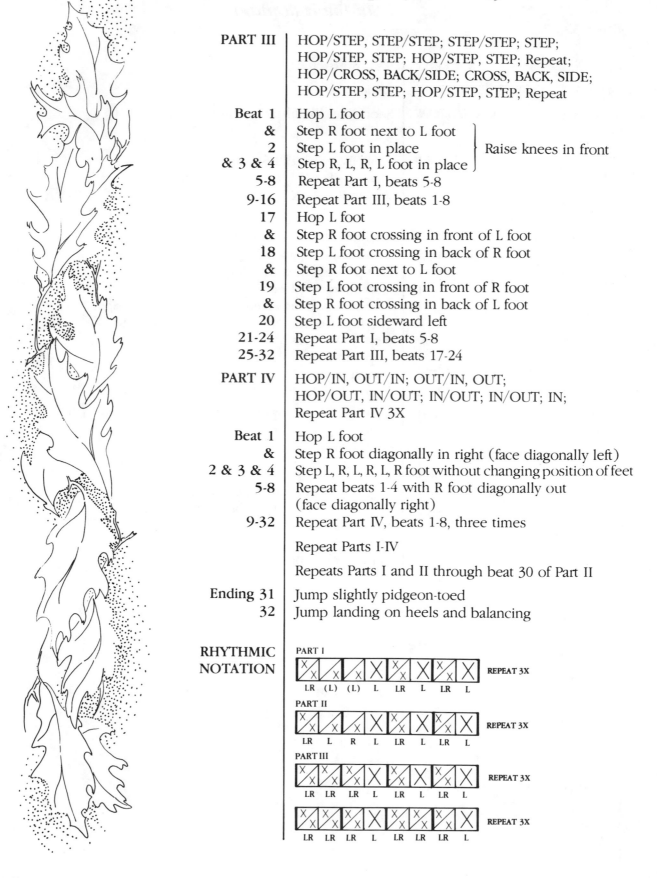

PART I · REPEAT 3X
LR (L) (L) L LR L LR L

PART II · REPEAT 3X
LR L R L LR L LR L

PART III · REPEAT 3X
LR LR LR L LR L LR L

REPEAT 3X
LR LR LR L LR LR LR L

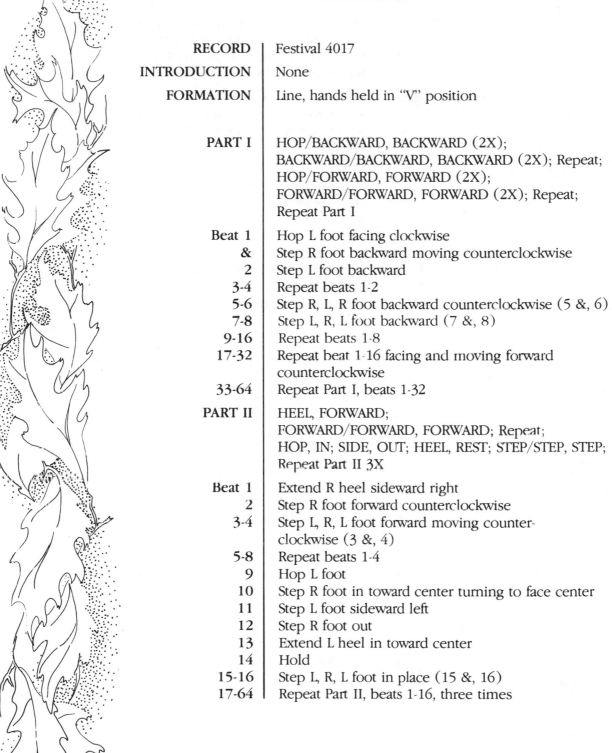

Četvorka
Macedonia

RECORD	Festival 4017
INTRODUCTION	None
FORMATION	Line, hands held in "V" position

PART I	HOP/BACKWARD, BACKWARD (2X); BACKWARD/BACKWARD, BACKWARD (2X); Repeat; HOP/FORWARD, FORWARD (2X); FORWARD/FORWARD, FORWARD (2X); Repeat; Repeat Part I
Beat 1	Hop L foot facing clockwise
&	Step R foot backward moving counterclockwise
2	Step L foot backward
3-4	Repeat beats 1-2
5-6	Step R, L, R foot backward counterclockwise (5 &, 6)
7-8	Step L, R, L foot backward (7 &, 8)
9-16	Repeat beats 1-8
17-32	Repeat beat 1-16 facing and moving forward counterclockwise
33-64	Repeat Part I, beats 1-32
PART II	HEEL, FORWARD; FORWARD/FORWARD, FORWARD; Repeat; HOP, IN; SIDE, OUT; HEEL, REST; STEP/STEP, STEP; Repeat Part II 3X
Beat 1	Extend R heel sideward right
2	Step R foot forward counterclockwise
3-4	Step L, R, L foot forward moving counter- clockwise (3 &, 4)
5-8	Repeat beats 1-4
9	Hop L foot
10	Step R foot in toward center turning to face center
11	Step L foot sideward left
12	Step R foot out
13	Extend L heel in toward center
14	Hold
15-16	Step L, R, L foot in place (15 &, 16)
17-64	Repeat Part II, beats 1-16, three times

(continued)

Četvorka (continued)

PART III	HEEL, FORWARD; FORWARD/FORWARD, FORWARD; FORWARD, IN; CROSS, OUT; LEAP, REST; STEP/STEP, STEP; LEAP, REST; STEP/STEP, STEP; Repeat Part III 3X
Beat 1	Extend R heel sideward right
2	Step R foot forward counterclockwise
3-4	Step L, R, L foot forward (3 &, 4)
5	Leap R foot forward
6	Leap L foot diagonally in
7	Leap R foot crossing in front of L foot
8	Leap L foot out
9	Leap R foot next to L foot (lift L foot in front of R leg)
10	Hold
11-12	Step L, R, L foot in place (11 &, 12)
13-16	Repeat beats 9-12
17-64	Repeat Part III, beats 1-16, three times
PART IV	HEEL, FORWARD; FORWARD/FORWARD, FORWARD; HOP, IN; SIDE, OUT; SIDE/BACK, SIDE; HOP, CROSS; SIDE, OUT; BOUNCE/BOUNCE, BOUNCE; Repeat Part IV 3X
Beats 1-4	Repeat Part III, beats 1-4
5-8	Repeat Part II, beats 9-12
9	Step L foot sideward left
&	Step R foot crossing in back of L foot
10	Step L foot sideward left
11	Hop L foot
12	Step R foot crossing in front of L foot
13	Step L foot sideward right
14	Step R foot out
15-16	Bounce both heels 3 times (15 &, 16)
17-64	Repeat Part IV, beats 1-16, three times

Četvorka *(continued)*

PART V	TOUCH, LIFT; TURN/TURN, TURN; Repeat 3X; HOP, IN; SIDE, OUT; BOUNCE/BOUNCE, IN (2X); STEP, SLAP (2X); HOP/OUT, OUT; OUT, SLAP; Repeat Part V 3X
Beat 1	Touch R toe sideward right
2	Lift R foot behind L leg (knee bent)
3-4	Step R, L, R foot turning 1/2 right
5-16	Repeat beats 1-4, three times alternating feet and facing direction out and in
17	Hop L foot
18	Step R foot in toward center
19	Step L foot sideward left
10	Step R foot out
21	Bounce R heel 2 times
22	Step L foot in
23-24	Repeat beats 21-22
25	Step L foot next to R foot with leap
26	Slap R foot in
27-28	Repeat beats 25-26 with opposite footwork
29	Hop R foot
&	Step L foot out
30	Step R foot out
31	Step L foot out
32	Slap R foot in
33-128	Repeat Part V, beats 1-32, three times

RHYTHMIC NOTATION

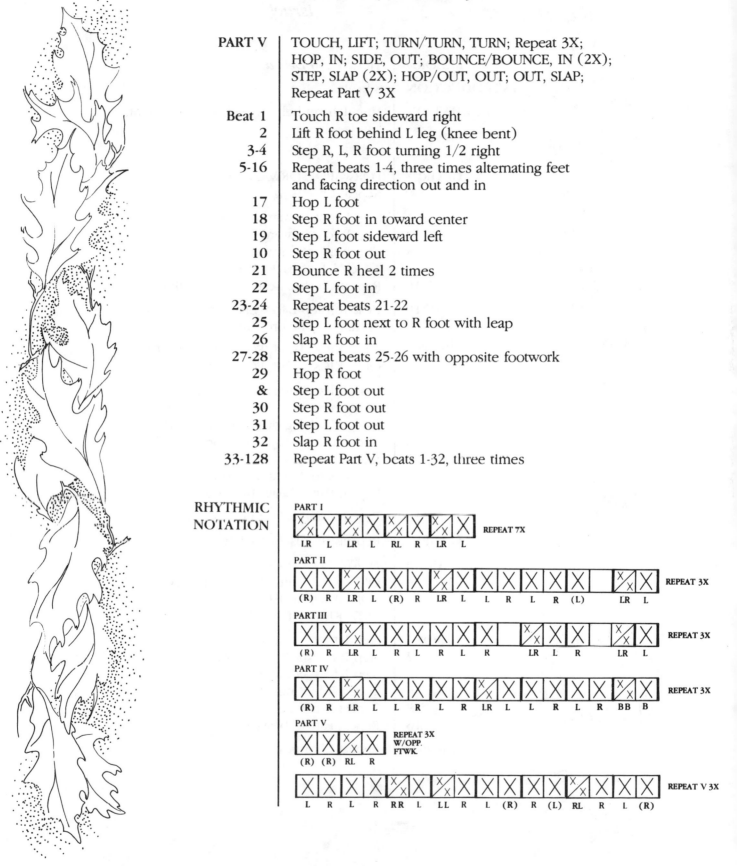

Debka Druz
Israel

RECORD	Tikva T-100 *Debka*
INTRODUCTION	8 beats
FORMATION	Line, L hand behind back, R arm straight, hands joined
CHORUS	FORWARD, FORWARD, TOUCH, TOUCH; Repeat Chorus 3X
Beat 1	Step L foot forward counterclockwise
2	Step R foot forward
3	Touch L foot forward
4	Touch L foot backward
5-16	Repeat Chorus, beats 1-4, three times
NOTE	Beat 16, step L foot backward (change of weight occurs only before Part I).
PART I	OUT, KICK, HEEL/FORWARD, TOUCH; Repeat 2X OUT, KICK, HEEL/FORWARD, CLOSE
Beat 1	Leap R leg diagonally sideward out (L leg bent with foot against R leg)
2	Straighten L leg diagonally forward left
3	Touch L heel diagonally forward left
&	Leap L foot forward
4	Touch R foot next to L foot
5-16	Repeat Part I, beats 1-4, three times
NOTE	Beat 16, step R foot next to L foot.
CHORUS	Repeat Chorus, beats 1-16
PART II	FORWARD, CLOSE, IN, TOUCH; OUT, KICK, HEEL/FORWARD, CLOSE; FORWARD, CLOSE, IN, TOUCH; OUT, KICK, HEEL/FORWARD, CLOSE
Beat 1	Step L foot forward
2	Step R foot next to L foot
3	Step L foot sideward in
4	Touch R foot next to L foot
5-8	Repeat Part I, beats 1-4
9-16	Repeat Part II, beats 1-8
CHORUS	Repeat Chorus, beats 1-16

Debka Druz *(continued)*

PART III	HEEL/FORWARD, CLOSE; HEEL/FORWARD, CLOSE; JUMP, HOP, HEEL/FORWARD, CLOSE; Repeat Part III
Beat 1	Touch L heel forward
&	Leap L foot forward
2	Step R foot next to L foot
3-4	Repeat beats 1-2
5	Jump in place
6	Hop R foot in place
7-8	Repeat beats 1-2
9-16	Repeat Part III, beats 1-8
CHORUS	Repeat Chorus, beats 1-16 and turn line to side-by-side formation
PART IV	TOUCH/SIDE, TOUCH, SWING, SIDE; Repeat 3X
Beat 1	Touch L foot in front of R foot
&	Leap L foot sideward left (line side by side)
2	Touch R foot next to L foot (one may use a squat)
3	Describe an arc close to the floor with R leg
4	Step R foot sideward right
5-16	Repeat Part IV, beats 1-4, three times

RHYTHMIC NOTATION

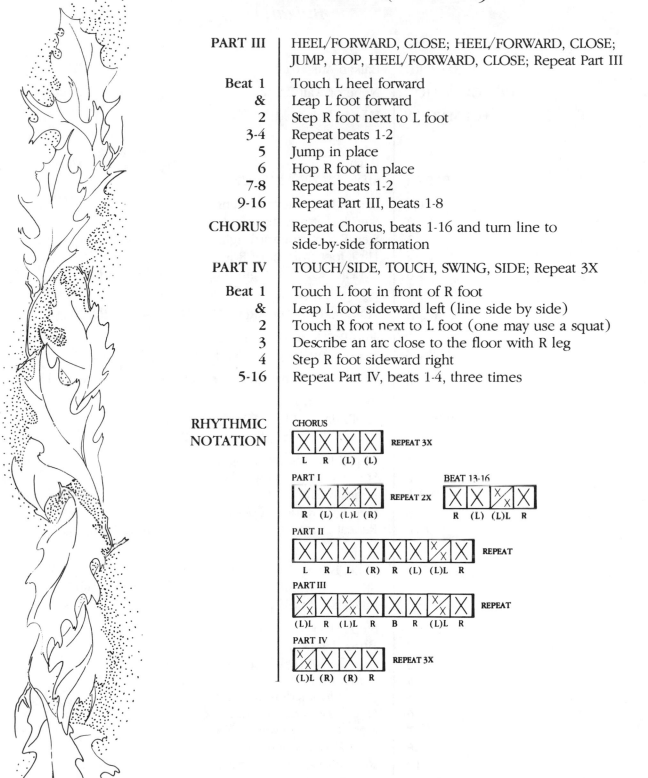

Dobroluško Horo
Bulgaria

RECORD	Balkan Arts 701
INTRODUCTION	None or wait 22 beats
FORMATION	Line in belt hold

	Bavno
PART I	SIDE, CLOSE; SIDE, LIFT; SIDE, LIFT
Beat 1	Step R foot sideward right
2	Step L foot next to R foot
3	Step R foot sideward right
4	Lift L foot in front of R leg
5-6	Repeat beats 3-4 beginning L foot sideward left
	Dai Go Zhivo
PART II	FORWARD, FORWARD; SIDE, HOP; SIDE, HOP
Beats 1-2	Run R, L foot forward counterclockwise
4-6	Repeat Part I, beats 3-6 adding a hop with the lift
NOTE	Parts I and II may be done as many times as desired.
	Tri Na Desno
PART III	SIDE, BACK; SIDE, BACK; SIDE, BACK; STEP/STEP, STEP; Repeat Part III
Beat 1	Step R foot sideward right
2	Step L foot crossing in back of R foot
3-6	Repeat beats 1-2 two times
7-8	Step R, L, R foot in place
9-16	Repeat beats 1-8 sideward left beginning L foot
	Hisfirli
PART IV	STEP, BRUSH; HOP, CLOSE; SIDE, BACK; SIDE, HOP; SIDE, BACK; SIDE, HOP; SIDE, BACK; SIDE, HOP; SIDE, BACK; SIDE, HOP
Beat 1	Step R foot in place
2	Brush L foot in
3	Hop R foot pedaling backward with L foot
4	Step L foot next to R foot
5	Step R foot sideward right
6	Step L foot crossing in back of R foot
7	Step R foot sideward right
8	Hop R foot lifting L foot
9-12	Repeat beats 5-8 sideward left beginning L foot
13-20	Repeat beats 5-12

Dobrolŭsbko Horo (continued)

PART V	STEP, HOP; STEP, HOP
Beat 1	Step R foot, lift L foot behind R foot
2	Hop R foot, swing L foot in
3-4	Repeat beats 1-2 beginning L foot
	Repeat Part IV, beats 1-20
NOTE	Repeat beats 1-4 as many times as desired.
PART VI	IN, IN; CLICK, REST; IN, IN; CLICK, REST; OUT, OUT; CLICK, REST; OUT, OUT; CLICK, REST
Beat 1	Step R foot in toward the center
2	Step L foot in
3-4	Click R foot to L foot
5-8	Repeat beats 1-4
9-16	Repeat Part V, beats 1-8, moving out away from the center
17-36	Repeat Part IV, beats 1-20
NOTE	Beats 1-4 may be repeated any number of times moving in and a like number of times moving out, i.e., 3 in, 3 out; 2 in, 2 out.
	Parts III, V, and VI may be done in any order and as many times as desired.

RHYTHMIC NOTATION

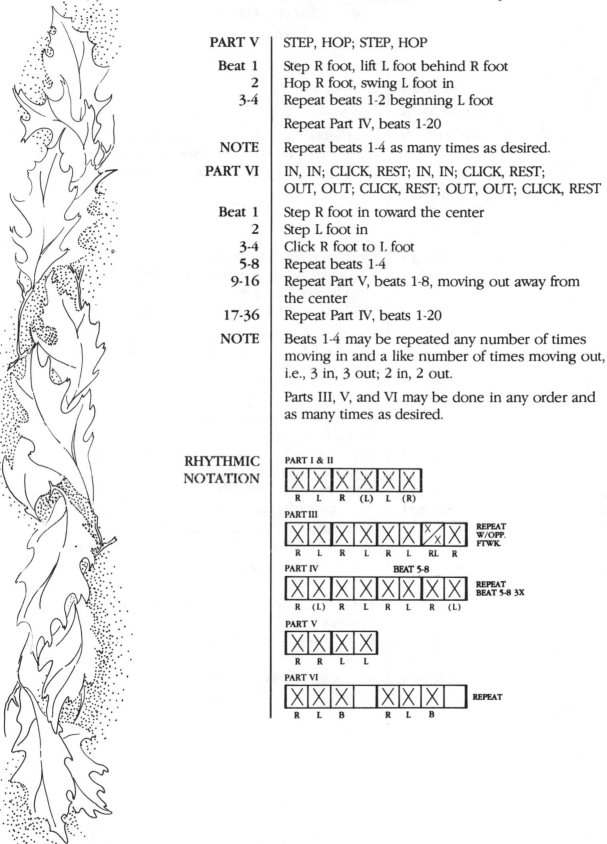

Dodi Li
My Beloved is Mine
Israel

RECORD	LP *Hora*
INTRODUCTION	None
FORMATION	Couples facing each other; women's left hand and men's right hand held; footwork given for men; opposite footwork for women
ALTERNATE FORMATION	Circle, no hands held
CHORUS	SIDE, SIDE, CROSS, PIVOT; FORWARD, REST, FORWARD, CLOSE; BACKWARD, CLOSE, SIDE, REST; SIDE, SIDE, CROSS, REST; Repeat Chorus
Beats 1-3	Yemenite beginning L foot
4	Pivot on L foot to face forward counterclockwise
5-6	Step R foot forward
7	Step L foot forward
8	Step R foot next to L foot
9	Step L foot backward
10	Step R foot next to L foot
11-12	Step L foot sideward left turning to face partner
13-16	Yemenite beginning R foot
17-32	Repeat Chorus, beats 1-16
PART I	SIDE, SIDE, CROSS, PIVOT; FORWARD, PIVOT; BACKWARD, 2; 3, 4; SIDE, REST; SIDE, SIDE; CROSS, REST; Repeat Part I
Beats 1-6	Repeat Chorus, beats 1-6 pivoting on beat 6 to face clockwise
7-10	Step L, R, L, R foot backward (change to opposite hand hold)
11-16	Repeat Chorus, beats 11-16
17-32	Repeat Part I, beats 1-16
CHORUS	Repeat Chrous, beats 1-32

Dodi Li (continued)

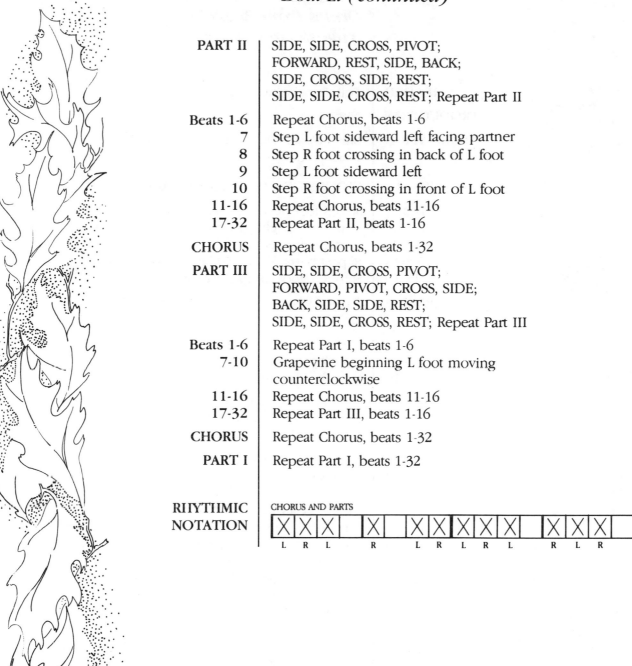

PART II	SIDE, SIDE, CROSS, PIVOT; FORWARD, REST, SIDE, BACK; SIDE, CROSS, SIDE, REST; SIDE, SIDE, CROSS, REST; Repeat Part II
Beats 1-6	Repeat Chorus, beats 1-6
7	Step L foot sideward left facing partner
8	Step R foot crossing in back of L foot
9	Step L foot sideward left
10	Step R foot crossing in front of L foot
11-16	Repeat Chorus, beats 11-16
17-32	Repeat Part II, beats 1-16
CHORUS	Repeat Chorus, beats 1-32
PART III	SIDE, SIDE, CROSS, PIVOT; FORWARD, PIVOT, CROSS, SIDE; BACK, SIDE, SIDE, REST; SIDE, SIDE, CROSS, REST; Repeat Part III
Beats 1-6	Repeat Part I, beats 1-6
7-10	Grapevine beginning L foot moving counterclockwise
11-16	Repeat Chorus, beats 11-16
17-32	Repeat Part III, beats 1-16
CHORUS	Repeat Chorus, beats 1-32
PART I	Repeat Part I, beats 1-32

RHYTHMIC NOTATION

CHORUS AND PARTS

X X X X X X X X X X X X
L R L R L R L R L R L R

Drmeš Iz Zdenčine
Drmeš from Zdenčine
Yugoslavia (Croatia)

RECORD	Folk Dancer MH 3030
INTRODUCTION	None
FORMATION	Small closed circles in a reverse basket, L arm under
PART I	CLOSE/SIDE, (14X); ACCENT, ACCENT
Beat 1	Step R foot next to L foot (knee slightly bent)
&	Step L foot slightly sideward left on ball of foot (straighten knees)
2-14	Repeat beats 1& moving clockwise, 13 times
15-16	Step R, L foot with an accent
PART II	IN, FORWARD (7X); ACCENT, ACCENT
Beat 1	Step R foot in toward center ⎱
2	Step L foot forward clockwise ⎰ Croatian walk
3-14	Repeat beats 1-2 six times
15-16	Step R, L foot with an accent
PART III	CROSS, HOP/FORWARD (8X); IN, REST; SIDE; REST; SIDE, REST; CROSS, HOP/FORWARD (4X); CROSS, HOP
Beat 1	Step R foot in front of L foot
2	Hop R foot
&	Step L foot forward clockwise
3-16	Repeat beats 1-2, seven times
17-18	Step R foot in toward the center with an accent
19-20	Step L foot sideward left with an accent (turn to face counterclockwise)
21-22	Step R foot sideward right with an accent
23-30	Repeat beats 1-2 four times beginning L foot
31-32	Step hop L foot, crossing L foot in front of R foot
RHYTHMIC NOTATION	

Drmeš Medley
Yugoslavia (Croatia)

RECORD	NAMA 1
INTRODUCTION	None
FORMATION	Closed circle, back basket

Drmeš Iz Zdenčine

PART I	CLOSE, SIDE (14X); ACCENT, ACCENT; IN, FORWARD (7X)
Beat 1	Step R foot next to L foot bending R knee
&	Step L foot slightly sideward left straightening knees
2-14	Repeat beats 1 &, thirteen times, moving clockwise
15	Accent R foot next to L foot
16	Accent L foot next to R foot
17	Step R foot in toward the center
18	Step L foot slightly forward left (body faces center)
19-30	Repeat beats 17-18, six times moving clockwise
PART II	FORWARD, HOP/FORWARD (8X); FORWARD, PIVOT; ACCENT, REST; ACCENT, REST; FORWARD, HOP/FORWARD (4X); FORWARD, HOP
Beat 1	Step R foot forward with accent moving clockwise
2	Hop R foot
&	Step L foot forward
3-16	Repeat beats 1-2 seven times moving clockwise
17	Step R foot forward with accent
18	Pivot on R foot to face counterclockwise
19-20	Accent L foot next to R foot
21-22	Accent R foot next to L foot
23-30	Repeat beats 1-2 four times counterclockwise with opposite footwork
31	Step L foot forward
32	Hop L foot
	Repeat Parts I, II, I
TRANSITION	Step R foot forward counterclockwise

Kriči, Kriči, Tiček

PART I	HOP/FORWARD, FORWARD (8X)
Beat 1	Hop R foot
&	Step L foot forward counterclockwise
2	Step R foot forward
3-16	Repeat beats 1-2, seven times

(continued)

Drmeš Medley (continued)

PART II	FORWARD (7X); PIVOT; FORWARD (8X)
Beats 1-7	Step L, R, L, R, L, R, L foot forward clockwise
8	Pivot L foot to face counterclockwise
9-16	Step R, L, R, L, R, L, R, L foot forward counterclockwise
PART III	Repeat Part I, beats 1-16 in opposite direction with opposite footwork
PART IV	Repeat Part II, beats 1-16 in opposite direction with opposite footwork
	Repeat Parts I-IV, Part I
TRANSITION	Step L foot foward clockwise and turn to face center
	Kisa Pada
PART I	CROSS, SIDE (16X)
Beat 1	Step R foot crossing in front of L foot (moving clockwise)
2	Step L foot sideward left on ball of foot
3-32	Repeat beats 1-2, fifteen times
PART II	CLOSE, BOUNCE/BOUNCE; SIDE, BOUNCE/BOUNCE; Repeat Part II 7X
Beat 1	Step R foot next to L foot bending R knee
2	Bounce both heels 2 times, knees straight
3	Step L foot slightly sideward left bending L knee
4	Bounce both heels 2 times
5-32	Repeat beats 1-4, seven times
PART I	Repeat Part I, beats 1-32
RHYTHMIC NOTATION	

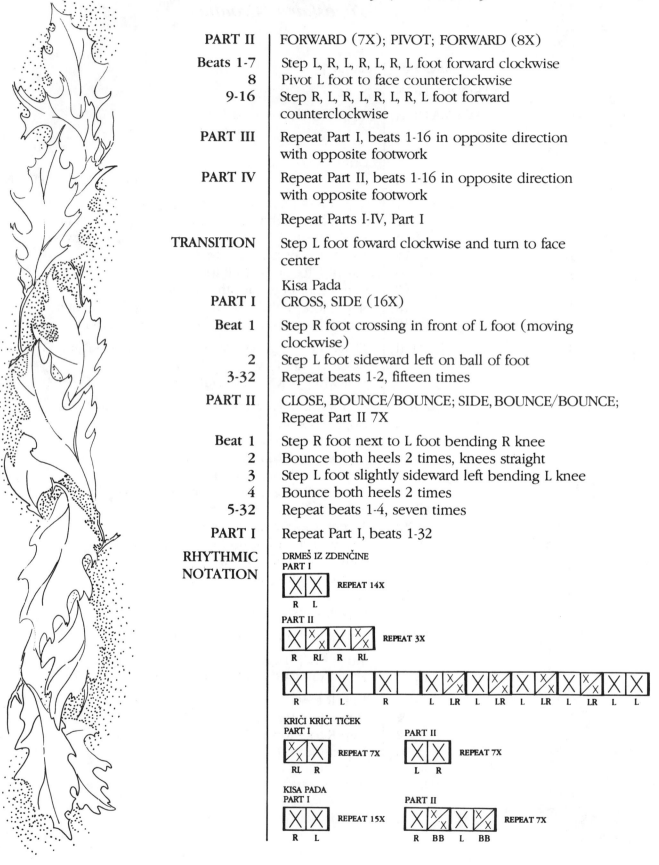

Dror Yikra
Call for Freedom
Israel

RECORD	Hadarim 3 *Back from Israel* Eretz Zavat; Tikva T-145 *Party*
INTRODUCTION	Varies with recording selected
FORMATION	Circle, hands joined or use shoulder hold
PART I	SIDE, BACK, SIDE/CROSS, SIDE/BACK; SIDE/SIDE, CROSS; Repeat; BEND/STRAIGHTEN, BEND/STRAIGHTEN; Repeat Part I
Beat 1	Step R foot sideward right
2	Step L foot crossing in back of R foot
3	Step R foot sideward right with a slight leap
&	Step L foot crossing in front of R foot (bend knees)
4	Step R foot sideward right
&	Step L foot crossing in back of R foot
5-6	Yemenite beginning R foot sideward right
7-12	Repeat beats 1-6 moving clockwise (begin L foot)
13	Step R foot next to L foot (bend and straighten knees)
14	Bend and straighten knees
15-28	Repeat Part I, beats 1-14
PART II	IN/HOP, CROSS; IN/HOP, CROSS; SIDE/SIDE, CROSS; SIDE/SIDE, CROSS; SIDE/SIDE; IN/HOP, IN; SNAP, SNAP, SNAP; OUT/CLOSE, IN; OUT/CLOSE, IN; TURN, 2, 3, 4; Repeat Part II
Beat 1	Step hop R foot in toward center; hands at sides
2	Step L foot crossing in front of R foot (cross wrists in front of body)
3-4	Repeat beats 1-2
5-6	Yemenite beginning R foot
7-8	Yemenite beginning L foot
9	Touch R foot next to L foot
10	Step R foot sideward right with a lunge then, Step L foot sideward left
11	Step hop R foot in
12	Step L foot in and go down into a squatting position (snap fingers in with wrists crossed)
13	Snap fingers right side
14	Snap fingers left side
15	Snap fingers in
16	Step R foot out away from center
&	Step L foot next to R foot

(continued)

Dror Yikra (continued)

17	Step R foot in toward center
18-19	Repeat beats 16-17 beginning L foot
20-23	Step R, L, R, L foot turning body one full turn clockwise; snap fingers with step and bend knee after each step
24-46	Repeat Part II, beats 1-23

RHYTHMIC NOTATION

Floricica
Little Flower
Romania (Mutenia)

RECORD	Nevofoon 12153 *Romanian Folkdances*
INTRODUCTION	None
FORMATION·	Closed circle, hands held in "V" position
PART I	SIDE/BACK; SIDE/BACK; SIDE/BACK; SIDE/STAMP; SIDE/BACK; SIDE/STAMP; SIDE/BACK; SIDE/STAMP; Repeat Part I
Beat 1	Step R foot sideward right
&	Step L foot crossing in back of R foot
2-3	Repeat beats 1 & two times
4	Step R foot sideward right
&	Stamp L foot
5	Step L foot sideward left
&	Step R foot crossing in back of L foot
6	Step L foot sideward left
&	Stamp R foot
7-8	Repeat beats 5-6 sideward right beginning R foot
9-16	Repeat beats 1-8 beginning L foot

Floricica (continued)

PART II	IN/HOP, OUT/HOP; SIDE/CLOSE, SIDE/HOP; SIDE/CLOSE, SIDE/CLOSE; SIDE/STAMP, IN; IN/HOP, OUT/HOP; SIDE/CLOSE, SIDE/HOP; SIDE/CLOSE, SIDE/CLOSE; SIDE/STAMP, IN
Beats 1 &	Step hop R foot in
2 &	Step hop L foot out
3-4	Schottische R foot sideward right (side/close, side/hop)
5-6	Side close sideward left 2 times beginning L foot
7	Step L foot sideward left
&	Stamp R foot
8	Step R foot slightly in with a lunge, accenting the step (L foot brought up skater's style)
9-16	Repeat Part II, beats 1-8 beginning L foot
RHYTHMIC **NOTATION**	

PART I

X	X	X	X	X	X	X	X	X	X
X	X	X	X	X	X	X	X	X	X

RL   RL   RL   R(L)   LR   L(R)   RL   R(L)

REPEAT W/OPP. FTWK.

PART II

RR   LL   RL   RR   LR   LR   L(R)   R

REPEAT W/OPP. FTWK.

Haroa Haktana
Little Shepherdess
Israel

RECORD	Tikva T-69 *Dance Along with Sabras*
INTRODUCTION	16 beats
FORMATION	Circle, facing center; arms down and close to body; no hands held
PART I	Circle moves counterclockwise throughout Part I JUMP, HOP (6X); SIDE, BOUNCE, SIDE, BOUNCE; Repeat Part I
Beat 1	Jump on both feet with feet slightly apart
2	Hop R foot turning 1/2 to right; end facing out (body turns clockwise)
3	Jump

(continued)

Haroa Haktana (continued)

4	Hop L foot turn 1/2 to left to face center; be sure to progress counterclockwise (body turns clockwise)
5	Jump
6	Hop R foot, continue with another 1/2 turn to left to face out (body turns counterclockwise)
7-8	Jump hop L foot, turn body 1/2 turn to right (R shoulder moves backward; body turning clockwise)
9-10	Jump hop R foot turning 1/2 turn (body continues clockwise turn)
11-12	Jump hop L foot turning 1/2 turn to end facing center (body continues clockwise)
13-14	Step R foot sideward right and bounce (snap fingers on beat 14, arms overhead)
15-16	Step L foot sideward left and bounce (snap fingers on beat 16)
17-32	Repeat Part I, beats 1-16
PART II	IN, HOP, IN, HOP; OUT, HOP, OUT, HOP; SIDE, BOUNCE, SIDE, BOUNCE; Repeat; IN, HOP, SCISSOR, SCISSOR; STEP, HOP, TOGETHER, REST
Beats 1-2	Step hop R foot in toward center, R shoulder toward center
3-4	Step hop L foot in toward center, L shoulder toward center
5-6	Step hop R foot away from center keeping L shoulder toward center
7-8	Step hop L foot away from center; R shoulder toward center
9-12	Repeat Part I, beats 13-16
13-24	Repeat Part II, beats 1-12
25-26	Step hop R foot kicking L foot in and low
27	Step L foot kicking R foot out
28	Step R foot kicking L foot out
29-30	Step hop L foot bringing R knee up
31-32	Step on R foot with slight accent; weight now on both feet

RHYTHMIC NOTATION

PART I

X	X	X	X	X	X	X	X	X	X	X	X	X	X	X	X	REPEAT
B	R	B	L	B	R	B	L	B	R	B	L	RL	R	LR	L	

PART II

X	X	X	X	X	X	X	X	X X	X X	X	REPEAT
R	R	L	L	R	R	L	L	RL	LR	L	

X	X	X	X	X	X	X	
R	R	L	R	L	L	B	

Hashachar
The Dawn
Israel

RECORD	Hadarim 3 *Back from Israel*
INTRODUCTION	8 beats
FORMATION	Individuals in a circle facing center; do not join hands

PART I	SIDE, CROSS; SIDE/SIDE, CROSS/HOP; SIDE, CROSS; SIDE, CROSS; SIDE/SIDE, CROSS, HEEL; Repeat Part I
Beat 1	Step L foot sideward left
2	Step R foot crossing in front of L foot; snap fingers, wrists crossed
3-4	Yemenite beginning L foot
&	Hop L foot
5	Step R foot sideward right
6	Step L foot crossing in front of R foot; snap fingers, wrists crossed
7-8	Repeat beats 5-6
9-10	Yemenite beginning R foot
11	Touch L heel diagonally left
12-22	Repeat Part I, beats 1-11
PART II	OUT/CLOSE, IN; OUT/CLOSE, IN, BRUSH/HOP, OUT/IN; HEEL, HEEL; HEEL, HEEL; JUMP/HOP, OUT; OUT, OUT; SIDE/SIDE, CROSS; HEEL, HEEL; JUMP/HOP, IN/OUT; OUT, OUT; SIDE/SIDE, CROSS
Beat 1	Step L foot out away from center
&	Step R foot next to L foot
2	Step L foot in toward the center
3-4	Repeat beats 1-2 beginning R foot
5	Brush L foot in
&	Hop R foot
6	Step L foot out
&	Step R foot in
7	Touch L heel in
8-10	Rotate L foot to right, left, right
11	Jump on both feet
&	Hop L foot
12-14	Step R, L, R foot out
15-16	Yemenite beginning L foot
17	Touch R heel in
18	Rotate R foot to left

(continued)

Hashachar (continued)

19	Jump on both feet
&	Hop L foot
20	Step R foot in
&	Step L foot out
21-22	Step R, L foot out
23-24	Yemenite beginning R foot

RHYTHMIC NOTATION

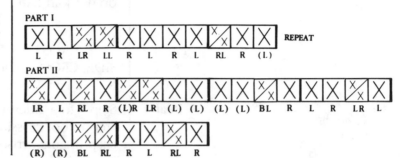

Hopa, Hopa
Yugoslavia (Croatia)

RECORD	Kola E404
INTRODUCTION	None
FORMATION	Small circles, front basket, L arm under

PART I FORWARD, HOP; CROSS, HOP; SIDE, HOP;
SIDE, BOUNCE/BOUNCE; SIDE, BOUNCE/BOUNCE;
SIDE, BOUNCE/BOUNCE; SIDE, BOUNCE/BOUNCE;
SIDE, BOUNCE/BOUNCE; SIDE, BOUNCE/BOUNCE;
SIDE, BOUNCE/BOUNCE; SIDE, BOUNCE/BOUNCE

Beats 1-2	Step hop L foot diagonally forward left (facing center)
3-4	Step hop R foot crossing in front of L foot
5-6	Step hop L foot sideward left
7	Step R foot slightly sideward right bending knee
8	Bounce both feet legs straight 2 times
9	Step R foot slightly sideward right
10	Bounce both feet legs straight 2 times
11-14	Repeat beats 7-10 sideward left beginning L foot
15-18	Repeat beats 7-10

Beats 7-10 bracketed: Drmeš

RHYTHMIC NOTATION

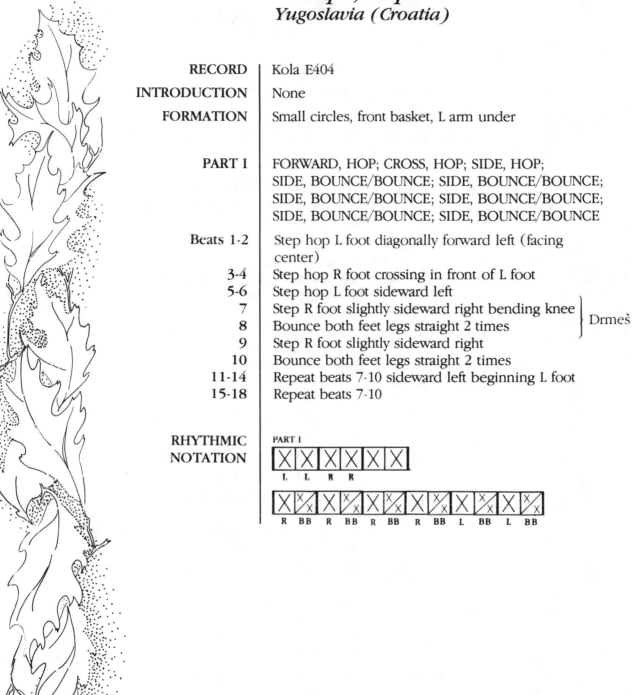

Hora Chemed
Hora of Delight
Israel

RECORD	Hadarim 3 *Back from Israel*
INTRODUCTION	8 beats
FORMATION	Circle, facing counterclockwise, hands joined
PART I	JUMP, JUMP, FORWARD, BRUSH; HOP, FORWARD, FORWARD/FORWARD, FORWARD; Repeat Part I 3X
Beats 1-2	Jump 2 times angling knees left then forward (Debka Jump)
3-4	Step L foot forward counterclockwise, brush R foot forward with accent
5	Hop L foot
6	Step R foot forward (slight leap) counterclockwise
7	Step L foot forward
&	Step R foot forward
8	Step L foot forward
9-32	Repeat Part I, beats 1-8, three times then release hand hold
PART II	FORWARD, FORWARD, FORWARD, REST (3X); FORWARD, FORWARD, FORWARD, SIDE
Beats 1-3	Step R, L, R foot forward leaning body right (out)
4	Hit back of R hand against palm of L hand (in front of R shoulder)
5-7	Step L, R, L foot leaning body left (in)
8	Hit back of L hand against palm of R hand (in front of L shoulder)
9-16	Repeat Part II, beats 1-8; beat 16 step R foot sideward right (face center and join hands)
PART III	SIDE, SIDE, CROSS, HOP; SIDE, CROSS, TOGETHER, BOUNCE; Repeat Part III
Beats 1-3	Yemenite beginning L foot
4	Hop L foot
5	Step R foot sideward right with a leap
6	Step L foot crossing in front of R foot
7-8	Step R foot next to L foot transferring weight to both feet (bounce heels)
9-16	Repeat Part III, beats 1-8

Hora Chemed (continued)

RHYTHMIC
NOTATION

PART I

| X | X | X | X | X | X | X̸ | X | REPEAT 3X
| | | | | | | X̸ | |

B   B   L   (R)   L   R   LR   L

PART II

| X | X | X | | X | X | X | |

R   L   R   L   R   L

| X | X | X | | X | X | X | X |

R   L   R   L   R   L   R

PART III

| X | X | X | X | X | X | X | REPEAT

L   R   L   L   R   L   B   B

Hora Eilat
Israel

RECORD	Tikva 104 *Dance for Fun*
INTRODUCTION	Pickup plus 16 beats
FORMATION	Circle, hands joined

PART I	FORWARD, FORWARD; FORWARD, HOP; BACKWARD, HOP; BACKWARD, FORWARD; Repeat Part I
Beat 1	Run L foot forward counterclockwise
2	Run R foot forward counterclockwise with a leap
3-4	Step hop L foot forward turning 1/2 to face clockwise (body turns counterclockwise)
5-6	Step hop R foot backward counterclockwise
7	Step L foot backward
8	Step R foot turning to face counterclockwise
9-16	Repeat Part I, beats 1-8
PART II	FORWARD, FORWARD; FORWARD, HOP; SIDE, SIDE; SIDE, HOP; Repeat Part II
Beat 1	Run L foot forward counterclockwise
2	Step R foot forward counterclockwise with a leap
3-4	Step hop L foot forward counterclockwise and turn to face center
5	Step R foot sideward right swaying right
6	Step L foot sideward left swaying left
7	Step R foot sideward right swaying right
8	Hop R foot turning to face counterclockwise
9-16	Repeat Part II, beats 1-8

(continued)

Hora Eilat (continued)

PART I	Repeat Part I, beats 1-16 (end facing clockwise)
PART III	FORWARD, HOP; FORWARD, HOP; SIDE, HOP; SIDE, SIDE; CROSS, HOP; FORWARD, HOP; JUMP, BACKWARD; BACKWARD, BACKWARD; Repeat Part III
Beats 1-2	Step hop L foot forward clockwise
3-4	Step hop R foot forward clockwise and turn to face center
5-6	Step hop L foot sideward left
7-9	Yemenite beginning R foot
10	Hop R foot
11-12	Step hop L foot forward clockwise
13	Jump facing clockwise
14-16	Step R, L, R foot backward kicking opposite leg forward, moving counterclockwise
17-32	Repeat Part III, beats 1-16. Beat 32 turn to face counterclockwise to begin dance again

RHYTHMIC NOTATION

PART I

X	X	X	X	X	X	X	X	REPEAT
L	R	L	L	R	R	L	R	

PART II

X	X	X	X	X	X	X	X	REPEAT
L	R	L	L	R	L	R	R	

PART III

X	X	X	X	X	X	X	X	X	X	X	X	X	X	X	X	REPEAT
L	L	R	R	L	L	R	L	R	R	L	L	R	R	L	R	

Horat Hasor
Tenth Anniversary Debka
Israel

RECORD	Tikva T-69 *Dance Along With Sabras*
INTRODUCTION	16 beats
FORMATION	Line, hands joined
PART I	FORWARD, 2; 3, 4; IN, OUT, IN, HOP; FORWARD, 2; 3, 4; OUT, IN, OUT, HOP; Repeat Part I
Beats 1-4	Step L, R, I, R foot forward moving counterclockwise
5	Step L foot in toward center (facing counterclockwise)
6	Step R foot out
7	Step L foot in
8	Hop L foot
9-16	Repeat beats 1-8 beginning R foot
PART II	SIDE, REST; SIDE, CROSS; SIDE, CROSS; SIDE/SIDE, CROSS; JUMP, JUMP; JUMP, HOP/STAMP; IN, REST; OUT, CLOSE; Repeat Part II
Beats 1-2	Step L foot sideward left (facing center)
3	Leap R foot sideward right
4	Step L foot crossing in front of R foot
5-6	Repeat beats 3-4
7-8	Yemenite beginning R foot
9-11	Jump 3 times
12	Hop L foot
&	Stamp R foot
13-14	Step R foot in with an accent
15	Step L foot out
16	Step R foot next to L foot
17-32	Repeat Part II, beats 1-16

RHYTHMIC NOTATION

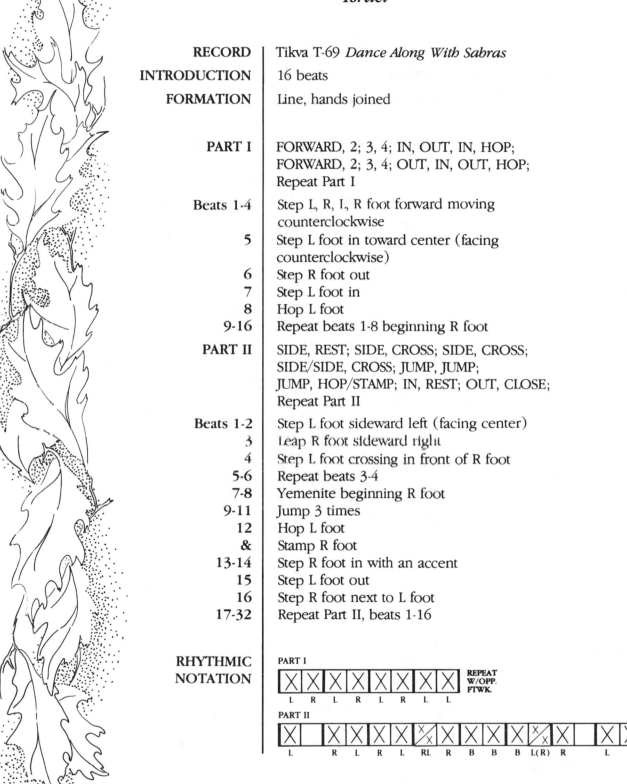

Im Ninalu
If They Were Locked Out
Israel

RECORD	Eretz Zavat
INTRODUCTION	10 beats
FORMATION	Lines facing the same direction
PART I	SIDE, TOUCH; SIDE, TOUCH; SIDE/HOP, CROSS/SIDE; HOP/CROSS; SIDE/SIDE; CROSS, TOUCH; Repeat Part I 2X
Beat 1	Step R foot slightly sideward right
2	Touch L foot in front of R foot
3	Step L foot slightly sideward left
4	Touch R foot in front of L foot
5	Step hop R foot sideward right
6	Step L foot crossing in front of R foot
&	Step R foot sideward right
7	Hop R foot
&	Step L foot crossing in front of R foot
8-9	Yemenite beginning R foot
10	Touch L foot next to R foot
11-20	Repeat Part I, beats 1-10 beginning L foot in opposite direction
21-30	Repeat Part I, beats 1-10 beginning R foot
NOTE	End with a step L foot next to R foot
PART II	SIDE, OUT; FORWARD, IN; Repeat Part II 3X
Beat 1	Step R foot sideward right
2	Step L foot out to face clockwise
3	Step R foot forward clockwise
4	Step L foot in
5-16	Repeat Part II, beats 1-4, three times

Square

```
4 ┌─────┐ 1
  │     │
  │     │
3 └─────┘ 2
```

Im Ninalu (continued)

PART III	SIDE/SIDE, CROSS; SIDE/SIDE, CROSS; IN/HOP, CLOSE; Repeat Part III
Beats 1-2	Yemenite beginning R foot
3-4	Yemenite beginning L foot
5	Step hop R foot in turning 1/4 right
6	Step L foot next to R foot
7-12	Repeat Part III, beats 1-6
NOTE	Last time dance executed, keep repeating Part III.
RHYTHMIC NOTATION	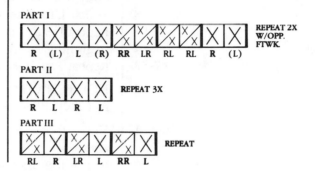

PART I

R (L) L (R) RR LR RL RL R (L)   REPEAT 2X W/OPP. FTWK

PART II

R L R L   REPEAT 3X

PART III

RL R LR L RR L   REPEAT

Jeftanovičevo Kolo
Jeftanovič's Dance
Yugoslavia
(Bosnia and Vojvodina)

RECORD	Folk Dancer MH 1012
INTRODUCTION	None
FORMATION	Broken circle, hands held in "V" position
PART I	HOP/SIDE, CLOSE; SIDE, HOP; Repeat Part I 7X
Beat 1	Hop L in place
&	Step R foot slightly sideward right
2	Step L foot next to R foot
3	Step R foot slightly sideward right
4	Hop R foot
5-32	Repeat Part I, beats 1-4, seven times alternating direction and footwork

(continued)

Jeftanovičevo Kolo (continued)

PART II	FORWARD, FORWARD; SIDE, TOUCH; SIDE, TOUCH; SIDE, TOUCH; Repeat Part II 3X
Beat 1	Step R foot moving forward counterclockwise
2	Step L foot moving forward counterclockwise
3	Step R foot sideward right
4	Touch L foot next to R foot
5	Step L foot sideward left (diagonally away from center)
6	Touch R foot next to L foot
7	Step R foot sideward right (diagonally away from center)
8	Touch L foot next to R foot
9-16	Repeat beats 1-8 to the left beginning L foot
17-32	Repeat Part II, beats 1-16
PART III	HOP/FORWARD, FORWARD (6X); ACCENT, REST, STAMP, REST; Repeat Part III
Beat 1	Hop L foot extending R slightly forward and low
&	Step R foot moving forward counterclockwise
2	Step L foot moving forward counterclockwise
3-12	Repeat beats 1-2, five times
13-14	Step R foot with an accent and turn to face center
15-16	Stamp L foot turning to face clockwise
17-32	Repeat Part III, beats 1-16 to the left beginning R foot

RHYTHMIC NOTATION

PART I

X	X	X	X	REPEAT 7X W/OPP. FTWK.
LR	L	R	R	

PART II

X	X	X	X	X	X	X	X	REPEAT 3X W/OPP. FTWK.
R	L	R	(L)	L	(R)	R	(L)	

PART III

X	X	X	X	REPEAT 2X
LR	L	LR	L	

X		X		REPEAT III W/OPP. FTWK.
R		(L)		

Kasapsko Oro
Macedonia

RECORD	Worldtone 10009
INTRODUCTION	None
FORMATION	Broken circle, belt hold with R arm under
PART I	FORWARD, FORWARD; FORWARD/FORWARD, FORWARD; HOP/STEP, REST/STEP; FORWARD/FORWARD, FORWARD; Repeat Part I 7X
Beats 1-2	Step R, L foot forward moving counterclockwise
3-4	Step R, L, R foot forward (3, &, 4)
5	Hop R foot
&	Step L foot forward
6	Hold
&	Step R foot forward
7-8	Step L, R, L foot forward (7, &, 8)
9-64	Repeat Part I, beats 1-8, seven times
PART II	FORWARD, FORWARD; FORWARD/FORWARD, SIDE; SIDE, CROSS/BACK; SIDE/CROSS, BACK; FORWARD, FORWARD; FORWARD/FORWARD, SIDE; SIDE, SIDE/CROSS; BACK/SIDE, CROSS; Repeat Part II
Beats 1-2	Step R, L foot forward moving counterclockwise
3	Step R, L foot forward
4	Step R foot sideward right
5	Step L foot sideward left
6	Step R foot crossing in front of L foot
&	Step L foot crossing in back of R foot
7	Step R foot sideward right
&	Step L foot crossing in front of R foot
8	Step R foot crossing in back of L foot
9-12	Repeat beats 1-4 clockwise beginning L foot
13	Step R foot sideward right
14	Step L foot sideward left
&	Step R foot crossing in front of L foot
15	Step L foot crossing in back of R foot
&	Step R foot sideward right
16	Step L foot crossing in front of R foot
17-32	Repeat Part II, beats 1-16

(continued)

Kasapsko Oro (continued)

PART III	FORWARD, FORWARD; FORWARD/FORWARD, SIDE; HOP/OUT, REST/BOUNCE; OUT/SIDE, CROSS; Repeat Part III 3X
Beats 1-4	Repeat Part II, beats 1-4
5	Hop R foot
&	Step L foot out away from center
6	Hold
&	Bounce L heel
7	Step R foot out
&	Step L foot sideward left
8	Step R foot crossing in front of L foot
9-16	Repeat beats 1-4 moving clockwise beginning L foot
17-32	Repeat Part III, beats 1-16
	Repeat Part II
	Repeat Part I 4 times
	Repeat Part III

RHYTHMIC NOTATION	

PART I

REPEAT 7X

R   L   RL   R   RL   R   LR   L

PART II

REPEAT W/OPP. FTWK.

R   L   RL   R   L   RL   RL   R

PART III

REPEAT 3X W/OPP. FTWK.

R   L   RL   R   RL   L   RL   R

Kisa Pada
Yugoslavia

RECORD	Monitor MF 326 Side 1, Band 1
INTRODUCTION	None
FORMATION	Front basket, L arm under, middle fingers joined
PART I	CROSS, SIDE (8X)
Beat 1	Step R foot crossing in front of L foot
2	Step L foot sideward left (slight leap)
3-16	Repeat beats 1-2 seven times

Kisa Pada (continued)

PART II	CROSS, HOP/STEP (8X)
Beat 1	Step R foot crossing in front of L foot
2	Hop R foot raising L hip keeping L leg close to R leg, twist body
&	Step L foot next to R foot
3-16	Repeat Part II, beats 1-2, seven times
PART III	STEP, BOUNCE/BOUNCE; STEP, BOUNCE/BOUNCE (8X)
Beat 1	Step on R foot bending R knee (move L foot sideward left)
2	Bounce both heels 2 times (feet are separated)
3	Step on L foot (move R foot next to L foot)
4	Bounce both heels 2 times (feet are together)
5-16	Repeat Part III, beats 1-2, three times
PART IV	IN, BOUNCE/BOUNCE; OUT, BOUNCE/BOUNCE; Repeat Part IV, 4X
Beat 1	Step R foot in toward center
2	Bounce R heel two times
3	Step L foot out from center
4	Bounce L foot two times
5-16	Repeat Part IV, beats 1-4, three times
PART V	CROSS, STEP (8X)
Beat 1	Step R foot crossing in front of L foot
2	Step L foot in place bending L knee, keep R knee bent as step is taken
3-16	Repeat beats 1-2, seven times
PART VI	FORWARD, FORWARD (8X)
Beats 1-2	Run R, L foot forward moving clockwise
3-16	Repeat beats 1-2, seven times

RHYTHMIC NOTATION

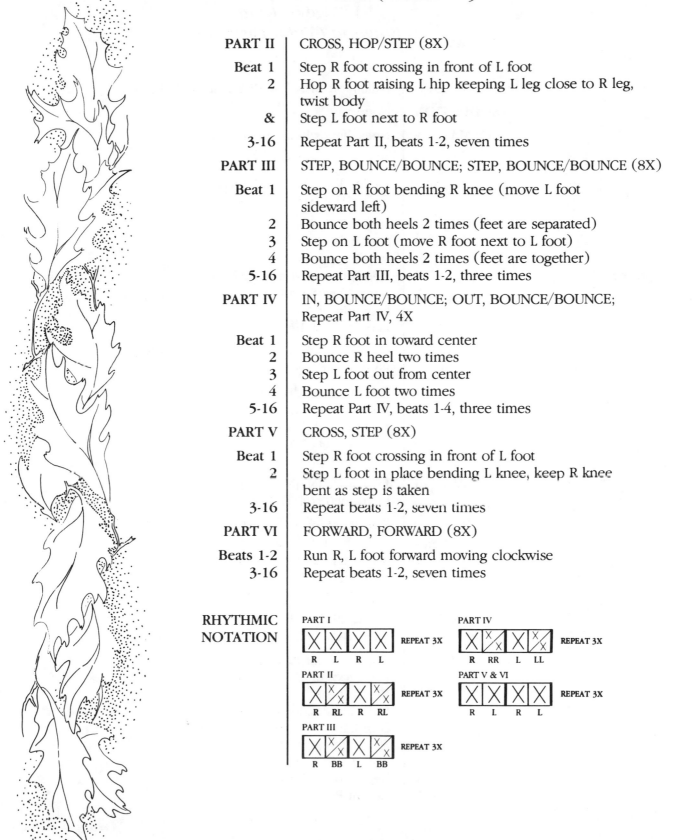

Kulsko Horo
Village of Kula
Bulgaria (Vidin District)

RECORD	Balkanton BHA 734 *Bulgarian Folk Dances*
INTRODUCTION	None
FORMATION	Lines, hands held "W" position
PART I	IN, IN; IN/STEP, STEP; OUT, OUT; OUT/STEP, STEP; Repeat
Beats 1-2	Step R, L foot in toward the center
3	Step R foot in
&	Step L foot next to R foot
4	Step R foot next to L foot
5-8	Repeat beats 1-4 moving out from the center beginning L foot
9-16	Repeat Part I, beats 1-8
PART II	HEEL, LIFT; BOUNCE/BOUNCE, BOUNCE; Repeat Part II 3X
Beat 1	Touch R heel diagonally right
2	Lift R foot in front of L leg
3-4	Bounce both heels 3 times
5-8	Repeat beats 1-4 with opposite footwork
9-16	Repeat Part II, beats 1-8
PART III	IN, IN; IN/IN, IN/STAMP; OUT, OUT; OUT/OUT, OUT/STAMP; Repeat
Beats 1-2	Step R, L foot in toward center
3 & 4	Step R, L, R foot in
&	Stamp L foot next to R foot
5-8	Repeat beats 1-4 moving away from center
9-16	Repeat Part II, beats 1-8
PART IV	HEEL, LIFT; HEEL, LIFT; SIDE/BACK, SIDE/STAMP; SIDE/BACK, SIDE/STAMP; Repeat
Beat 1	Touch R heel diagonally right
2	Lift R foot in front of L leg
3-4	Repeat beats 1-2
5	Step R foot sideward right
&	Step L foot crossing in back of R foot
6	Step R foot sideward right
&	Stamp L foot next to R foot
7-8	Repeat beats 5-6 beginning L foot
9-16	Repeat Part IV, beats 1-8

Kulsko Horo *(continued)*

PART V	SIDE, BACK; SIDE/BACK, SIDE/STAMP (4X); SIDE/BACK, SIDE/BACK; SIDE/BACK, SIDE/STAMP; Repeat; SIDE/BACK, SIDE/STAMP; SIDE/BACK, SIDE/STAMP; SIDE/STAMP, SIDE/STAMP; SIDE/STAMP, STAMP; Repeat PART V
Beat 1	Step R foot sideward right
2	Step L foot crossing in back of R foot
3	Step R foot sideward right
&	Step L foot crossing in back of R foot
4	Step R foot sideward right
&	Stamp L foot next to R foot
5-16	Repeat beats 1-4 three times reversing footwork and direction
17-19	Repeat beats 3 & three times
20	Repeat beats 4 &
21-24	Repeat beats 17-20 sideward left beginning L foot
25-26	Repeat beats 3-4
27-28	Repeat beats 25-26 sideward left beginning L foot
29	Leap R foot sideward right
&	Stamp L foot next to R foot
30	Repeat beats 29 & sideward left
31	Repeat beats 29 &
32	Stamp L foot
33-64	Repeat Part V, beats 1-32 beginning L foot sideward left
PART VI	IN/IN, IN/STAMP; IN/IN, IN/STAMP; IN/IN, IN/STAMP; TWIST, TWIST; OUT/OUT, OUT/STAMP; OUT/OUT, OUT/STAMP; OUT/OUT, OUT/STAMP; TWIST, TWIST; Repeat Part VI
Beat 1	Step R, L foot in toward center
2	Step R foot in
&	Stamp L foot next to R foot
3-6	Repeat beats 1-2 two times
7	Bring L leg behind bent R knee, twist hips left turning L knee out
8	Straighten body
9-16	Repeat beats 1-8 moving out beginning L foot
17-32	Repeat Part VI, beats 1-16
PART I	Repeat Part I, beats 1-8
PART II	Repeat Part II, beats 1-8
PART III	Repeat Part III, beats 1-8
PART IV	Repeat Part IV, beats 1-8

(continued)

Kulsko Horo (continued)

PART V | Repeat Part V, beats 1-8 and 17-32
           | Repeat Part V, beats 1-8 and 17-32 beginning L foot
PART VI | Repeat Part VI, beats 1-16

RHYTHMIC NOTATION

PART I

REPEAT 3X W/OPP. FTWK.

R   L   RL   R

PART II

REPEAT 3X W/OPP. FTWK.

(R)   (R)   BB   B

PART III

REPEAT 3X W/OPP. FTWK.

R   R   RL   R(L)

PART IV

REPEAT

(R)   (R)   (R)   (R)   RL   R(L)   LR   L(R)

PART V

REPEAT 3X W/OPP. FTWK.   REPEAT W/OPP FTWK

R   L   RL   R(L)   RL   RL   RL   R(L)

REPEAT V

RL   R(L)   LR   L(R)   R(L)   L(R)   R(L)   (L)

PART VI

REPEAT 3X W/OPP. FTWK.

RL   R(L)   LR   L(R)   RL   R(L)   (L)   (L)

Marhaba
Welcome
Israel (Arabic)

RECORD	MIH3 *Dance with Moshiko*
INTRODUCTION	8 beats
FORMATION	Circle facing counterclockwise, hands held down
PART I	FORWARD, HOP/STEP, FORWARD, FORWARD; FORWARD, SWIVEL, SWIVEL, ACCENT; Repeat Part I 3X
Beat 1	Step L foot forward moving counterclockwise
2	Hop L foot
&	Step R foot forward moving counterclockwise
3-4	Step L, R foot forward counterclockwise
5	Step L foot forward counterclockwise and bring R foot next to L foot
6	Twist heels and hips right, weight on balls of feet
7	Twist to straight position
8	Accent R foot next to L foot bending knees
9-32	Repeat Part I, beats 1-8, three times
PART II	FORWARD/CLOSE, FORWARD (2X); TOGETHER, CHUG, ACCENT, REST; TOUCH, TWIST, TOUCH, TWIST; FORWARD, HOP/FORWARD, STAMP, REST; Repeat Part II
Beats 1-2	Two step forward counterclockwise beginning L foot
3-4	Two step forward counterclockwise beginning R foot
5	Step L foot next to R foot
6	Chug backward on both feet
7-8	Accent R foot in place, knee bent (L knee bent and pointed diagonally right, hips twisted slightly)
9	Touch L heel diagonally left as hips untwist
10	Bring L knee back to position on beats 9-10
11-12	Repeat beats 9-10
13	Step L foot forward
14	Hop L foot backward
&	Step R foot forward
15-16	Stamp L foot next to R foot
17-32	Repeat Part II, beats 1-16

(continued)

Marhaba *(continued)*

PART III	FORWARD, FORWARD, FORWARD, OUT; TOUCH, IN, STAMP, OUT; STAMP, REST, BEND, REST; STAMP, BEND, STAMP, REST
Beats 1-3	Step L, R, L foot forward counterclockwise (bouncy steps); clap with step
4	Step R foot diagonally out; clap with step
5	Touch L foot next to R foot facing center; clap with touch
6	Step L foot in toward center
7	Stamp R foot
8	Step R foot out away from center
9	Stamp L foot
10	Rest
11-12	Bend R knee and raise L leg sharply with bent knee
13	Stamp L foot straightening R knee
14	Bend R knee raising L leg sharply
15	Stamp L foot straightening R knee
16	Rest

RHYTHMIC NOTATION

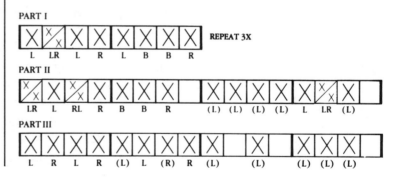

Mîndrele
Sweet Girl
Romania (Oltenia)

RECORD	Noroc Vol I "Hai La Joc" 8-measure introduction
FORMATION	Circle or open circle of women, hands held in "W" position
METER	6/8 S = Slow *S'er = Slower* Q = Quick
PART I	FORWARD/close, *FORWARD* (2X); *FORWARD*, BACKWARD/close; BACKWARD/close, *BACKWARD*; *SIDE*, SIDE/cross; SIDE/back, *SIDE*; Repeat Part I

Measure	Beat	
1	S	Step R foot forward counterclockwise
	Q	Step L foot next to R foot
	S'er	Step R foot forward
2		Repeat measure 1 beginning with L foot
3	*S'er*	Step R foot forward and turn 180° to face clockwise
	S	Step L foot backward counterclockwise
	Q	Step R foot next to L foot
4	S	Step L foot backward
	Q	Step R foot next to L foot
	S'er	Step L foot backward
5	*S'er*	Step R foot sideward right (swaying right)
	S	Step L foot sideward left (swaying left)
	Q	Step R foot crossing in front of L foot
6	S	Step L foot sideward
	Q	Step R foot crossing in back fo L foot
	S'er	Step L foot sideward
7-12		Repeat Part I, measures 1-6

(continued)

Mindrele (continued)

PART II		*BRUSH*, BACKWARD/close; BACKWARD/close, *BACKWARD*; Repeat; *CROSS, SIDE; BACK, SIDE;* SIDE/side, CROSS/side; BACK/side, *CROSS;* Repeat Part II

Measure	Beat	
1	*S'er*	Brush R foot across in front of L foot while bending and straightening L leg
	S	Step R foot backward counterclockwise
	Q	Step L foot next to R foot
2	S	Step R foot backward counterclockwise
	Q	Step L foot next to R foot
	S'er	Step R foot backward
3-4		Repeat measures 1-2 in opposite directions beginning with L foot
5	*S'er*	Step R foot crossing in front of L foot
	S'er	Step L foot sideward
6	*S'er*	Step R foot crossing in back of L foot
	S'er	Step L foot sideward
7	S	Step R foot sideward right (swaying right)
	Q	Step L foot sideward left (swaying left)
	S	Step R foot crossing in front of L foot
	Q	Step L foot sideward left
8	S	Step R foot crossing in back of L foot
	Q	Step L foot sideward left
	S'er	Step R foot crossing in front of L foot (turning to face center)
9-16		Repeat Part II, measures 1-8

PART III		*IN, IN*; IN/in, *IN;* *TOUCH, TOUCH; TOUCH*, OUT/out; *OUT, TOUCH*; OUT/out, *OUT;* bounce/SIDE, cross/BACK; bounce/SIDE, cross/BACK; Repeat Part III

Measure	Beat	
1	*S'er*	Step R foot in toward center
	S'er	Step L foot in
2	S	Step R foot in
	Q	Step L foot in
	S'er	Step R foot in
3	*S'er*	Touch L foot in front of R foot
	S'er	Touch L foot sideward left

Mîndrele (continued)

4	*S'er*	Touch L foot in front of R foot
	S	Step L foot out from center
	Q	Step R foot out
5	*S'er*	Step L foot out
	S'er	Touch R foot in front of L foot
6	S	Step R foot out
	Q	Step L foot out
	S'er	Step R foot out
7	Q	Bounce R foot (chukche)
	S	Step L foot sideward
	Q	Step R foot crossing in front of L foot
	S	Step L foot crossing in back of R foot
8		Repeat measure 7 beginning with L foot
9-16		Repeat Part III, measures 1-8 beginning with L foot

RHYTHMIC NOTATION

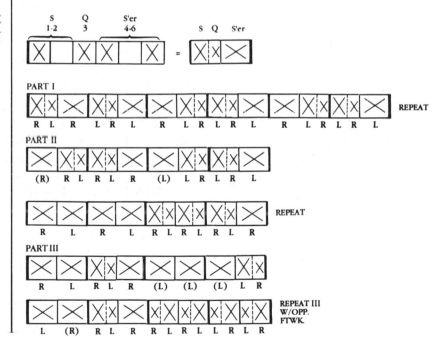

Moja Diridika
Yugoslavia

RECORD	Monitor MF 327 F4003X45
INTRODUCTION	16 beats
FORMATION	Front basket, left arm under
PART I	CROSS, HOP, SIDE, HOP; BACK, HOP, SIDE, HOP; Repeat Part I
Beats 1-2	Step hop R foot crossing in front of L foot
3-4	Step hop L foot sideward left
5-6	Step hop R foot crossing in back of L foot
7-8	Step hop L foot sideward left
9-16	Repeat Part I, beats 1-8
PART II	CROSS, SIDE (8X)
Beat 1	Step R foot crossing in front of L foot
2	Step L foot sideward left
3-16	Repeat beats 1-2, seven times
PART I	
Beats 1-16	Repeat Part I, beats 1-16
PART III	SIDE, BOUNCE/BOUNCE (8X)
Beat 1	Step R foot slightly sideward right ⎫
2 &	Two bounces with feet together ⎬ Drmeš
	(weight on both feet, legs straight) ⎭
3	Step L foot in place, bending knee
4 &	Two bounces with feet together
5-16	Repeat Part III, three times

RHYTHMIC NOTATION

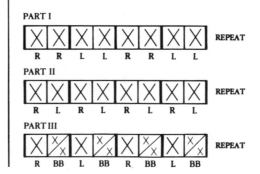

Pentozális
Five Dizzying Steps
Greece (Crete)

RECORD	Tikva 131 *Greek Dance Party*
INTRODUCTION	8 beats
FORMATION	Line or broken circle, shoulder hold
INTRO	IN, TOUCH; OUT, TOUCH; SIDE, TOUCH; IN, TOUCH
Beat 1	Step L foot diagonally in left
2	Touch R foot behind L foot
3-4	Step R foot diagonally out right (touch L foot)
5-6	Step L foot sideward left (touch R foot)
7-8	Step R foot diagonally in right (touch L foot)
	Basic
PART I	IN, HOP; OUT, SIDE/CROSS; BACK, SIDE/CROSS; BACK, HOP
Beat 1	Step L foot diagonally in left
2	Hop L foot swinging R foot in
3	Step R foot diagonally out right
4	Step L foot sideward left
&	Step R foot crossing in front of L foot
5	Step L foot crossing in back of R foot
6	Step R foot sideward right
&	Step L foot crossing in front of R foot
7	Step R foot crossing in back of L foot
8	Hop R foot lifting L foot in front of R leg
	Slap
PART II	IN, HOP; OUT, SIDE/CROSS; BACK, SIDE; SLAP, SLAP
Beats 1-5	Repeat Basic, beats 1-5
6	Leap R foot sideward right
7-8	Slap L foot twice in front of R foot (straight knee)
	Scissor
PART III	IN, HOP, OUT, SIDE/CROSS; BACK, STEP/STEP; STEP, HOP
Beats 1-5	Repeat Basic, beats 1-5
6 & 7	Step R, L, R foot in place (kick L, R, L in)
8	Hop R foot lifting L foot in front of R foot
NOTE	Beat 5 begins scissor with R kick in

(continued)

Pentozális (continued)

VARIATION I	Double scissors IN, HOP; OUT, STEP/STEP; STEP, STEP/STEP; STEP, HOP
	First set of 3 scissor kicks on beats 4 & 5
VARIATION II	Triple scissors IN, HOP; OUT/STEP, STEP/STEP; STEP/STEP, STEP/STEP; STEP, HOP
	Scissor kicks occur on beats 3-7 (9 scissor steps)
PART IV	Leaps IN, HOP; OUT, IN; OUT, IN; SIDE, HOP
Beats 1-2	Repeat Basic, beats 1-2
3	Leap R foot out swinging L foot slightly across L foot
4	Leap L foot in swinging R foot in
5-6	Repeat beats 3-4
7	Step R foot sideward right
8	Hop R foot lifting L foot in front of R leg
PART V	Jump Swing IN, HOP; OUT, SIDE/CROSS; BACK, JUMP; HOP, HOP
Beats 1-5	Repeat Basic, beats 1-5
6	Jump with feet slightly apart
7	Hop R foot bringing L foot up behind
8	Hop R foot swinging L foot in
NOTE	Do each part a often as desired.

RHYTHMIC NOTATION

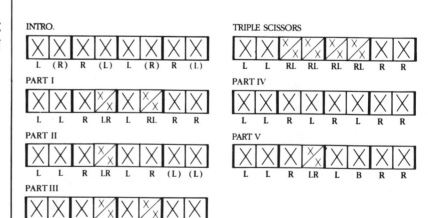

Porunceasca
Bulgaria (Vidin District)

RECORD	BG 1002
INTRODUCTION	None
FORMATION	Short lines, 4-8 persons, belt hold, R arm under
PART I	PUSH, PUSH, SIDE/BACK, SIDE (4X); IN/CLOSE, IN (4X); HOP/OUT, OUT, HOP/OUT, OUT; HOP/OUT, OUT/STAMP; HOP/OUT, OUT; SIDE/CLOSE, SIDE/STAMP (2X); SIDE/STAMP, SIDE/STAMP, SIDE/CLOSE, SIDE/STAMP; SIDE/CLOSE, SIDE/STAMP (2X); SIDE/STAMP, SIDE/STAMP; SIDE/CLOSE, SIDE
Beats 1-2	Extend R leg 2 times with a pushing motion (weight on L foot)
3	Step R foot sideward right
&	Step L foot crossing in back of R foot
4	Step R foot sideward right
5-16	Repeat beats 1-4, three times
17	Step R foot in toward center
&	Step L foot closing behind R foot
18	Step R foot in
19-24	Repeat beats 17-18, three times
25	Hop L foot
&	Step R foot away from center
26	Step L foot away from center
27-28	Repeat beats 25-26
29-30	Repeat beats 25-26 adding a stamp on the "&" of beat 30
31-32	Repeat beats 25-26
33	Step R foot sideward right
&	Step L foot next to R foot
34	Step R foot sideward right
&	Stamp L foot next to R foot
35-36	Repeat beats 33-34 beginning L foot
37	Step R foot sideward right
&	Stamp L foot next to R foot
38	Repeat beats 37&
39-40	Repeat beats 33-34
41-48	Repeat beats 33-40 beginning L foot
RHYTHMIC NOTATION	

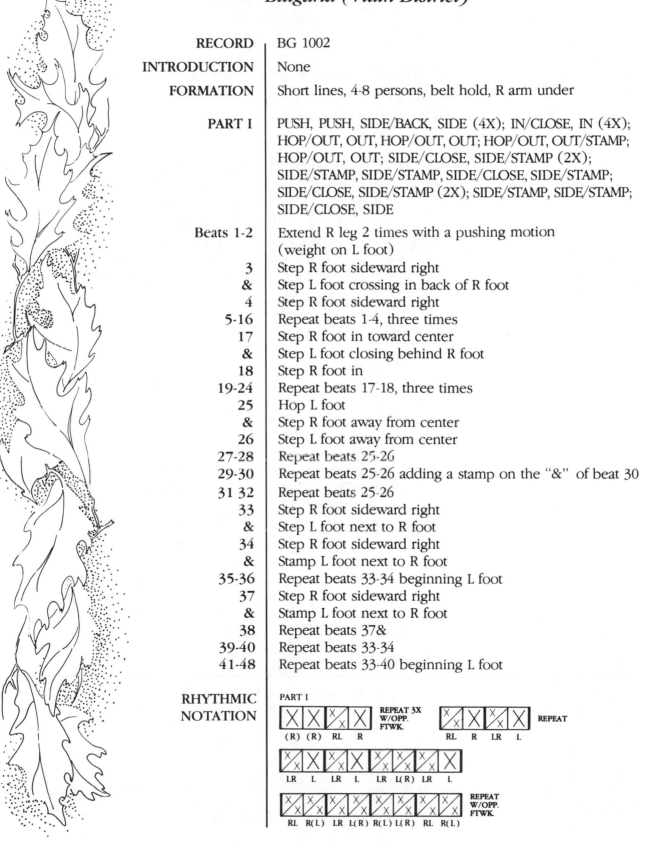

Povrateno
Forward and Back
Macedonia

RECORD	Yugoslavia Dance and Song LPM-GT: 101
INTRODUCTION	None
FORMATION	Lines in "T" position
PART I	FORWARD, REST; BACKWARD, REST; FORWARD, LIFT; FORWARD, LIFT; SIDE, REST; BEND, STRAIGHTEN; BOUNCE, BOUNCE; OUT, LIFT
Beats 1-2	Lunge R foot forward; keep L toe on floor
3-4	Step L foot backward, bend and lift R leg
5	Step R foot forward counterclockwise
6	Bend and lift L foot in front of R leg
7	Step L foot forward
8	Bend and lift R foot in front of R leg
9-10	Step R foot sideward right
11	Bend R knee
12	Straighten R knee and move L foot in an arc to behind R knee
13-14	Bounce R heel 2 times
15	Step L foot out
16	Lift R foot in front of L leg
PART II	FORWARD, REST; BACKWARD, REST; FORWARD/FORWARD, FORWARD; FORWARD/FORWARD, FORWARD; SIDE, REST; BEND, STRAIGHTEN; BOUNCE, BOUNCE; OUT, LIFT
Beats 1-4	Repeat Part I, beats 1-4
5-6	Step R, L, R foot forward counterclockwise (running "three")
7-8	Step L, R, L foot forward (running "three")
9-16	Repeat Part I, beats 9-16
PART III	HOP/FORWARD, FORWARD; HOP/FORWARD, FORWARD; FORWARD/FORWARD, FORWARD; FORWARD/FORWARD, FORWARD; SIDE, REST; BEND, STRAIGHTEN; BOUNCE, BOUNCE; OUT, LIFT
Beat 1	Hop L foot
& 2	Step R, L foot forward counterclockwise
3-4	Repeat beats 1-2
5-16	Repeat Part II, beats 5-16

Povrateno *(continued)*

PART IV	HOP/FORWARD, FORWARD; HOP/FORWARD, FORWARD; FORWARD/FORWARD, FORWARD; FORWARD/FORWARD, FORWARD; SIDE, REST, BOUNCE, BOUNCE/step; STEP/step, STEP, STEP, HOP
Beats 1-8	Repeat Part III, beats 1-8
9-10	Leap R foot sideward right lifting L foot in front of R leg and hold (don't bounce on R foot)
11-12	Bounce R heel 2 times
a	Step L foot in place
13&	Step R foot in place
a	Step L foot in place
14	Step R foot in place
15	Leap L foot in place lifting R foot in front of L leg
16	Hop L foot turning to face counterclockwise
PART V	HOP/FORWARD, FORWARD; HOP/FORWARD, FORWARD; FORWARD/FORWARD, FORWARD; FORWARD/FORWARD, FORWARD; SIDE, SIDE, SIDE, HOP; HOP/step, STEP/step, STEP, SIDE
Beats 1-8	Repeat Part III, beats 1-8
9	Leap R foot sideward right lifting L foot in front
10	Leap L foot sideward left lifting R foot in front
11	Leap R foot sideward right lifting L foot in front
12	Hop R foot
13 &	Hop R foot
a	Step L foot in place
14 &	Step R foot in place
a	Step L foot in place
15	Step R foot in place
16	Leap L foot sideward left lifting R foot in front

(continued)

Povrateno (continued)

NOTE	Do each part three times to fit with the record.

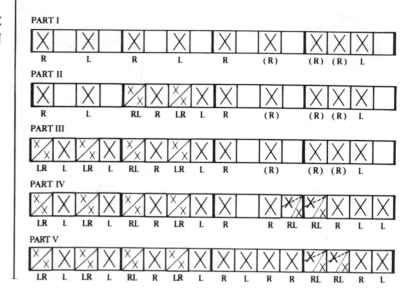

RHYTHMIC NOTATION

PART I ... R L R L R (R) (R) (R) L

PART II ... R L RL R LR L R (R) (R) (R) L

PART III ... LR L LR L RL R LR L R (R) (R) (R) L

PART IV ... LR L LR L RL R LR L R R RL RL R L L

PART V ... LR L LR L RL R LR L R L R R RL RL R L

Preplet
(Mangupsko Kolo)
Yugoslavia (Serbia)

RECORD	Kolo 406
INTRODUCTION	None
FORMATION	Broken circle, hands joined in "V" position
PART I	SIDE/CLOSE (4X); STEP, STEP/STEP, TOGETHER, REST; Repeat Part I 3X
Beat 1	Step R foot on ball of foot sideward counterclockwise, facing diagonally right
&	Step L foot next to R foot (knee bend)
2-4	Repeat beats 1 &, three times
5	Step R foot facing center bending R knee
6 &	Step L, R foot in place on balls of feet
7-8	Close feet lowering heels (do not click heels)
9-16	Repeat beats 1-8 sideward clockwise beginning L foot
17-32	Repeat Part I, beats 1-16

Preplet (continued)

PART II	SIDE/BACK, SIDE/CROSS; SIDE/BACK, SIDE; IN/OUT, IN; OUT/IN, OUT; Repeat Part II 3X
Beat 1	Step R foot sideward right with straight knee
&	Step L foot crossing in back of R foot
2	Step R foot sideward right
&	Step L foot crossing in front of R foot
3	Step R foot sideward right
&	Step L foot crossing in back of R foot
4	Step R foot sideward right
5	Step L foot slightly in toward the center
&	Step R foot slightly out
6	Step L foot slightly in
7	Step R foot slightly out
&	Step L foot slightly in
8	Step R foot slightly out
9-16	Repeat beats 1-8 sideward left beginning L foot
17-32	Repeat Part II, beats 1-16
PART III	HOP/FORWARD, FORWARD (3X); STEP/STEP, STEP; Repeat Part II 3X
Beat 1	Hop L foot facing diagonally counterclockwise
&	Step R foot forward counterclockwise
2	Step L foot forward counterclockwise
3-6	Repeat beats 1-2, two times
7	Step R foot in front of L foot cutting L foot out
&	Step L foot in back of R foot cutting R foot in
8	Step R foot in front of L foot cutting L foot out
9-16	Repeat beats 1-8 moving left beginning R foot
17-32	Repeat Part III, beats 1-16

RHYTHMIC NOTATION

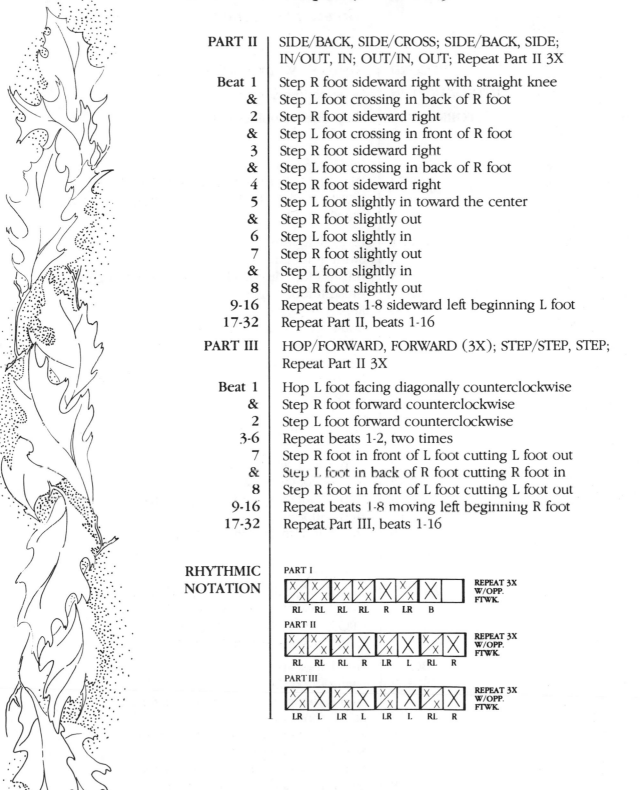

Rebetic Hasápikos
Greece (Panhellenic)

RECORD	Worldtone WT10025 *Oniro Demeno*
INTRODUCTION	None or 16 beats
FORMATION	Short lines, shoulder hold

Basic step

PART I
IN, SWING; BRUSH, BRUSH; BRUSH, BRUSH;
BOUNCE, OUT; BOUNCE, OUT; BOUNCE, SIDE;
CROSS, BACK; IN, IN

Beat	
1	Lunge L foot in
2	Swing R foot in
3	Brush R foot diagonally across in front of L foot
4	Brush R foot diagonally right in
5-6	Repeat beats 3-4
7	Bounce L heel slightly lifting R foot in front of L leg
8	Step R foot out
9	Bounce R heel slightly lifting L foot in front of R leg
10	Step L foot out
11	Bounce L heel slightly lifting R foot in front of L leg
12	Step R foot sideward right
13	Step L foot crossing in front of R foot
14	Step R foot crossing in back of L foot
15	Step L foot in
16	Step R foot in crossing to the outside of the L foot

Grapevine

PART II
IN, SWING; CROSS, SIDE; BACK, SIDE;
CROSS, SWING; CROSS, SIDE; BACK, SIDE;
CROSS, REST; TOGETHER, REST;
JUMP, REST; JUMP, REST; IN, IN

Beat	
1	Step L foot in
2	Swing R foot in
3	Step R foot crossing in front of L foot
4	Step L foot sideward left
5	Step R foot crossing in back of L foot
6	Step L foot sideward left
7	Step R foot crossing in front of L foot
8	Swing L around in front of R foot
9	Step L foot crossing in front of R foot
10	Step R foot sideward right
11	Step L foot crossing in back of R foot

Rebetic Hasápikos *(continued)*

12	Step R foot sideward right
13-14	Step L foot crossing in front of R foot
15-16	Close R foot to L foot putting weight on both feet
17-18	Jump in
19-20	Jump out
21	Step L foot in
22	Step R foot in and to the outside of the L foot

Forward

PART III IN, IN; JUMP, CROSS; OUT, OUT; OUT, REST; OUT, REST

Beat 1	Step L foot in
2	Step R foot in
3	Jump with feet apart
4	Step R foot crossing in front of L foot
5	Step L foot out
6	Step R foot out
7-8	Step L foot out, lifting R foot in front
9-10	Step R foot out, lifting L foot in front

Turns

PART IV CROSS, REST; PIVOT/STEP; REST;
CROSS, REST; PIVOT/STEP, REST; BRUSH, BRUSH;
BRUSH, BRUSH

Beats 1-2	Step L foot crossing in front of R foot
3-4	Turn counterclockwise 1/2 pivoting on L foot and step on R foot
5-8	Repeat beats 1-4
9	Brush L foot in
10	Brush L foot out
11-12	Brush L foot in, out

(continued)

Rebetic Hasápikos (continued)

PART V	Cherkessiya CROSS, BACK; SIDE, CROSS; BACK, SIDE; IN, IN; Repeat; IN, REST; OUT, CLOSE; IN, REST; OUT, CLOSE; CROSS, PIVOT; IN, HIT; IN, IN
Beats 1-6	Double Cherkessiya beginning L foot crossing in front of R foot
7-8	Repeat beats 15-16 of Basic
9-16	Repeat beats 1-8
17-18	Lunge L foot in going down with R knee almost to floor
19	Step R foot out
20	Step L foot next to R foot
21-24	Repeat beats 17-20 with opposite footwork
25	Step L foot crossing in front of R foot beginning clockwise turn
26	Pivot clockwise on L foot (complete full turn)
27	Step R foot in
28	Hit outside of L shoe with L hand
29-30	Repeat beats 15-16 of Basic
NOTE	The Basic is done unless another part is called and return to Basic after any part is executed unless instructed to repeat that part or to do another part.

RHYTHMIC NOTATION

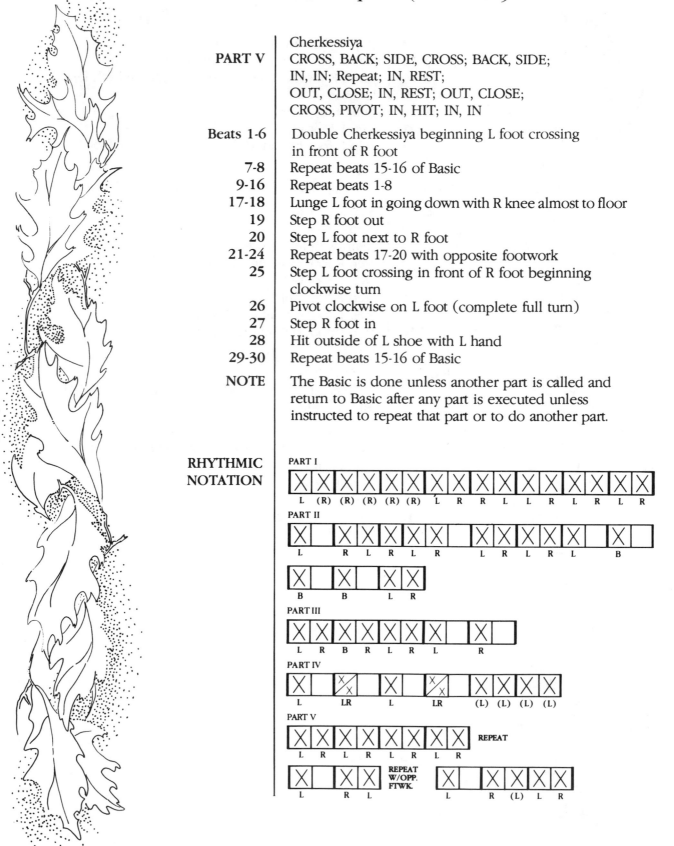

Rustemul
Romania

RECORD	NAMA #1
INTRODUCTION	4 measures, dance begins on "&" of measure 4
FORMATION	Line, hands joined in "V" position Arms swing in and out
METER	6/8 6, 1-2, 3, 4-5 Quick, Slow, Quick, Slow (QSQS)
NOTE	The first Quick (Q) is an up beat from the previous measure
PART I	hop/SIDE, cross/BACK; Repeat; hop/SIDE, cross/BACK; out/IN, cross/BACK; Repeat Part I

Measure	Beat	
	Q	Hop L foot in place raising R knee
1	S	Step R foot sideward right
	Q	Step L foot crossing in front of R foot
	S	Step R foot crossing in back of L foot
	Q	Hop R foot
2	SQS	Repeat measure 1, beats SQS with opposite footwork
	Q	Hop L foot
3	SQS	Repeat measure 1, beats SQS
	Q	Step L foot diagonally out
4	S	Step R foot in
	Q	Step L foot crossing in front of R foot
	S	Step R foot crossing in back of L foot
	Q	Hop R foot
5-8		Repeat Part I, measure 1-4 with opposite footwork

(continued)

Rustemul (continued)

PART II | hop/SIDE, cross/BACK; Repeat;
leap/IN, close/IN; hop/IN, close/IN;
hop/ACCENT, rest/OUT; close/OUT, close/OUT;
hop/SIDE, cross/BACK; hop/SIDE, cross/BACK

Measure	Beat	
	Q	Hop L foot
1-2		Repeat Part I, measure 1-2
	Q	Leap R foot and turn body to face diagonally right
3	S	Step L foot sideward in toward the center
	Q	Step R foot next to L foot
	S	Step L foot sideward in
	Q	Hop L foot turning to face diagonally left
4	SQS	Repeat measure 3, beats SQS
	Q	Hop R foot turning to face diagonally right
5	S	Accent L foot toward center
	Q	Hold
	S	Step R foot sideward out
	Q	Step L foot next to R foot
6	S	Step R foot sideward out
	Q	Step L foot next to R foot
	S	Step R foot sideward out
	Q	Hop R foot
7-8		Repeat Part I, measures 1-2, reversing footwork
9-16		Repeat Part II, measures 1-8, reversing direction and footwork

Rustemul (continued)

PART III		hop/FORWARD, hop/FORWARD; Repeat; hop/SIDE, cross/BACK; hop/SIDE, cross/BACK; hop/OUT, hop/OUT; hop/SIDE, cross/BACK; Repeat Part III

Measure	**Beat**	
	Q	Hop L foot
1	S	Step R foot forward right
	Q	Hop R foot
	S	Step L foot forward right
	Q	Hop L foot
2	SQSQ	Repeat measure 1 SQSQ
3-4		Repeat Part I, measures 1-2
	Q	Hop L foot
5	S	Step R foot out behind L heel
	Q	Hop R foot
	S	Step L foot out behind R heel
	Q	Hop L foot
6		Repeat Part I, measure 1
7-12		Repeat Part III, measures 1-6 reversing direction and footwork
NOTE		The dance sequence to this record is as follows: Part I, II, III, I, II, I, III, I, II, I, III.

RHYTHMIC NOTATION

PART I

L R L R R L R L L R L R L R L R   REPEAT

PART II

L R L R R L R L R L R L L R L R R

L   R L R L R R L R L L R L R   REPEAT II W/OPP. FTWK.

PART III

L R R L L R R L L R L R R L R L L

R R L L R L R   REPEAT III W/OPP. FTWK.

Santa Rita
Mexico

RECORD	Express
INTRODUCTION	Pick up
FORMATION	Couples in ballroom position facing counterclockwise; man's back to center of circle, man's step given; woman opposite footwork except where noted
PART I	FORWARD/CLOSE, FORWARD (4X); CROSS, CROSS; STAMP/STAMP, ACCENT; SIDE/CLOSE, SIDE; STAMP, STAMP; Repeat Part I
Beats 1-8	Four polka steps (two steps) beginning L foot forward counterclockwise
9	Step L foot across in front of R foot "twist" (facing partner)
10	Step R foot across in front of L foot "twist"
11 &	Stamp L foot 2 times
12	Step L foot with accent
13	Step R foot sideward right moving clockwise
&	Step L foot next to R foot
14	Step R foot sideward right
15-16	Stamp L foot 2 times
17-32	Repeat Part I, beats 1-16
PART II	SIDE/CLOSE, SIDE; CROSS, CROSS; Repeat Part II 7X
Beat 1	Step L foot sideward left
&	Step R foot next to L foot
2	Step L foot sideward left
3	Step R foot crossing in front of L "twist" ⎫ Broken ankle
4	Step L foot crossing in front of R "twist" ⎭ step
5-32	Repeat Part II, beats 1-4, seven times alternating direction and footwork

Santa Rita (continued)

PART III	POLKA (16X)
Beats 1-32	Free style couple polka
PART IV	Partners hold both hands and use same footwork TOWARD/STEP, STEP; AWAY/STEP, STEP; Repeat 7X
Beats 1-2	Balance R foot toward partner with R shoulders adjacent
3-4	Balance L foot away from partner
5-6	Man balance R foot toward partner turning woman counterclockwise under his R arm; both are now side by side
7-8	Balance L foot out in tucked position
9-12	Balance R foot in and L foot out in tucked position
13-14	Man balance R foot in untucking woman
15-16	Balance L foot out away from one another
17-18	Balance R foot toward partner (L shoulders adjacent)
19-20	Balance L foot away from partner
21-22	Man balance R foot toward partner turning woman clockwise under his L arm
23-24	Balance L foot out in tucked position
25-32	Balance R foot in and L foot out in tucked position 2 times (do not untuck)
PART V	STEP/STAMP, BOUNCE/STAMP (4X); SIDE/CLOSE (7X); TOGETHER; Repeat Part V
Beats 1-8	Four taconazo steps beginning R foot Taconazo step: Step R foot, stamp L heel next to R foot, raise and lower R heel, stamp L heel again
9-16	Seven push steps beginning R foot and bounce both feet on beat 16 Push step: Step R foot sideward right, step on L ball of foot with heel turned out (uneven rhythm)
17-32	Repeat beats 1-16 beginning L foot
BRIDGE	TURN, 2, 3, 4; TURN, 2, 3, 4
Beats 1-4	Woman turns to her left side (man's R hand, woman's L hand still are held)
5-8	Both turn, releasing hands, and return to ballroom position

(continued)

Santa Rita (continued)

	Moving counterclockwise around circle; woman opposite footwork
PART VI	CHERKESSIYA; CHERKESSIYA; FORWARD, 2, 3, 4; 5, 6, 7, 8; Repeat Part VI 3X
Beats 1-8	Cherkessiya twice, man beginning forward L foot; woman backward R foot; man's L hand pumps woman's R hand at waist level
9-16	Eight crazy walks beginning L foot (woman R foot backward); man turns unsupported heel out, woman turns unsupported ankle over
17-64	Repeat PART VI, beats 1-16, three times
PART VII	HOP, HOP; SIDE/CLOSE, SIDE; CROSS, CROSS; TOGETHER, BOUNCE; Repeat Part VII 3X
Beat 1	Hop R foot extending L heel diagonally sideward
2	Hop R foot crossing L toe in front of R foot
3-4	Slide L foot sideward left (side, close, side)
5-6	Step R foot crossing in front of L foot, step L foot crossing in front of R foot
7	Close R foot to L foot (weight on both feet)
8	Bounce on both feet
9-32	Repeat Part VII, beats 1-8, three times alternating direction and footwork
PART I	Repeat Part I
PART II	Repeat Part II
PART I	Repeat Part I

RHYTHMIC NOTATION

PART I

LR L RL R LR L RL R L R (L)(L) L RL R (L) (L)   REPEAT

PART II

LR L R L   REPEAT 7X W/OPP. FTWK.

PART III & IV

LR L RL R   REPEAT 7X

PART V

R(L) R(L)   REPEAT 3X W/OPP. FTWK.

RL RL RL RL RL RL RL B   REPEAT V

PART VI

L R L R   REPEAT 15X

PART VII

R R LR L R L B B

Sapari
Israel

RECORD	1 FC 1 *Na'arah*
INTRODUCTION	8 beats
FORMATION	Line, R arm straight and L arm bent with the hand in middle of the back
PART I	FORWARD/2/3, BRUSH (2X); FORWARD/BRUSH (2X); FORWARD/2, 3/TOGETHER; SNAP, SNAP; FORWARD/2, 3/BRUSH (2X); FORWARD/BRUSH (2X); FORWARD/2, 3/TOUCH
Beats 1-2	Step R, L, R foot forward moving counterclockwise
&	Brush L foot forward
3-4	Repeat beats 1-2 beginning L foot
5	Step R foot forward
&	Brush L foot forward
6	Repeat beats 5 & beginning L foot
7-8	Step R, L, R foot forward
&	Bring feet together weight on both
9-10	Snap fingers to the right then to the left
11-18	Repeat beats 1-8, ending with a touch of R foot as the line turns side by side facing in
PART II	SIDE, CROSS; SIDE/SIDE, TOUCH; UP, OUT/OUT; IN/IN, TOGETHER; SNAP, SNAP; SIDE, CROSS; SIDE/SIDE, TOUCH; UP, OUT/OUT; IN/IN, TOGETHER; JUMP, FORWARD/FORWARD (4X); SIDE, CROSS; SIDE/SIDE, TOUCH; UP, OUT/OUT; IN/IN, TOGETHER
Beat 1	Step R foot sideward right
2	Step L foot crossing in front of R foot
3 &	Step R, L foot side to side right and left
4	Touch R foot next to L foot
5	Raise R knee up
6	Step R, L foot out
7	Step R, L foot in
8	Bring feet together weight on both
9-10	Snap fingers right side then left side
11-18	Repeat beats 1-8
19	Jump on both feet
20	Run L, R foot to the left, kick legs up behind
21-26	Repeat beats 19-20 three times alternating direction
27-34	Repeat beats 1-8

(continued)

Sapari (continued)

PART III	SIDE, TOUCH; BACK, TOGETHER; BOUNCE/BOUNCE, SIDE; CROSS/SIDE, CLOSE; SIDE, TOUCH; BACK, TOGETHER, BOUNCE/BOUNCE, SIDE; CROSS/SIDE, TOGETHER; JUMP, BOUNCE/CROSS (2X), SIDE; SIDE/SIDE, CROSS; SIDE/SIDE, CROSS; FORWARD/BACKWARD, CLOSE
Beat 1	Step L foot sideward left
2	Touch R foot in front of L foot
3	Step R foot crossing in back of L foot
4	Step L foot next to R foot weight on both feet
5	Bounce both heels 2 times
6	Step L foot sideward left
7	Step R foot crossing in front of L foot
&	Step L foot sideward left
8	Step R foot next to L foot
9-16	Repeat beats 1-8 ending with weight on both feet
17	Jump on both feet
18	Bounce R heel
&	Step L foot crossing in front of R foot
19-20	Repeat beats 17-18
21	Step R foot sideward right
22	Step L foot sideward left
&	Step R foot sideward right
23	Step L foot crossing in front of R foot
24-25	Repeat beats 22-23 beginning R foot
26	Step L foot forward facing counterclockwise
&	Step R foot backward clockwise
27	Step L foot next to R foot

RHYTHMIC NOTATION

PART I

									SNAP	SNAP	REPEAT WITHOUT SNAPS

RL   R(L)   LR   L(R)   R(L)   L(R)   RL   RB

PART II

								SNAP	SNAP

R   L   RL   (R)   (R)   RL   RL   B

												REPEAT

R   L   RL   (R)   (R)   RL   RL   B   B   LR   B   RL

R   L   RL   (R)   (R)   RL   RL   B

PART III

								REPEAT

L   (R)   R   B   BB   L   RL   R

B   RL   B   RL   R   LR   L   RL   R   LR   L

Šestorke from Bela Palanka
Yugoslavia

RECORD	Kola 406
INTRODUCTION	None or begin with any phrase
FORMATION	Lines in belt hold, R hand under
PART I	FORWARD, HOP; FORWARD, HOP; SIDE, CLOSE; SIDE, CLOSE; HOP/CROSS, BACK; SIDE, CLOSE; HOP/CROSS, BACK; SIDE, HOP; HOP/CROSS, BACK; SIDE, CLOSE; HOP/CROSS, BACK; SIDE, HOP
Beats 1-2	Step hop R foot forward moving counterclockwise
3-4	Repeat beats 1-2 beginning L foot
5	Step R foot sideward right
6	Step L foot next to R foot (L-arch near R toe)
7-8	Repeat beats 5-6
9	Hop L foot
&	Step R foot crossing in front of L foot
10	Step L foot crossing in back of R foot
11-12	Repeat beats 5-6
13-14	Repeat beats 9-10
15	Step R foot sideward right
16	Hop R foot
17-24	Repeat beats 9-16 with opposite footwork beginning R foot

RHYTHMIC NOTATION

PART I

X	X	X	X	X	X	X	X
R	R	L	L	R	L	R	L

X/X	X	X	X	X/X	X	X	X
LR	L	R	L	LR	L	R	R

REPEAT W/OPP. FTWK.

Shiru Hashir
Sing the Song
Israel

RECORD	Tikva 117 *Potpourri*
INTRODUCTION	12 beats
FORMATION	Line facing counterclockwise, hands joined
PART I	FORWARD, FORWARD; SIDEWARD, SIDEWARD; SIDEWARD, SIDEWARD; FORWARD, HOP; BACKWARD, BACKWARD, BACKWARD; FORWARD, HOP; STEP/STEP, STEP; Repeat Part I

Beats 1-2	Run R, L foot forward, body low
3-6	Run R, L, R, L foot side to side, body up
7-8	Step hop R foot forward; kick the L leg forward on hop
9-11	Run L, R, L foot backward
12-13	Step hop R foot forward; kick L leg forward on hop
14-15	Step L, R, L foot in place
16-30	Repeat Part I, beats 1-15

	Face center
PART II	SCUFF, SIDE (4X); SIDE, REST, BACK, HOP (4X); CROSS, BACK; SIDE, CROSS; BACK, SIDE; CROSS, BACK; SIDE, FORWARD; BACKWARD, BACKWARD

Beat 1	Scuff R heel in place
2	Leap R foot sideward right
3-4	Repeat beats 1-2 to the left
5-8	Repeat beats 1-4
9-10	Step R foot sideward right; bend body down swinging arms out
11-12	Step hop L foot crossing in back of R foot, body up, arms swing in

Shiru Hashir (continued)

13-24	Repeat beats 9-12, three times
25	Step R foot crossing in front of L foot
26	Step L foot crossing in back of R foot
27	Step R foot sideward right
28-30	Repeat beats 25-27 beginning L foot
31-33	Repeat beats 25-27
34	Step L foot moving counterclockwise
35	Step R foot backward moving counterclockwise (leaping to make turn)
36	Step L foot backward and turn to face counterclockwise to begin dance

RHYTHMIC NOTATION

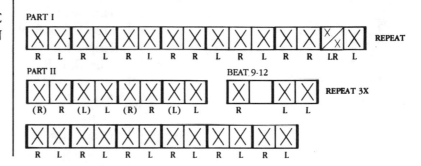

Sitno Zhensko
Bulgaria (Thrace)

RECORD	Vitosha *Folkdances of Bulgaria*
INTRODUCTION	Begin after pause
FORMATION	Short lines, belt hold
PART I	HOP/FORWARD, HOP/FORWARD; HOP/FORWARD, FORWARD/FORWARD; Repeat Part I 3X
Beat 1	Hop L foot
&	Step R foot forward counterclockwise
2	Hop R foot
&	Step L foot forward counterclockwise
3	Hop L foot
& 4	Step R, L, R foot forward counterclockwise
5-8	Repeat beats 1-8 beginning hop R foot
9-16	Repeat Part I, beats 1-8 and turn to face center
PART II	HOP/HEEL, HOP/TOE; HOP/HEEL, HOP/OUT; HOP/OUT, HOP/OUT; Repeat Part II
Beat 1	Hop L foot
&	Touch R heel in
2	Hop L foot
&	Touch R toe out
3	Hop L foot
&	Touch R heel in
4	Hop L foot
&	Step R foot out
5	Hop R foot
&	Step L foot out
6 &	Hop L foot, step R foot out
7-12	Repeat Part II, beats 1-6 beginning hop R foot

Sitno Zhensko (continued)

PART III	IN/CLOSE, IN; IN/CLOSE, IN; CROSS/SIDE, CROSS/SIDE; CROSS/SIDE, CROSS; CROSS/SIDE, CROSS/SIDE; CROSS/SIDE, CROSS; CROSS/SIDE, CROSS/SIDE; CROSS/SIDE, CROSS
Beats 1-2	Two step R foot in toward center
3-4	Two step L foot in toward center
5	Step R foot crossing in front of L foot
&	Step L foot sideward left
6-7	Repeat beats 9-10, two times
8	Step R foot crossing in front of L foot and swing L foot around
9-12	Repeat beats 5-8 beginning L foot
13-16	Repeat Part III, beats 5-8

(beats 5–8 bracketed as **Seven**)

NOTE	During the "sevens" look in the opposite direction from the direction in which you are moving.
PART IV	IN/CLOSE, IN; IN/CLOSE, IN; HOP, HOP/OUT; HOP/OUT, STEP/STEP; Repeat Part IV
Beats 1-2	Two step R foot in toward center
3-4	Two step L foot in
5	Hop L foot extending R foot forward off floor with heel down
6	Hop L foot
&	Step R foot out
7	Hop R foot
&	Step L foot out
8	Step R, L foot in place
9-16	Repeat Part IV, beats 1-8

RHYTHMIC NOTATION

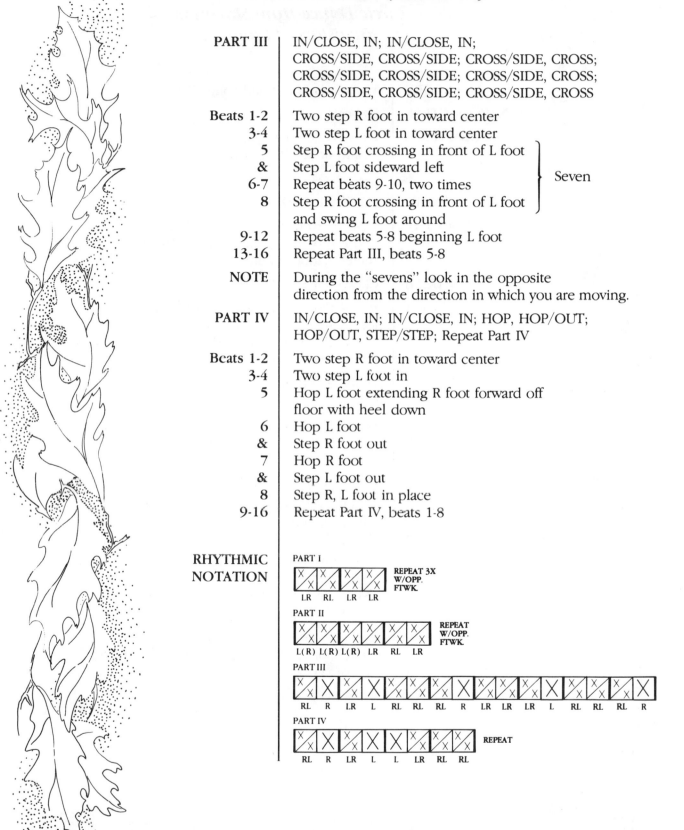

PART I

LR RL LR LR   REPEAT 3X W/OPP. FTWK.

PART II

L(R) L(R) L(R) LR RL LR   REPEAT W/OPP. FTWK.

PART III

RL R LR L RL RL RL R LR LR LR L RL RL RL R

PART IV

RL R LR L L LR RL RL   REPEAT

Slavonsko Kolo
Circle Dance from Slavonija
Yugoslavia (Croatia)

RECORD	Yugoslavia Dance and Song LPM-GT 101
INTRODUCTION	32 beats
FORMATION	Front basket moving clockwise (L arm under, R arm over)
PART I	FORWARD (16X)
Beats 1-16	Walk 16 even steps clockwise beginning R foot (no up-down motion); R foot points to center, L foot forward
PART II	CROSS, SIDE (8X)
Beat 1	Step R foot crossing in front of L foot, foot pointed center (bend knees)
2	Slight leap L foot sideward left (straighten knees)
3-16	Repeat Part II, beats 1-2, seven times
PART III	FORWARD HOP (8X)
Beat 1	Step R foot forward clockwise
2	Hop R foot swinging L foot in front of R leg
3-16	Repeat Part III, beats 1-2, seven times (alternate feet on step hops)
PART IV	CROSS, HOP/STEP (8X)
Beat 1	Step R foot crossing in front of L foot with an accent
2	Hop R foot twisting body right (keep knees close together)
&	Step L foot next to R foot
3-16	Repeat Part IV, beats 1-2, seven times
PART V	BOUNCE, BOUNCE/BOUNCE (8X) IN, HOP; IN, HOP; IN, HOP; IN, HOP; OUT, HOP; OUT, HOP; OUT, HOP; OUT, HOP; Repeat Part V

Slavonsko Kolo (continued)

Beat 1	Bounce R heel (move L foot sideward left) ⎫
2 &	Step L foot to left so weight on both and ⎬ Slavonsko Drmeš
	bounce heels twice
3	Bounce L heel (bring R foot to L foot)
4 &	Step R foot so weight on both feet and
	bounce heels twice
5-16	Repeat beats 1-4 three times
17	Step R foot in toward center
18	Hop R foot swinging L foot in front of R leg
19-24	Step hop L, R, L foot in toward center;
	beat 24 keep R foot behind L leg
25-32	Step hop R, L, R, L foot out
33-64	Repeat Part V, beats 1-32
PART VI	JUMP, BOUNCE/BOUNCE (8X);
	IN, HOP; IN, HOP; IN, HOP; IN, HOP;
	OUT, HOP; OUT, HOP; OUT, HOP; OUT, HOP;
	Repeat Part VI
Beat 1	Jump on both feet, bending knees
2 &	Bounce both heels twice
3-16	Repeat beats 1-2 seven times
17-32	Repeat Part V, beats 17-32
33-64	Repeat Part VI, beats 1-32
	Repeat Parts I-VI
	Repeat Parts I-II
	Repeat Parts I-II slowing to end feet together

RHYTHMIC NOTATION

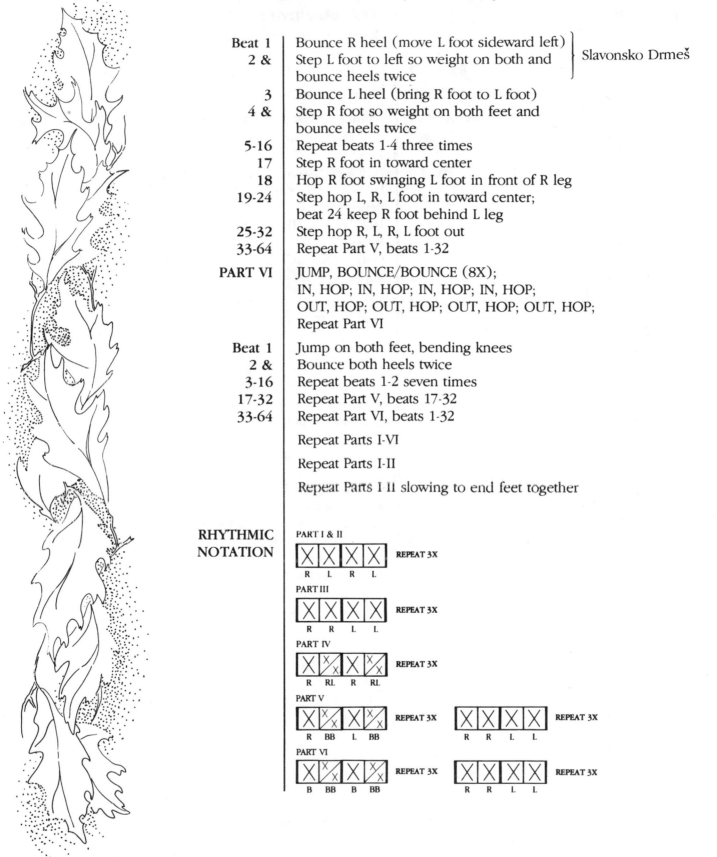

Szakăcsně Tănc
Hungary

RECORD	Qualiton LPX 18007 (Side A, Band 4)
INTRODUCTION	None
FORMATION	Women in open circle, facing counterclockwise

PART I	FORWARD, REST, FORWARD, REST;
	FORWARD, FORWARD, STEP/STEP, STEP;
	Repeat 3X
	IN, REST, IN, REST; IN, IN, STEP/STEP, STEP;
	Repeat;
	OUT, REST, OUT, REST; OUT, OUT, STEP/STEP, STEP;
	Repeat Part I;
Beats 1-2	Step R foot forward counterclockwise extending heel before step
3-4	Step L foot forward counterclockwise extending heel before step
5	Step R foot diagonally forward right (keep L foot close to R foot)
6	Step L foot diagonally forward left (keep R foot close to L foot)
7-8	Cifra R foot turning to face clockwise (step R, L, R foot)
9-16	Repeat beats 1-8 moving clockwise (opposite footwork)
17-32	Repeat beats 1-16
33-48	Repeat beats 1-8 twice moving toward center of circle; turn to face out on beats 47-48
49-64	Repeat beats 1-8 twice moving out of circle; turn to face center on beats 63-64
65-96	Repeat beats 1-32

Szakăcsně Tănc *(continued)*

	Fast melody
PART II	TURN, TURN; TURN, TURN; STEP/STEP, STEP; FORWARD, 2, 3, JUMP; Repeat; IN/CLOSE, IN; IN/CLOSE, IN; OUT/CLOSE, OUT; OUT/CLOSE, OUT; SIDE, CLICK; TURN, TURN; STEP/STEP, CLICK; Repeat; Repeat Part II 2X

Beat 1	Step R foot with knee bent beginning a full turn clockwise
2	Step L foot straight knee completing full turn clockwise
3-4	Repeat beats 1-2
5 &	Step R, L foot in place
6	Leap R foot extending L foot diagonally toward center of circle
7-9	Run L, R, L foot forward clockwise
10	Jump knees bent
11-20	Repeat beats 1-10
21-24	Two leaping style two steps in toward center of circle, beginning R foot
25-28	Two leaping style two steps out away from center of circle
29-30	Single csardas right
31	Step R foot pivoting clockwise, raise L foot behind R foot
32	Step L foot completing full turn, raise R foot in front of L foot
33 &	Leap R, L foot in place
34	Click heels
35-48	Repeat beats 21-34
49-144	Repeat Part II, beats 1-48, two times

Beats 1-4: } Turning Rida

RHYTHMIC NOTATION

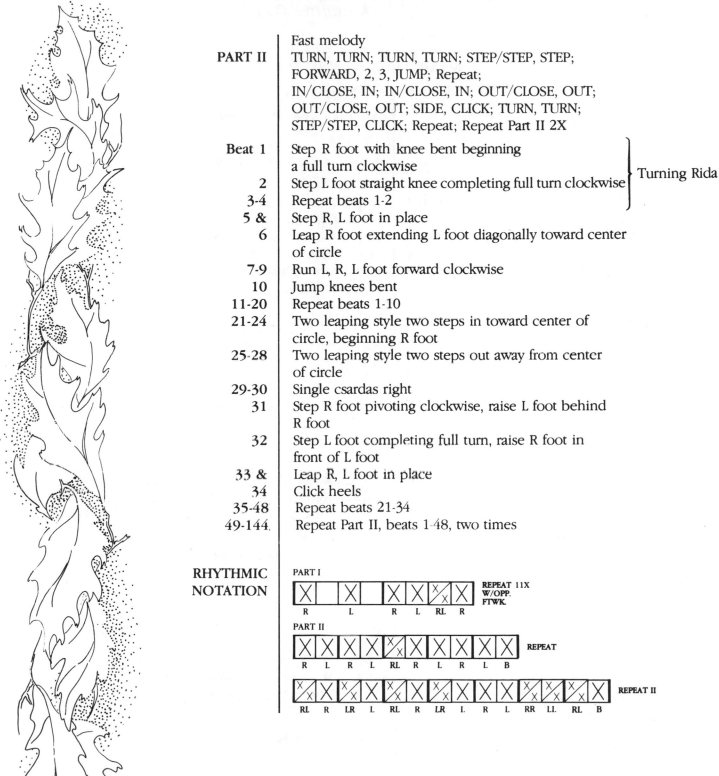

PART I

REPEAT 11X W/OPP. FTWK.

R L R L RL R

PART II

R L R L RL R L R L B

REPEAT

RL R LR L RL R LR L R L RR LL RL B

REPEAT II

Trei Pazeşte de la Bistret
Romania (Oltenia)

RECORD	Noroc Vol. I *Hai La Joc*
INTRODUCTION	32 beats
FORMATION	Short lines, shoulder hold
PART I	OUT/CLOSE, IN/SCUFF; ACCENT, STAMP; Repeat Part I 3X
Beat 1	Step R foot out
&	Step L foot next to R foot
2	Step R foot in toward center
&	Scuff L foot in
3	Step L foot with accent
4	Stamp R foot
5-16	Repeat beats 1-4 three times
PART II	CROSS/SIDE, BACK/SIDE (2X); CROSS/SIDE, CROSS/SIDE, CROSS/SIDE, CROSS (3X)
Beats 1-4	Two grapevine steps moving clockwise beginning R foot
5-8	One seven moving clockwise (CROSS/SIDE, CROSS/SIDE, CROSS/SIDE, CROSS)
9-12	One seven moving counterclockwise
13-16	One seven moving clockwise
PART III	SIDE, CROSS/BACK, SIDE/CROSS, BACK (2X); SIDE, CROSS/BACK, SIDE/CROSS, BACK/SIDE; CROSS/SIDE, CROSS/SIDE, CROSS/SIDE, CROSS
Beat 1	Leap L foot sideward left
2	Step R foot crossing in front of L foot
&	Step L foot crossing in back of R foot
3	Step R foot sideward right
&	Step L foot crossing in front of R foot
4	Leap R foot crossing in back of L foot (kicking L foot)
5-8	Repeat beats 1-4
9-12	Repeat beats 1-4 adding a step L foot slightly sideward left on the "and" of beat 4
13-16	One seven moving clockwise
PART IV	Repeat Part II, beats 1-16 beginning L foot to the right

Trei Pazeşte de la Bistret (continued)

RHYTHMIC NOTATION

PART I

X X X X X — **REPEAT 3X**

RL R(L) L (R)

PART II

X X X X X X X — RL RL RL RL

X X X X — **REPEAT 2X W/OPP. FTWK.** — RL RL RL R

PART III

X X X X X — **REPEAT** — L RL RL R

X X X X X X X X X X X X — L RL RL RL RL RL RL R

Vrni Se Vrni
Come Back, Come Back
Yugoslavia (Macedonia)

RECORD	Festival FM 4005
INTRODUCTION	32 beats
FORMATION	Circle, hands joined in "W" position

PART I	FORWARD, REST, BACKWARD, FORWARD;
	FORWARD, REST, BACKWARD, FORWARD;
	FORWARD, REST, FORWARD, REST, SIDE, REST, LIFT, REST;
	Repeat;
	FORWARD, REST, FORWARD, REST, SIDE, REST, LIFT, REST;
	FORWARD, REST, FORWARD, REST; SIDE, REST, LIFT, REST

Beats 1-2	Step R foot forward counterclockwise
3	Step L foot backward
4	Step R foot forward
5-6	Step L foot forward
7	Step R foot backward
8	Step L foot forward
9-10	Step R foot forward
11-12	Step L foot forward
13-14	Step R foot sideward right
15-16	Lift L foot in front of R leg
17-32	Repeat beats 1-16 clockwise beginning L foot
33-36	Step R, L foot forward counterclockwise
37-38	Step R foot sideward right
39-40	Lift L foot in front of R leg
41-44	Step L, R foot forward clockwise
45-46	Step L foot sideward left
47-48	Lift R foot in front of L leg

(continued)

Vrni Se Vrni *(continued)*

PART II	Lower arms to "V" position HOP/FORWARD, FORWARD (2X); FORWARD/CLOSE, FORWARD; FORWARD/CLOSE, FORWARD; HOP/IN, REST, OUT, OUT; DROP, REST; STEP/STEP, STEP; Repeat Part II
Beat 1	Hop L foot
&	Step R foot forward counterclockwise
2	Step L foot forward counterclockwise
3	Hop L foot
&	Step R foot forward counterclockwise
4	Step L foot forward counterclockwise
5-6	Two step R foot forward counterclockwise
7-8	Two step L foot forward counterclockwise
9	Hop L foot facing center
&	Step R foot in toward center
10	Rest
11	Step L foot out from center
12	Step R foot out on ball of foot
13-14	Lower R heel
15-16	Step R, L, R foot in place
17-32	Repeat Part II, beats 1-16

RHYTHMIC NOTATION

PART I

X		X	X	X		X	X	X		X		X		X		REPEAT W/OPP. FTWK.
R		L	R	L		R	L	R		L		R		(L)		

X		X		X		X		REPEAT W/OPP. FTWK.
R		L		R		(L)		

PART II

X/X	X	X/X	X	X/X	X	X/X	X	X/X	X	X	X	X	X/X	X	REPEAT
LR	L	LR	L	RL	R	LR	L	LR		L	R	R	LR	L	

Vulpiuţa
The Little Fox
Romania (Oltenia)

RECORD	Nevofoon 15005 *Romanian Folkdances*
INTRODUCTION	32 beats
FORMATION	Closed circle facing center, hands held in "V" position

PART I	IN, HOP, OUT, HOP; IN, 2, 3, HOP; SIDE, HOP, SIDE, HOP; OUT, 2, 3, HOP
Beats 1-2	Step hop in beginning L foot
3-4	Step hop out beginning R foot
5-8	Schottische in beginning L foot
9-10	Step hop diagonally sideward out beginning R foot
11-12	Step hop sideward left beginning L foot
13-16	Schottische diagonally right out beginning R foot
PART II	FORWARD, HOP; FORWARD, HOP; SIDE, CLOSE; SIDE, CLOSE; SIDE, CLOSE; FORWARD, HOP; FORWARD, HOP; FORWARD, FORWARD
Beats 1-2	Step hop L foot forward clockwise beginning L foot
3-4	Step hop R foot forward clockwise
5-10	Side close sideward left 3 times beginning L foot
11-12	Step hop L foot clockwise
13-14	Step hop R foot counterclockwise
15	Step L foot forward counterclockwise
16	Leap R foot forward
PART III	CROSS, SIDE, BACK, SIDE; FORWARD, 2, 3, HOP; Repeat Part III
Beats 1-4	Grapevine beginning L foot crossing in front of R foot
5-7	Run L, R, L foot counterclockwise
8	Hop L foot turning to move clockwise, body low
9-16	Repeat Part III, beats 1-8 clockwise

(continued)

Vulpiuṭa (continued)

PART IV	IN, HOP; IN, HOP; OUT, 2, 3, HOP; CROSS, SIDE; CROSS, SIDE; CROSS, SIDE; CROSS, HOP
Beats 1-2	Step hop L foot in toward center of circle
3-4	Step hop R foot in turning 1/2 left on hop to face out of circle
5-8	Schottische beginning L foot moving out of circle (join hands again)
9	Step R foot crossing in front of L foot moving counterclockwise (facing out)
10	Step L foot sideward left
11-14	Repeat beats 9-10 two times
15-16	Step hop beginning R foot turning left to face center

**RHYTHMIC
NOTATION**

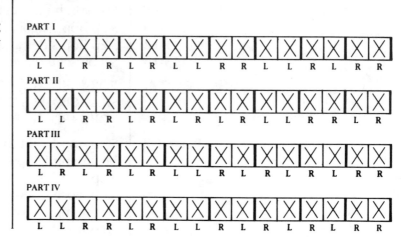

PART I

L L R R L R L L R R L L R L R R

PART II

L L R R L R L R L R L L R R L R

PART III

L R L R L R L L R L R L R L R R

PART IV

L L R R L R L L R L R L R L R R

Bičak
Bulgaria

RECORD	Balkanton BHA 734 *Bulgarian Folk Dances*
INTRODUCTION	None or 4 measures
FORMATION	Segregated lines or broken circles. Men in shoulder hold. Women in "W" position
METER	14/16 (9/16 + 5/16) 1-2, 1-2, 1-2, 1-2-3 + 1-2, 1-2-3 Quick, Quick, Quick, *Slow*, Quick, *Slow* (QQQSQS)

Basic

PART I   BOUNCE, FORWARD, BOUNCE, *FORWARD*,
SIDE, *IN*;
BOUNCE, OUT, BOUNCE, *OUT*, FORWARD,
FORWARD

Measure	Beat	
1	Q	Bounce L heel (chukche)
	Q	Step R foot forward moving counterclockwise
	Q	Bounce R heel (chukche)
	S	Step L foot forward and turn to face center
	Q	Step R foot sideward right
	S	Step L foot in toward center
2	Q	Bounce L heel (chukche)
	Q	Step R foot out from center
	Q	Bounce R heel
	S	Step L foot out
	Q, S	Step R, L foot forward counterclockwise

Twist

PART II   BOUNCE, FORWARD, BOUNCE, *FORWARD*,
SIDE, *IN*;
BOUNCE, OUT, BOUNCE, *OUT*, TWIST, *TWIST*

Measure	Beat	
1		Repeat Part I, measure 1
2	QQQS	Repeat Part I, measure 2 (QQQS)
	Q	Twist heels right
	S	Twist heels left

(continued)

Bičak (continued)

PART III		Rock
		BOUNCE, FORWARD, BOUNCE, *FORWARD*
		BACKWARD, *FORWARD*;
		SIDE, REST, BACK, *SIDE*, BOUNCE, *CROSS*;
		OUT, IN, OUT, *IN*, BOUNCE, *CROSS*;
		OUT, IN, OUT, *IN*, BOUNCE, *CROSS*

Measure	Beat	
1	Q	Bounce L heel
	Q	Step R foot forward counterclockwise
	Q	Bounce R heel
	S	Step L foot forward
	Q	Step R foot backward
	S	Step L foot forward and turn to face center
2	QQ	Step R foot sideward right and hold
	Q	Step L foot crossing in back of R foot
	S	Step R foot sideward right
	Q	Bounce R heel bring straight L leg in front of R leg
	S	Step L foot crossing in front of R foot bending knee; bring R leg up behind
3	Q	Step R foot out away from center
	Q	Step L foot in toward center
	Q	Step R foot out
	S	Step L foot in
	Q	Bounce L heel bring straight R leg in
	S	Step R foot in front of L foot bending knee; bring L leg up behind
4		Repeat measure 3 beginning R foot and turn to face counterclockwise on final step

Bičak (continued)

		Leap
PART IV		BOUNCE, FORWARD, BOUNCE, *FORWARD*, FORWARD, *FORWARD*;
		HOP, FORWARD, JUMP, *FORWARD*, FORWARD, *SIDE*;
		Repeat

Measure	Beat	
1	QQQS	Repeat Part I measure 1 (QQQS)
	QS	Step R, L foot forward counterclockwise
2	Q	Hop L foot
	Q	Step R foot forward
	Q	Jump with L foot ahead of R foot
	S	Leap R foot forward
	Q	Leap L foot forward and turn to face center
	S	Leap R foot sideward right (lift L foot in front of R leg)
3-4		Repeat Part IV, measures 1-2 moving clockwise beginning with a bounce on R heel

RHYTHMIC NOTATION

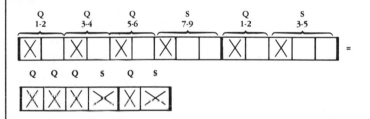

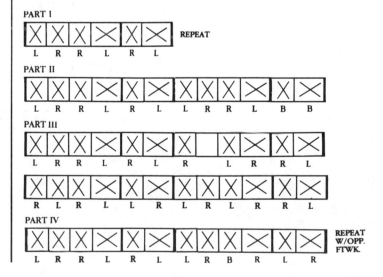

Dajčovo Horo
Village Dajčovo
Bulgaria

RECORD	XOPO 301
INTRODUCTION	None or 4 measures
FORMATION	Broken circle, hands held in "V" position
METER	9/16 1-2, 3-4, 5-6, 7-8-9 Quick, Quick, Quick, *Slow* (QQQ*S*) Dajčovo step HOP, STEP, STEP, *STEP*
Step Q	Hop L foot
Q	Step R foot next to L foot
Q	Step L foot next to R foot
S	Step R foot next to L foot
NOTE	Begin each repeat with the opposite foot. Dajčovo steps may be done in place, in a diamond pattern as below, or in other patterns
Measure 1	One Dajčovo moving diagonally forward left beginning hop L foot
2	One Dajčovo moving diagonally forward right beginning hop R foot
3	One Dajčovo moving diagonally backward right beginning hop L foot
4	One Dajčovo moving diagonally backward left beginning hop R foot

RHYTHMIC NOTATION

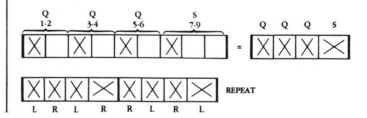

Delčevsko Horo
Bulgaria (Macedonia)

RECORD	BG 1001
INTRODUCTION	Short lines, belt hold, R arm uner
METER	7/16
	1-2, 3-4, 5-6-7
	Quick, Quick, *Slow*, (QQS)

PART I	HOP, FORWARD, *FORWARD*;
	HOP, FORWARD, *FORWARD*;
	HOP, SIDE *BACK*; SIDE, LIFT, *HOP*;
	HOP, SIDE, *BACK*; SIDE, LIFT, *HOP*;
	SIDE, LIFT *HOP*; SIDE, LIFT, *HOP*;
	SIDE, SIDE, *CROSS*; HOP, PIVOT, *CROSS*

Measure	Beat	
1	Q	Hop L foot
	Q	Step R foot forward counterclockwise (bend knees) } Limping style
	S	Step L foot forward
2		Repeat measure 1 and turn to face center
3	Q	Hop L foot
	Q	Step R heel sideward right
	S	Step L foot crossing in back of R foot
4	Q	Step R foot sideward right
	Q	Raise L leg in front with bent knee
	S	Hop R foot, keep L foot raised
5-6		Repeat measures 3-4 beginning hop R foot and moving left
7		Repeat measure 4
8		Repeat measure 4 beginning L foot
9	Q	Step R foot sideward right
	Q	Step L foot sideward left
	S	Step R foot crossing in front of left with an accent, bring L foot up behind R leg
10	QQ	Hop R foot turning to face counterclockwise straightening L foot forward sharply, straightening body
	S	Step L foot crossing in front of R foot and turn to face counterclockwise

(continued)

Delčevsko Horo (continued)

RHYTHMIC NOTATION

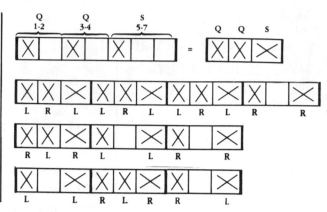

Deninka
Yugoslavia (Macedonia)

RECORD	XOPO X329 *Ordan Sedi*
INTRODUCTION	8 measures
FORMATION	Open circle, hands joined in "W" position
METER	7/8 1-2-3, 4-5, 6-7 *Slow*, Quick, Quick (*SQQ*)
PART I	*BOUNCE*, FORWARD, FORWARD; *FORWARD*, 2, 3; *FORWARD*, 2, 3; *FORWARD*, CROSS, BACK; *BOUNCE*, SIDE, CROSS; *BACK*, SIDE, REST; *CROSS*, BOUNCE, BOUNCE; *IN*, BOUNCE, BOUNCE; *OUT*, BOUNCE, BOUNCE

Measure	Beat	
1	*S*	Bounce (chukche) L foot (R foot in front slightly off floor)
	Q	Step R foot forward counterclockwise
	Q	Step L foot forward
2	S	Step R foot forward counterclockwise
	QQ	Step L, R foot forward
3	S	Step L foot counterclockwise
	QQ	Step R, L foot forward
4	S	Step R foot forward counterclockwise and turn to face center
	Q	Step L foot crossing in front of R foot
	Q	Step R foot crossing in back of L foot

Deninka (continued)

5	*S*	Bounce (chukche) R foot (facing center)
	Q	Step L foot sideward left
	Q	Step R foot crossing in front of L foot
6	*S*	Step L foot crossing in back of R foot with slightly bent knee and rise up in preparation for next step
	QQ	Step R foot sideward right bending knee and rise up
7	*S*	Step L foot crossing in front of R foot with slightly bent knee
	QQ	Touch R foot next to L foot and bounce 2 times on L foot
8	*S*	Step R foot in toward center
	QQ	Touch L foot next to R foot and bounce 2 times on R foot
9	*S*	Step L foot out away from center
	QQ	Touch R foot next to L foot and bounce 2 times on L foot

RHYTHMIC NOTATION

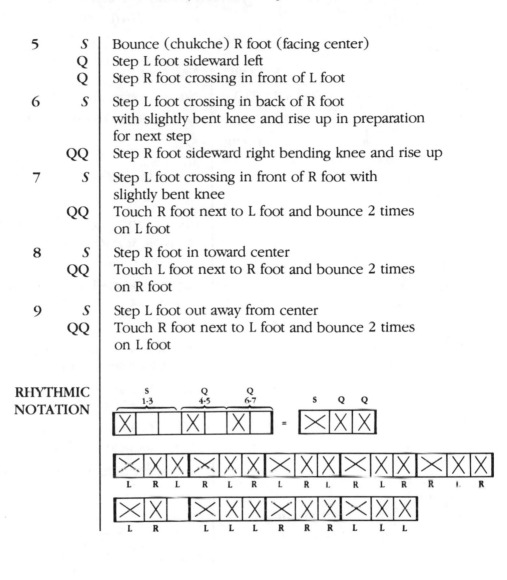

Jambolsko Pajduško Horo
Bulgaria

RECORD	NAMA #1
INTRODUCTION	None or begin any time
FORMATION	Broken circle, hands joined "V" position
METER	5/16
	1-2, 3-4-5
	Quick, *Slow* (Q,*S*)

PART I		CROSS, *SIDE* (3X); HOP, *CLOSE*;
		SCISSOR, *SCISSOR*; HOP, *OUT* (3X)

Measure	Beat	
1	Q	Step L foot crossing in front of R foot
	S	Step R foot sideward right
2-3		Repeat measure 1, two times
4	Q	Hop R foot in place raising L knee slightly
	S	Step L foot next to R foot
5	Q	Step R foot kicking L leg in
	S	Step L foot kicking R leg in
6	Q	Hop L foot bringing R foot in back of L heel
	S	Step R foot close in back of L heel
7-8		Repeat measure 6, two times alternating footwork

RHYTHMIC NOTATION

Karsilimas
Face-to-Face
Turkey

RECORD	Folklore Dances of the Middle East M7C23590 *Rampi Rampi*
INTRODUCTION	1 measure
FORMATION	Partners standing face-to-face, no hands held Men raise and spread arms Women place the backs of the hands on the hips
METER	9/8 1-2, 3-4, 5-6, 7-8-9 Quick, Quick, Quick, *Slow* (QQQ*S*)
PART I	FORWARD, 2, 3, *LIFT*; FORWARD, 2, 3, *LIFT*; Repeat Part I

Measure	Beat	
1	Q	Step R foot forward right facing diagonally right (move away from partner)
	Q	Step L foot forward right
	Q	Step R foot forward right
	S	Lift L foot in front of R leg (toe touching floor)
2		Repeat measure 1 beginning L foot (end facing center)
3-4		Repeat measure 1-2 moving toward partner

NOTE	Part I may be varied by using turns on any measure desired.
VARIATION I	IN, 2, 3, *LIFT*; IN, 2, 3, *LIFT*; OUT, 2, 3, *LIFT*; OUT, 2, 3, *LIFT*; Repeat Variation I

Measure	Beat	
1		Step in toward partner beginning R foot
2		Step in toward partner beginning L foot (end with R shoulders adjacent)
3-4		Repeat measure 1-2 returning out to place
5-6		Repeat measure 1-2 moving toward partner (end with L shoulders adjacent)
7-8		Repeat measure 1-2 returning out to place *(continued)*

Karsilimas *(continued)*

VARIATION II	IN, 2, 3, LIFT; FORWARD, 2, 3, LIFT; OUT, 2, 3, LIFT; FORWARD, 2, 3, LIFT; Repeat Variation II

Measure	**Beat**	
1-4		Step in toward partner, pass R shoulders, move back-to-back, pass L shoulders, return to place
5-8		Repeat measure 1-4 passing L shoulders first

VARIATION III	FORWARD, 2, 3, *LIFT*; TURN, 2, 3, *LIFT*; IN, 2, 3, *LIFT*; OUT, 2, 3, *LIFT*; Repeat Variation III

Measure	**Beat**	
	1	Repeat Part I, measure 1
	2	Step L, R, L foot turing full turn left toward partner
	3	Step R, L, R foot in toward partner
	4	Step L, R, L foot out away from partner
	5-8	Repeat Variation III, measures 1-4

RHYTHMIC NOTATION

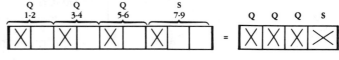

PART I & VARIATIONS

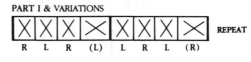

Krustenkilska Ruchenitsa
Bulgaria (Shope region around Sofia)

RECORD	Folk Dancer MH 3057
INTRODUCTION	16 measures.
FORMATION	Broken circle, hands joined in "V" position
METER	7/8
	1-2, 3-4, 5-6-7
	Quick, Quick, *Slow* (QQS)
PART I	HOP, BACKWARD, *BACKWARD*;
	HOP, BACKWARD, *BACKWARD*;
	FORWARD, FORWARD, *FORWARD*;
	FORWARD, BACKWARD, *FORWARD*;
	SIDE, REST, *HOP*; HOP, SIDE, *CROSS*; HOP, SIDE, *BACK*;
	SIDE, REST, *HOP*; HOP, HOP, *IN*; HOP, HOP, *IN*

Measure	Beat	
1	Q	Hop L foot backward (facing clockwise, moving counterclockwise)
	Q	Step R foot backward moving counterclockwise
	S	Step L foot backward moving counterclockwise
2		Repeat measure 1 and pivot to face counterclockwise
3	Q	Step R foot forward counterclockwise
	Q	Step L foot forward counterclockwise
	S	Step R foot forward counterclockwise
4	Q	Step L foot forward ⎫
	Q	Step R foot backward ⎬ Rocking step
	S	Step L foot forward ⎭
5	Q	Step R foot sideward right or hop L foot, step R foot (skip step)
	Q	Hold
	S	Hop R foot extending L foot in front of R leg
6	Q	Hop R foot in place
	Q	Step L foot sideward left
	S	Step R foot crossing in front of L foot (bend knees)
7	Q	Hop R foot in place
	Q	Step L foot sideward left
	S	Step R foot crossing in back of L foot
8	Q	Step L foot sideward left or hop R foot, step L foot (skip step)
	Q	Hold
	S	Hop L foot, extend R foot in (straight knee)

(continued)

Krustenkilska Ruchenitsa (continued)

9	Q	Hop L foot with R foot extended in
	Q	Hop L foot with R foot extended in
	S	Step R foot slightly in
10		Repeat measure 9 beginning hop R foot

RHYTHMIC NOTATION

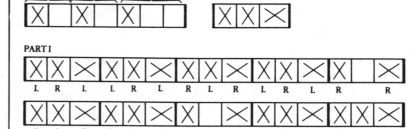

PART I

Lakhana
Greece (Pontos)

RECORD	Folklorist LP1
INTODUCTION	2 measures
FORMATION	Line, hands joined in "V" position
METER	9/16
	1-2, 3-4, 5-6, 7-8-9
	Quick, Quick, Quick, *Slow* (QQQS)
PART I	SIDE, REST, CLOSE, *SIDE*;
	CROSS, REST, SIDE, *CROSS*

Measure	Beat	
1	QQ	Step R foot sideward right
	Q	Step L foot next to R foot
	S	Step R foot sideward right
2	QQ	Step L foot crossing in front of R foot
	Q	Step R foot sideward right
	S	Step L foot crossing in front of R foot

Lakhana (continued)

PART II		hop/*SIDE*, BACK, *SIDE*; hop/*CROSS*, SIDE, *CROSS*
1	Q'er	Hop L foot
	S	Step R foot sideward right
	Q	Step L foot crossing in back of R foot
	S	Step R foot sideward right
2	Q'er	Hop R foot
	S	Step L foot crossing in front of R foot
	Q	Step R foot sideward right
	S	Step L foot crossing in front of R foot

PART III		HOP, SIDE, BACK, *SIDE*; HOP, CROSS, SIDE, *CROSS*
1	Q	Hop L foot
	Q	Step R foot sideward right
	Q	Step L foot crossing in back of R foot
	S	Step R foot sideward right
2	Q	Hop R foot
	Q	Step L foot crossing in front of R foot
	Q	Step R foot sideward right
	S	Step L foot crossing in front of R foot

NOTE	Each part may be executed any number of times in any order.

**RHYTHMIC
NOTATION**

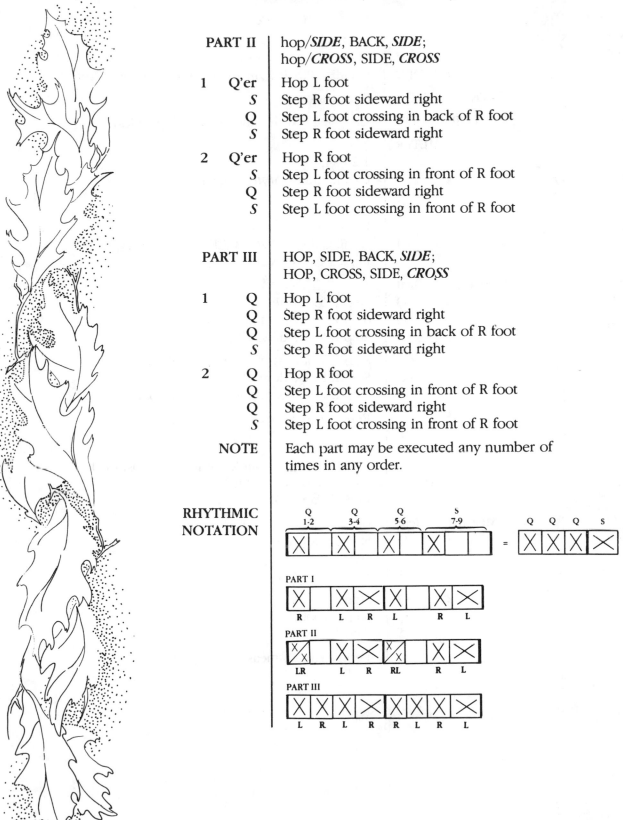

Laziko
Greece

RECORD	Polydisc PLS 201 *An Intersection of Greek Dances*
INTRODUCTION	8 measures
FORMATION	Line, begin with hands held "V" position
METER	7/8
	1-2, 3-4, 5-6-7
	Quick, Quick, *Slow* (QQS)

		Basic
PART I		SIDE, CROSS, *SIDE*; BACK, SIDE, *CROSS*;
		Repeat Part I 3X

Measure	Beat	
1	Q	Step R foot sideward right
	Q	Step L foot crossing in front of R foot
	S	Step R foot sideward right
2	Q	Step L foot crossing in back of R foot
	Q	Step R foot sideward right
	S	Step L foot crossing in front of R foot
3-8		Repeat Part I, measures 1-2, three times

		Rock (arms in shoulder hold—"T" position)
PART II		OUT, IN, *OUT*; IN, OUT, *IN*;
		Repeat Part II 3X

Measure	Beat	
1	Q	Step R foot out
	Q	Step L foot in
	S	Step R foot out
2	Q	Step L foot in
	Q	Step R foot out
	S	Step L foot in
3-8		Repeat Part II, measures 1-2, three times

Laziko (continued)

		Swing ("T" position continued)
PART III		SIDE, CROSS, *SIDE*; SIDE, BACK, *SIDE*; Repeat Part III 2X
Measure	**Beat**	
1	Q	Step R foot sideward right
	Q	Step L foot crossing in front of R foot
	S	Step R foot sideward right—swing L leg across in front of R leg
2	Q	Step L foot sideward left
	Q	Step R foot crossing in back of L foot
	S	Step L foot sideward left—swing R leg across in front of L leg
3-6		Repeat Part III, measures 1-2, two times

		Accent ("V" position)
PART IV		FORWARD, FORWARD, *ACCENT*; Repeat Part IV 7X
Measure	**Beat**	
1	Q	Step R foot forward moving counterclockwise
	Q	Step L foot forward moving counterclockwise
	S	Accent R foot forward
2-8		Repeat Part IV, measure 1, seven times alternating footwork

		Touch
PART V		FORWARD, FORWARD, *TOUCH*; Repeat Part V 7X
Measure	**Beat**	
1	Q	Step R foot forward moving counterclockwise
	Q	Step L foot forward
	S	Touch R foot next to L foot bending body forward
2-8		Repeat Part V, measure 1, seven times

		Twist ("W" position)
PART VI		FORWARD, FORWARD, *TOUCH*; Repeat Part VI 5X
Measure	**Beat**	
1	Q	Step R foot forward moving counterclockwise
	Q	Step L foot forward and pivot to face center
	S	Touch R foot next to L foot (facing center)
2-6		Repeat Part VI, measure 1, five times

(continued)

Laziko (continued)

Circle ("V" position)

PART VII   OUT, IN, *CLOSE*; Repeat Part VII 7X

Measure	Beat	
1	Q	Step R foot slightly out
	Q	Step L foot slightly in
	S	Step R foot next to L foot circling L leg around to the left and behind R foot
2-8		Repeat Part VII, measure 1, seven times alternating footwork

RHYTHMIC NOTATION

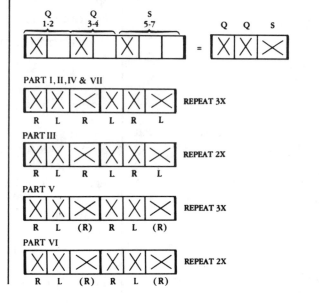

Lilka
Western Bulgaria
Eastern Serbia
(Dajčovo Family)

RECORD	Vitosha *Folk Dances of Bulgaria*
INTRODUCTION	None
FORMATION	Short lines, belt hold
METER	9/16
	1-2, 3-4, 5-6, 7-8-9
	Quick, Quick, Quick, *Slow (QQQS)*

Dajčovo step
HOP, STEP, STEP, *STEP*

Q	Hop L foot
Q	Step R foot
Q	Step L foot
S	Step R foot
NOTE	Alternating footwork is used.

Measure	Beat	
1		One Dajčovo step moving counterclockwise, beginning hop L foot
2		One Dajčovo step moving counterclockwise, beginning hop R foot
3		One Dajčovo step moving out (facing center)
4		One Dajčovo step moving in
5		One Dajčovo step moving diagonally out right facing diagonally left
6-10		Repeat measures 1-5 with opposite footwork in opposite direction

RHYTHMIC NOTATION

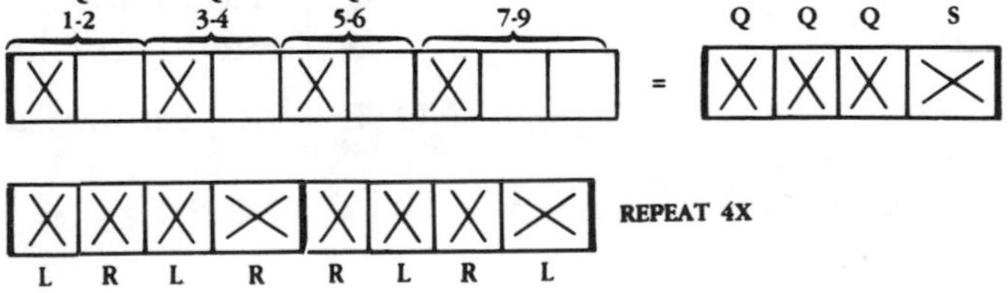

REPEAT 4X

Plevensko Dajčovo Horo
Bulgaria

RECORD	XOPO
INTRODUCTION	None
FORMATION	Lines, belt hold with R arm under
METER	9/8
	1-2, 3-4, 5-6, 7-8-9
	Quick, Quick, Quick, *Slow* (QQQ*S*)
PART I	STEP, IN, OUT, *OUT*; IN, IN, OUT, *OUT*; SIDE, STAMP, SIDE, *STAMP*; OUT, IN, IN, *OUT*; OUT, IN, IN, *OUT*; HOP, OUT, HOP, *OUT*

Measure	Beat	
1	Q	Step R foot in place
	Q	Step L foot in toward the center
	Q	Step R foot out from center
	S	Step L foot out from center
2	Q	Step R foot in
	QQ*S*	Repeat measure 1, QQS
3	Q	Leap R foot sideward right
	Q	Stamp L foot next to R foot
	Q	Leap L foot sideward left
	S	Stamp R foot next to L foot
4	Q	Step R foot out
	Q	Step L foot in
	Q	Step R foot in
	S	Step L foot out
5		Repeat measure 4
6	Q	Hop L foot
	Q	Step R foot behind L foot
	Q	Hop R foot
	S	Step L foot behind R foot

Reel style (for measure 6)

NOTE	Repeat measures 1-6 as often as desired.

Plevensko Dajčovo Horo (continued)

PART II		HOP, SIDE, CROSS, ***BACK***; SIDE, BACK, SIDE, ***BACK***; HOP, OUT, HOP, ***OUT***; HOP, SIDE, CROSS, ***BACK***; Repeat Part II

Measure	Beat	
1	Q	Hop L foot
	Q	Step R foot sideward right
	Q	Step L foot crossing in front of R foot
	S	Step R foot crossing in back of L foot
2	Q	Step L foot sideward left
	Q	Step R foot crossing in back of L foot
	Q	Step L foot sideward left
	S	Step R foot crossing in back of L foot
3	Q	Hop R foot
	Q	Step L foot behind R foot
	Q	Hop L foot
	S	Step R foot behind L foot
4		Repeat measure 1 with opposite footwork beginning hop R foot
5-8		Repeat Part II, measures 1-4
NOTE		Repeat Part II as often as desired.

PART III		SIDE, BACK, SIDE, ***CROSS***; Repeat; CROSS, SIDE, CROSS, ***SIDE***; HOP, OUT, HOP, ***OUT***

Measure	Beat	
1	Q	Step R foot slightly sideward right
	Q	Step L foot crossing in back of R foot
	Q	Step R foot sideward right
	S	Step L foot crossing in front of R foot
2		Repeat measure 1
3	Q	Step R foot crossing in front of L foot
	Q	Step L foot sideward left
	Q	Step R foot crossing in front of L foot
	S	Step L foot sideward left
4	Q	Hop L foot
	Q	Step R foot behind L foot
	Q	Hop R foot
	S	Step L foot behind R foot

(continued)

Plevensko Dajcŏvo Horo (continued)

RHYTHMIC NOTATION

Q 1-2	Q 3-4	Q 5-6	S 7-9		Q	Q	Q	S
X	X	X	X		X	X	X	X

PART I

X	X	X	X	X	X	X	X	X
R	L	R	L	R	L	R	L	R	(L)	L	(R)

X	X	X	X	X	X	X	X	X
R	L	R	L	R	L	R	L	L	L	R	R	L

PART II

X	X	X	X	X	X	X	X	X	X	X	REP
L	R	L	R	L	R	L	R	R	L	L	R	R	L	R	L

PART III

X	X	X	X	X	X	X	X	X	X	X	X
R	L	R	L	R	L	R	L	R	L	R	L	R	L	L	R	R	L

Tino Mori
Macedonia

RECORD	Folkraft 1557
INTRODUCTION	None
FORMATION	Circle or broken circle, hands held head height and in slightly toward center
METER	7/8 1-2-3, 4-5, 6-7 Slow, Quick, Quick (SQQ) or 1-2, 3, 4-5-6-7 Quick, Quicker, Slower (Q, Q'er, S'er)
PART I	FORWARD, *LIFT*; FORWARD/close, ***FORWARD***; SIDE, *LIFT*; SIDE, *LIFT*; SIDE, ***BACK***; SIDE, *LIFT*; CROSS/side, ***CROSS***; IN, ***OUT***; OUT, *LIFT*; FORWARD/close; ***FORWARD***; IN, ***OUT***; OUT, *LIFT*; SIDE, ***REST***; SIDE, ***REST***; SIDE, ***REST***; SIDE, ***SIDE***

Tino Mori *(continued)*

Measure	Beat	
1	S	Step R foot forward counterclockwise
	S'er	Lift L foot in front of R leg (swinging motion)
2	Q	Step R foot forward
	Q'er	Step L foot next to R foot
	S'er	Step R foot forward
3	S	Step R foot sideward right
	S'er	Lift L foot in front of R leg (swinging motion)
4		Repeat measure 3 with opposite footwork to the left
5	S	Step R foot sideward right
	S'er	Step L foot crossing in back of R foot
6		Repeat measure 3
7	Q	Step L foot crossing in front of R foot
	Q'er	Step R foot sideward right
	S'er	Step L foot crossing in front of R foot
8	S	Step R foot in toward the center
	S'er	Step L foot out away from center
9	S	Step R foot out
	S'er	Lift L foot in front of R leg (swinging motion)
10	Q	Step L foot forward clockwise
	Q'er	Step R foot next to L foot
	S'er	Step L foot forward
11-12		Repeat measures 8-9
13		Step L foot sideward left (sway)
14		Step R foot sideward right (sway)
15		Step L foot sideward left (sway)
16	S	Step R foot sideward right (sway)
	S'er	Step L foot sideward left (sway)
	NOTE	The instrumental interludes have 12 measures. Omit the dance steps for measures 13-16 and substitute the following for measure 12: S—Step R foot out, S'er—Step L foot next to R foot.

(continued)

Tino Mori (continued)

RHYTHMIC NOTATION

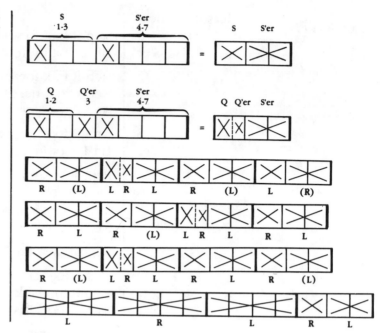

Glossary

Language-to-Movement Terms

Basic Locomotor Movements

HOP A transfer of weight from one foot to the *same* foot. Executed with an even beat. May be done in place or proceed in any direction. (If the hopping foot is changed, a leap is performed.)

JUMP A transfer of weight from one or both feet to *both* feet. Executed with an even beat. May be done in place or proceed in any direction.

LEAP A transfer of weight from one foot to the other foot. Both feet are off the floor in the transfer. Greater height or distance is used than in the run. Executed with an even beat. May proceed in any direction.

RUN A transfer of weight from one foot to the other foot. Both feet are off the floor momentarily before the transfer of weight. Executed with an even beat which often is faster than the beat used for the walk. May proceed in any direction.

WALK A transfer of weight from one foot to the other foot. One foot always is in contact with the floor. Executed with an even beat which allows the same amount of time between each step. May proceed in any direction.

Basic Locomotor Movement Combinations

GALLOP A forward or backward movement. One foot steps then the other foot closes; the step takes more time than the close (uneven rhythm). The same foot always leads. The easiest of the basic locomotor combinations.

SKIP A combination of a step and a hop executed in an uneven rhythm. Same rhythmic pattern as the gallop and slide. The time interval of the hop is shorter than the step. The skip may proceed in any direction. The leading foot changes with each skip.

SLIDE A sideward gallop. Same rhythmic pattern as the gallop. The same foot leads sideward followed by a close of the opposite foot. The side step takes more time than the close (uneven rhythm).

Other Movement Terms

BUZZ TURN A movement in which partners, using the shoulders-waist or social dance position, turn 360° in a forward direction with a series of steps using divided beats. The right foot leads.

CAMEL ROLL A movement from the forward foot to the backward foot to the forward foot again. The hips describe a movement in the shape of a "C."

CHARLESTON STEP (simplified) A step forward, a forward kick of the free leg, a step backward from the kick, and a touch of the free leg backward.

DEBKA JUMP A sequence of two jumps. On the first jump, the knees angle diagonally left. On the second jump, the knees are forward.

DO-SA-DO A partner movement in which partners move toward one another, pass right shoulders back to back, and then move backward to place.

ELBOW SWING A partner movement in which partners hook elbows and walk, run or skip around in a forward direction, turning 360°.

FIGURE EIGHT A series of steps which describe the floor pattern of an "8."

GRAND RIGHT AND LEFT Partners face each other and begin to move around the circle in opposite directions giving right hands to each other, then alternating left and right hands with each person in turn.

HORSE TROT A "leaping" movement in which the legs bend and reach forward for each new step.

PARTNER BEAT Two persons move together with the same tempo.

RIGHT HAND STAR Dancers move in a forward direction clockwise with right hands joined in the middle.

SCISSORS KICKS A forward or backward kicking movement of the legs in which the kicks occur in sequence.

SIDEWARD CAMEL ROLL Feet step from side to side and hips move in "C" from side to side.

Language-to-Dance Vocabulary

Weight Transfer Terms

ACCENT   A forceful step on the designated foot.

AROUND   A step on the designated foot to begin a sequence of steps that travel around a partner as in a do-sa-do.

AWAY   A step on the designated foot to move apart from a partner as partners face one another.

BACK   A step on the designated foot crossing in back of the other foot.

BACKWARD   A step on the designated foot moving away from the facing direction (clockwise or counter-clockwise) around a circle or one behind the other in a line.

CHANGE   A step on the designated foot to begin a change of partners or change of places between two people.

CLOSE   A step on the designated foot to bring it next to the other foot. May occur in any direction.

CROSS   A step on the designated foot crossing in front of the other foot.

CUT   A step consisting of a forceful movement toward the supporting leg causing the supporting leg to come off the floor with the knee straight.

FORWARD   A step on the designated foot moving in the facing direction (clockwise or counterclockwise) around a circle or one behind the other in a line.

IN   A step on the designated foot toward the center of a circle or in the facing direction when standing side by side in a line.

OUT   A step on the designated foot away from the center of a circle or away from the facing direction when standing side by side in a line.

SHUFFLE   A step from one foot to the other maintaining contact with the floor.

SIDE   A step on the designated foot perpendicular to the facing direction. Dancers are facing center in a circle or side by side in a line.

SIDEWARD   A step on the designated foot per-pendicular to the facing direction. Dancers are one behind the other in a circle or line. (In a circle, OUT and IN might be substituted.)

SKATE   A step on the designated foot which slides the foot against the floor.

STEP   A weight transfer to the designated foot in place (next to the other foot).

SWAY   A step on the designated foot sideward with a movement of the upper body in the same direction.

SWIVEL   The toes and heels move sideward either together (toes then heels) or toes of one foot and heels of the other in an alternating motion.

TOGETHER   A step on the designated foot without lifting the other foot. Weight now is on both feet.

TOWARD   A step on the designated foot move closer to a partner as partners face one another.

TURN   A step on the designated foot which moves the body clockwise or counterclockwise 90° or 180° with a single weight transfer or a step which begins a multi-step rotation (90°, 180° or 360°).

Nonweight Transfer Terms

BEND   A motion of the supporting leg toward the floor as the knee bends.

BICYCLE   A movement of one leg as if it were pedaling a bicycle. May be a forward or backward motion.

BOUNCE   A movement of one or both heels which raises and lowers them to the floor. May be thought of as a jump or hop which doesn't leave the floor.

BRUSH   A motion of the designated foot against the floor.

CHUG   A movement of the supporting leg (generally backward) with the foot kept in contact with the floor.

CHUKCHE   A motion of the supporting leg that raises and lowers the heel.

CLICK, HEEL CLICK   A forceful motion of the designated foot against the other foot while it is on the floor or in the air.

DIG   A forceful motion of the designated foot to the floor with the front part of the foot contacting the floor.

DRAW   A movement which slides the free foot along the floor up to the supporting foot.

DROP   A forceful movement of the raised heel to the floor.

HEEL   A motion of the designated heel against the floor.

HIT   A motion of one or two hands to the foot or to the partner's hands.

HOOK   A motion of the designated foot against the back of the supporting knee causing the knee to bend.

KICK   A motion of the designated leg in front, back or to the side of the body involving a straightening of the knee.

LIFT   A motion of the designated leg in front of the body involving a bent knee. The lower leg is angled in front of the supporting leg.

PIVOT   A motion of the designated foot against the floor which turns the body to face a new direction.

PUSH   A motion that straightens a raised leg so that it moves diagonally to the floor. The weight is maintained on the other leg during the pushing motion.

SCUFF   A motion similar to a brush that brings the heel against the floor as the leg moves in front of the body.

SLAP   A forceful motion of the whole foot against the floor executed with the leg straight out from the body.

SNAP   A snapping motion of the fingers of one or both hands.

STAMP   A forceful motion of the designated foot against the floor.

STRAIGHTEN   A movement which straightens one or both knees from a bent position.

SWING   A movement that brings the leg in with the knee relaxed. The heel of the supporting foot is often raised as the leg swings.

TOE   A motion of the designated toes against the floor.

TOUCH   A motion of the designated toes or heel against the floor.

UP   A motion of the designated leg in front of the body begun by raising the knee.

Dance Patterns

BUMBLE BEE   STEP/STEP, STEP, or Quick TWO STEP

DOUBLE TRAVEL   CROSS, SIDE, CROSS, PIVOT

FIVES   SIDE/BACK (2X), SIDE/STAMP

SEVENS   SIDE/BACK (3X), SIDE/STAMP

SINGLES   CROSS, CROSS

THREES   SIDE/BACK, SIDE/STAMP

CIFRA
In place   SIDE/BACK, CROSS*
Moving   FORWARD, CLOSE, FORWARD, REST

CSÁRDÁS
Single   SIDE, CLICK
Double   SIDE, CLOSE, SIDE, CLICK

DRMEŠ   BEND, BOUNCE/BOUNCE

GRAPEVINE   CROSS, SIDE, BACK, SIDE
Reverse   BACK, SIDE, CROSS, SIDE
Uneven   CROSS, REST/SIDE, BACK, SIDE

GRAPEVINE PATTERN   SIDE, CROSS, SIDE, BACK or SIDE, BACK, SIDE, CROSS

HARMONICA   CROSS, BACK, SIDE, HOP

HOP/STEP, STEP   HOP/STEP, STEP

KOLO STEP   HOP/SIDE, CLOSE; SIDE, HOP

MIXED PICKLE   FORWARD,* REST, FORWARD, FORWARD

POLKA   HOP, FORWARD,* CLOSE, FORWARD

RIDA
Closed   CROSS, SIDE
Open   SIDE, CROSS

SCHOTTISCHE   WALK, WALK, STEP, HOP

STEP HOP   STEP, HOP

STEP HOP/STEP   STEP, HOP/STEP

THREE   FORWARD,* 2, 3, REST

TWO STEP   FORWARD,* CLOSE, FORWARD, REST

WALTZ   FORWARD,* FORWARD, CLOSE

YEMENITE   SIDE, SIDE, CROSS, REST

TRIPLE TRAVEL   CROSS, SIDE, CROSS, SIDE, CROSS, PIVOT

ZORBA   CROSS, SIDE, BACK, SIDE, CROSS, PIVOT

Dance Steps

CHERKESSIYA
Single   IN, OUT, OUT, IN
Double   CROSS, BACK, SIDE, CROSS, BACK, SIDE

*Other facing or traveling directions may be substituted.

Nonpartner Formations

BELT HOLD   Dancers wear belts loosely fastened around their waists. With palms toward the floor, dancers grasp the belt of the person on either side of them in front of the hip (fingers go over the belt). The right arm is over the neighbor's left arm for moving right. The left arm is over the neighbor's right arm for moving left.

BROKEN CIRCLE   Dancers are arranged in a single circle with one place in which the hands are not joined, thus establishing a leader.

CIRCLE   Dancers are arranged in a single circle with or without hands joined.

FREE FORMATION   Dancers are scattered around the dance sapce in a random pattern.

LINE   Dancers stand side by side. Line may be short with three to five dancers or long with one leader.

OPEN CIRCLE   Dancers are arranged in circle formation but hands are not joined during the dance.

Partner Formations

DOUBLE CIRCLE (PARTNERS FACING EACH OTHER)   Partners are arranged around a circle. Outside partner faces toward the center (IN) and inside partner faces away from the center of the circle (OUT).

FRONT BASKET   Dancers stand in a circle or line and spread their own arms sideward in front of the persons on either side. Hands are joined with persons one beyond the dancer on each side. The underneath arm corresponds to the traveling direction. (If the basket moves right the right arm is under.)

HEADS   The two sets of partners in a square set who face each other across the set; one set of heads has their backs to the music. (See *Square set* illustration.)

LONGWAYS SET, CONTRA LINE   Partners are in a double line facing each other or facing the head of the set.

REVERSE BASKET   Same as front basket with hands joined in back of the dancer on each side. The arm on top corresponds to the traveling direction.

SIDES   The two sets of partners in a square set who face each other and are not heads. (See *Square set* illustration.)

SINGLE CIRCLE   Partners stand side by side in a single circle facing toward the center or around the circle.

SQUARE SET   Eight persons (four couples) are arranged so that one couple is on each side of a square facing the center.

STAR   Four or more persons all join right or left hands in the middle of their circle.

Group Formations and Handholds

ESCORT HOLD   Dancers are side by side or diagonally forward of one another. The hand in the moving direction hooks the bent elbow of the person ahead. The other hand is at the waist, elbow bent, with the back of the hand on the hip. Occasionally the escort hold requies dancers to be very close together in which case the arm in the moving direction is underneath the neighbor's arm.

LINE AND CIRCLE "T" (SHOULDER HOLD)   Arms are extended sideward at shoulder level to the near shoulders of the dancer on either side. Elbows are straight. Right arms are in back and left arms in front.

LITTLE FINGER   Little fingers are joined at shoulder level. The left hand takes the neighbor's right little finger hooking it from the back.

"U"   Hands are joined as in the "W" position, and arms are raised above the head.

"V" (KOLO HOLD)   Hands are joined with arms down. The left palm faces to the rear (OUT) and the right palm faces to the front (IN). The left palm is on top.

"W"   Hands are joined at shoulder level with elbows bent. The right hand supports the neighbor's left hand. A convenient way to form this handhold is to take the "V" position as described and raise the arms.

Partner Positions and Handholds

BACK HOLD   Hands are joined behind partners' backs. Dancers assume the elbow swing position with right hips adjacent. Each person extends the left hand behind the back to join the partner's hand.

DOUBLE SHOULDER   This modification of the shoulder-waist position is used when two males or two females are partners. Dancers hold each other's shoulders.

ELBOW SWING   Partners hook right or left elbows to walk, run, or skip.

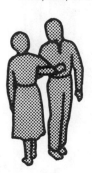

ISRAELI TURN Partners stand with right hips adjacent to one another. Right arms are extended in front of partner, holding the partner at the waist. Left arms are held high.

SHOULDER BLADE Facing each other, dancers hold partner at the shoulder blades (woman's arms above man's arms).

SHOULDER-WAIST Partners face each other. Male holds the female at her waist. Female's hands are on the male's shoulders.

SKATER'S HOLD or CROSS-HAND HOLD Partners are side by side with right hands joined in front of the right partner and left hands joined in front of the left partner. Right hands are joined on top and left hands are joined underneath. A promenade is sometimes danced in this position.

SOCIAL DANCE (CLOSED POSITION) Partners face each other. Male holds the female's right hand in his left hand. Male's right hand holds the female's back above the waist. The female's left hand is placed on the male's right shoulder.

VARSOVIENNE or PROMENADE Partners are side by side with the male to the left of the female. Right hands are held at the female's right shoulder (male's right arm is straight across female's shoulders). Left hands are joined in front of the male with the female's left arm straight. (This position does not require a coed setting.)